# AN ADDRESS IN PARIS

BLACK LIVES IN THE DIASPORA:
PAST / PRESENT / FUTURE

# AN ADDRESS IN PARIS

## EMPLACEMENT, BUREAUCRACY, AND BELONGING IN HOSTELS FOR WEST AFRICAN MIGRANTS

### AÏSSATOU MBODJ-POUYE

Columbia University Press *New York*

Columbia University Press
*Publishers Since 1893*
New York    Chichester, West Sussex
cup.columbia.edu

Library of Congress Cataloging-in-Publication Data
Names: Mbodj-Pouye, Aïssatou, author.
Title: An address in Paris : emplacement, bureaucracy, and belonging
in West African hostels / Aïssatou Mbodj-Pouye.
Description: New York : Columbia University Press, [2023] |
Includes bibliographical references and index.
Identifiers: LCCN 2023014398 | ISBN 9780231211420 (hardback) |
ISBN 9780231211437 (trade paperback) |
ISBN 9780231558907 (ebook)
Subjects: LCSH: West Africans—France—Social conditions. |
West Africans—Dwellings—France. | Immigrants—France—
Social conditions. | Black people—France—Social conditions. |
France—Race relations. | France—Emigration and immigration.
Classification: LCC DC718.A34 M36 2023 |
DDC 305.896/6044—dc23/eng/20230607
LC record available at https://lccn.loc.gov/2023014398

Cover design: Elliott S. Cairns
Cover image: Jane Ali / Alamy Stock Photo

# CONTENTS

# ABBREVIATIONS

| | |
|---|---|
| ADEF | Association pour le développement des foyers du bâtiment et des métaux |
| AFRP | Association des foyers de la région parisienne |
| AFTAM | Association pour la formation des travailleurs africains et malgaches |
| AOF | Afrique occidentale française |
| APL | Aide personnalisée au logement |
| APUR | Atelier parisien d'urbanisme |
| ARS | Agence régionale de santé |
| ASSOTRAF | Association pour l'aide sociale aux travailleurs africains |
| ASTI | Associations de solidarité avec les travailleurs immigrés |
| ATL | Aide transitoire au logement |
| ATMF | Association des travailleurs maliens en France |
| BAS | Bureau d'aide sociale |
| CAF | Caisse d'allocations familiales |
| CGT | Confédération générale du travail |
| CILPI | Commission interministérielle pour le logement des populations immigrées |
| CNL | Confédération nationale du logement |

| | |
|---|---|
| CNLI | Commission nationale du logement immigré |
| CODAF | Coordination départementale des affaires frauduleuses |
| COPAF | Collectif pour l'avenir des foyers |
| DAL | Droit au logement |
| DIHAL | Délégation interministérielle à l'hébergement et à l'accès au logement |
| FAS | Fonds d'action sociale |
| FEANF | Fédération des étudiants d'Afrique noire en France |
| GRDR | Groupe de recherche et de réalisations pour le développement rural |
| HLM | Habitat à loyer modéré |
| INSEE | Institut national de la statistique et des études économiques |
| MOUS | Maîtrise d'œuvre urbaine et sociale |
| MRAP | Mouvement contre le racisme et pour l'amitié entre les peuples |
| OP | Organisation politique |
| PCF | Parti communiste français (French Communist Party) |
| PSU | Parti socialiste unifié |
| PTFTM | Plan de traitement des foyers de travailleurs migrants |
| RESF | Réseau éducation sans frontières |
| RMI | Revenu minimum d'insertion |
| Sonacotra | Société nationale de construction pour les travailleurs |
| UCFML | Union des communistes de France marxiste-léniniste |
| UGTSF | Union générale des travailleurs sénégalais en France |
| UNAFO | Union nationale des associations gestionnaires de foyers de migrants, renamed Union professionnelle du logement accompagné in 2009 |

# AN ADDRESS IN PARIS

# INTRODUCTION

I n *Black Manoo*, a novel set in the cosmopolitan area of Belleville in Paris at the end of the twentieth century, the main character, freshly arrived from Abidjan, makes his way into the French capital.[1] As part of his daily routine, Black Manoo visits a *foyer*, a facility for male migrants, to buy a cheap plate of *mafé*, a rice dish made with peanut sauce emblematic of West African cooking. In a short and caustic chapter, the Franco-Ivorian novelist Gauz retraces how the foyers originated in the political project of controlling migrants from colonial Algeria, and later sub-Saharan Africa, and how French authorities maintained migrants within the cities only to keep an eye on them. While tapping into the typical image of the foyer as an African village, Gauz also depicts the foyer as a "child of the republican order"—and contends that a French industrialist invented mafé in the colonial era.

Situating the foyers within French national history while acknowledging their prominence among diasporic West Africans, Gauz's literary account aptly captures the tension at the heart of this unique housing system. Set in the 1990s, the novel also bears witness to a past situation: the specific building he refers to—a dilapidated facility located on "rue

David D'Angers"—was replaced in 2014 with a brand new facility called a "*résidence sociale*," no longer offering a restaurant service. Over the past twenty years, such new buildings have been gradually replacing the seven hundred foyers built in French cities during the twentieth century. Institutions in charge of managing immigration have designed these new residences to be distinct from the old foyers: they provide autonomous studios in place of multiple rooms, offer many fewer collective spaces, and are open to disadvantaged men and women of all social and ethnic backgrounds.

Taking the moment of this transformation as a starting point to investigate a sixty-year-old story, in this book I scrutinize the ruptures and continuities in the life of the West African foyers. I explore how, beginning in the 1950s, they were established as key migration infrastructures by administrative actors in charge of migration and urban policies as well as by the migrants themselves; and how their future has been disputed, both inside and outside, since the late 1990s. An anthropological approach makes it possible to unpack the ambivalent attachments to these buildings that the foyers' inhabitants have developed over time, exploring the afterlives of bureaucratic practices and housing policies initially designed to contain migrants.

## A WEST AFRICAN DIASPORA

With a focus on the foyers' black residents, I investigate how the racialized management of (post)colonial migrants materialized in these buildings and contributed to the consolidation of communities sharing a common geographical origin; and how, conversely, foyer inhabitants contested and displaced the categories imposed upon them. I tease out the identities assigned to these men, and the identities they claimed, exploring how these inter-twined dimensions have evolved across time.

Sub-Saharan Africans arriving in France in the late 1950s to early 1960s as labor migrants came from a specific region, the Senegal River Valley. In 1960, this area, formerly under French colonial rule as part of French West Africa (Afrique Occidentale Française [AOF]), constituted the peripheral zones of the newly independent states of Mali, Senegal, and Mauritania.[2] In 1970, most of the sub-Saharan migrants were still from the Senegal River Valley, with Soninke (64 percent) and Haalpulaar (14 percent) ethnic backgrounds.[3] In this region, social organization relied on agricultural work as well as on the mobility of young men in search of cash, often in seasonal cycles but at times for longer-term displacements. For centuries, the axis of mobility had been long-distance trade routes between the Sahara and the coast of the Gulf of Guinea; during the colonial era, it had evolved into migration toward areas where export crops or industrial work developed. As a general term, I designate migrants from this region as "West Africans," even though their area of origin covers only a tiny area of this subregion of the African continent. In so doing, I follow other scholars working on migrants from the same area who have emphasized the relevance of dealing with West Africans from the Sahel as a group in consideration of their relative internal homogeneity beyond national and ethnic distinctions, and of the way in which they were often assigned a common identity by outsiders.[4]

Heirs to a much older black presence in France, these migrants came to be known as "black African workers" (French: *travailleurs noirs africains*), distinguished from the far more numerous North African workers who had been in France since the beginning of the twentieth century. During the Algerian War (1954–1962), French authorities had developed the foyer system to lodge and control North African labor migrants; this housing system ensured the availability of a male migrant labor force whose presence was envisaged as temporary. When the condition of black migrants became an issue in the early 1960s, they replicated this type of housing, but in separate buildings. Hence racial categories were crucial in the constitution of the foyers; however, they did not strictly follow any color line: in the early 1960s, the authorities also organized the migration of black French nationals from the Caribbean, but consciously avoided lodging them in the foyers, developing specific options for them to access social housing. Although these black citizens were discriminated against, not conflating them with black African migrants was a key concern for the administration.[5]

In the 1980s, African migration in France became much more diverse, and the previously established migratory flow altered after the economic crisis and the political decision to "suspend" labor immigration in 1974. At that time, even as the black population of Paris diversified, the foyers themselves remained populated through family and ethnic networks, both because of the internal dynamics of the migratory networks and as a result of unchanging administrative practices in the foyers. Hence the foyers remained significant for West African migrants: in 1999, around 31 percent of the Malian and Mauritanian migrants in the Paris region resided in foyers, and nearly 14 percent of the Senegalese did so.[6]

Ties between the foyers and the residents' villages of origin consolidated progressively thanks to specific institutions; namely, hometown-based associations whose development was encouraged in France in the 1980s. Furthermore, the foyers have become rallying points for the communities of West African families living outside the foyers, many of their members becoming or being French citizens, notably those born in France. In addition, the foyers welcomed much more varied crowds, such as the occasional visitors epitomized in *Black Manoo* or Muslims of all origins joining a religious service in their prayer rooms.

The experience of diaspora is thus integral to the history of the foyers, and I illuminate its changing contours across generations, contributing to a growing scholarship on "new African diasporas."[7] But, as Tiffany Ruby Patterson and Robin Kelley importantly noted, "the linkages . . . that tie the diaspora together must be articulated and are not inevitable [and] are always historically constituted."[8] The foyers constituted neither ethnic enclaves premised on a narrowly defined common identity nor a melting pot where all black populations of France would have come together. If understood as meaning transnational communities, the foyers were undoubtedly formative of diasporas, providing the material and social conditions for the transnational networks, not only at the level of localities but in regional and even transethnic dynamics too. If understood as conveying the meaning of wider ties across regional identity and identification with a black or African diaspora, the foyers illustrate changing configurations where fragmentation as much as cooperation must be pinpointed, as Félix Germain indicated in his study of African and Caribbean migrants in postwar Paris.[9]

## A (POST)COLONIAL METROPOLIS

Since the 1950s, Paris has gone from a postwar city in reconstruction and colonial metropolis to a largely gentrified global city. This book is a journey around the French capital and its twenty districts (French: *arrondissements*), as well as the adjacent towns where migrants have circulated, worked, and lived. Since the 1950s, the geographical borders of inner Paris have not changed despite occasional administrative and political reorganizations. In contrast, the wider "Paris region" constitutes a geographical area whose administrative name and contours have changed. Within this area, I focus on Paris and postindustrial cities in the three adjacent "departments" (French: *départements*) where migrants live, notably Seine-Saint-Denis, to quote the administrative divisions in place since 1968.[10]

The Paris region has always attracted a significant number of foreigners, but their share in the population of the region rose from 5.2 percent in 1954 (compared to a national rate of 4.1 percent) to 11.9 percent in 1999 (compared to a national rate of 5.6 percent). Taking into account not only foreigners but immigrants more broadly, recent figures indicate that 18.5 percent of the population of the Paris region are immigrants, twice the share of the immigrant population at the national level.[11] Paris (20 percent) is slightly above the regional average, and the Department of Seine-Saint-Denis has an even larger proportion of immigrants (29 percent). Among these immigrants concentrated in the Paris region, half were born on the African continent, most in Algeria, Morocco, and Tunisia, followed by sub-Saharan countries, notably Mali; conversely, 60 percent of sub-Saharan Africans in France live in the Paris region.[12] My focus on Paris and its surroundings thus corresponds to the centrality of the capital in the dynamics of West African migration; furthermore, it allows an understanding of the several administrative scales in which issues of housing and management of migrants, framed by national policies, have been dealt with, debated, and contested.

## THEORIZING MIGRATION FROM THE FOYERS

Key to the public imagination of sub-Saharan migration to France, the foyers have also played a formative role in Africanist scholarship and French migration studies.[13] In Europe, migrant laborers first featured as part of a history of workers in the 1970s.[14] As Marxist analysts sought to demonstrate that imperialist relations with the former colonial powers caused African emigration, the foyers symbolized the neocolonial exploitation of manpower whose reproduction was ensured by domestic households in their countries of origin.[15] Scholars followed migrants from their Parisian foyers to their villages of origin to further root such analysis in an understanding of the social organization of emigration societies.[16] Critically engaging with Marxist assumptions, the historian François Manchuelle insisted on the *longue durée* sociocultural dynamics of migration.[17] In parallel, and with a bias toward ethnic and cultural factors, the anthropologist Jacques Barou contributed to the production of knowledge on the foyers through public commissions as well as academic studies.[18] Although French sociology of that time generally did not tackle racial dimensions, an interest in interethnic relations developed in the specialized literature on migrant housing.[19]

After the suspension of labor migration in 1974 in the context of the economic crisis and mounting politicization of migration as an issue, authorities offered limited opportunities for family reunion and framed immigration in the new discourse of integration.[20] As a result, West African communities diversified in the 1980s: beyond foyer residents, families now lived in French cities. Contributing to discussion on the notion of "integration" in academic studies, the sociologist Mahamet Timera studied the dynamics of settlement through and beyond the foyers.[21] With the advent of the development dimension in migration policies, studies analyzed the involvement of migrants in development activities in their home countries and the importance of the foyers in such activities.[22] Decentering the foyers as fieldwork sites and research topics, scholars sought to investigate other forms of African migration than the typical figure of the masculine unskilled labor migrant, with research focusing on women and migrants from other social and geographical backgrounds.[23] Informed by the transnational turn in migration studies, other scholars still used the foyers as entry points for investigating social and political dynamics that spanned across borders.[24]

The foyers have been contentious sites from the beginning, with early political protests that this book contributes to pinpointing. The most well-known episode is the emblematic nationwide rent strike in Sonacotra-run foyers (1973–1979).[25] As historical and sociological studies began to tease out continuities in the racialized management of (post)colonial migrants, the historiography of this episode has been thoroughly renewed.[26] Recent studies further recast the political activism of West African migrants in wider transnational dynamics, including their previous political socialization on the African continent.[27]

As a result of the tightening of migratory policies since the 1970s, migrant activism shifted from housing to claims for legal residence. Undocumented migrants reclaimed their status of "*sans-papiers*" as the main ground for political action.[28] Migrants from Tunisia and Turkey were at the front of these struggles in the 1970s, but West Africans became the visible face of the sans-papiers movement in the summer of 1996 when the police violently evacuated three hundred of them (among which ten were on hunger strike) from the Church of Saint-Bernard in Paris. The articulation, and at times tension, between these two interrelated struggles is a key theme of this book.

Following Tyler Stovall's plea for histories of African diasporas that fully acknowledge the role of the nation-state, I place the French state, through the foyers, at the heart of West African experiences in Paris, further demonstrating that "the heterogeneity of the African diasporic condition is in part grounded in diverse national cultures and histories."[29] The foyers offer a unique vantage point from which to analyze the changing meanings of race from the late colonial era to the resurgence of the "black question" in the French public sphere in the 2000s, benefiting from a renewed scholarly interest in the plural experience of blackness in France.[30]

## INSTITUTION AND EXPERIENCE: THE FOYER, *SYSTEM* AND *MODEL*

Foyers are housing facilities monitored by the state, either directly or through state-subsidized associations, and a web of public policies target these places and their inhabitants.[31] In a comparative perspective, they stand in stark contrast with housing arrangements for migrants in the private sector generally described in the literature, such as the "vertical villages" analyzed by Paul Stoller in New York City or the "bachelor rooms" for migrants in Istanbul studied by Kristen Biehl.[32] Considering the foyers as institutions serves to grasp the importance of the French state (understood as myriad administrative actors with distinct agendas rather than as a coherent entity) in their creation, as part of wider migration and urban policies. However, although a line of scholarship aligns the foyer with camps and other places of confinement for postcolonial migrants and displaced people, I consider such a disciplinary view of the foyer system to have only partial value because it obscures the social and spatial practices of their inhabitants.[33]

The notion of institution is pivotal in building an analysis of the foyers in their dual aspect as key parts of a French administrative system for managing migrants and as nodal points in West African migratory networks.[34] I move from institution to infrastructure when I need to emphasize their materiality and instability.[35] Infrastructure is enduring and often outlasts the projects that initially led to its establishment. Furthermore, urban infrastructures are contentious sites where people make "the lived experience of unequal provisioning and differentiated belonging in cities" as much as they learn the possibility of "claims to social membership, political belonging, and rights to modernity in terms of infrastructure, whether imaginary, potential, or derelict."[36]

The duality of the foyers as migrant and state institutions, on one hand, and the political resonance of the notion of infrastructure, on the other, help bridge the view of the foyers as an administrative system with the approach of the individual and collective experiences of their inhabitants that form the core of this book's material. *Experience* refers to the lived engagement with the foyers as buildings and urban crossroads, as administrative spots and culturally meaningful landmarks.

Attention to experience encompasses two perspectives. First, this book stems from ethnographic fieldwork aimed at understanding the relationship of my interlocutors to the foyers as dwellings. In this respect, "*foyer*" is an ambiguous term in French: from an original meaning of "hearth," it designates, on one hand, a household (a typical domestic space) and, on the other hand, "a set of establishments that offer accommodation and services to residents who, for one reason or another, are not able to access their own accommodation."[37] I also offer ethnographic evidence of the ambiguous rapport to the foyer: multifaceted, in that migrants with distinct backgrounds and trajectories may view it very differently; and ambivalent, in the sense that the same person can express contradictory feelings of comfort and disgust toward this place, depending on what he compares it with and which aspect of it he emphasizes.[38] I contribute to emerging discussions on the home-migration nexus by empirically exploring the full relationship to these migrant "homes"—provisional or enduring, lifelong dwellings or short-term shelters.[39]

Second, by focusing on the experience of the foyer, I engage with the changing meanings that these places have represented in the lives of generations of men. They have been consolidated into what I call a "model," referring to the social and cultural meanings of the foyers in West African migratory dynamics. A model of the foyers emerged as the crystallization of practices of mobility, of established ways of living together, and of social expectations on conduct within and outside the foyers. I pinpoint the historical evolution of this model: how it developed as a hegemonic reference in the 1970s, and how it became one of the possible life paths, often deemed outdated, for younger migrants. The value of this model also stemmed from the possibilities (or lack thereof) of imagining and pursuing a meaningful life outside the foyers; hence this social and cultural formation has been deeply shaped by structural factors, notably the mobility regimes and economic possibilities and social promotion prospects of the time.

Gender lies at the junction of the foyer as system and model. French state services and the other agencies that established the foyers designed them for "isolated men" (French: *hommes isolés*): foyers were all-male facilities by definition, and in earlier times visits by women were forbidden. The model of the foyer, rooted in social and cultural expectations of success for male migrants, rested on the idea that migration was a path to an achieved masculinity. Exploring this junction, Marxists anthropologists and Claude Meillassoux in particular touched on a key point regarding the foyers, whose endurance rested on the convergence of institutional arrangements reflecting France's economic needs in terms of a cheap labor force and sociocultural expectations, whereby international migration was viewed as sustaining social reproduction in the emigration locales.[40]

Feminist scholars have highlighted the importance of gender in migration dynamics since the 1980s, sparking attention to the position of women in migration and a wider interest in the interrelation of gender roles and migratory dynamics.[41] This scholarship subsequently inspired a fresh look at male migration understood as rooted in gendered identities potentially affected by mobility.[42] Studies on West African female migrants have become more and more informed by gender scholarship, but a gendered take on West African masculinities in migration to France is much less developed.[43]

## SPATIAL AND TEMPORAL DISJUNCTIONS

In the central part of this book, I thoroughly detail the demolition-reconstruction of a foyer and scrutinize the various positions of the residents as well as those of the professional and institutional actors. A classic topic of the sociology of housing, rehabilitations as part of urban renewal projects have been studied in postindustrialized cities across the world. The dismantling of public housing in the United States has been the subject of a wealth of studies paying attention to the racial dimensions of such processes, and in France the social effects of a nationwide urban renewal plan in 2003 have been critically investigated, with studies showing that the intention of creating mixed-income blocks or neighborhoods has not succeeded.[44] The case of the foyers brings in institutional stakeholders and discourses that are at play in the wider field of social housing, but it also evidences broader dynamics of the management of postcolonial migrants that I approach with an anthropological lens in the vein of Andrew Newman's study of urban renewal in a section of northern Paris.[45]

I trace the history of the foyers through the uncertain times of decolonization of French West Africa, whose termination the historian Frederick Cooper marks in 1974, when mobility agreements negotiated in the aftermath of the 1960 independence of countries such as Mali, Senegal, and Mauritania were suspended.[46] Residents situate their experience in the complex albeit unequal relationship that ties West Africa to France.[47] By devoting space to the nuanced ways in which the residents remember this time, I go beyond the focus on practices of control and surveillance that characterize some of the existing scholarship on the foyers and West African migrants.[48] As the ethnography of the foyers' renovation demonstrates, historical arguments were not always efficient in inflecting the foyers' present-day management; however, these discourses contributed to the strength of foyer collectives, which have facilitated their preservation in the city over decades.

In the 1980s, structural adjustment programs implemented in West Africa rendered other paths of social and economic success more uncertain, and migration to Europe remained significant and extended to other regional and social groups. Migration networks relied increasingly on the foyers in a context of heightened control over their mobility. These networks were driven by migrants' plans, where work remained a central consideration, although the jobs in question changed from industry to services, such as cleaning and catering—still fueling a flux of labor migrants in a post-Fordist context.

My research thus points to the asynchrony between, on one hand, policies that frame the foyers as "relics," bearing witness to a past historical moment when postcolonial migrants were needed and, on the other hand, a still dynamic West African migration. As material traces of past arrangements, foyers are akin to the "imperial debris" that inspire Ann Laura Stoler to consider the "uneven pace with which people can extricate themselves from the structures and signs by which remains take hold."[49] The endurance of foyer model after the end of the guest-worker system testifies precisely to such disjunctions.

This vantage point allows me to qualify the switch observed from migration policies centered on workers to a consideration of the suffering body.[50] The renovation scheme that transformed the foyers into residences attests to an inclusion of migrants into a larger category of persons "in need." However, foyer inhabitants strongly resist such an assignation and sometimes obtain practical recognition of the fact that most of them are still active, neither retired nor unemployed. Moreover, although gaining documents on health grounds was a novelty in the 2000s, work-based legalization processes have again been promoted in the last decade.[51] Only a tiny percentage of migrants' regularizations occur on health grounds.[52] Likewise, analysis of conjugal histories of foyer inhabitants reveals that some of them attempt to legalize their status through marriage to a French citizen. But rather than a shift from work to the family as a way to gain legal status in Europe, I emphasize how migrants navigate the intricacies of French laws and make use of both options. Work remains central, as an identity and a project in the lives of foyer inhabitants. "Frontline" workers, which the COVID-19 pandemic brought back to the world's attention, are largely migrants, with sectors such as cleaning, catering and food-delivery services, and segments of the construction industry drawing heavily on undocumented migrants.

Given the relative stability of foyer populations, these historical shifts, directly experienced by many men in these sites, fuel intergenerational debates and comparisons. These are notably reflected in the varying ability of foyers to be place-making spaces.

## CONCEPTUALIZING BELONGING
## THROUGH EMPLACEMENT

The ethnographic inspiration for this book lies in the demands made by many foyer inhabitants to be treated as "*Parisiens*" (or "*Dyonisiens*" in Saint-Denis, "*Boulonnais*" in Boulogne-Billancourt), which I heard in contentious moments as well as in ordinary conversations. Such assertions of belonging were enmeshed with other loyalties, notably transnational attachments. They were at odds with dominant national political discourses of exclusion or, at best, selective inclusion—a fact that my interlocutors were well aware of. As they enunciated such claims of belonging, they often confronted them with clear-headed statements on the difficulties in accessing the legal status of documented resident or citizen.

From this empirical starting point, one avenue would be to contest present-day political and media representations of the foyers. Since the 1990s, such representations have consolidated around a critique of "communitarianism," defined as the tendency of individuals to relate to ethnic or religious communities rather than to the unique national community. West African foyers, viewed as places of informal activities outside of French law and as shelters for undocumented migrants, typified this threat[53]—and still loom large when the issue of immigrant integration is discussed in French public debate. In addition, the presence of collective spaces of Islamic worship within their walls subjected them to a political management of Islam rife with ambiguities. Thus the history of the foyers intersects with two key elements of the French political model: the notion of "the Republic" and the idea of *laïcité* (a French word for secularism). Scholars of contemporary France have highlighted that racialized dynamics lie at the heart of the imagined colorblind French Republic,[54] and they have pointed to the crystallization of the issue of national identity around Islam. As the anthropologist Mayanthi Fernando summarizes it, investigating present-day France requires one to proceed "by not taking the republic for granted as a coherent or stable formation" and by "examin[ing] how secularism and republicanism coalesce despite—or, more precisely, through—their immanent contradictions."[55] The foyers offer an ideal observatory for such inconsistencies because they make it possible to trace the shifting attitudes adopted by the French state toward its (post)colonial migrants and evidence the contradictory demands that their inhabitants faced.

As consubstantial topics to the history of the foyers that are intensely debated in the context of their present-day endings, such issues form part of the story told in the following pages. Yet my analytical take is different: following the experiential thread put forward earlier, I focus on the lived experience of the city that substantiates claims of belonging, exploring how an urbanite identity was once sustained by the foyers, and the processes that weakened it—what I define as the dynamics of urban emplacement.

Emplacement is a process whereby one comes to feel part of an environment, to build a "sense of place."[56] My elaboration of the notion of urban emplacement emphasizes three layers: affective (the feeling of familiarity when moving within the area delineated through this process), epistemic (the knowledge and skills that allow living, navigating, and staying there), and discursive (the naming practices shared at the level of a group and the stories about one's arrival and adaptation). The affective dimension of emplacement intersects with legal and political dimensions but does not align with them: emplacement requires a sense of legitimate belonging that does not need to be rooted in economic and legal property, nor in political rights and legal status, because it can be supported by alternative representations of ownership. The process of emplacement does require, however, a perceived security and an imagined ability to stay for some time in this place. Emplacement implies the ability to embark on defensive actions to protect one's right to remain in the area (or one's family, group of residence, etc.). Knowledge and skills encompass abilities to navigate the part of the city in which one is emplaced, as well as the social capital accumulated through life in a neighborhood and a city, which together constitute a resource to maintain oneself in this place. Rooted in engagement with the materiality of the built and urban environment, emplacement also deeply shapes verbal practices. As in rural landscapes, urban place-making goes with the production of toponymy, which can borrow from existing names but often reworks them; "narratives of emplacement" crucially contribute to building a sense of belonging and the ability to share it with others.[57]

Temporal and spatial, emplacement is also simultaneously an individual experience and a shared one, with the existence of a community that might be as tiny as a group of peers or the family about which narratives of emplacement are told.[58] Dynamics of emplacement likewise determine distinct scales at which these components of belonging operate: one's safe zone might extend to a few blocks, whereas the claim to be part of an area can target the neighborhood or the city; although these might evolve, the notion that there are boundaries delimiting inside and outside is crucial.[59]

Focusing on migrants' emplacement in a foreign city adds an additional layer to this general description because emplacement needs to be articulated with displacement. In this respect, a useful point of departure is the now classic definition of "transnational migration [as] the process by which immigrants forge and sustain simultaneous multi-stranded social relations that link together their societies of origin and settlement."[60] Considering the foyer both as a site of urban emplacement and as a transnational node, I seek to understand the changing articulation of these two facets of the foyer. The foyer as a social model obviously supports international mobility: offering a shelter to newcomers, informal systems of cash transfers, help in obtaining a job, and more generally encouragement to pursue a migratory project. But scrutinizing emplacement highlights other aspects, such as the knowledge that inhabitants acquire of their neighborhood and their partial incorporation into local social networks, all of which can reinforce, as much as distract from, transnational commitments.

In both cases, mobility lies at the heart of the dynamics: the transnational character of migration is predicated on forms of connection and circulation; emplacement requires moving in the city. I focus on how these forms of mobility intersect. In particular, I trace a change from a productive articulation of these two forms of mobility for older residents to younger ones who experience far more blockages at a time when immobility is part and parcel of the migrant experience.[61] While examining urban foundation narratives, I also trace how spatial practices and understandings travel; as Michel Agier reminds us, even when the making of the city involves the creation of local identities, those remain "movable."[62] Recently, theoretical innovation in this vein has refined the approach to the dialectics between mobility and immobility and emphasized the dynamics of place-making.[63] To this scholarship primarily based on ethnographic projects among people on the move, I add a reflection on place-making grounded on the perspectives of generations of migrants who have lived within a city for more than half a century.

## THE ADDRESS: EMPLACEMENT THROUGH BUREAUCRACY

To explore the dynamics of emplacement, I follow a seemingly insignificant attribute of a domicile: the address. The address is a political technology that renders legible both the city, projecting each home onto an administrative grid, and the population, subjecting each individual to the obligation to declare as his residence one such identified place of living.[64] An address primarily identifies a place, but its administrative uses have made it a component of the identification of persons. The address combines two distinct values: as a place name (indexing a specific location in the city) and as a title (attesting to a domicile establishing particular rights).

In the course of my research, my attention was drawn to identifying the address at several moments. To begin, recollections of the foyers were saturated by addresses of the places my interlocutors had lived. Beyond its indexical role when made material by a street sign, an address in its referential use is a toponym that designates a unique location in the city. The fact that most foyers are metonymically named by the name of the street on which they are located renders such toponyms omnipresent in the narratives about the foyers. In accounts of the early days of the foyers, street addresses functioned as mnemonic markers in the progressive acquisition of a sense of place in the city.

Beyond urban circulation, having an address meant access to the service of postal distribution. The importance of an address appears in stories about letters received, but even more in accounts of failed mail distribution, a key point of contention in the foyers from the 1960s to the present. The postal address ties a person to an identified domicile, but such a relation could be disputed, and the local staff of a foyer, in charge of distributing mail, often contested accommodation by refusing to distribute mail to unofficial inhabitants. In discussions about administrative procedures more generally, the address again featured prominently: it is one of the tokens of identification that appears on all official documents, which are repeatedly requested from an individual in administrative contexts.

In the era of irregularized migration, migrants are subjected to dense administrative scrutiny in order to get documents. The administrative injunction to provide a valid address has become a vital question for migrants. A type of residence (in the sense of domicile) can allow or block access to residence in the sense of legal permission to stay in a country. Rooted in anthropological approaches to bureaucracy, I examine and compare these distinct meanings of the address and their evolution across time, considering a token of identification rarely studied as such.[65]

## ENTERING, CIRCULATING, AND SPENDING TIME WITHIN A "MEN'S SPACE"

Foyers have long been part of my geography of Paris. My father was a student in the capital when I was a child, and he would take me to have lunch in a foyer canteen when I visited him. More than a decade later, in the late 1990s, when I was a student myself, I volunteered to offer literacy classes in several foyers. When I designed a project on West African memories of migration in 2010, the foyers seemed to be an obvious place to start. But my attempts to enter the place through my father's acquaintances failed, and I was similarly unable to reconnect with the participants of the literacy classes. Hanging around did not seem to be an effective strategy, given the hierarchical organization of the foyers and the often tense relations between a foyer's established residents, on one hand, and the more marginal visitors and inhabitants who occupied the halls and collective spaces, on the other. I first tried to present my research projects to foyer representatives (French: *délégués*) in Montreuil, a city east of Paris that is home to a number of foyers and has an important community of Malian migrants and their descendants. However, these first interlocutors received me politely but unenthusiastically—oversolicited as they were by journalists, artists, and students. There were lesser known foyers in the nineteenth arrondissement where I lived, and I chose to focus on these neighboring facilities rather than on the emblematic Montreuil foyers.

In this book I rely on an ethnography of two foyers in Paris—Foyer Lorraine and Foyer D'Hautpoul—which are named after the streets where they are located. Over the course of 2011, I conducted a series of interviews with an open-ended set of questions on what life in the foyers meant for men of different generations. During 2012, the issue of the two foyers' upcoming renovations became a concern for my interlocutors. I had initially received only elusive answers when trying to document the history of the foyers, but discourses on the shared past of these two buildings suddenly arose continuously. Residents began to tell intriguing stories about the 216 bis, a foyer that older residents had moved from in 1979, which was named after its address—216 bis rue Saint-Denis (Paris, second arrondissement).[66] This moment was a turning point in my project, propelling me into two distinct temporal directions: a historical study prompted by the resurfacing of these memories, and an ethnographic approach to the renovation process, which I followed from the first meetings informing residents of the project in 2012 to the closure of the two foyers in 2014 and 2015.

Beyond this case study, from 2011 to 2020 I visited more than fifty foyers in Paris and the three adjacent departments.[67] I had several reasons for expanding my fieldwork research. First, I was drawn to the archives while searching for elements on the 216 bis foyer, but I embarked on a larger historical study conducting historical interviews in many locations. Second, as I tried to encompass the views and practices of the various institutional and political actors, I became aware of my limitations in the cases of Foyer Lorraine and Foyer D'Hautpoul. My acquaintance with the residents there was such that institutional actors always assumed I was on the residents' side and would therefore circulate relevant information to them.[68] Investigating other sites enabled me to gain other perspectives. I negotiated access to a series of "steering committees" convened by the municipality of Paris to discuss the renovation process of the foyers one by one. This allowed me to meet actors with whom I later managed to negotiate interviews. Seeking to observe the multiple phases of the renovation process, I also attended meetings during which social workers interviewed residents prior to the renovation.

Finally, the focus on the renovation led me to spend time with délégués during public appearances, but I had little access to other aspects of their lives or to the experience of less established members of the foyer residential community. So I sought occasions to initiate fieldwork relationships in more peripheral spaces, such as the premises of one neighborhood association where many young foyer inhabitants spent time, and I joined a support group for sans-papiers attached to another Parisian foyer. This extension of my ethnographic project led me to "reenter" the field and to build ethnographic relationships beyond

Foyer Lorraine and Foyer D'Hautpoul. Although a focus on the same foyer would have been ideal, this was impractical due to the exclusive form fieldwork relationships often took, which reflects both the specificities of these sites and the singularity of my position—two dimensions to which I now turn.

Foyers are all-male residences; they are masculine spaces by definition and are places where one mostly encounters men. At the time of my fieldwork, they were no longer places that excluded women. From reserved buildings with internal rules prohibiting female visitors, they had evolved into places where women, if invited, were free to circulate. In a typical visit, I generally did not meet other women, but I sometimes crossed paths with female social workers, who carefully stayed in their offices or meeting rooms, and with activists, relatives, or girlfriends, and occasionally with sex workers.[69] Some women were particularly at ease: I was sitting among a crowd of five in a room one afternoon when a hawker who regularly toured Foyer Lorraine to sell bottles of ginger and hibiscus juice jokingly engaged with the attendance; she then left her baby, whom she had been carrying on her back, under the men's watch for almost an hour—one in particular seemed to take great pleasure in gently bouncing the baby on his lap while his mother went on with her rounds.

Beyond the empirical fact of the occasional presence of other women, this anecdote indicates that the absence of women and children is not something sought by foyer men but is rather a condition with which they live. Descriptions of men-only spaces hostile to the presence of women did not apply to the foyers. These spaces enabled the gathering together of men from different generations and varied social statuses (measured in terms of both occupations in France and social categories in the emigration society) who were bound by varying degrees of kinship and other social relations. Hence the foyer space was stratified, and notions of shame were at play *between* the men living there. In the old buildings, where rooms hosted several men, any visitor could show up at almost any time, and the room was not primarily conceived of as a private space. Although the space was reorganized by a guest's presence, it was already fit for a visit: no dirty linen lying on the ground, no undone beds, and certainly no posters of naked women on the walls.[70]

Even so, foyers were mainly homosocial environments and, moreover, living spaces, and the textbook ethnographic injunction of "being there" posed specific issues. The solutions I found are partly shared by other women ethnographers and are partly tied to my *halfie* status, as my debut at Foyer D'Hautpoul evidences.[71] I was conducting a series of recorded interviews with residents, a technique I later abandoned in favor of informal conversations but that was a good way to look purposeful at that time. The délégué who had agreed to help me with my project introduced me to seventy-five-year-old Demba, who had lived in the foyer for thirty years.[72] At the end of our one-hour recorded interview, Demba told me: "When you come back to the foyer, don't hesitate to ask me other questions. Even if you come to see someone else, you should drop by and say, 'Hi, Papa.'" As I turned off the recorder and mentioned that I could understand some Wolof, Demba told me warmly that I should have said so from the beginning.[73] Upon my next visit, he retold me the life story that had been the substance of our first interview, but this time in Wolof. Speaking Wolof inverted the linguistic asymmetry that had prevailed in our French exchange: he was the one who could explain words that I did not understand and teach me proverbs in Wolof. Demba is the first person I remember greeting with a genuflection (Wolof: *sukk*), a gesture that came to me before I even had time to reflect on it, a reminiscence of what my cousins and aunts used to do, and instructed me to do, in Dakar when greeting older relatives.[74]

In the foyer, my identity as the daughter of an immigrant from Senegal prevailed over the fact that my mother was white French—in stark contrast to my general experience in Senegal and Mali, where my Western origin dominates and I am often racialized as white (Wolof: *tubaab*; Bamanan: *tubabu*). My interlocutors sometimes explicitly tied my presence and efforts to the status of "second-generation" children. As I introduced my research in a foyer room, a visitor who lived with his family outside the foyer emphasized that what I was doing was "good," explaining: "We are so happy to see that some of our children manage to pursue further studies."

However, the discourses of inclusion ("We are the same") and the genealogical inquiries that I was subjected to situated me within a shared history of West African emigration to France rather than within fixed social hierarchies. The fact that I would sukk while greeting Demba did not mean that my interlocutors expected me to comply with "West African social rules" (such rules vary from rural to urban to diasporic settings). My interlocutors selectively drew on the shared and composite cultural repertoire of the foyer in light of what each of them imagined about my cultural knowledge and social skills. To give a characteristic example, my patronym "Mbodj" unlocks a potential type of joking relationship between me and people bearing specific patronyms (a pattern that recurs throughout the West African Sahel). Yet I only became aware of this connection when a man I had known for a long time met my father and immediately teased him; it struck me that he had never established such a rapport with me, probably fearing that I would not be comfortable responding. In contrast, Dramane, my age-mate and someone who became a friend, playfully relied on the repertoire of the client/patron relationship on the basis of a status group assignation inferred from my patronym. This reflects my ambivalent status as much as the reality of the heterogeneous milieu of the foyer, characterized by bubbles of social and cultural familiarity and wider spaces of less stable cultural and linguistic translations.

Following my meeting with Demba, I quickly assumed the habit of calling most of the men whom I perceived to be much older than me "*tonton*" (a familiar French term for "uncle") as well as most of the délégués who were notably in their fifties and sixties. Being a "dutiful daughter," to quote again from Lila Abu-Lughod, offers a definite place and position; yet the deference associated with it obviously limits the range of questions one can ask, and the things that one can do.[75] Furthermore, as I came to know Demba better over repeated visits, I observed that the other inhabitants of this room, whom he called "the kids" (Wolof: *xale yi*) but were men in their thirties and forties, kept their distance with me. This points to another key characteristic of foyer men's social relationships: their compartmentalization. At the level of the room, the West African understanding that a stranger must have one single host prevailed. When I met someone comfortable enough to introduce me to his roommates, I could spend some time with them, but the hierarchy of proximity was fixed: the person I had come to know first was my point of reference, and the others rarely tried to establish more than superficial relationships with me. This logic also operated at the level of the foyer: when I stepped into Foyer D'Hautpoul, some men would come to tell me that Demba was not there and would be confused if I explained that I was visiting someone else.

Although I felt safe in the foyers, my interlocutors developed protective strategies that attested to the possible inappropriateness of my presence if I were to transgress the limits they had carefully set. At Foyer D'Hautpoul, Yero, a fifty-year-old délégué who acted as a broker for my research, took me very freely into his room and regularly invited me to join him at the café around the corner where he spent many hours. However, at dusk he generally became anxious and asked who was picking up my kids from school, a question I soon understood to be purely rhetorical and a polite invitation for me to go home. Issues around my respectability as a married woman were even more explicit in my relationship with younger men: Dramane bluntly asked me during our first conversation at a café, "Is your husband aware that you are here?" As I mumbled a positive but vague answer, I realized that developing this informal dimension of fieldwork could be challenging. I alternated between moments when I stuck to the expected gendered norms, such as complying with Yero's concern that I should leave the foyer before nighttime, and others when I provisionally ignored concerns over my reputation to reach out to foyer inhabitants whose own relationship to the foyer and its norms was ambivalent. In this respect, leaving the foyer was crucial: in a classic approach of urban ethnography, I followed some of my interlocutors to a variety of places beyond the foyer, from benches at the park or cafés to laundromats and barber shops.

Finally, my ability to be regularly on-site depended on the proximity of the foyers to my own places of work or living. In this respect, my field sites tended to mirror my own moves within Paris. From 2011 to 2013, I lived a five-minute walk from both Foyer D'Hautpoul and Foyer Lorraine; not only could I visit my interlocutors on a daily basis but inadvertently bump into them in my daily activities. When I moved to a neighboring city located North of Paris, I found myself near the Saint-Ouen Foyer, whose process of renovation I followed over the course of regular visits. At that time, my office was in Ivry, and I also spent a lot of time at neighboring Foyer Masséna (Paris, thirteenth arrondissement). When my office moved to Aubervilliers in 2019, I worked some hundred meters from

Foyer Fillettes and regularly had lunch in its restaurant. This description of my moves speaks to the possibility of finding a nearby foyer almost everywhere in the Paris region —with enough knowledge or observational skills, Parisian geography can be reconfigured around foyers as meaningful landmarks and resource-rich locales.

# I

# COMMUNITIES IN
# THE MAKING

The birth of the foyers was a response to the arrival of labor migrants from West Africa in the early 1960s. Use of the foyers, as buildings and as a way to manage migrants from former African colonies, was consolidated in the 1970s. Despite challenges from residents and their political allies, the foyer system persisted beyond the period of economic growth (1945–1973) and after the suspension of labor migration in 1974. In the 1990s, at a time of tightening immigration rules and politicization of migration issues, French authorities sought to renovate and profoundly reorganize "black African foyers."

Part 1 traces the evolution of the "community" paradigm from the 1960s to the 1970s, from a guide for public action in the management of (post)colonial migrants to a depreciative feature. Chapter 1 describes the racialized treatment of West Africans, which was informed by assumptions about the community-based arrangement of their lives. Pinpointing the continuities between colonial administrative practices and forms of management of the postcolonial migrants, this chapter shows that the organization of communities on the basis of localities of origin was a joint operation between West African brokers and French institutional actors.

Chapter 2 investigates the paradoxical stabilization of the foyers as a segregated system of housing at a time when economic labor immigration was suspended in France. New buildings were erected to host West African migrants in Paris during this decade, which contrasted with the improvisation of earlier times.

As a result of the problematization of immigration in France in a context of economic crisis and anxieties around the identity of the French Republic, the community-based dynamics of the foyers came under public scrutiny. Meanwhile, migratory dynamics made the foyers nodal points in West African mobility patterns. Chapter 3 explores the internal significance of the foyers for West African diasporas, including the development of Islamic places of worship within their walls. Bringing together internal dynamics and external discourses, this chapter sheds light on the design of a renovation scheme in the late 1990s, at a time when the communitarianism epitomized by West African foyers appeared to be a threat to French identity.

# 1

## IMPROVISING THE FOYERS

Franco-African Institutions of Migration (1958–1967)

*Bakary Traoré came from Somankidi, a Soninke village on the right bank of the Senegal River, west of the city of Kayes.*[1] *He arrived in Marseille in 1960 just weeks before the Mali Federation gained independence from France, thus entering French territory "with his ID card of French Soudan," as he recalls. After traveling by train to Paris, he first lived in the eighteenth arrondissement at 33 rue Polonceau, a dormitory managed by a fellow Malian and where other migrants from his village lived. At that time, West Africans also lived in other places, notably a basement at 32 rue Petit, which Traoré describes as "the first foyer of France." In 1966 or 1967, Traoré and others in his dormitory met a member of the Missionaries of Africa society (also known as the White Fathers). This Catholic priest helped them find alternative housing. Traoré recalls how Demba Saounera, a Soninke migrant from Sobokou, a village on the other bank of the Senegal River, led the discussions with the priest. In 1967, they all moved to this newly opened foyer, located in an old building at 216 bis rue Saint-Denis in central Paris (second arrondissement).*

**Samba Sylla** *was born in 1948 in Diataya, a village to the east of Kayes.*[2] *Sylla migrated to France in 1965, also arriving at the port of Marseille before traveling to Paris. He spent his first night in Paris at 36 rue de la Sablière (fourteenth arrondissement) but lived in several other places after that, including rue Polonceau. According to Sylla, the initiative leading to their relocation to 216 bis involved the Catholic priest as well as various brokers, including two Malian doctors. Soninke residents hailing from the three villages of Sobokou, Somankidi, and Diataya and living in disparate parts of Paris came together and learned to live together at 216 bis: "That's the place where we stuck together," Sylla said. Later on, Haalpulaar and Wolof migrants from Senegal joined them at this foyer.*

**Moussa Kanté** *arrived in France from Mali via Dakar in 1967 and found lodging in the fourteenth arrondissement in an underground accommodation where most migrants from Sobokou stayed.*[3] *Although he was of Khassonke origin and from another village, he had family ties with migrants from Sobokou and had spent time in the house collectively run by migrants from this village in Dakar. In the fourteenth arrondissement, he met Senegalese from Soninke villages such as Waoundé, Moudéri, and Dembacané (who would later move to Boulogne-Billancourt, next to the Renault auto factory where many of them worked). In 1968, Kanté left the fourteenth arrondissement for the 216 bis foyer. "That's the way we relocated: 216 bis was the place where everybody who'd come [to France] was reunited. We'd meet in the factories, and we'd bring them over. We told those from Diataya whom we'd met at Renault, 'We have a new place.' We informed comrades at other factories, such as Viandox, as well* *as those living in the surroundings, such as on the cul-de-sacs near rue Petit."*

The stories of these three Malian migrants give us a glimpse into the urban trajectories of migrants in Paris and other nearby municipalities in the 1960s. Each narrative mentions multiple addresses, and the broader set of stories recounted by the migrants I interviewed conveys a sense of central places often mentioned as much as it delineates a more scattered geography of transient residences. The notion of the "first African foyer" in Paris is significant: it testifies to the migrants' way of telling the history of their migration as one with foundations, rooted in specific places.[4]

A history of shared workplaces and intense movements within Paris accounts for the form of regrouping that occurred at the foyers. The three villages that most of the residents of 216 bis came from were not geographically close to each other (figure 1.1), nor were they historically connected prior to the migration era. The union of these migrants was forged in places of work and residence in Paris. Beyond the shared Soninke ethnicity of the initial group, a number of Haalpulaar migrants from several villages on the Senegalese-Mauritanian border, as well as Wolof migrants, joined the initial residents.[5] This story illustrates the crucial role of migrant networks in international migration. As defined by Douglas Massey, "Migrant networks are sets of interpersonal ties that link migrants, former migrants, and nonmigrants in origin and destination areas by ties of kinship, friendship, and shared community origin."[6] Beyond these well-known dynamics, I argue that the very experience of mobility throughout the city was also crucial to the migrants' sense of forging a community.

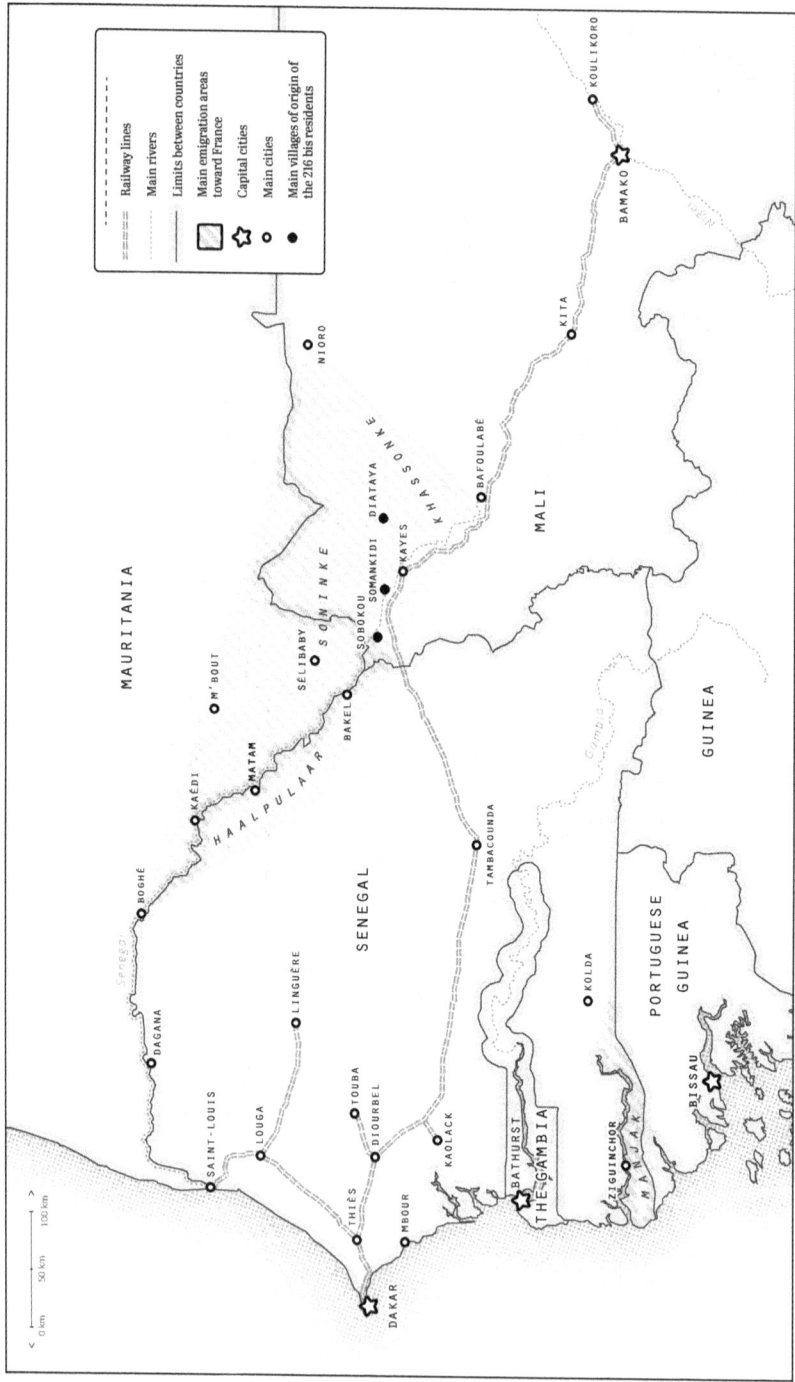

**FIGURE 1.1** Main departure areas of West African migrants arriving in France in the 1960s.

*Source:* Adapted from Souleymane Diarra, "Les travailleurs africains noirs en France," *Bulletin de l'Institut fondamental d'Afrique noire* 30, no. 3 (July 1968). © Jeremy Masse,

## URBAN PIONEERS IN HOTELS
## AND BASEMENTS

The arrival of West African workers in France as African colonies gained independence followed older forms of mobility. Heir to a longer Atlantic history that had brought a few thousand blacks to France throughout the eighteenth century, some West Africans were established in French cities from the early twentieth century.[7] During and after World War I, sailors had settled in ports such as Bordeaux and Marseille, some of them becoming café or hotel owners in a highly diverse black population.[8] In the interwar period, students and intellectuals were part of the cultural and intellectual Parisian scene, and they forged ties with people coming from other parts of the French Empire, as well as with other black men and women such as African Americans, in a socially diverse milieu.[9] The population of French West Africans in France in 1926 was reported to be barely two thousand people, a number that was probably underestimated.[10] After World War II, professional opportunities for West African sailors emerged in France. Some demobilized soldiers from the colonies stayed on, a few of them forming families with French women, notably in southern parts of the country.[11]

In the early 1960s, a new facet of West African migration suddenly became visible: the "black African worker," which attracted intense press coverage that focused on the poor living conditions of these men.[12] The first arrivals in search of industrial jobs can be traced to the mid-to-late 1950s, first to the department of Seine-Maritime (in cities such as Rouen and Le Havre) and then toward the Paris region.[13] Estimating the number of black African workers in France proved difficult, given the lack of registration and their high mobility: in 1963, press articles quoted estimates ranging from 10,000 to 70,000.[14] That same year, the Prefecture de la Seine counted 22,100, of whom 12,000 lived in the Paris region, followed by 6,000 in Marseille and its wider department, 2,000 in Bordeaux, 800 in Rouen, and 500 in Le Havre.[15] Although still probably underestimated, these figures provide a sense of the spatial distribution of West African migrants. They were a small group in comparison, notably, to Algerians, whose population in France was about 445,000 in 1963.[16] Nonetheless, the numbers over time attest to rapid growth: by 1967 the authorities counted 40,000 West African workers.[17]

This influx occurring in a short span of time was due to the conjunction of several factors. After World War II, France had huge labor needs in the industrial and construction sectors. As happened in other European countries, French workers had the opportunity to access better-skilled jobs, leaving low-skilled jobs to newcomers.[18] In the 1950s and early 1960s, in addition to migrants from Italy, Spain, and Portugal, labor migration from Algeria, begun in the 1930s, developed.[19] However, starting in 1954, the Algerian War led the French government to renew its control over their mobility, fears of political agitation deterred employers from recruiting them, and some Algerians returned home to fight with the National Liberation Front. In recognition that the African colonies had been crucial to France's ability to win World War II, West Africans as newly recognized French citizens could circulate relatively freely within the French Empire.[20] Most of these migrants came through their own networks, although the presence of recruiters in African ports was occasionally reported.[21]

The independence of Mali, Senegal, and Mauritania in 1960 did not constitute a major break in the rules over mobility. In fact, for fear of retaliation on her expatriate community, France negotiated a fairly liberal mobility regime. In 1963 and 1964,

French authorities signed conventions with these three countries concerning "the circulation of persons," requiring newcomers to present a labor contract and a medical certificate—but those coming as "tourists" only needed to present an identification card and a return ticket.[22]

As previously stated, these migrants came from specific regions: the largest number came from the Upper Senegal River Valley, primarily members of the Soninke ethnic group; the second largest were the Haalpulaar, also from the Senegal River Valley;[23] other pioneers of West African migration included Manjak migrants from the Casamance region in Senegal and from Guinea Bissau.[24]

This regional specialization is a feature of many migratory histories throughout the world. It is tied to earlier histories of mobility, which had delineated paths of circulation, notably from the Upper Senegal Valley to the coastal cities, especially Dakar. It also reflects the specificities of the social organization of emigrant societies: the temporary migration of young men supplemented their household revenue with cash, enabling them to accumulate enough to marry upon return. In the early 1960s, migrants needed to pay their boat fare; some could work in Dakar to fund their own travel, and others waited for a relative or a friend already in France to send them their ticket.

West Africans reaching Paris at the turn of the sixties found a city still suffering from a serious housing shortage despite postwar reconstruction efforts.[25] As in other major French cities, its outskirts were filled with *bidonvilles* (shantytowns) where North Africans, Portuguese, and poor French families were housed, which already constituted a political concern.[26] Within the cities, a variety of housing types existed, often with low levels of comfort. *Garni* or *meublé* (a furnished room), a type of accommodation that had hosted internal French migrants and working-class populations since the nineteenth century, had found new currency during the housing crisis of the 1950s.[27]

The West African newcomers lodged wherever they could find space in the city. In an enumeration that seems to cover every possible kind of shelter in a deindustrializing city, the sociologist Souleymane Diarra lists "basements, attics, cafés, ballrooms, sheds, former stables, outhouses, workshops, and abandoned factories."[28] In hotels, they not only occupied rooms left vacant by Algerians but also stayed in previously uninhabited spaces such as basements.[29] Bunks were built that allowed two and occasionally three beds, thus maximizing the numbers of tenants in the same space but creating problems of air circulation and poor access to shared bathrooms, which often only provided cold water.

West Africans occupied parts of the city in which earlier migrants were already present, and their places of residence were mapped onto the geography of neighborhoods populated by working-class Parisians: the eastern and northern areas of the city, notably the nineteenth arrondissement; more central parts of the city; and working-class areas immediately surrounding Paris where many factories still stood. Some streets and cul-de-sacs came to be systematically occupied. In the nineteenth arrondissement alone, Souleymane Diarra counted 2,100 black Africans in forty-four garnis and five hotels.[30] Newcomers joined other family members, covillagers, or migrants who came from the same region or who spoke the same language. This led to a process of concentration both in terms of emigration affecting specific localities and of the grouping of migrants from the same locality in a limited number of lodgings.

These dynamics borrowed from institutions of hospitality toward newcomers that had sustained long-distance trade networks over centuries.[31] Modes of organizing collective life replicated those adopted in urban places of emigration. In Dakar, as mentioned in Moussa Kanté's opening narrative, migrants from the inland lodged in dormitories or buildings with people from the same village or small region. These had been known since the nineteenth century as "rooms" (French: *chambre*; Soninke: *konpe*; Pulaar: *suudu*).[32] In these spaces, the migrants set up "cash boxes" (French: *caisse*) that were used to pay for collective meals, to which all men working in Dakar as well as migrants returning from Central Africa or France would contribute a fixed amount. Newcomers looking for a job in the city could find room and board while searching for employment, and would-be migrants could prepare for their journey. In Paris, these dimensions of collective organization and mutual help proved crucial. Hierarchical relations shaped the handling of money: new migrants would hand over their pay slips to an elder, who would divide it up, some going to the collective cash box, some being sent to the family back home, and the remaining given back to the worker as pocket money.

In Paris, the private sector was the first to absorb the newcomers. It was a lucrative market with a variety of configurations, from hotel owners renting empty rooms to complex arrangements involving owners, managers, and brokers. Among 202 privately run facilities listed by the authorities in 1963, 156 were owned by North Africans, thirty-five by Europeans (who generally entrusted Algerians to manage them), and eleven by fellow West Africans.[33] The coexistence with North African owners and Algerian returnees after the end of the Algerian War generated frictions. Algerians were eager to take back their living spaces and jobs, provoking competition with African migrants. Tensions were sometimes articulated in relation to wider historical dynamics, especially the racial stigmatization of black people in North Africa and parts of West Africa, and Algerian resentment over the participation of West African soldiers on the French side during the Algerian struggle for independence.[34] Violent episodes occurred, such as in July 1963, when arguments over a minor incident developed into a street battle between Mauritanians and Algerians in Saint-Denis, injuring twenty-four men.[35] In recounting these historical incidents, my interlocutors tied frictions in the foyers to events in the workplace, where they were subjected to unequal and racialized recruitment processes.[36]

The minority of eleven facilities involving West African landlords or managers is probably underestimated.[37] Some of the identified African landlords ran very large facilities.[38] Others were in charge of several: for example, 4 rue du Rhin (180 beds) was opened and managed by war veteran Lassana Diagouraga, a man from Diaguily married to a French woman;[39] Diagouraga, who had also installed several dormitories in other hotels in the eighteenth and nineteenth arrondissements, appears in the archival record as renting a former grocery shop in the eighteenth arrondissement where twenty-two men lived in eighty square meters. He explained to the police that he had been approached by the Mauritanian representative in France to act as a "social delegate" for his brothers from Mauritania, Senegal, and Mali who had come to work in France. These African landlords held an ambivalent position: they were figures of success who inverted the racial hierarchy. But their failures were held up as examples of exploitation in morally-loaded terms.[40] Furthermore, residents resented the landlords' close relations with African national authorities.

The issue of crowded living conditions for African workers became widely publicized during the winter of 1962–63, and authorities began plans to develop government-subsidized housing as an alternative to this uncontrolled private market.

## RESPONDING TO EMERGENCY: SPECIALIZED ASSOCIATIONS AND THE CREATION OF BLACK FOYERS IN THE 1960s

In 1963, several associations subsidized by public funds began providing African workers with accommodation, improving their conditions, and giving rise to a housing system for West Africans that was to last decades. When the housing of West African migrants emerged as a problem, France had already had experience providing collective housing for single migrant laborers, mainly from Algeria and secondarily from Tunisia and Morocco; migrants from these countries were subsumed under the colonial era category of "North Africans."[41] Government officials continued these policies by adopting the "foyer" as a form of housing, but they decided not to mix West African migrants with those from North Africa. West Africans were generally managed by ad hoc associations; in a few instances, associations involved in the housing of North Africans and other migrants designed separate facilities for workers from sub-Saharan Africa.

A foyer was a type of collective housing for single men that had existed in France since the beginning of the twentieth century.[42] During the interwar period, French authorities extended this kind of subsidized housing to North Africans by building six foyers in Paris and neighboring industrial towns.[43] After World War II, an association covering the Paris region gave new momentum to this project and contributed to the establishment of fourteen foyers for North Africans.[44] In 1956, in the midst of the Algerian War, authorities established a semipublic company, the National Society for the Construction of Housing for Algerian Workers and Families (Société nationale de construction de logements pour les travailleurs originaires d'Algérie et leurs familles [Sonacotral]).[45] This was part of a network of institutions targeting so-called French Muslims from Algeria at a time when social assistance and repression were intertwined.[46] Having previously been dealt with by the Ministry of Labor, the issue of housing Algerians now came under the remit of the Ministry of the Interior. Using foyers for housing had several advantages. First, they had low construction costs and offered low rents. Second, they allowed authorities to keep immigration under control; they were designed to make family reunion more difficult by housing male immigrants outside of lodging suitable for families. Finally, they kept migrants concentrated in sites that facilitated the operation of educational projects, social assistance, and surveillance.

In 1963, as part of a wider trend to extend services and facilities created for Algerians to other migrants, Sonacotral was expanded and renamed National Society for the Construction of Housing for Workers (Société nationale de construction de logements pour les travailleurs [Sonacotra]) to reflect its mandate to accommodate workers of all origins. Despite this change, Sonacotra avoided housing black African workers. Sonacotra administrators believed North Africans were individualistic, and they encouraged this perceived characteristic by offering individual rooms. In contrast, they viewed West Africans as prone to organizing themselves in groups and communities, a dimension that they did not want to deal with.[47]

In parallel with developing foyers along these lines, authorities discussed whether to promote the concentration or the dispersal of migrants. A 1968 report asserted that "dilution" in small facilities was preferred and that the acceptable proportion of foreigners was 10 to 15 percent of the population.[48] Eventually, an organized concentration of migrants categorized as "black

Africans" prevailed; this policy was guided by racialized assumptions about the differences between migrants from North Africa and sub-Saharan Africa and the fear of tensions between these two groups.[49]

Another line of distinction separated black Africans from black Caribbeans: in the early 1960s, French authorities organized labor migration flows from French overseas territories, notably the Caribbean islands of Guadeloupe and Martinique, as well as the island of Réunion in the Indian Ocean. They opened dedicated community centers and developed housing policies for these migrants to facilitate their access to social housing and the private market. These black French citizens were consciously separated and distinguished from black African workers, arguably by fear of feelings of "frustration" among the Caribbeans in a context in which they experienced racism on a daily basis.[50]

Among myriad associations, the two that opened the most foyers in the 1960s were the Association for Technical Training of African and Malagasy Workers (Association pour la formation technique de base des travailleurs africains et malgaches [AFTAM]), which ran eleven foyers, and Support and Dignity for African Workers (Soutien et dignité aux travailleurs africains [Soundiata]), which oversaw six foyers (figure 1.2). Both were typical of specialized associations focusing on the support of West Africans.[51]

AFTAM was created in 1962 by high-ranking civil servants working in the emerging arena of foreign aid and international cooperation, such as Stéphane Hessel, its first president.[52] The vice president was Solange Faladé, born in Dahomey, a psychoanalyst and leader of the Federation of Students from Black Africa in France (Fédération des étudiants d'Afrique noire en France [FEANF]) in the 1950s. Other members had been involved in decolonization movements, and the board included

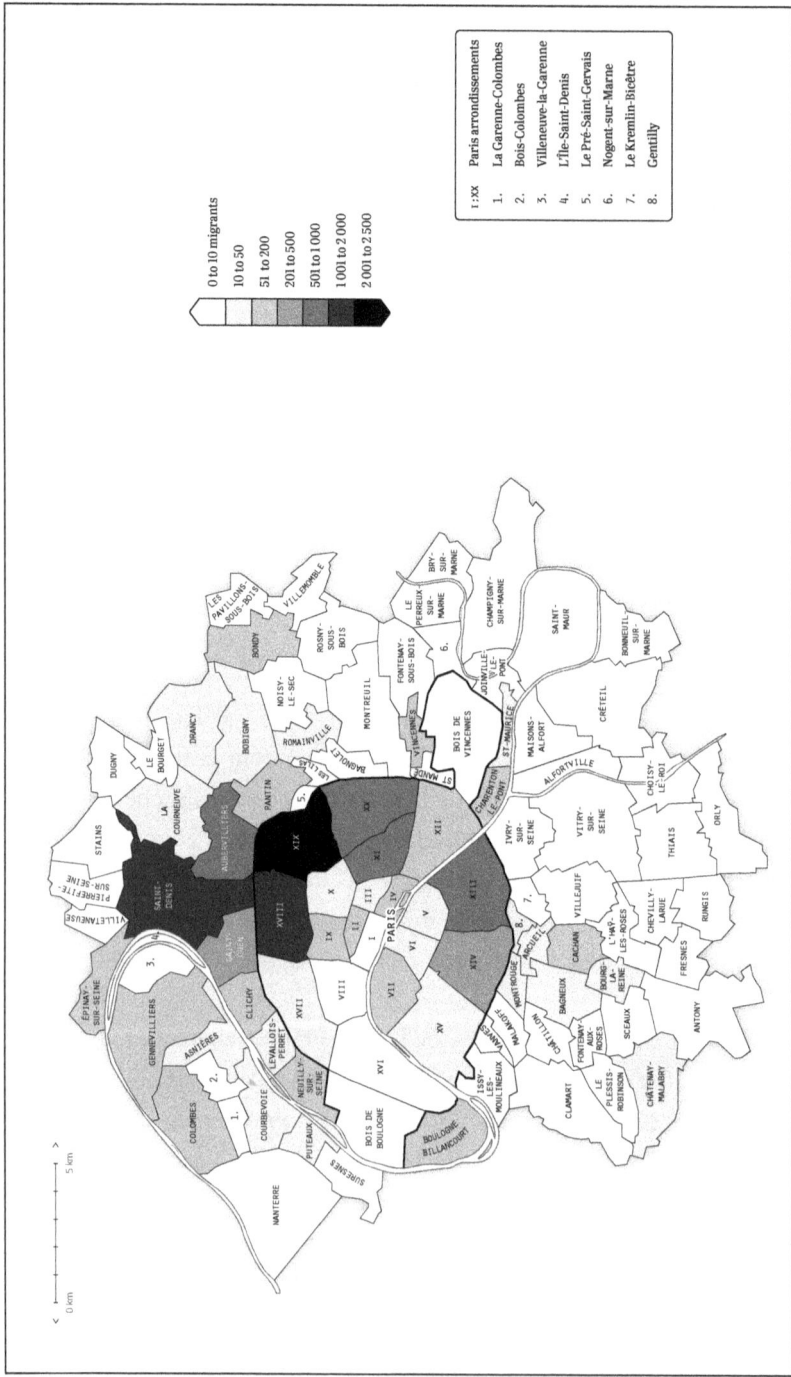

**FIGURE 1.2** West Africans in private lodging houses and café-hotels in the Paris area (early to mid-1960s).

*Source:* Adapted from Souleymane Diarra, "Les travailleurs africains noirs en France," *Bulletin de l'Institut fondamental d'Afrique noire* 30, no. 3 (July 1968).

delegates from several ministries, the prefecture, and three African embassies.[53]

AFTAM set itself the task of "training Africans with the aim of absorbing them as workers in France but with the prospect of their return to Africa."[54] Although its initial goal was to create an organization to help migrants find jobs and to offer training, it was swiftly caught up in the pressing need to house African workers. To deal with the issue of housing, AFTAM laid out the following recommendations:

> With the prospect of their returning to their countries of origin . . . [we should] provide them with living conditions that are the least different from those they have always known and will go back to upon their return. . . . They live in village communities with chiefs, customs, and laws. Within such communities, they feel at ease surrounded by people who understand them and speak the same language. . . . Lodgings need to be of the community type, offering comfort but not luxury, so as to avoid maladjustment upon their return.[55]

Establishing foyers deemed "adapted" to the presumed living conditions of the migrants in Africa became a motto of AFTAM projects throughout the 1960s. Such paternalistic principles guided the design of the living space, with a preference for collective forms such as dormitories.

Soundiata, the other prominent association involved in the creation of African foyers, including the one at 216 bis, grew out of slightly different networks but adopted a similar philosophy. Soundiata was created in 1963 in Catholic aid networks, with members of the White Fathers, a missionary congregation active in Africa; retired military officers; and civil servants and members of associations and trade unions with Catholic leanings.[56] The role of the White Fathers was highlighted in a report by a Malian official on his tour of the living conditions of his compatriots in France in the early 1960s. He noted that Father Bollinger, who had served in Mali, was "fluent in the Bamanan language."[57] The specific interest in Mali of the founders of the association influenced the choice of the association's name, which was both an acronym and a reference to a major historical figure in West Africa, the king Soundiata Keïta. Its first president was Robert Buron, a former minister who was first a Christian Democrat before gravitating toward socialism and becoming active in aid networks. The White Father Pierre Laridan, who had also served in Mali, was the association's secretary general at the time. Discussions initially involved more radical French and African activists who left Soundiata because they wanted the foyers to be managed by the residents, not by the association.[58]

Like AFTAM, Soundiata opted for foyers that would respect the community character that it saw as rooted in the migrants' home societies. It provided foyer residents with social support, such as assistance with administrative issues, and invited French and African volunteers to work with a team of African workers and local-level managers.

This account of these associations challenges the notion that they were only "shell associations" (French: *associations bidons*), a form of criticism that arose in the late 1960s and persisted into the 1970s.[59] As the 216 bis narratives recall, this was a time of experimentation. Mainly French administrators but also African intellectuals met a majority of unskilled migrant laborers from West Africa, an encounter shaped by the French political and administrative framework in managing migrants, but from which emerged an original formula—that of the African foyer (figure 1.3).

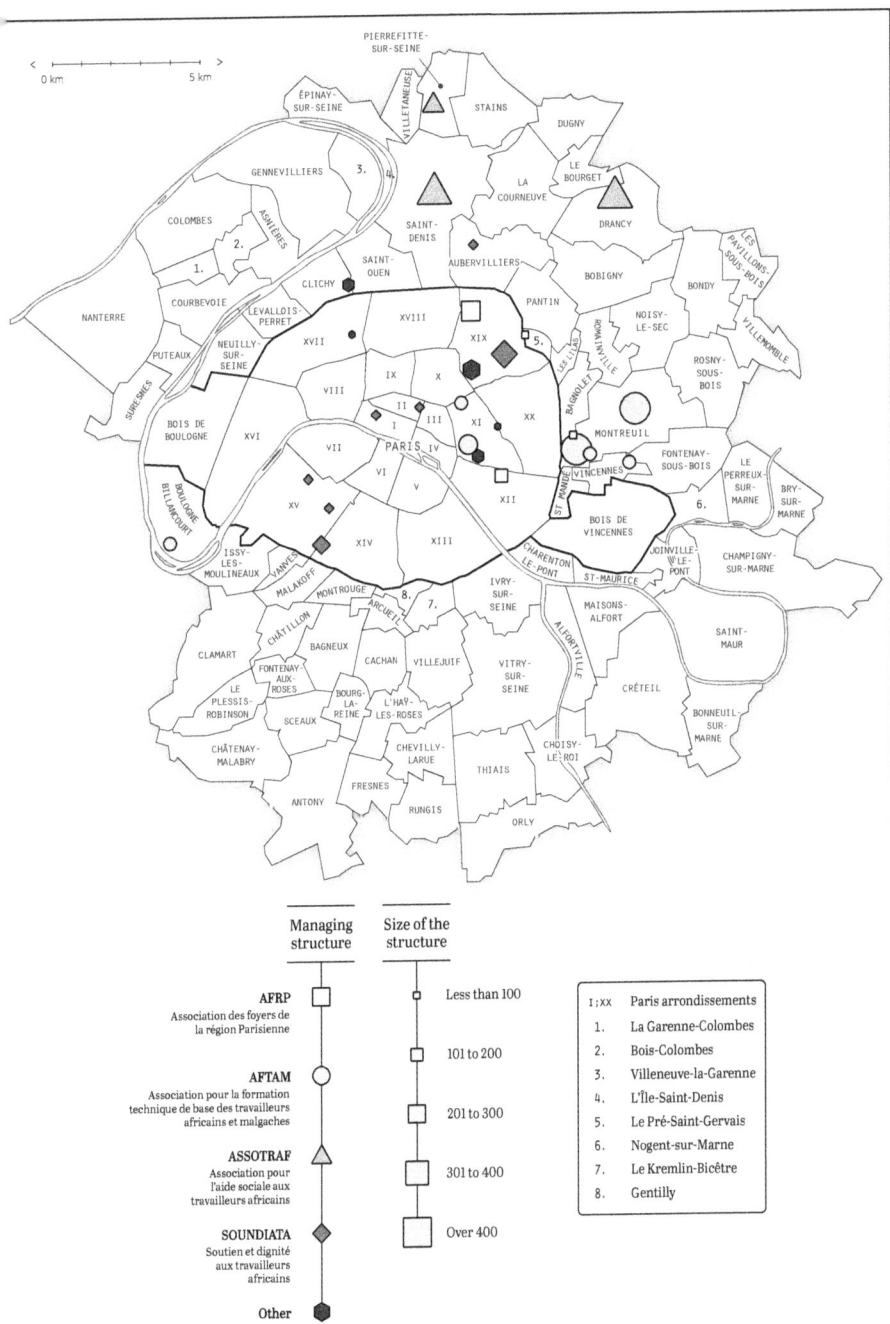

**FIGURE 1.3** Foyers opened for "black Africans" in the Paris area (1963–1969).

*Note*: This map covers a period when the administrative division around Paris changed, from the Seine Department (represented here) to newly created departments in January 1968.

*Sources: Logement collectif à caractère non lucratif des travailleurs à Paris et dans les trois départements limitrophes*, Prefecture of Paris, October 1968; Hélène Béguin, "Héberger des migrants ou gérer des logements? L'Aftam et ses 'foyers d'Africains noirs' (1962–2012)," PhD diss., University of Paris Est, 2015. © Jeremy Masse, Aïssatou Mbodj-Pouye.

Two other associations dealt with black African workers in the Paris region. As part of a long tradition of employers providing lodging for their workers, the African Workers' Social Aid Association (Association pour l'Aide sociale aux travailleurs africains [ASSOTRAF]) was started by Georges Larché, an industrialist in French Senegal and a former deputy of the colony.[60] In 1966–67, ASSOTRAF opened three large housing facilities in neighboring municipalities in north Paris: Pierrefitte, Saint-Denis, and Drancy.[61] The Paris Region Foyers' Association (Association des foyers de la région parisienne [AFRP]), which had initially been devoted to housing for North Africans, opened separated facilties for sub-Saharan migrants.[62]

All these associations received public funding from the Social Action Fund (Fonds d'action sociale [FAS]), another institution that extended its activities from assisting and controlling Algerian migrants to other groups from elsewhere.[63] They also sought support from municipal governments: for example, the municipality of Paris let Soundiata occupy, free of rent, a former industrial building located at 214 rue Raymond Losserand (fourteenth arrondissement), which came to be known as Foyer Losserand.[64] When granting this authorization in 1963, the prefect admitted that the municipality had a future project (within "2 or 3 years") to reclaim the structure for building a highway, demonstrating how such arrangements were perceived as being only short-term solutions, even though, in the end, Foyer Losserand remained in place until 1974.[65] The assumption that these solutions would be short-lived was behind the policy of reusing industrial and military buildings in makeshift arrangements.

At 216 bis rue Saint-Denis, the structure Soundiata established as the foyer was a former commercial building dating from the eighteenth century that had been converted into living space just after World War II.[66] Soundiata's limited financial capacity led them to first opt for joint ownership and to occupy only the basement and first three floors of the six-story building. White working-class tenants occupied the rest of the building. An incident recounted by several interlocutors was the death of one of the French tenants living alone on one of the upper floors, whose corpse was only discovered after several days. This anecdote elicited comments about the risk of living alone—a risk averted by collective life in the foyers.

Beyond the choice of collective facilities (an option that can also be interpreted as a pragmatic decision given scarcity of resources), the way that some associations organized internal life in the foyers was based on proclamations of respect for African social organization. The choices made regarding local staff, notably the director, were crucial because this employee was the person who dealt with residents on a daily basis. AFTAM recruited two Malian female social workers, and Soundiata promoted some residents to the position of director.[67] This contrasts with the Sonacotra policy of recruiting former colonial military personnel to run its foyer.

## AFRICAN BROKERS, AFRICAN GOVERNMENTS, AND CREATION OF THE FOYERS

A key figure of the opening of 216 bis was Demba Saounera, who came from Sobokou and was a *sakke*, a status group within Soninke society associated with brokerage.[68] Arriving in Paris in 1958, he was among the pioneers. He had connections with many other West African migrants and seemed knowledgeable about Parisian urban life. His renown as the founder of the foyer at 216 bis traveled back to his home village: when I visited his widow in Sobokou in 2017, she showed me his framed photograph hanging on the wall, telling me how he had "opened a foyer in France."[69] Perspectives on the foyers held by their inhabitants highlight their agency at all levels, as this story told by M'Pama Siby, who came from a different region, demonstrates:

I heard that the history of the foyer goes back to Modibo [Keïta]. Modibo, the first president of Mali, decided to create foyers for Africans in France in 1963. King Hassan II of Morocco, Boumediene of Algeria, Senghor of Senegal, Bourguiba of Tunisia, and the leader of Mauritania, they accepted the idea. . . . I myself arrived in France in 1968; our first place was 5 rue de Reuilly. African migrants had requested the opening of this place; the boss was an Algerian, and there were bedsteads; it was disgusting! Men from Gadiaga [a province between Bakel and Kayes] had opened it. I come from Diongaga near Yélimané [outside Gadiaga], but I went there because my older brother had joined them from Marseille in 1958, a time when there were no Africans in Paris. [Siby names the eight men in the first group of arrivals, among them Demba Saounera.]

I then asked Siby, "How did you move from there to here, Foyer Masséna [thirteenth arrondissement]?"

The French agreed to build this building when Mamadou Diarra, a former government minister in Mali, came to 5 rue de Reuilly during an official mission on behalf of Moussa Traoré [the second president of Mali, brought to power after a coup in 1968]. Thanks to him and Woussou Bathily, the village head who lived with us at 5 rue de Reuilly, the French agreed to find us a foyer. Here, there were factories building army tanks [Panhard factories]. In 1970, this foyer was erected in the place of barracks for Arabs who worked in the factory.[70]

Siby's narrative attests to a trajectory some migrants took in Paris that was distinct from, but intersected with, the one involving residents of 216 bis. It fits into the geography of the establishment of West African communities in Paris in which reference to Soninke or Haalpulaar polities is prominent, at a time when covillagers in France rarely exceeded a handful, and when regional grouping prevailed.[71] The chronology of events at 5 rue de Reuilly-Masséna, which opened in 1958, was similar to that surrounding the move to 216 bis. But this narrative emphasizes the role of African officials.

A few foyers resulted from the direct action of African authorities. The two best-documented cases are located outside Paris in the industrial cities of Rouen (Seine-Maritime) and Roubaix (Nord-Pas-de-Calais). In 1960, Rouen's African community consisted of 1,000 Senegalese, 350 Mauritanians, and a few other West Africans from Mali, Côte d'Ivoire, and Guinea. Pierre Landemaine, a local political figure from the ranks of a Catholic party, the Popular Republican Movement, had supported the creation of an association for Senegalese workers, and a first foyer had been established in 1957. A friend of Senegal's president Léopold Sédar Senghor, Landemaine became the representative of the region's Senegalese embassy, and in 1960 he negotiated the opening of another facility called the Senegalese and Mauritanian Workers' Shelter as part of an urban renewal project.[72] This foyer was later replaced by a new facility with a mosque located on rue Moïse, inaugurated in 1968 with much fanfare, an event attended by Mauritanian president Moktar Ould Daddah. The Rouen cases illustrate the interaction between municipal actors concerned with urban renewal, Catholic networks involved in Africa, and African heads of state.

In Roubaix, the project involved a key figure of Senegalese associations, the activist Sally N'Dongo, who had founded the

General Union of Senegalese Workers (Union générale des travailleurs sénégalais en France [UGTSF]) in 1964.[73] Roubaix's foyer opened in 1965 under the remit of an association run by Senegalese from the UGTSF.[74] The administrative record shows that official collaboration and the approval of Senegalese and Mauritanian embassies were also key elements of the project.[75] Nonetheless, the UGTSF accounts suggest that they viewed migrants' concerns differently from the prevailing consensus among other associations regarding the cultural peculiarity of West Africans. UGTSF stated, "For a long time it has been believed, simplistically, that Africans needed community housing. This is absolutely not true. Many would be satisfied with not being too dispersed."[76]

But Siby's reflections are rooted in his experience of the opening of a foyer in Paris, suggesting that the involvement of African authorities went beyond these two documented cases. In the early 1960s, African officials sought to position themselves as providers of assistance and housing to their citizens, but their success was uneven. On one hand, they sometimes responded to calls for migrant support issued by French authorities,[77] on the other, they faced a degree of opposition from their constituents who had migrated to France, a key point that Siby does not mention. West African migrants sought to evade control by the authorities of their countries of origin during a time of one-party rule and military regimes. The defiance of migrants at their embassies' interventions in their lives is conspicuous in the record. This is in part because African governments tended to limit emigration or even, in the case of Mali, prohibit it as a form of "desertion" from the newly independent country.[78] In 1965, officials from Mali, including the mayor of Kayes and the Malian consul in France, toured several foyers in the Paris region, reiterating Mali's official position against migration and inviting unemployed migrants to move back to their country. Along with a similar intervention from a Senegalese official, these tours stirred anxiety among Malian and Senegalese migrants, who feared that collusion between their government and French authorities could result in organized repatriation.[79]

Furthermore, under Modibo Keïta, the Malian consulate attempted to monitor Malians in France through the Association of Malian Workers in France (Association des Travailleurs Maliens en France [ATMF]). In 1966, the Malian consul visited several foyers in Montreuil, requiring the residents to register at the consulate and show their membership cards for the ATMF and for the Union soudanaise-Rassemblement démocratique africain, then the single ruling party in Mali. French administrative and police records indicate that the foyer residents deemed such requirements to be inappropriate in light of the authorities' lack of concrete involvement in improving the migrants' conditions.[80] Another group, the Association of Malian Students and Interns in France (Association des Étudiants et Stagiaires Maliens en France), actively opposed Keïta's regime.[81] As for Senegalese interventions, Sally N'Dongo seems to have relied on the Senegalese authorities until 1965. But when the authorities began creating other associations that they intended to control more closely, N'Dongo became more and more vocal in criticizing their lack of assistance and their collusion with French services.

Notwithstanding these internal tensions, the French system of assistance for migrants did not leave much space for African authorities to act in favor of their emigrants. In 1964, in a letter to the prime minister, the Minister of the Interior signaled that a nephew of President Senghor, alarmed by the situation of his compatriots he had visited in France, was looking for funds in Dakar to improve their conditions. The letter also reported that

Malian president Keïta had promised to subsidize the foyers in France.[82] For fear of political interference if foreign structures aimed at delivering such assistance were established on French soil, the Minister of the Interior insisted on the need to accelerate the French institutional response (notably through FAS) to improve social assistance for migrant workers. Only then would it be diplomatically possible to ask Malian and Senegalese authorities to restrict their efforts to their "traditional roles as foreign representatives."

Siby's assertion about President Keïta's prominent role concerns a short period when African authorities made promises they could not keep, in part because French authorities objected to such activities. More broadly, Siby's idea that decisions on the fate of African migrants were made at a higher level is congruent with the way African and French governments closely monitored the conditions and political mood of African migrants. Jacques Foccart, Secretary General for African Affairs from 1958 to 1974, actively reported on such matters to President De Gaulle and later to President Pompidou.

Siby's account also sheds light on the wide-ranging social backgrounds of the African brokers involved in creation of the foyers. Some were community members with specific skills and authority, such as Woussou Bathily and Demba Saounera. Others came from outside the community of West African workers, such as the two Malian medical doctors, Dr. Keïta and Dr. Soumaré; Samba Sylla also mentions that African students from FEANF helped him find literacy classes.[83]

The position of African students and intellectuals vis-à-vis their less educated countrymen, and their solidarity toward or disassociation from them, is both a classic historiographic issue and a debate of the era.[84] In 1962 or 1963, the Bureau for the Study of African Realities (Bureau d'étude des réalités africaines), founded by a group of African students and headed by the Senegalese sociologist Jean-Pierre N'Diaye, convened a discussion on the topic of African migrations in Paris. They invited personalities from the African embassies, as well as intellectuals such as Sembene Ousmane, a former dock worker in Marseille turned novelist and filmmaker.[85] Their discussions were both theoretical, asking notably if African migrations were instances of neocolonialism to be discouraged, and practical, offering material help and support to their fellow workers. They were vocally critical of the pitiful tone characterizing the press coverage on the workers' conditions in the winter of 1962–63. Among the speakers, Sally N'Dongo seems to have been the only one to embark on concrete plans to design foyers and radically change these conditions. Nonetheless, the encounter between a highly diverse student milieu (far more diverse than the workers in terms of their national origins but also gender, with the added presence of women) and the workers in the foyers serves to situate these communities in the making within wider diasporic networks. The presence of Sembene Ousmane further points to sociological profiles of autodidacts who blur the clear-cut distinction between workers and students. These issues would regain prominence both during and after the May 1968 movement in France.

## MOVING TO A FOYER IN THE 1960s

By recalling the role of African actors in the migrant initiatives of the 1960s, a more complex picture of the foyers emerges. Scrutinizing the periods when migrants moved from one residence to another, in this section I nuance the emphasis of existing scholarly accounts on the dynamics of surveillance and control at work during these periods.[86] Taking my lead from interviews that highlight the agency of migrants in "finding" the 216 bis foyer, I reconsider the administrative records as evidence of often unsuccessful attempts to control a mobile population. West Africans were determined to carve a place for themselves in the city and forged political alliances with African and French actors who would play crucial roles in later developments.

Undoubtedly, the authorities intended to render West Africans more countable and knowable, and ultimately to be better equipped to discipline these unruly migrants. Moving them from hotels, basements, and other privately run dilapidated lodgings to foyers supervised by public agencies and funded by subsidized associations provided occasions for the French government to do so. These relocations occurred under the supervision of the prefecture, notably its Technical Assistance Service.[87] The fact that relocations facilitated control is salient when one considers the coupling of such operations with health interventions in a population among which the prevalence of TB reached a worrisome 10 percent.[88] At a 1965 conference on the health of black African workers, a speaker explained how one way to treat reluctant migrants for TB was to take advantage of new foyer openings.[89] But the unwillingness of migrants to comply with health mandates was also widely noted: in 1963, while offering to detect TB, AFTAM and Malian doctor Abdoulaye Keïta were barred by West Africans in the nineteenth arrondissement from accessing their accommodation.[90]

The earlier instances of organized protest were directly tied to relocation projects. In 1963, a committee pulled together local associations, political organizations from left to center, and Catholic priests and organizations to oppose the imminent expulsion of ninety West African workers from a hotel in the thirteenth arrondissement.[91] This case attests to wide-ranging political alliances well beyond involvement of the main workers' organization, the French Communist Party, and its parent organization, the General Confederation of Labor trade union.[92]

In some cases, African organizations played a key role. In 1964, West Africans mobilized in Saint-Denis under the guidance of Galadio Camara, the ATMF representative, indicating that the association had some legitimacy at the local level. Claiming to speak on behalf of black Africans across the Seine-Saint-Denis department, he not only wrote leaflets but also engaged in a steady exchange of letters with the municipality, advocating for the construction of a foyer for one thousand West African workers in the city.[93] In 1965, Sally N'Dongo actively supported West African migrants who protested against their housing conditions in several places, reporting to the African consulates and helping residents pursue legal actions.[94] He further demanded that Senegalese authorities look into some relocations undertaken by the prefecture. The Senegalese consul appears to have been more convinced by explanations provided by the prefecture. He argued that these moves represented relocations to better places rather than evictions and that the prefecture had the full agreement of the African workers. The consul further accused Sally N'Dongo of being an exploitative lodger.[95] N'Dongo denounced the fact that his letter, which included named individuals, had been sent to the prefecture, and he denied any accusation of financial exploitation. Beyond the intricacies of UGTSF's changing relationship with the Senegalese authorities, the case suggests that the rehousing processes were ambivalently perceived, involving a dimension of coercion as well as adherence from workers eager to find better living conditions. As previously noted, when 216 bis opened in 1967, the migrants were willing to move in and even convinced other migrants to do so.

In 1967, a report described West African communities as "withdrawn, closed in on themselves," observing that "these tribes live grouped together in isolated colonies, unable to integrate, and many of their representatives appear to be uprooted with regard to our society."[96] In addition to the racist overtones and ignorance of the ability to forge alliances across the political spectrum among African and French organizations, this document can be read as a first step in erasing the role of dedicated associations and French authorities in forging such communities in the first place. The assumption of closed-off African communities unable to "integrate" into French society became a key argument in later views of the foyers.

## CONCLUSION: SECURING AN ADDRESS

As the problem of precarious migrant accommodation was exacerbated in the context of a national housing shortage, associations opened dedicated foyers for West African migrants. From 1963 onward, a public response to the problem developed, with the government providing financial support to specialized associations deemed better equipped to deal with black Africans. These associations worked with West African residential communities that were in the process of organizing themselves at the grassroots level and were capable of exercising leverage through representatives ranging from workers with literacy skills or other aptitudes to students and activists. Rather than stories of alienation, my interlocutors told foundational narratives of emplacement in the city.

The foundational dimension of these narratives is twofold. First, the migrants claimed the foyers as their own because of arrangements made between African and French authorities in the postcolonial era, linking specific ways institutions dealt with them to a shared imperial history. Second, migrants referred to the foyers as places where they came to establish new rules among themselves; the 216 bis residence was the place where they got to know each other and created a residential community that only partly overlapped with ethnic and regional ties.

Migrants lodged in foyers in the suburbs or on the outskirts of the capital often portray themselves as "pioneers" (French: *défricheurs*) in areas that were sparsely populated and mostly industrial.[97] More generally, interviews were suffused with stories of migrants progressively gaining a place in the city through acquaintances they made at work or in cafés, and through increased familiarity with new urban styles. Tied to their high labor mobility, the intensity of their movements within the city is evidenced by the trajectories of Traoré, Sylla, and Kanté, which opened this chapter. These narratives of emplacement echo West African historical accounts of villages moving from one location to a more propitious one.

This sense of becoming a city dweller is integral to the meaning of having an address and accounts for the importance of this reference. Inscribed on a piece of paper, the address was initially viewed as a talisman: for many newcomers who were illiterate, at least in French, a piece of paper with an address was shown to a passerby to get directions to a foyer or a factory.[98] After joining literacy classes or becoming more confidently oriented in the city, the migrant would memorize the address instead.

These stories must be read against the role of addresses in the archival record as a means of control: a list of places where West African workers could be found; identification of some men under surveillance by providing their domicile. In West Africans' recollections of access to housing in Paris in the 1950s and 1960s, the administrative purpose of the address for identification and surveillance is wiped out. Here, I am inspired by the anthropologist Laura Bear, who asked in her research among

Anglo-Indian railway families, "How in people's account of connectedness does one kind of proof (institutional) become converted into emotional and experiential proof."[99] Administrative proof of one's link to a place becomes converted into evidence of a collective gain and of emplacement in the city.

# 2

# MODERN BUILDINGS

Political Challenges, Administrative Anxieties, and the
Consolidation of the Foyer System (1968–1979)

I n 1975, the Soundiata association built a fire escape on one
of the foyers it managed, the old industrial building located
at 216 bis rue Saint-Denis. Soundiata had lodged West
African men in the basement and on the first two floors with
white French tenants occupying the upper floors, but in 1972
it took over the whole six-floor building, converting all family
flats into dormitories. Vast spaces on the ground floor included
a TV room as well as a kitchen with several cooking stations.
The basement offered collective rooms used for meetings and
literacy classes. Centrally located within Paris, 216 bis became
a place of encounter for African workers and students drop-
ping by to purchase a meal from the kitchen or attend a political
meeting in the basement (see figure 2.1).

Building a fire escape proved urgent in a decade marked by
deadly fires in several foyers. The fire escape was one attempt
among several to reduce risks and patchy refurbishment on a
deteriorating building. Indexed by police surveillance as one of
the strongholds of political agitation among West Africans, 216
bis also raised public order concerns. In 1975, a report estimated
that it hosted twice its registered population of 184 residents, and

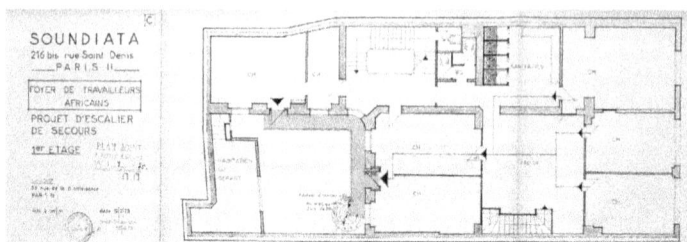

**FIGURE 2.1** A 1975 architectural drawing of the first floor of Foyer 216 bis, featuring rooms used as dormitories and shared sanitary facilities.

*Source*: Archives de Paris 1178 W 2900.

it was one of the facilities classified by the authorities and Soundiata as being in urgent need of renovation. In 1979, the residents were relocated to two newly erected foyers in the nineteenth arrondissement.[1]

Although the administrative record ascribes the installation of a fire escape to a request from safety officers, Samba Sylla, who was then one of this foyer's délégués, recalled that the residents had asked for such equipment and claimed it as their own victory. Combining administrative records with interviews with former 216 bis inhabitants, this chapter foregrounds the active part residents took in the process leading up to their relocation. Their actions crucially shaped policies designed at municipal and national levels about the foyers.

To understand this particular move as indicative of wider trends, several factors need to be considered. First, political activism took on a new dimension after the political upheavals of May 1968. Second, at an institutional level, the foyers consolidated as a system throughout the 1970s despite decisive changes in the situation of postcolonial migrants in France, notably, the 1974 decision to "suspend" labor migration as the

French economy entered recession. Third, gendered identities and social and sociocultural expectations of success shaped West Africans' adhesion to the foyer system, and their emplacement in the city took on new dimensions in the 1970s. Finally, all these dynamics took place in an urban setting, a modernizing metropolis trying to get rid of its slums, and translated into material choices in terms of architecture and interior design, as the collective spaces and dormitories of the 216 bis attest. Considering all these layers is crucial in understanding what the "modern" character of the new foyers asserted by institutional actors and the inhabitants themselves meant.

## UNREST IN WEST AFRICAN FOYERS, MAY 1968

May 1968 was a turning point in the politicization of immigrants' struggles in France.[2] Participation of immigrants in the events of May 1968 remained limited, although some of them did take part in the strikes, as Samba Sylla recalls:

> In '68, I was on a picket line in Malakoff, as a worker at the Roux-Combaluzier elevator factory. I wasn't a trade union representative, but I was part of the movement. There were at least fifteen Africans, mostly Malians. They were unskilled workers [*manoeuvres gros travaux*]. But I was a warehouse clerk, in charge of the elevator spare parts.[3]

May 1968 and its aftermath propelled new activists into the foyers. High school or university students arriving in France who were involved in African 1968 events, notably in Senegal, made the foyers a site of transnational political action.[4] In France, protests in the foyers took place at the same time as struggles for decent or better housing across various types of accommodation, from bidonvilles to student and young worker facilities.[5] The post-1968 years were also marked by new forms of political involvement by migrants in their workplaces, and activist connections made there fueled struggles in the foyers.[6]

The foyers became a competitive ground for recruitment between myriad political organizations at a time of deep political change. Although the French Communist Party (PCF) and the General Confederation of Labour (CGT) were influential in some foyers, the communists' stance toward migrants had always been ambivalent.[7] The PCF was firmly entrenched in the Paris "Red Belt," a string of working-class municipalities run by communist mayors since the 1930s.[8] Interfering with municipal ambitions to renovate and modernize their working-class districts, the arrival of poorly housed migrants posed an acute dilemma between the perceived need to protect the more established working-class by limiting the migrants' precarious installation and international solidarity with these new working-class elements. In a 1969 written public statement, communist mayors in the Paris region objected to the concentration of immigrants in their municipalities resulting from slum clearances.[9] This position was premised on the assumption that the concentration of immigrants over a certain threshold impeded integration.[10] As a result, in 1975, the sympathy of West Africans toward the communists diminished in favor of old and new actors.[11]

In a continuation of their early involvement, Senegalese members of the Union générale des travailleurs sénégalais en France (UGTSF) remained active within the foyers, as did the Associations de solidarité avec les travailleurs immigrés (ASTI) and antiracist movements like the Mouvement contre le racisme et pour l'amitié entre les peuples (MRAP).[12] The Parti Socialiste Unifié (PSU) also supported several struggles.[13] But the early

1970s primarily saw the emergence of leftist groups, themselves highly divided along ideological stances. Those with particular influence in the foyers included the following: the Maoist Gauche Prolétarienne; the Union des communistes de France marxiste-léniniste (UCFML), also Maoist; the Trotskyist Ligue Communiste; and after 1971 the Révolution! organization born of a Ligue Communiste schism, from which the Révolution Afrique group stemmed.[14]

In 1969, in the context of this political pressure cooker, authorities expressed a new anxiety toward West Africans. Two sites polarized police surveillance as well as activist involvement: the ASSOTRAF-run Foyer Pinel in Saint-Denis (six hundred beds) and a privately owned facility in Ivry (five hundred beds). In May, protests erupted in Foyer Pinel.[15] Inhabitants complained of inadequate mail delivery and transferring of phone calls and asked for a change of sheets twice a month. They condemned barring literacy instructors access to the foyer and accused the foyer director of racism. The local ASTI and the communist municipality assisted in organizing meetings between the residents, the ASSOTRAF, and the authorities. Despite these talks, in June the police arrested three leaders of this movement. They expelled two Malians and detained a third leader, Boubacar Bathily, a French citizen born in Senegal, who was accused of threatening to kill the director. Many organizations denounced the expulsions and Bathily's arrest, notably the CGT trade union, which launched collective action, including a petition signed by five thousand individuals.[16] Released after one month in jail, Bathily managed to get his job back at the Renault auto factory thanks to CGT support.

At the other end of Paris, down south, protests arose in Ivry's private foyer.[17] Similarly to Saint-Denis, the director, Garba Traoré, concentrated the anger of the residents. In early 1969, a pamphlet threatened a rent strike if conditions were not improved. Traoré not only increased the rent but further infuriated residents when he banned all outside visitors in July.[18] A rent strike ensued, and the manager retaliated by cutting off the supply of water and electricity.

Beyond these two high-profile cases, an investigation into thirty-one foyers in the summer of 1969 identified eight of them as "self-managed," and protests continued in twenty-one others across the Paris region.[19] In July, the Paris prefecture counted five "agitated African foyers" within the capital, among which was 216 bis.[20] Authorities attributed this new situation in part to the influence of African students and French leftists, but they also pinpointed a changing profile of foyer representatives.[21] These dynamics played out at 216 bis: representatives had originally been designated by each community—sometimes referred to as a "sector," sometimes "canton," in reference to an administrative subdivision in colonial French West Africa— but a new generation of more politicized délégués was emerging who rejected the idea of representing only their community and connected with activist groups.

After a year marked by various forms of political protests in foyers and the emergence of new activist networks, the deaths of five West African workers—four Senegalese and one Mauritanian—in a private foyer in Aubervilliers during the night of January 1, 1970, sparked even wider public emotion.[22] The five migrants died of asphyxiation because they had lit coal to cope with the cold, a practice observed and signaled as potentially dangerous in several reports over a decade.[23] This tragic event brought intense press coverage, including articles based on investigations in foyers in and around Paris as well as a TV debate,[24] and it became a landmark moment for French and African activists. It shed light on the ongoing protests, and one Ivry foyer delegate appeared on national television on January 14.[25]

Collective protests were often sparked by claims about the mundane details of everyday foyer life, from improved sanitation facilities to orderly mail distribution—thus highlighting yet another role of the address, the ability to get one's postal mail—but they fueled a wider political demand for better treatment of immigrants in France. New immigration laws tightened conditions of entry, notably the Circulaires Marcellin-Fontanet in 1972, which tied residency in France to proof of employment, but these legal texts were ultimately abandoned after migrants protested.[26] Activism in the foyers went way beyond national issues, with activists espousing pan-African causes such as the independence struggles of Portuguese African colonies.

The 1970s also witnessed heightened political and racial tensions: in June 1973, a meeting of the far-right organization Ordre Nouveau was held at the Mutualité, in the Latin Quarter, with the motto "Stop uncontrolled immigration". This episode is well known both for the counterdemonstration organized by leftists and antiracist groups, leading to violent confrontations with the police, and for its political consequences: the banning of both Ordre Nouveau and the Ligue communiste.[27] Interviews with foyer residents and activists shed further light on the climate of fear that surrounded the event: activists and residents feared that 216 bis, not far from the Mutualité, could be a target for Ordre Nouveau's members, and they organized watches around the foyers throughout the night.[28]

## BEFORE AND BEYOND THE "SONACOTRA" RENT STRIKE

The topic of detailed studies, the "Sonacotra" rent strike (1973–1981) has marked the history of postcolonial migration by its magnitude: with up to thirty thousand foyers residents refusing to pay their rent at its peak (a majority of whom lived in Sonacotra-run facilities) and large street demonstrations, this coordinated rent strike had wide-ranging effects and constitutes a landmark in activist memory.[29]

Even though the myriad protests that had affected West African foyers prior to the Sonacotra rent strike did not coalesce into a unified movement, some attempts were made by West African residents and activists to develop a concerted course of action.[30] The first movement targeting one managing structure developed in AFTAM-run foyers, mainly populated by West Africans, where a rent increase in autumn 1974 set off a generalized rent strike across fourteen of the thirty-seven foyers managed by the association. Although some officers had been warning of the possible "extension" of rent strikes to North Africans for a year, the problem was first addressed as an issue of "black foyers."[31] Administrative sources ascribed the precedence of mobilizations in West African foyers to their looser control; the authorities were caught off guard as they had constantly underestimated the political potential of black workers. Furthermore, the architecture of these facilities often offered large collective spaces. In addition, West Africans were affected by the economic crisis earlier than workers from the Maghreb, making them more sensitive to rent increases.[32]

As with the AFTAM movement, the Sonacotra rent strike began at a time of successive rent increases, when the economic crisis had already degraded workers' earnings. Beyond economic motives, other demands included revision of the internal rules in order to obtain the right to visitors; dismissal of racist local managers (at the Sonacotra, 95 percent of foyer directors were former military who had served in colonial wars); and recognition of resident representatives. This led to the overarching request to enjoy the same rights as ordinary "tenants," an entirely new demand.

Continuity between protest within West African foyers and the Sonacotra movement is palpable. Among the first Sonacotra foyers to strike were some of the few where West Africans resided, even though Sonacotra only hosted a small number of West Africans (3.9 percent of its residents were from sub-Saharan Africa in 1971).[33] This is notably the case of Foyer David Siqueiros (Saint-Denis), a facility hosting West African residents coming from a dilapidated private facility on rue Gaston Philippe.[34] This case suggests that West Africans, who had experienced poorer albeit less tightly controlled housing conditions in their previous locations, were prone to mobilize. The leaders of the Sonacotra were mainly men from Portugal, Algeria, Morocco and Tunisia, more represented in the foyers run by this structure, but they also counted a few West Africans.[35]

Created in 1975, the "Committee for the coordination of Sonacotra foyers on strike" later welcomed foyers from other managing structures.[36] Under this committee, which had nationwide networks, foyer conditions became the topic of activist expertise and knowledge production, notably on the legal level. In April 1976, the authorities expelled eighteen residents considered leaders, an event that served to publicize the protest (sixteen of them were allowed back in 1977 when the decision was overturned on appeal). The climax was reached in 1979, when the committee rallied together 130 foyers. However, after a peak in 1978 and 1979, the movement declined sharply. Ultimately, the residents made gains in some areas, such as the right to hold meetings in the foyers, but they did not obtain the same legal status as tenants.

## THE PARADOXICAL STABILIZATION
## OF THE "FOYER FORMULA"

Combined with urban policies initiated in 1970, the institutional and political responses to mobilization in the foyers ultimately contributed to the consolidation of the foyer system in a wider context of economic crisis and changing immigration policy. The 1970 fire in Aubervilliers had prompted a governmental response to the scandal of migrants' dire living conditions: in February 1970, Prime Minister Jacques Chaban-Delmas visited basements hosting West Africans and a bidonville in Aubervilliers and announced his decision to get rid of these types of housing, reviving a policy of slum clearance initiated in the 1950s. A law was passed a few months later in July 1970, accompanied by the creation of a permanent interministerial structure on the issue.[37]

In parallel, immigration became a political issue, and the idea of controlling mobility, specifically those of Algerians and sub-Saharan immigrants, gained momentum in the wider context of the economic crisis and rising unemployment. This led to the decision to suspend economic migration in July 1974. As administrative regulations governing conditions on entry and residence in France for African migrants were brought into line with the general system, a residence permit became a mandatory requirement for West African migrants.[38] Economic difficulties at the national level did not mean that job opportunities dwindled evenly. For instance, it was in the 1970s that recruitment by Renault extended significantly toward Senegalese in particular, with the erection of dedicated foyers in Boulogne-Billancourt.[39] Likewise, waste collection municipal services recruited West African workers in the 1970s, initially as "seasonal workers," but many stayed.[40] In such services with strong local work cultures, they often joined unions and engaged in collective action, notably in a series of strikes in the 1970s that enabled them to gain more stable work positions.

The same period of the early 1970s was characterized by a peak in building new foyers. AFTAM reached its maximum capacity in 1975, with 10,827 beds in thirty-nine foyers, after a sharp increase between 1971 and 1975; and Sonacotra in 1976 had 69,975 beds in 262 facilities all over France.[41] From 1970, foyer construction benefited from funding previously reserved for social housing and adopted stricter norms. In areas where immigrant workers were numerous, this translated into a new density of foyers: thus, in the newly created Department of Seine-Saint-Denis, between 1968 and 1973 the number of foyers grew from seventeen to fifty-three, and from 4,449 beds to 15,163.[42]

This conjunction of restrictions on immigration and acceleration of foyer construction was not coincidental. The will to diminish migration flows went hand in hand with the idea of enhancing the living conditions of migrants already present in France. The ambition was also to deprive foyer activists of grounds for their claims with the enhanced levels of comfort in new-built facilities. In 1971, André Postel-Vinay drafted a memo in favor of the "foyer formula." He was then president of AFTAM, and later briefly became Secrétaire d'Etat aux travailleurs immigrés in 1974.[43] Postel-Vinay supported the foyer system for practical and ideological reasons:

> [The foyer formula] is justified by the convenience of grouping immigrant workers around the collective service they need (medical control, literacy, social assistance, etc.). It is also justified by the unsuitability of many of them to life in France.[44]

This normative statement on the inadaptability of the migrants ascribed the exclusionary effects of the foyers to the migrants themselves, and it disguised as sociological analysis a political refusal to provide suitable conditions to postcolonial migrants. The document also introduced practical advice, recommending that foyers offer one to three beds per room. It reasserted the ambition to limit the facilities to 150 to 200 beds, a theme of reports from the 1960s, but pragmatically acknowledged that financial viability was better ensured with facilities of 300 beds or more.

Postel-Vinay's program provides insights into crucial aspects of foyer policy, notably the way it recognizes the exceptionality of the foyer, while at the same time suggesting forms of normalization. Such an idea remained at the core of the foyers' political management long after Postel-Vinay was replaced in his position as Secrétaire d'Etat aux travailleurs immigrés by Paul Dijoud in 1976. However, Dijoud's policy ran against Postel-Vinay's idea that France had a moral and material debt toward immigrants who had contributed to the wealth of the country.[45] Dijoud revised the ambitious plan for the construction of foyers downward in 1976, although he accepted the necessity to provide 25,000 to 30,000 beds in the Paris region.[46]

The fragile tendency toward normalization or de-singularization materialized in the legal framework around the foyers.[47] This was notable in the decision to extend the possibility of housing benefits to foyers' residents, first in 1977 as an experiment and then more widely in 1979. The government used this as a strategy to end the Sonacotra conflict, in a context of financial crisis surrounding the foyers, although its application proved cumbersome.[48] Funded by the Family Benefit Funds (Caisse d'allocations familiales), the "individualized housing allowance" (Aide personnalisée au logement [APL]) was subject to conditions both on the beneficiary (whose salary had to be below a certain amount) and on the type of housing, which only some foyers could meet (for instance, dormitories did not meet this criterion).[49] At the national level, a policy of developing the foyers prevailed in the 1970s, but a discourse on black African populated foyers as "a problem" also emerged, ascribing difficulties in managing some facilities not to the legal and political framework that gave rise to them but to the ethno-racial specificity of these residents.

## DIVERGING VIEWS ON THE PROBLEM OF AFRICAN FOYERS

From fears surrounding the new political activism of sub-Saharan residents at the beginning of the 1970s, in the second half of the decade authorities shifted to anxiety regarding the social and cultural problems created by these migrants' ways of inhabiting the foyers. In 1973, Georges Gorse, the newly nominated Ministry of Labour, commissioned a memo "on the problems foyer management by African workers in the Paris region." This document noted that the policy previously conducted had "paved the way for the creation of groups of men living in a closed circuit, with entrenched behavior and habits completely at odds with the receiving society's common ways of life. These men seem more concerned with racial solidarity than hygiene rules and healthy financial management."[50]

The memo further denounced the poor state of some foyers, a condition blamed on their "dramatic over-occupancy," while also suggesting that even "modern" and well-managed foyers could go on strike. It finally proposed to "disseminate black African workers into multiethnic foyers." This memo is important because it described the workings of the foyers as being the opposite of French mores. It attested to a rising anxiety over black African workers among high-ranking civil servants in charge of immigration. It also introduced the issue of black Africans' hosting practices, subsumed here as "racial solidarity." The epithet "clandestine," previously an attribute given to lodgings provided by unscrupulous landlords, came to be applied to individuals.

This document is repeatedly quoted in scholarship on the foyers, in studies that have examined the treatment of West Africans in the limited time frame of the early 1970s, when Sonacotra managers looked down on their associative counterparts and blamed them for a situation they thought would not touch them. This memo has been read as evidence of the isolated resurfacing of older themes.[51] Against such a reading, I see this document as part of a wider field of analyses and recommendations on the future of West African foyers. Always present, racialized assumptions led to very different solutions, and the recurring theme of the dispersion of African immigrants was only one of the options discussed.

In the Paris region, the debate unfolded around two main positions. Stemming from the services of the prefecture, a first discursive strand echoed at the regional level the main theme of the 1973 memo. It was notably expressed by Marc Roberrini, a former colonial officer and prominent figure in the slum clearance processes and an expert on immigrant housing issues from 1965 to the 1980s.[52] Roberrini was a hands-on person, used to handling delicate situations on the ground with any resources available: for instance, during discussions over the relocation of the Ivry foyer residents, he challenged the representativeness of one of his interlocutors by publicly asking if he himself was actually living in the dormitory; and he devoted a lot of energy to differentiating the various "clans" he had identified;[53] he is even reported to have used retaliatory measures, such as preventing a particularly vocal foyer representative from obtaining a job when negotiating the fate of the foyer at 51 rue de Charonne in 1975.[54]

Roberrini focused on what he termed the "appropriation" of the foyers by West African residents that had resulted in loss of control over these spaces.[55] Monitoring the situation in the first Sonacotra foyers to strike, Foyer Romain Rolland (Saint-Denis), he suggested that West Africans were trying to "organize the basis of an irregular and tribal immigration." He concluded by recommending that the maximum number of West Africans admitted to mixed foyers should be fifteen.[56] This unrealistic suggestion echoed the more general discourse on the necessity to "disperse" West African "concentrations" that had resulted from the prevailing laissez-faire. In the mid-1970s, associative foyers often reached high numbers of residents: thus, in 1975, the department of Seine-Saint-Denis alone had four facilities with over 600 beds, two between 500 and 600, and two others between 400 and 500. In Paris, foyers were generally smaller, but twelve foyers offered between 150 and 310 official beds.[57]

Opposite Roberrini's style of handling the foyers, an alternative paradigm arose from emerging ethnological studies. Authors of in-depth studies of West African communities in France, such as Jacques Barou and Michel Samuel, contributed to the institutional body of expertise on African foyers.[58] Barou's approach relied heavily on the notion of "tribes" (French: *ethnies*), through which he apprehended the population of the foyer.[59] In 1975, he was commissioned by the newly created CNLI to produce a study on the rehousing of black Africans in the Paris region, which resulted in a twenty-seven-page memo.[60] Barou emphasized the importance of producing a form of housing "adapted" to what he understood as the cultural needs of the population considered—a population whose "adaptation" in France was in turn the problem to be solved. His analysis was based on the assumption that "in general, African personality remains collective and the individual only realizes himself through adhesion to a community." He described West Africans as aspiring primarily to remain in close-knit communities. As a result, he recommended the creation of "specific foyers," meaning not only foyers for West Africans but, as far as possible, foyers populated by homogeneous ethnic groups.

His proposal for rehousing 216 bis is telling in this respect. Alarmed by the condition of this foyer, he suggested dealing first with the unregistered inhabitants (which he calculated as equal to the number of official residents: 184) and recommended that their rehousing be conducted along ethnic lines: the forty-four "Toucouleurs" [Haalpulaar] could be sent to a new facility in the fourteenth arrondissement (Foyer Gergovie), where they would meet compatriots from the same Matam district in Senegal; the other group of "Sarakolé" [Soninke] could form the bulk of a Sonacotra foyer that was to be transformed into an African foyer (Foyer Duée, twentieth arrondissement). Throughout the report he designed options primarily around ethnic considerations, offering guidelines for a super concentration and rejoining village communities.

The idea of "dispersing" the population of West African foyers did not become generalized; nor did Barou's hyperconcentration along ethnic lines materialize. The prevailing practice was the construction of facilities providing around two hundred beds where communities previously living together more or less stayed together. The idea of separating West Africans and North Africans, based on long-standing arguments around their mutual hostility, gained new strength after violent incidents polarized the two communities in 1975 in Villejuif. In July, there was a fight between Malians and Algerians in this foyer, resulting in two dead among the Algerians and the immediate rehousing of the

Malian residents to other foyers.[61] Oblivious to the role played by the French state in the divergent treatment of these populations, administrators emphasized "ancestral rivalries."[62]

Eventually, Roberrini abandoned his advocacy for scattering West African communities: in 1976, he acknowledged that the trend of constructing new foyers was "irreversible" and pragmatically stated the need to erect new facilities.[63] Another tragic event accelerated this tendency: during the night of September 14, 1977, a criminal fire at Foyer Sedaine (Paris, eleventh arrondissement) cost the lives of three residents and injured fifty of them.[64] This prompted authorities to find solutions to the problem of "dilapidated foyers," whose state of emergency the fire at Sedaine recalled.[65] A construction plan had been adopted in 1976, with a large part earmarked for housing sub-Saharan Africans in Paris.[66] As a result, the construction of specific structures for West African residents developed in the capital. Before scrutinizing the case of the new foyers that replaced 216 bis, let us first address the question of why the foyer system, as it was consolidated in the mid-1970s, remained of interest to West African migrants themselves.

## "HOMMES ISOLÉS": THE FOYER IN MIGRANTS' LIVES AND PROJECTS

The changing demographics of West African migration crucially shaped not only the administrative perception and institutional response to their presence but the experience and expectations of the migrants. In the late 1950s and early 1960s, the pioneers were young: in 1963, almost 70 percent were under thirty and only 6.5 percent over forty.[67] In the early 1970s, the average age of departure remained low, between fifteen and twenty-five, but some migrants stayed for some time in France or returned after their first trips, thus slowly changing the age distribution in France.[68] In 1975, 56 percent were under thirty and 10 percent over forty.[69] This affected their marital status: estimated at 70.7 percent in 1963, the percentage of unmarried men dropped to 44.5 percent in 1975.[70]

As early as 1963, a few women migrated as wives.[71] This remained a minority phenomenon, however. Furthermore, celibacy was built into the foyer system through the administrative designation of "isolated" (French: *isolé*). Dormitories did not provide spaces for intimacy, and internal rules generally prohibited female visitors.[72] A fear of homosexual relations also pervades the administrative record.[73]

De facto celibacy and life in the foyers did not mean that migrants avoided sexual and affective relationships in France. Sources regarding sexual practices are limited, and administrative remarks on the topic contain particularly strong racial stereotypes.[74] This contrasts with how my interlocutors portray themselves in the 1960s and 1970s as being fully part of Parisian leisure life. Nicknamed Otis or Johnny, in reference to their favorite singers, some had already been immersed in a cosmopolitan urban youth culture in Dakar or Bamako. Hence, Alassane Ba, having arrived from Mali in 1977, recalled how 216 bis was within walking distance of the excitement and glamour of city nightlife. "At the time, we were all *yéyé* [a French pop music style of the 1960s], so you should have seen us, well dressed, going out on the Grands Boulevards every weekend."

Beyond this flavorful evocation of the pleasures of Paris, some encounters led to unions. Given the small number of African women, most stories of girlfriends or wives involve French women, some of them of Caribbean origin, many being French white women. Although frowned upon by a majority of the

French population, relationships with French girlfriends developed.[75] Some led to marriages, which were occasions to leave the foyer. In 1971, Postel-Vinay indicated that 10 percent of foyer departures took place "in order to live with a French woman or a foreign woman already established in France [or because] . . . of sufficient earnings to rent an independent room."[76]

However, the bulk of West African migrants still lived in the foyers in the 1970s, and most of them who were married had their wives back in the home country.[77] Hence, until the mid-1970s, life in the foyer was defined by two converging assumptions. The institutional reduction of the migrant to his identity of productive worker echoed, on the part of the emigration society, an ideal of a temporary life abroad whose social significance rested on what a migrant could achieve back home. Marxist scholars have located migrant men at the intersection of two systems of domination: a global labor order and domestic relations.[78] From the organization of departure to life in France, hierarchical relations and expectations of respect toward elders prevailed. Premised on return, migration also allowed single men to fulfill their socially expected breadwinner role, typically by marrying during their first return visit. However, contrary to earlier depictions of migrants handing over their salary to elder men in the foyers, many of my interlocutors arrived in the late 1960s, emphasized the relative freedom of their first years until the mid-1970s.

In his *longue durée* approach to Soninke migration, Manchuelle has powerfully contradicted the view of African migrations as "the result of poverty engendered by colonial rule," demonstrating that Soninke were comparatively wealthy when they engaged in long-distance migration.[79] Emphasizing the agency of migrants, Manchuelle puts to the fore social dynamics, such as the desire of younger men to be independent from their elders, combined with what he calls the patriarchal ideal. Migration thus relates ambivalently to social reproduction. On one hand, it calls for personal involvement, fueled by competitive tendencies and narratives of individual achievement[80] and, on the other hand, it is a socially sanctioned process whose ultimate goal is the fulfillment of obligations in the society of emigration. In this understanding of migration, gendered notions of work and labor play a key role.[81] In light of these considerations, Meillassoux's statement that migrants invest at home because of their subaltern status in the immigration society appears truncated, missing the strong incentives male migrants receive to perpetuate a social order in which their migration experience is an asset.[82] But these distinct perspectives converge on the central figure of the migrant as a breadwinner motivated by the prospect of establishing a dominant position back home. In this perspective, the foyer constituted an ideal place for newcomers because community and family control could apply, even if migrants could momentarily escape it.

## FROM 216 BIS TO LORRAINE AND D'HAUTPOUL

The story of the fire escape at the beginning of this chapter is only one instance of the numerous frictions between the residents and Soundiata.[83] It is this contentious terrain that shaped the 1979 move. According to Samba Sylla, "the residents' committee asked for rehousing within Paris." He added that the location suggested, on rue de Lorraine in the nineteenth arrondissement, was unappealing because leaving a central location in Paris for the north of the capital equated to moving "to the bush," but that they finally accepted the idea.[84]

The architect Anthony Béchu was commissioned to build two foyers: the one on rue de Lorraine, intended to host 216 bis residents (figure 2.2), and the one on nearby rue d'Hautpoul, whose initial purpose was to host residents from the adjacent Foyer David D'Angers.[85] Based in Paris at that time, Béchu had designed a number of projects on the African continent, notably in Algeria and Cameroon.[86] His former construction manager recalled that he designed about ten foyers and emphasized the quality of the construction of Lorraine and D'Hautpoul as "three-star hotels."[87]

That construction manager also remembered meetings with the residents (among which he included "African mamas," probably the cooks). The team took into account what he termed "the ethnically defined needs of the users." As an example of one such adaptation, he recalled how residents asked that beds should not be visible from the entrance. He suggested that some of the residents' wishes were integrated into the concept—although it is not clear if this only affected the furniture layout or also the spatial design.

The layout of the two foyers followed the model of "*unités de vie*," whereby two rooms shared toilets and showers as well as a communal cooking space.[88] In the case of Foyer Lorraine, the design of the "*unités de vie*" was complicated because another construction was underway on the plot when Béchu was commissioned for the project, and foundations had already been laid for an ordinary social housing project for family apartments.[89] Béchu had to adapt his foyer plan to this earlier design, with the result that the space shared by two bedrooms was extremely reduced and cooking was only possible while standing. In Foyer D'Hautpoul, erected from scratch, he had the latitude to design proper unités de vie, and the shared space before the rooms could accommodate several seats.

FIGURE 2.2 Front view of Foyer Lorraine, 1979.

*Source:* Archives de Paris 1178 W 2959.

The change affecting Lorraine's designation, from ordinary social housing to a foyer, caused some emotion among the authorities, who signaled that some of Foyer D'Hautpoul's neighbors had taken legal action against it.[90] Alongside a petition bearing 410 signatures, one neighbor wrote to Jacques Chirac, the newly elected mayor of Paris, "I am the voice of a neighborhood in turmoil: a building that one could describe as savage is under construction at 29 rue d'Hautpoul." Diluted among technical arguments surrounding the building's noncompliance, fear of migrants lay at the heart of the judicial memo, which stated that the projected foyer "runs counter to public interest in patent contradistinction to the vocation and interest of the surroundings. The whole neighborhood . . . is of residential type and cannot bear the presence of a foyer."[91] That the nineteenth arrondissement could be labeled "residential," with an implicit exclusion of immigrant lodgings, attests to the ambitions of its 1970s inhabitants rather than its actual history.[92]

In addition to these actions, the wooden board displaying mandatory information on the construction was burned down. Nonetheless, in contrast to many cases in which local authorities canceled building projects, such opposition did not hinder the building of the two foyers.[93] These struggles, which probably involved only a limited part of the population, were not even mentioned in the residents' narratives. On the contrary, they emphasized how they had gotten used to their previous neighborhood, with one even signaling that their departure from rue Saint-Denis was experienced as a loss by the shopkeepers around.[94]

More important, the residents' narratives focused on a key point of the relocation process: the fate of the unofficial residents (French: *clandestins*). After the opening of Lorraine in March 1979, which led to the installation of 216 bis's official residents, the old foyer was not closed, and Soundiata came under pressure to find a solution for its clandestins. Despite police intervention, the residents managed to win the case, led by a team of vocal délégués and backed by activists from Révolution Afrique and MRAP, among other organizations. The victory was multifaceted: the clandestins were offered beds; they were assigned to Foyer D'Hautpoul, in place of the residents of Foyer David D'Angers;[95] the residents even managed to impose their criteria for designating clandestins: a pay slip was enough to prove one's ability to pay for the room, and no residence permit could be requested; the délégués produced their own list of residents, giving way to a trick attributed mainly to Haalpulaar residents, who managed to include friends and relatives who did not live in the old foyer.[96]

Resistance continued until the moment of entering Foyer D'Hautpoul: the residents notably secured a working space for tailors within the new foyer.[97] They initially refused to sign the new contracts, which were criticized as "mimicking Sonacotra internal rules." Although the outcome is unclear, the rejection of the new contracts is ascribed by the activist Geneviève Petauton to the wider context of repression in the context of the Sonacotra movement: the move to Foyer D'Hautpoul occurred in November 1979, at a time when the Sonacotra strikers were opposing a prospective law that would have tightened the conditions of their stay (stipulating, in particular, that losing one's job would result in the loss of their right to stay in a foyer).[98]

Finally, a key feature of residents' narratives surrounding the move is the emphasis on collective action transcending ethnic divisions. The ability to form a collective beyond lines of kinship and shared village or regional origin is often highlighted. The former délégué Bakary Traoré stated: "We own the foyer, we fought, we are not sheep. We have different languages but we fought together."[99] The insistence on the foyer being "one" and residents being "the same" can be read as an acknowledgment of the work that had been needed to overcome actual differences. As developed in Part 2, these narratives of 216 bis acquire further significance in the context of their utterance in the early 2010s, when the future of the two foyers was being debated and when aging délégués looked back nostalgically to a time of greater solidarity and political achievements. However, the fact that the two buildings shared the same representatives for a time attests to the unifying character of a shared life and struggle.

## CONCLUSION: BUILDING MODERN FOYERS IN THE LATE 1970s IN PARIS

"We wanted 'a modern foyer:' that was our motto," recalled Alassane Dieng, a former délégué of Foyer Lorraine. The notion of "modern foyers," a trope of residents' stories, captures the political claims for decent housing, and beyond that for social and political rights, that forcefully emerged in the 1970s. Protests in the foyers brought together residents from all origins, but the fight for the foyers took on a specific meaning for West African migrants who had few other options in the city. Rooted in the foyer system and corresponding to patriarchal norms of migration from the Senegal River Valley, male migration was still unquestioned. As a result, West African migrants deemed the new structures as progress.

The notion of "modern foyers" also had some currency within the institutions.[100] The existence of such administrative category suggests that other foyers remained below common standards, such as makeshift accommodation in wooden barracks as well as facilities providing dormitories, which could still be found in Paris and other municipalities at that time. Even "modern" and built as such, foyers continued to be designed with lower standards than ordinary social housing. Moreover, the modern character of some foyers went along with persisting racialized perceptions of the population for whom these facilities were designed: their peculiarities accounted for specific architectural arrangements, and their inadaptability to French society justified the whole foyer system.[101]

These contradictions did not prevent the system from being at its peak in the 1970s for the whole country. The late 1970s even saw the construction of new structures in Paris, several projects being completed by the beginning of the 1980s, with ten foyers due in 1979 and more than three thousand new beds planned between 1979 and 1981.[102] Overlooking this short period when institutions collaborated to build specialized facilities, the derogatory view of the foyers' unruly appropriation by West Africans prevailed and consolidated in later decades.

# 3

# PERMANENCE AND DECAY

African Foyers, from Solution to Problem
(1980s–1990s)

Having arrived in France from Bamako in 1977, Amadou, a former high school student, was active in the mobilizations surrounding the move from the 216 bis foyer to the new facilities in the nineteenth arrondissement. His elder brother, who had married a French woman and left the foyer, nonetheless attended the official inauguration of Foyer Lorraine in March 1979. According to Amadou, on this occasion his brother told Lionel Stoléru, the *Secrétaire d'Etat aux travailleurs immigrés*, "We're not immigrants, we're at home in France" [French: *on est chez nous*].

This anecdote highlights the historical changes as well as the distinct relationship to the foyers that prevailed at Foyer Lorraine and Foyer D'Hautpoul. In contrast to 216 bis, a building progressively converted into a shelter for migrants who did not anticipate staying in France for long, these two foyers were built in 1979 and designed for a population expecting to spend part of their adult life there. These foyers opened at a time when migrants of more diverse social and educational backgrounds became political actors claiming a right to live in France. That Amadou attributes the provocative line to his brother, who lived outside the foyer, is also telling because it situates the foyer as one type of housing, among others, where West African migrants lived. The changing demographics of West African migration are key to understanding the dynamics at the end of the twentieth century. Finally, the notion of being "at home" is ambiguous: the very fact of its assertion suggested that it was not self-evident, and such a declaration stood in contradiction to the category of "*foyer de travailleurs migrants*" that maintained these new buildings as distinct from ordinary ones—not to mention the presence of Stoléru, a high-ranking official who was known for promoting the return of migrants to their country of origin.

The process of moving into Foyer Lorraine and Foyer D'Hautpoul occurred in a context of deteriorating economic conditions, and tightening immigration laws led to further uses of the foyers as shelters for undocumented newcomers. The election in 1981 of François Mitterrand, the first socialist president of postwar France, resulted in some pro-immigrant actions: abandonment of the infamous measures in favor of return; establishment of a ten-year resident permit; freedom of association extended to foreigners; and regularization of 130,000 undocumented migrants.[1] However, the number of expulsions continued to increase in the years after 1981, and in 1983 immigrant controls were tightened. Founded in 1972, the xenophobic National Front (Front National) made important electoral gains in the 1983 municipal elections, becoming a key player in mainstream politics. In these circumstances, administrative anxieties over West African foyers, which began in the 1970s, consolidated to the point that the foyers appeared to be an outdated mode of dealing with postcolonial migrants by the mid-1990s.

In parallel, sub-Saharan African migrations became much more diverse in terms of nation of origin. The 1990 national census counted 235,000 sub-Saharan Africans in France, of which

43,692 were Senegalese and 37,693 Malians, followed by sub-stantial populations from Zaire, Cameroon, and Côte d'Ivoire. In contrast to their overwhelming numerical dominance as late as the mid-1970s, Malians, Mauritanians, and Senegalese only represented around 37 percent of black Africans in France by 1990.[2] But the foyers did not open their doors to the new waves of African immigrants; where they shared the space with other migrants, generally from the Maghreb, West Africans tended to occupy beds and rooms left vacant by others.[3]

In what follows, I not only keep track of changing policies but also turn my gaze to the foyer communities and ask: How did the foyers become a place of living for West Africans in the long run? The dialectics between provisional and permanent lie at the heart of the dynamic of labor migration. Institutions empha-size the provisional nature of the presence of migrants, and the migrants themselves and the families left behind reiterate this idea when focusing on the horizon of return.[4] Before 1974, this jointly maintained illusion was inscribed in an economic con-text of cheap labor needs as well as in migrants' social practices. The product of an initial convergence of these varying interests, the foyer system, once adopted as a social model, rendered this provisional perspective more lasting. As material infrastruc-ture, foyers took on a life of their own, hence my emphasis on "permanence."

Once new and modern, these buildings became poorly man-aged and dilapidated after a few decades. Although rarely spe-cific in terms of dates, residents' depictions of the "Soundiata period" provide a sense of how the foyers evolved during the era between installation in 1979 and the change of managing struc-ture in the 2000s.[5] Having arrived from Mali in 1981, Karamoko, whose sharp look illuminated a face framed by carefully main-tained sideburns, recalled the comforts of Lorraine (figure 3.1):

**FIGURE 3.1** Two residents of Foyer Lorraine relax in their room, 1984.

*Source*: Photo by Jacqueline Geering.

At the time, it was Soundiata [that ran the foyer]. There was someone we knew who replaced the sheets. When you needed a broom or a mop, you asked him, he'd give you one. Since Soundiata left, the foyer is shit. At that time?! [Wolf-whistling] When you enter, on your left, on your right, there are gardens everywhere. At dawn, there are lamps lighting up from inside the lawn. People used to take pictures of themselves on the lawn, in front of the flowers. But when too many people came, the grass, the flowers died.

For Karamoko, the changes at institutional levels (the end of Soundiata) directly translated into an inability to properly maintain the place, which was reflected in the absence of permanent (known) staff and the absence of basic equipment they could use to clean their rooms. The foyer's deterioration is also ascribed to the increased number of inhabitants. The foyers' "modern" phase thus appears to have been short-lived; the 1980s and 1990s corresponded to times of crisis in terms of the arrival of migrants as much as to institutional neglect.

## PERPETUATING THE FOYERS AT THE TIME OF FAMILY REUNION

After the suspension of labor migration in 1974, the authorities took timid measures to allow family reunions in the late 1970s. After Mitterand's election, more favorable measures prevailed until 1984, coinciding with a relative opening of housing opportunities in low-income housing organizations.[6] In 1974, migrant women from Mali, Mauritania, and Senegal accounted for 14 percent of the migrants of these countries in France, but the number grew to 40 percent in 1990, mainly due to the arrival of spouses joining their husbands.[7] As a result, the foyers shifted from the numerically predominant to a minority housing type for these migrants. Rather than a general shift from the foyers to ordinary social housing, however, the process resulted in a sustained attachment on behalf of West African migrants to the foyers, along with a growing number of immigrants living with their families outside.

Family reunion was not a smooth process. One of the conditions for family reunion eligibility was that foyer residents who intended to bring their spouses to France had to find an apartment before their wives could join them.[8] However, a few women and families did take up residence in foyers in arrangements that prompted a strong administrative response.[9] In addition to the bureaucratic requirements, plans to bring one's wife over often faced opposition from relatives: parents feared that monetary contributions would drop down, and mothers resented the departure of their daughters-in-law who performed a significant share of domestic work.[10] Demba, who arrived in France in 1974, emphasized that after his mother died only his sisters lived in the family compound; he felt that if his wife had joined him there would no longer have been anyone left back home. Women sometimes tried to get away with family decisions by using an illness as a reason to move. These testimonies demonstrate that family reunion was not merely a discussion between spouses but involved family members and relatives who were economically dependent on remittances, with varying outcomes according to family configurations and migrant trajectories.

For a migrant in France, the social and moral evaluation of a departure from the foyer is variously assessed in the literature. In his investigation of Haalpulaar migrant trajectories, Hamidou Dia notes that until the 1980s leaving the foyer for an apartment was socially valued; whereas in the early 1990s difficulties in

France rendered "community inscription" more useful.[11] Mahamet Timera points to the way Soninke migrants viewed family reunion with suspicion, indicating that the "first ones to take such a decision found themselves more or less isolated, sometimes openly stigmatized."[12] These discrepancies attest to the varying moral and social evaluations of the meanings of migration and possible avenues of success under difficult and shifting circumstances. In general, the initial appeal of family reunion seemed to give way to more nuanced assessments of family life in France.

As demonstrated for many other migration settings, the arrival of wives and children prompted men to stiffen the moral values of the society of origin, notably gender norms, rendering conjugal life in France fraught with misunderstandings.[13] The fact that many West African men stayed in the foyers must be explained as much by their adhesion to the foyer model as by the dire housing conditions the reunited families faced and the lack of prospects for upward social mobility in France. In the 1980s, the economic crisis deepened, creating a difficult context for newly reunited couples. In addition, opportunities to access social housing shrunk. Management in social housing projects relied on racial categorization, and black African families were rated low on the list.[14] In the 1980s, renovation programs enacted forms of selection based on ethnic criteria.[15] Outside social housing projects, West African families often found themselves in degraded privately owned lodgings, and their access to property remained very limited.[16]

At the same time, restrictions on the legal possibilities for entering France led to an increase in clandestine arrivals. Newcomers experienced mounting restrictions on mobility from West Africa to France. Many entered on a tourist visa and subsequently experienced a period of illegality before gaining a more stable residence permit. For undocumented migrants, the foyer became a base from which to find their first jobs and attempt to regularize their situation. Growing unemployment also meant that collective life, limiting expenses and offering comparatively cheap accommodation, proved a precious advantage.

These changes in the distribution of West African migrants in France provided the foyers with new roles as centers for diasporic communities in the making. The presence of families outside the foyer inaugurated visiting circuits, with foyer residents having opportunities to call on their families as well as host visitors on weekends. The foyers' collective spaces were used for events such as naming ceremonies, marriages, and other festivities. In addition, collective arrangements such as contributions for village cash boxes took on a new urgency at the end of the 1970s.

The 1973 drought in the Sahel constituted a turning point in its effect on livelihoods in the emigration zone and long-term migration patterns. This intersected with the emergence of the "migration-development nexus," defined by Jean-Philippe Dedieu as the way "French governmental bodies and NGOs started to frame public policies linking migration and development."[17] Village-based associations developed when foreigners were granted the right to form associations in 1981. These associations became pivotal in the development of their regions of origin, and the old system of cash boxes remained, taking new responsibilities such as the repatriation of corpses, a practice initiated in the 1980s and 1990s.[18] Meeting places for these associations as well as their declared headquarters were most often located in the foyers. The meetings were joined by migrants living outside the foyers, not only working-class men but occasionally educated members of the transnational village, perpetuating the role of the foyer as a place of exchange across classes and situations.[19]

## THE INNER WORKINGS OF THE FOYERS:
## SOCIAL HIERARCHIES IN MIGRATION

Soninke and Haalpulaar societies are characterized by their hierarchical organization, which rests on statutory distinctions between "freemen" and "slaves," with endogamous groups devoted to artisanal activities representing an intermediary status. Although slavery was formally abolished in French West Africa in 1905, the inheritance of slave status, and inherited statuses in general, still weigh on ordinary practices, from marriage options to ritual and material obligations.[20] In this section I investigate the historical role of the foyers in the persistence of these social categories in migration in France.

The first issue to address is the extent to which the foyer populations comprised the same distribution of statutory groups as the societies of emigration. Members of all status groups migrated, but existing scholarship suggests that members of dominant groups were the first to become involved in migration to urban cities and then France, and that subaltern groups, notably those of slave descent, entered international migration with a delay.[21] However, the extent to which this situation lasted is subject to contrasting assessments. Michel Samuel's evaluation of the relative weight of social groups in locales of departure and in emigration communities within France attests to major local variations, with one documented case in which ex-slaves dominated migration to France and were even overrepresented (the Soninke village of Tuabou in Senegal), and other cases in which ex-slaves constituted a minority of the emigration community.[22] After initial difficulties in emigrating, Michel Samuel speculates that there may have been a rush from lower categories toward France because access to work was generally not mediated by social relations.[23] Francine Kane and André Lericollais even suggest "that slaves emigrate a little more than nobles and casted people."[24] This is in line with more recent evidence from the economist Jean-Luc Demonsant, who demonstrates that "belonging to a low status family raises the probability of migrating"; however, he emphasizes that dominant families secure the migration of some of their comembers, and that these migrants are more likely to remit than members of subaltern families.[25] In contrast, working in a Gambian Soninke village that was not primarily oriented toward migration to France, Paolo Gaibazzi highlights the obstacles preventing individuals from slave backgrounds to move (notably the smaller extent of their families compared to others), which lasted into the twentieth century.[26] This point needs to be investigated further, but such scattered evidence calls for a careful assessment of each local situation.

In the course of my historical interviews, I encountered men from all social backgrounds. Narratives of emigration occasionally mentioned the joint departure of migrants of distinct backgrounds, notably in a pair formed of a "noble" or "*naxamala*" with "his" slave.[27] Once in migration, existing studies and my own material converge on the idea that early forms of foyer organization rested on social hierarchies as materialized notably by status. Cooking, in particular, was initially a task performed by (young) men of subaltern status: ex-slaves and sometimes cobblers (Soninke: *garanko* [a *naxamala* group]).[28] They were partially or totally exempt from monetary contributions, depending on arrangements that varied from place to place.[29] The role entrusted to foyer chiefs and representatives by associative managers (see chapter 1) led to forms of control by these men over the allocation of beds, a process in which "nobles" could find some leverage over members of subordinate groups.

The 1970s were a turning point when men assigned to cooking duties contested the unequal distribution of domestic chores. This can be ascribed to the politicization of migrants in the course of organized protests in the foyer from the late 1960s onward, which acquainted some of them with ideologies advocating social equality. It may also have reflected longer-envisioned prospects of emigration and acknowledgment of the fact that migrants of all backgrounds shared similar working conditions in France. This last argument is not clear-cut, however, because it can support egalitarian discourses as much as it can foster a reactive reemphasis on the relevance of these vernacular distinctions within the foyers.

Whatever the precise trigger, outright disputes over unequal arrangements erupted in the early 1970s.[30] In the case of the Soninke region of Diafounou in Mali, the "revolt" led to meetings bringing together members of several villages. It began with young ex-slaves refusing to cook alone, asking either that the work be shared with all members of the group— thus including older ex-slaves—or that young members of all groups participate. The accounts diverge on the specific context of each village- or region-based struggle but overlap on key points: arguments combined age and social distinctions, and these events occasioned intense exchanges between the community in emigration and the village of origin. Migrants' relatives back home generally adopted a conservative stance because they feared retaliation, including exclusion from the village social organization and marriage circuits. Despite these dynamics, the outcome in most documented cases was participation of all young men in cooking; in other cases, collective cooking was simply abandoned.

At 216 bis cooking was organized at the community level and men from distinct localities came together, thus rendering establishment of direct patron–client links difficult. In addition, several of the main lineages represented in 216 bis and the later foyers were *ɲaxamalo* of the *sakke* status group; in the French emigrant community, some individuals remained attached through social links to specific "noble" families whose members did not live in the same foyer; in the foyer itself, they had played a decisive role in the foundation story of 216 bis. More generally, the team of délégués for these foyers comprised men of all social backgrounds, including some of slave descent.

My own reading of the situation is sensitive to the scale considered. At the level of foyer management, and in terms of collective organization, the 1970s were decisive in promoting new generations of representatives who explicitly denied currency to status group identity as far as managing affairs in France was concerned. This process was unevenly achieved across the foyers and was probably easier to implement in ethnically mixed foyers such as 216 bis. Unequal and exploitative arrangements could persist at the intermediate level of smaller communities, but in 216 bis as well as in Lorraine and D'Hautpoul residents of subaltern status could enjoy their own bed or rooms and make decisions regarding passing these spaces on to others.

Ultimately, this question is tied to a wider one—the kind of social control operated within the foyer, both at the level of the collective housing structure and that of extended families. Early descriptions suggest tight control and policing, in particular with young migrants handing over their salaries to the oldest member of their families, a system abandoned in the 1970s. However, the obligation to contribute to collective structures remained, together with forms of internal policing within the foyers where deviant behaviors were sanctioned, notably at a time when the shared reference to Islam regained traction.

## NEW USES OF THE FOYERS: ISLAMIC PLACES OF WORSHIP IN FRENCH CITIES

From the mid-1970s onward, an Islamic revival among West African migrants materialized in the development of prayer rooms in the foyers. These spaces were generally repurposed collective rooms. Upon opening, Foyer Lorraine and Foyer D'Hautpoul offered large communal rooms, none of which was dedicated to religious worship. Foyer Lorraine's first floor was comprised of two adjacent TV rooms that could be combined to form one 81 m² room: one 36 m² meeting room and a 50 m² "cultural room." Foyer D'Hautpoul also provided two TV rooms and one cultural room.[31] In 1983, however, Soundiata acknowledged the presence of a dedicated room for religious worship in both of these foyers instead of the TV rooms.[32] This period saw increasing demands for Islamic places of worship in the living and working spaces of postcolonial immigrants from the Maghreb and West Africa.

Islamic places of worship in French cities, and occasionally in foyers, predate these developments, notably with the erection of a few Muslim religious sites, such as the Mosquée de Paris in 1926 as part of a wider project to monitor (post)colonial migrants of Islamic faith.[33] There is early evidence of foyers with a dedicated place to worship (for example, a 1930 Moroccan foyer in Gennevilliers). With regard to West Africans, Mahamet Timera suggests 1966 as marking the opening of the first prayer room in the Clichy foyer; also in 1966, a newly opened ASSOTRAF foyer provided a prayer space.[34] Other scholars indicate that the first prayer room opened in a West African foyer dates back to 1967.[35] In fact, the late 1960s and early 1970s saw a flurry of initiatives, from improvised prayer rooms at best tolerated in basements to the official inauguration of a mosque as part of Foyer

Moïse in Rouen.[36] In Jacques Barou's account of Charonne's case, the residents went on strike because they wanted meat that would be sacrificed in accordance with Islamic ritual practice, and they also demanded a space for worship. As was the case in housing projects, managing structures tolerated the improvised installations and associative foyers tried to adapt the spaces to these new uses.[37]

When the Sonacotra movement began, requests for prayer rooms were already common and were listed among the demands made by Sonacotra rent strikers, as well as by West African residents beyond the Sonacotra strike.[38] Choukri Hmed rightfully notes that the strikers' public action did not rest on religious identity.[39] But while Hmed views demands by resident committees for prayer rooms as marginal, the archival evidence attests to a wider trend, at least among West African residents.[40]

These developments can be ascribed to internal dynamics in West African communities. At the beginning of the 1970s, Islamic reformist movements developed within Soninke societies in West Africa and in their diasporas.[41] At that time, most foyer residents did not regularly practice Islam. Mahamet Timera provides useful recollections from residents who explain this fact as being due to several factors, notably the notion that one's stay in France was to be short; the fact that it was impossible to practice dutifully; and the belief that practicing in bad conditions could "pollute" Islam.[42] Although modest at the end of the 1960s, the process of "re-Islamization" developed in the 1970s and gained momentum in the 1980s.[43] In the Soninke case, emigration communities in Congo and France have been pioneers in this process, which involves global connections, including students returning from Gulf countries and the intense circulation of news from the emigration locales to diasporic places.[44]

This Islamic renewal occasionally reignited tensions with Maghrebis, a dimension etched into the structure of the foyers by administrative practices; this materialized in the form of opposition to having black Africans leading collective prayer.[45] Among Soninke and Haalpulaar, distinct religious networks developed.[46] Among Soninke, the influence of the transnational Jamaat Tabligh movement, founded in India in 1927, has been central, as Moustapha Diop details: "At the end of the sixties, small groups of men, whose dress was by then judged eccentric . . . circulated among foyers (black Africans, Maghrebis) and incited them, in a convivial manner, to demand prayer rooms."[47] An imam involved in this process explained that he had first become acquainted with the movement in Le Havre, where he had lived. After arriving in Paris in 1986, he found that collective prayers had begun in Foyer Gergovie, and he further encouraged foyer inhabitants to attend.[48] He was also among the initiators of Friday prayer service in the foyer in 1993. The movement extended its activities to families living in the neighboring social projects. Its reformist approach was intended to correct Islamic practices imported from the homeland and to provide migrants as well as French citizens of immigrant backgrounds with a new Muslim identity.

Haalpulaar followed a different path, with the influential figure of Mansour Baro, a leader of the branch of the Tijaniyya Sufi order.[49] Baro began preaching in France in 1974, notably in the foyers of Boulogne-Billancourt, where he acted as a broker in obtaining authorization for Renault factory workers to pray at their place of work.[50] These diverging religious trajectories resulted in forms of specialization with regard to religious spaces in Lorraine and D'Hautpoul. Because Foyer D'Hautpoul hosted more Haalpulaar (many of them having been unofficial residents in 216 bis), this foyer became a stronghold of the Tijani networks, allowing them to engage in recitation practices after Friday prayer and during the month of Ramadan; on this yearly occasion, they paid for the trip of a scholar from Senegal.[51]

These boundaries do not preclude religious exchanges, and Soninke and Haalpulaar often partook in the same collective prayers. This internal diversity of West African Muslim communities was part of a broader "transnational spiritual economy" in which Islamic scholars and traditional healers both operated, with clients inside and outside the walls of the foyers.[52]

From the early 1970s, these internal dynamics invited new interest from political and administrative actors in the Islamic affiliation of postcolonial migrants. In September 1976, Paul Dijoud, Secrétaire d'État aux travailleurs immigrés, composed a memorandum aimed at "improving the living and working conditions of immigrants living in France" that encouraged the development of Islamic places of worship, notably in the foyers. This conjunction of relative institutional openness to providing the space and internal processes of religious renewal served to increase the spread of Islamic practice. By the mid-1980s, the overwhelming majority of foyers where Muslims lived were equipped with dedicated spaces, sometimes previously existing spaces converted into prayer rooms, sometimes even enhanced with an "Islamic touch" by the architect.[53] Until 1981, the majority of places of Islamic worship in France were located in foyers (197 in foyers and 180 in other locations). Both figures grew in the following years: openings outside foyers rose more sharply (to 381 in 1985), whereas the number of prayer rooms in foyers almost stagnated after 1983 (reaching 238 in 1985).[54]

Another effect of a wider policy promoting integration by taking into account cultural differences was the provision of "budgets d'animation" to each foyer, many of which went to buying sheep to be slaughtered for the Muslim feast of Eid.[55] "Animation" was a key word in foyer actions from the beginning, with literacy classes, film projections, and even holiday tours within France organized for the residents.[56] These activities were controlled to an extent that varied from one managing structure to another, but they could be quite strict. During the Sonacotra movement, protesters denounced the patronizing dimension of animation and demanded that residents should be able to control these budgets. In the 1980s, comanagement of the foyer's animation budget became routine. "We were happy in the new foyers," recalled one of my interlocutors, arrived in France in 1973, adding that "at the time of Soundiata, there was a small budget to organize events."[57]

After the Iranian Revolution and with global fears of Islamist threats, attitudes of tolerance and encouragement changed both in the management of the foyers and in workplaces.[58] This materialized in fears of fundamentalism.[59] The practices of ritual slaughtering were publicly denounced in the 1990s.[60] Soundiata's annual report for the year 1991 read:

> Until now, we never had any qualms about this topic [the provision of Islamic spaces of worship in foyers]; we even tried to respond favorably to these demands in order to offer these individuals who live as single men the means and spaces to observe their religion. However, we now ask ourselves if such an attitude is in line with the promotion of integration.[61]

Integration and religious practice began to be untied.

## OLD AND NEW CONCERNS IN THE 1980s: FINANCIAL ISSUES, "OVER-OCCUPANCY," AND ONGOING PROTESTS

The 1980s were marked by a tendency to de-particularize communities in terms of ethnic origin: in 1988, AFTAM changed its name to "Aftam—Accueil et Formation" and abandoned the reference to the African origin of its audience, redefining its mission to target all individuals "experiencing difficulties," a shift made by Sonacotra in 1976.[62] Managing structures tended to favor the recruitment of trained social workers to fulfill the function of foyer directors, and in associative foyers directors were no longer chosen from among residents.[63] This willingness to despecify the foyers conflicted with the tendency of West Africans to remain in the foyers, rendering the ethnic dimension of many foyers even more visible. In Paris and the surrounding cities, AFTAM, Soundiata, and ASSOTRAF foyers remained de facto West African foyers.

The material condition of the foyers was uneven. New facilities had opened in the 1970s, as evidenced by the foyers of Lorraine and D'Hautpoul, but some older foyers that had been opened in industrial buildings in the 1960s still stood, as did some barracks. At the same time, opportunities to erect new buildings shrunk; laws on decentralization, notably that of 1983, empowered mayors to issue construction permits, and they generally refused to authorize the building of new foyers.

Alongside these evolutions, new concerns emerged surrounding foyer populations. A 1989 internal survey within Soundiata requested the following details on each foyer:

> number of observed clandestine residents;
> number of external visitors at mealtimes;
> number of couples or families de facto living in the foyer;
> squatters.

Is the permanent or temporary presence of the following categories of people observed in the foyer?

cooks, kitchen assistants;

tailors;

blacksmiths;

hawkers;

propagandists;

procurers;

receivers, intermediaries;

drug users or dealers.

This list reflects the main anxieties of the era. This was the moment when the presence of families became problematized. The list also combines craftsmen activities (previously encouraged, including dedicated spaces where blacksmiths melted metal to make jewelry) and criminalized ones (such as drug dealing and procuring). Finally, surveillance of religious activities (by "propagandists") is also apparent.

Significantly, the first item listed is assessment of the number of clandestine residents. The predominant issue facing managing structures in the 1980s was "over-occupancy" in the foyers, a phenomenon identified as particularly pronounced in West African foyers.[64] Under the term "clandestine," the categories of illegal or undocumented (in terms of residency in the country) and unofficial (in terms of status in the foyer) overlap, as was the case regarding undeclared workers.[65] The fear of illegals as undocumented developed when residents became subject to residence permits, and foyers even anticipated the definitive change in policy: from early 1972 to 1974, the Préfet of Seine-Saint-Denis asked for increased controls of the black African population in the foyers.[66] As a result, in 1974 the policy change was approved based on the assumption that residence permits would allow for a better monitoring of the population of the foyers. Police controls expanded in the following years; for instance, the Préfet of

Seine-Saint-Denis approved a plan to inspect several foyers in the department in February 1975.[68] Such inspections repeatedly occurred during the 1980s and beyond, with an impressive police roundup in a Sonacotra foyer at La Verrière in 1991.[69]

The obsession with illegals went beyond the undocumented to designate undeclared residents too. The topic of many comments and assessments since the 1970s, these inhabitants became a focus of policies in the 1980s. Control went together with forms of tolerance in associative foyers. In 1986 Soundiata laid out its doctrine in the following terms:

> In the name of solidarity, turn a blind eye to over-occupation, so long as rents are collected in full . . . of course, do not treat *clandestins* as officials; ignore them, but use them as an ultimate weapon in negotiations. In cases of outstanding debts, have the over-occupants evicted.[70]

Other foyers had much stricter rules, notably the dozen Parisian foyers managed by the municipal social aid bureau (Bureau d'aide sociale [BAS]).[71] To be allocated a room, an applicant had to present a valid work certificate, and each resident needed to have an annual medical checkup. Furthermore, BAS tried to control the way one's bed or room could be passed on to another, as its managing director explained to the foyer directors:

> Let me remind you that no substitution can be carried out at the level of your facility. In the event of replacement, incomers need to present themselves at the Housing Bureau and supply the usual documentation. . . . Let me add, once again, that the residents, whoever they are, do not own their places.[72]

This reminder suggests that the administration had to fight against such practices, and it echoes present-day frictions and claims of "ownership," which later chapters explore. The explicit rejection of such practices contrasts with the way associations such as AFTAM and Soundiata systematized the transference of beds from one individual to a replacement of his choice, often involving the délégués in the process. Under pressure from the Paris municipality, BAS further sought to ensure that its facilities did not host undeclared and possibly undocumented migrants.[73] In early 1984, BAS set out to have police services carry out systematic inspections in all its foyers. Police interventions were imagined as a means to discriminate between illegal and legal immigrants, as well as to get rid of undeclared residents. But they were costly in terms of damaging relations between the managing structure and the residents.[74] Furthermore, inspections were not always effective, and control of the undeclared progressed at a finer scale, notably by the refusal to keep and distribute any mail not addressed to a declared resident.[75]

Although no general strike occurred after the Sonacotra movement, localized forms of dispute endured in the 1980s, at a time when legal proceedings against residents refusing to pay became widespread. In AFTAM-run foyers, the refusal to pay rent increases affected as many as three-quarters of AFTAM-run foyers from 1980 to 1985.[76] Other examples include lengthy periods of self-management, such as Foyer Bisson after it was abandoned by BAS in 1986.

From the mid-1980s to the 2000s, many managing associations withdrew from management of the foyers or divested themselves for financial reasons. As early as 1984, BAS sought to transfer management of the foyers to dedicated associations deemed more suitable to dealing with such structures. It transferred four foyers from 1986 to 1996, and the remaining seven in the following decade.[77] Throughout the 1980s and 1990s, some associations collapsed (such as AFRP and ASSOTRAF) and passed their foyers on to associations. Soundiata, rebranded in 2001 as Soundiata-Nouvelle, also experienced managing and financial difficulties, and it shut down in 2006. AFTAM has been managing Foyer Lorraine and Foyer D'Hautpoul since January 2007. This led to a new landscape and a concentration in terms of managing structures, with Sonacotra (renamed Adoma) and AFTAM (renamed Coallia) managing the vast majority of foyers in the 2000s.

## CONCLUSION: THE FOYERS AND THE REPUBLIC

The 1990s saw mounting public concern over sub-Saharan migration. Black Africans became more visible through the presence of families, which generated new debates, notably around polygynous households after this configuration was banned in 1993; at the same time, mobilizations and claims for decent housing from families also attested to the latter's political agency.[78] Immigration policies became stricter and the focus on "illegals" tightened after 1983 for the remainder of Mitterrand's presidency and following election of right-wing Jacques Chirac (1995–2007). In parallel, the idea of a "Muslim problem" developed.[79] These distinct trends situated the foyers and their inhabitants at the heart of public debates.

Public exposure of the foyers culminated in a report assigned by the prime minister to Henri Cuq, a right-wing member of Parliament in 1996. Although it was meant to encompass all foyers, Cuq explicitly targeted the "black African foyers" that

combine[d] over-occupation, all kinds of businesses, parallel economic activities, drug dealing, prostitution, public health problems (the spread of AIDS, the resurgence of tuberculosis, etc.). These are lawless zones where Africans recreate villages on tribal bases.[80]

This official report was suffused with racism; it portrayed black inhabitants of the foyers as responsible for troubles ranging from infractions to employment rules to major health concerns. It further established a racialized reading of the foyers according to which "aging" should be viewed as the principal problem regarding residents from the Maghreb, whereas issues relating to sub-Saharan residents focus on reforming their community-based ways of living. To this, Cuq added the role of the foyers in facilitating illegal immigration, as well as the possible presence in their prayer rooms of proponents of radical Islam. In sum he stated: "Most black African foyers . . . have established themselves as extraterritorial zones, subject to the authority of customary leaders, where Republican law is absent."[81] In terms of solutions, Deputy Cuq proposed stricter control of the foyers (combining checks on the inhabitants' legal status with checks on their status as regular residents); cessation of all activities such as crafts, commercial restaurants, etc.; and a sharp rejection on behalf of management structures of the community model of foyer organization. Strongly publicized, such measures would demonstrate the state's determination of its "rejection of communitarianism."[82]

The term "communitarianism," first used by French intellectuals during the 1980s, gained momentum in the mid-1990s.[83] A deprecatory term, it points to cultural and social dynamics in which allegiance to religious or ethno-racial communities is presumed more important than affiliation with the national community. Communitarianism is associated with an (imagined) American or Anglo-Saxon way of celebrating communities, which is contrasted with French republicanism.[84]

As Hélène Béguin usefully recalls, another key report from this period is the earlier memo on immigrant housing ("Le logement des immigrés," CNLI, 1994) by Pierre Pascal, which already identified black African foyers as problematic sites. However, Pascal's report had a different tone; it positively acknowledged the role of the foyers in the communities beyond its residents, going so far as to state that the foyers "fulfill several functions that contribute to [migrants'] integration."[85] Advocating for the foyers' preservation, the report recommended the renovation of the most derelict ones. In contrast, Cuq's report projected a dilution of the foyers into normal social housing.

This tension echoes the earlier divergences discussed in chapter 2 when I unearthed the ethnologically inspired stance that ran counter to the dominant view of control in the management of Parisian foyers. Although both influenced national policies, Cuq's report stirred controversies that gained wide media coverage and mobilized the foyer residents and their allies. In reaction to Cuq's report and the subsequent press coverage given to the foyer issue, long-term activists and délégués from the Sonacotra strike joined with social workers interested in the workings of African foyers to create the collective for the future of the foyers (Collectif pour l'avenir des foyers).[86] In 1997, against this backdrop of public debate attacking or defending the foyers, the French government launched a coordinated national plan to renovate the foyers. The implementation and effects of this plan on France's West African inhabitants are the topic of the following chapters.

# II

# PARTIAL ENDINGS

I n the 1990s the institutions in charge of the foyers changed how they viewed them: rather than seeing them as building community, they came to view them as problematic and impeding "integration," the new key concept in the management of immigrants. In opposition to a presumed insulation of the foyers (variously ascribed to the residents themselves or to the segregation dynamics they experienced), the institutions and managing structures set out to normalize these spaces and redefine their uses.

Part 2 traces how these assumptions operated in the renovation scheme. This nationwide plan altogether changed the destination, name, architecture, and juridical definition of the foyers. I analyze the uneven end of the foyers system through a detailed study of the moment of the move and unpack the contradictory demands residents as well as professional and institutional actors faced. The renovation scheme offered a stage where tensions set opposite institutions on one side and residents and their allies on the other, but neither of these blocks is monolithic. To understand the dynamics at play, it is particularly important to go beyond the stance of the délégués, who are vocal in defending the foyers but do not reflect the diversity of the positions of the foyers' population. Likewise, multiple institutions maneuver the renovation, with distinct agendas and understandings of the dynamics on the ground; within the same institution diverging views are important to apprehend.

The following chapters tie together the fate of buildings, administrative structures, and communities. Each layer comes with its own chronology and intersects with the others. Hence, when buildings appear to be decaying, they not only testify to institutional neglect and to unintended uses but to the active process of "ruination," which speaks to their status as relics, evoking a past time of full employment when migrant workers were sought after.

Before analyzing the renovation scheme, an overview of the preexisting situation is in order. What held foyer inhabitants together? Chapter 4 addresses this question through an analysis of the ways of inhabiting the old foyers before their renovation, as I observed them in the 2010s. Foyer communities were sociohistorical formations rooted in the premigration socialization of foyer inhabitants as much as in their migratory experience, all of this being reworked under the constraints of the physical and social space of the foyer.

Understanding the core dimensions of the foyer communities as well as lines of tension proves illuminating when considering how the renovation scheme was received and experienced by West African migrants. Chapter 5 provides a broad view of the moves, which involved a variety of actors. Confronting the evolution of public policies and managing practices in the foyers with the residents own understanding of the dynamics at stake enriches existing studies of the renovation that are rooted in political science and sociology.

Turning my gaze back onto the inner workings of the foyers, in chapter 6 I question the effects of this transformation on the collectives of residents living in the foyer. This moment when collectives constituted since the 1960s were dislocated offers a unique opportunity to provide a thick description of the foyers. Analyzing the nature of the ties between coresidents and their evolution, I demonstrate how the renovation process and the wider legal and administrative changes of the past two decades has inflected individual and family decisions and reshaped the forms of relatedness prevailing among migrants.

# 4

## TOLERATED BONDS

### Living Together in the Foyers

*As I step into the hall of the foyer in a cramped place in front of the elevator, I greet Assane. It is the first time that I am paying him a visit, having gotten to know him in demonstrations that he had participated in as a sans-papiers representative. I find him sitting on a chair selling international phone cards that he bought wholesale in the neighborhood of La Chapelle in Paris, an activity that he interrupts to welcome me. Age forty-three, he migrated from his hometown in Senegal only two years ago, quite recently compared to most of his peers. His maternal uncle, a former Renault worker, has found him a bed in a room adjacent to his. That day we first go to greet his uncle, although on subsequent visits we will not do so. Since this uncle is also his wife's father, Assane is highly deferential toward him and does not seek out his company. I will gradually discover the places where Assane spends his time in the foyer: the workshop of his longtime friend, a tailor, where we sit and have tea; the collective kitchen, where I get to know one of his friends, a woman working as a cook; the outside courtyard, where we eat grilled corn and exchange a few words with older men sitting on a bench; and a room where fellow villagers in their thirties or forties are living, located on another floor of the building.*

*It is not until some time later that I first enter this room, an hour before he and I are due to leave to join a demonstration. Four men are casually sitting or half-lying on the three beds, and I am invited to sit on one of the four chairs in the room. They all greet me politely and resume their previous discussions in Soninke, while Assane and I discuss the situation in their foyer in French. Anxious to have others join our conversation, I address the man sitting on the bed next to us, Mody, who is the same age as Assane and he joins our discussion. Our chatter is interrupted when Mody signals that the hour of the evening prayer is approaching. He turns down the volume a bit on the TV set and spreads out two prayer rugs in the center of the room. I apologetically push my chair out of the way, but Mody and Assane urge me not to move, assuring me that I will not disturb them. While they jointly perform the prayer, another man goes down to the collective prayer room, and the last one, Issa, nonchalantly continues preparing some spicy tea, filling the room with the scent of fresh ginger and cloves, before leaving the room to go smoke a cigarette. After the prayer, I attempt to exchange a few words with him in Wolof because I know that he comes from the same Senegalese village as Assane. But when Assane tells him that I can converse in Bamanan, Issa immediately switches to this language, thus excluding the other two who did not know it. Assane immerses himself in his cell phone until it is time to go to the demonstration. While we are getting ready to leave, I urge Issa to join us, but my authoritative tone only makes him laugh. Although he promises to do so, we both know he will not actually leave the comfort of his room to go out into the cold.*[1]

Several key features of the foyers as lived-in spaces emerge from these field notes. First, foyers were highly heterogeneous places where power relations between inhabitants determined rights to use the space, and the existence of multiple spaces also constituted a resource. Assane's circulation among them attests both to the possibilities offered by the foyer spaces and to his subaltern status as an unregistered resident and an undocumented migrant. Second, relationships were strongly shaped by references to kinship as well as status, gender, and age: my joking relationship with Issa (which we maintained on subsequent encounters) was made possible by the fact that he was much younger than I, whereas Assane, a few years older than I, never departed from his very respectful attitude, a demeanor he adopted as a condition for having me around in an almost all-male place. Third, living together did not involve an undifferentiated use of space. Rather, it implied ways of compartmentalizing a shared space to create bubbles of privacy for oneself or a pair, by switching to a language not shared by others, for example, or by retreating to a corner of a room.

Sensitive to the material and sensorial dimensions of life in the foyers as they stood before the renovation process, in this chapter I explore the nature of the groups consolidated through coresidence, scrutinizing the ties that hold coresidents together as much as the centrifugal forces that pull them apart. The analysis moves from consideration of the more mundane spatial practices—a horizontal view of these men's daily actions and movements within the foyer—to an exploration of kinship ties and the intergenerational transference of beds and rooms—a vertical view of the foyer's structure.

## PLURAL COMMUNITIES

Depicting the inhabitation of the foyers leads to several conflicting analytical tensions. To begin with, the status of the foyer as a home is ambiguous. On one hand, the often dilapidated status of the buildings engendered extremely bitter comments. Demba, who arrived in France in 1973 from Dolol, Senegal, and had lived for more than twenty years at Foyer D'Hautpoul, asserted that "a foyer is not a home, it's just a place of passage" (Wolof: *Foyer du kër, passage la rekk*). The anthropologist Catherine Quiminal stated that "the foyer has none of the attributes of a home" (notably due to the absence of women), but I prefer a more nuanced approach that pays attention to the way in which its inhabitants voiced a strong attachment to it.[2]

This was done in public settings, when they claimed the foyer as a "place of our own" (French: *chez nous*), a phrase that emphasized property and belonging. In addition to such claims, mundane practices also pointed to homemaking processes. Inhabitants and users actively maintained forms of sociability that they were aware did not prevail outside, for instance, while greeting others.[3] These salutations could be minimal and adapted to everybody, such as the generic *"Assalamu alaikum"* (a borrowing from Arabic widely used in West African countries) addressed to all the occupants of the elevator, or specific when greeting better-known people with the appropriate Soninke or Pulaar phrase.[4] Likewise, when attending a meeting in the foyer, many inhabitants would come in flip-flops and kaftans (wide-sleeved gowns) that constituted their indoor garment, which some would also wear outside although less frequently. This sense of a community sustained the understanding of the foyer community as resting on a bare minimum of consideration for one another. Historical and contemporary accounts evoked the fate of one resident dying alone without those in the next room being aware of it as something dramatic, something that should not happen in a foyer.

The second tension is between continuity and rupture in terms of inhabitants' premigratory experiences. All foyer inhabitants were migrants, but they ranged from the freshly arrived to men who had been in France for decades. Presuming continuity in terms of their ways of inhabiting the foyers would ignore their acquired experience of life in France and the specific nature of the foyers as historical constructs. When I borrow from African studies or take my lead from my knowledge of domestic West African settings, I am cautious not to replicate cultural assumptions that have historically served as hasty justifications to provide migrants with degraded lodging conditions.[5] Nevertheless, the foyer inhabitants' primary spatial socialization (and the associated relational skills embedded) shaped their conduct within the foyers, and I focus on how acquired modes of dwelling were remodeled under the social and physical constraints of the foyer.

Third, when trying to grapple with the kind of community constituted within the foyer, we need to be sensitive to the interplay between commonality and difference at distinct scales. Foyers were places where some men belonged to the same small or extended family, a number came from the same village, many shared the same ethnolinguistic background or partook in a looser "West African" identity, and West Africans and Maghrebis shared a postcolonial and Islamic background. These scales of belonging, of varying strength and meaning, converged in the creation of an "us" and a characterization of the foyer as a place where prevailing rules in French public space did not necessarily apply.

The few instances of West Africans and Maghrebis cohabiting that I encountered attested to an inclusive reference to Islam as a shared identity, and a minority one in the French context. In addition, the shared time within the foyer forged individual bonds between long-term coresidents of both origins. But I also observed oppositional stances based on racialized stereotypes on both sides. These can largely be explained by the fact that these groups were distinct in terms of demographics, with Maghrebis being, for the most part, old men constituting a shrinking population in foyers, whereas the West Africans tended to be more numerous. Furthermore, living in a foyer seemed negatively connoted for Maghrebi residents. A Moroccan that I met in Foyer Masséna explained how his presence there was the result of a downward trajectory: "I slipped into RMI [Revenu minimal d'insertion, a subsidy for people not entitled to unemployment benefits] and so arrived in the foyer," a configuration that could be observed among some West Africans, but only marginally.[6]

The "West African" transethnic identity in the foyers was also built on a similar reference to Islam, on a common regional origin (Senegal River Valley), and on more or less mutually translatable features throughout neighboring societies in the Sahel in terms of common general aspects of social organization and kinship systems. Soninke and Haalpulaar share the same basic kinship features, dominated by patrilineal descent and patrivirilocal residence. As previously indicated, both societies are stratified in statutory groups.

Knowledge of the inner workings of other groups was unevenly distributed; my older Haalpulaar interlocutors generally knew the statutory group of the Soninke families with whom they coexisted, whereas my younger interlocutors did not. Some sociocultural features had currency across several groups. Illustrating one ordinary usage of a pivotal linguistic and sociocultural item, thirty-year-old Souley, one of my Haalpulaar friends, used the term *"kaaw"* (Pulaar: maternal uncle, also used in Soninke) to address older Soninke men. Joking relations on the basis of patronyms or ethnic assignation tended to be established within groups, but occasionally straddled them. Migrants selectively drew from this shared repertoire to emphasize or downplay similarities.

Commonality beyond ethnicity was paradoxically emphasized in narratives of the most violent event (a homicide) that had occurred in one foyer between two men, a Haalpulaar and a Soninke, after a dispute over the use of a collective room degenerated, resulting in one's death and the other being jailed. One of my interlocutors insisted that this dramatic event had not resulted in exacerbated tensions between communities, but he also detailed his involvement in smoothing things over, which suggests that divisive tendencies had needed to be countered. This attests to the collective work undertaken to overcome ethnic differences whenever they surface.

## THE ENDURING ISSUE OF INHERITED SOCIAL STATUSES

The issue of statutory groups—a key point in the history of the foyers—deserves its own examination. This issue has gained recent attention as critical voices within West African communities have denounced the foyers as places of domestic labor exploitation and even physical abuse. Antislavery activists have targeted the situations in foyers as epitomizing this kind of reproduction and sometimes hardening of unequal rules. Since 2010, an association has listed cases of physical abuse based on the consideration of inherited statuses and pursued legal actions, notably regarding cases at Foyer Commanderie (nineteenth arrondissement) and in the foyer of Saint-Ouen.[7] Although not based on a systematic inquiry on this topic, my remarks provide a sense of the situation as I observed it while focusing on other issues. The subject is complicated: most foyer residents are reluctant to discuss these matters and tend to minimize the persistence of statutory distinctions; direct questioning on such issues can be perceived as offensive or elicit only vague answers; and beyond discourses, decoding embodied practices referring to unequal social statuses is an arduous task.[8]

In the course of my fieldwork, I did not encounter systematic relations of exploitation formalized at the level of the foyers, a point I further detail when considering the allocation of cooking. Foyer representatives hailed from all status groups. Furthermore, several of my interlocutors claimed an egalitarian stance, and my old interlocutor Demba professed: "When it comes to the situation here, we are all workers, there is no slave, no noble."[9] However, these considerations must be mitigated by some observations that I made in rooms where references to slave status, often in a seemingly joking mode, were ubiquitous.[10]

Statutory groups combined with many other registers, and no unilateral qualification of the foyer as a site of oppression held.[11] Assane, whom I introduce in the opening sequence of this chapter, was of slave descent and lived in a foyer where one of his paternal uncles (of the same status) was a prominent délégué. Assane had the possibility to leave the foyer because one of his brothers lived with his family in a midsized town in the west of France. He occasionally went there for month-long visits, but he told me that the foyer was preferable given the job opportunities available in the Paris region. Even when unemployed, he conducted several small business activities within the foyer: selling cards, as we have seen; but also temporarily cooking and selling food in a floor kitchen. He was also involved as one of the representatives of the foyer sans-papiers group; he related this political activity to his previous experience in local village politics, where he mentioned that customs (Soninke: *laada*) had prevented him from having the career that he desired.[12] From the hours spent in the room where he met his friends, I also noticed that he did not specifically endorse subaltern roles— Issa, the one brewing tea, was from a *naxamala* family. Assane's profile (and the fact that his uncle is a délégué) invalidates the notion that the foyer persists as a site where migrants of subaltern status are limited to lesser positions. However, this case suggests that other registers—here, the social capital built across generations—combined with (and could neutralize) the effects of status group categorizations.

In other circumstances, lower-status migrants expressed their desire to leave the foyer. Diaguily, from Mauritania and of *kome* (Soninke: slave) status, spent fifteen years living in a foyer before being able to move out from an environment that he characterized in terms of social control and his disproportionate participation in domestic chores.[13] In addition, foyers have remained the spaces where village associations convene and where issues regarding the whole village tend to be brought up and debated. Hence, when cases of intergroup marriages—which run counter to the endogamous rule still very much in place in West African societies—have been publicly dealt with, the foyers have been at the center of these debates.[14] As the sociologist Yaya Sy's intricate case studies demonstrate, such dramatic situations have led to the public reassertion of strict endogamous rules, but they have stirred up heated debates and offered opportunities, albeit limited, for critical voices to express themselves. As previously demonstrated in the debates over collective chores in the 1970s, which resulted in drastic changes, foyers offer spaces of shared life and are the main place where scattered members of diasporic communities meet and engage with one another, and they reflect existing power dynamics and their historical changes rather than imposing the permanence of rigid hierarchies.

## INTERNAL RULES AND *SUTURA*

Order in the foyer relied on explicit and implicit rules. Rules for cohabitation could be formalized in written internal rules—not the official version set by the managers but the translation by the délégués of collectively sanctioned rules. At Foyer Lorraine, a two-page document was adopted in 1994 to delimit the correct use of the collective gatherings: the organization of celebrations such as weddings and parties was forbidden, but "village meetings" and "cultural events" such as film screenings were authorized; it further set time restrictions on all collective activities and prohibited noisy behavior at night.[15] In another facility, the internal rules adopted by the residents further regulated interpersonal conflicts and stipulated that "the foyer committee is the competent authority in charge of settling disputes among residents. An individual found guilty will be fined €100."[16] It excluded intrafamilial conflicts, however—a point explained this way by a délégué: "If my son misbehaves, I punish him; this is no one else's business." The document established a chain of responsibility: families were responsible for maintaining order internally; a host was responsible for the acts of the individuals under his charge; and délégués took care of interfamily issues.

In most foyers such rules were unwritten, but the notion that délégués had to control "their" foyers was often expressed in collective meetings, especially when security issues arose in neighborhoods where drug dealing was widespread. At Foyer Lorraine, shortly before the renovation, the délégués tore apart a bike shed located in the foyer courtyard because it was a place where a mixed crowd of young foyer inhabitants and outsiders convened at night. In other foyers, watches were organized and the délégués made rounds, kicking out squatters. However, throughout my fieldwork, délégués also voiced their concern that maintaining such order was difficult and complained about the constant challenges to their authority. Thus the assertions of control and occasional actions should be understood against a larger backdrop of diminishing ability to enforce these collective rules.

Along with explicit rules that mostly targeted collective spaces, more pervasive norms of discretion prevailed in the foyers. Shame, a core value of West African ethics, regulated interpersonal relationships: for example, Assane avoided his uncle who was also his wife's father. This example of tricky cohabitation with in-laws was brought up by several of my interlocutors. The notion of shame also came into play with regard to accepted behavior in the foyer's collective spaces. Foyers were tied to the localities of origin of many inhabitants through dense interpersonal networks and a flux of exchange of news. Sanctions could be exerted on a migrant's family back home if, for instance, one tried to evade mandatory financial contributions to the village associations.[17] The steadiness of the circulation of news between the foyer and the village is still obvious, especially in the digital age. A friend of mine had the following bitter experience: he had married a French woman while hiding the fact that he already had a spouse in his village. While he was spending two months' vacation in his village (which he had framed to his French wife as a visit to his parents), one of their mutual acquaintances visited the French spouse and disclosed the reality to her. In a gesture of anger, the French wife sent photographs of their wedding to all my friend's Facebook contacts. When he was back in France, I discussed the situation with him. He said that he had not yet identified the snitch, but—assuming that it had to be one of his relatives—he would "make his life a misery in the village."[18]

In this respect, the foyer is an extension of close-knit communities, where the constraint of being under the constant gaze of others leads to a conscious effort to secure privacy. One sociocultural resource is the notion of *sutura*, an Arabic-derived term whose equivalent can be found in the West African languages used in the foyer (at least in Pulaar, Soninke, Wolof, and Bamanan). Sutura is generally defined as an emphasis on displaying respect for the others and for dominating norms in public, with inappropriate behavior reserved to private spheres. Souley, a former student who had spent several years in Dakar before coming to France, explained to me that drinking alcohol in the foyer was not a problem, but you should put your bottle of beer in a nontransparent bag before entering. He disapproved of the conduct of another student living in the foyer who, during Ramadan, drank from a water bottle in the hall. He commented that no one cared if he himself chose not to fast, but that displaying such behavior was disrespectful toward the elders. Sutura relied on an interplay between public and private that could fully operate in old foyers, which offered various kinds of spaces, from collective to intimate and across many intermediary ones.

## SPACE: CONSTRAINED, MULTIPLE, POLYVALENT

Two months before the closure of Foyer D'Hautpoul, I met Yero at the café La Piscine, where he spent most of his spare time, a few hundred meters from the foyer. Having arrived in France in 1991 from his hometown on the Senegalese bank of the Senegal River, Yero had first lodged a few months in the communal spaces

of Foyer D'Hautpoul before moving to a foyer located in La Verrière in the west of the Paris region, where he occupied the bed of
an absent resident. Following a large police operation in this foyer
a few months later, he moved back to Foyer D'Hautpoul, where
he finally secured a bed under his own name. Around fifty years
old, he was one of the younger members of the team of délégués.
We met at La Piscine as part of an ongoing project with photographer Anissa Michalon who was documenting life in the foyer
before the move. When we asked him to list the most important
places within the foyer, Yero suggested the prayer room because,
he said, "we are gathered here during prayers, always together, this
is a memory to preserve." He also mentioned other rooms: "We
meet in a room where we drink tea, but younger ones can't be with
older ones." Being together covered distinct realities depending
on the given space. Yero considered the prayer room a place where
distinctions did not matter, but he assumed that ordinary spaces
of sociability reflected age-group divisions.[19]

   This distinction was possible because the foyer offered multiple spaces and because spaces could be used in provisional
spatiotemporal arrangements. As my moves from one place to
another within Assane's foyer demonstrate, the dialectics of
inside/outside plays *within* the foyers: common spaces ranged
from dedicated collective areas, such as courtyards or indoor collective rooms, to spots occupied against their initial design, such
as stairway landings converted into sitting areas. Community-
oriented moments, such as meetings of hometown associations
or to receive condolences and arrange the repatriation of a body,
tended to occur in collective rooms. But some collective activities were distributed across foyer rooms: the informal system of
money transfers located in the foyers involved several individuals, and records were kept by a responsible party in one room
while many others kept an eye on the process.[20]

Rooms could have several functions: someone might sleep in one room but spend most of his time in another, as Assane did. Another of my interlocutors kept his luggage in the room that he had been greeted in upon arrival, but he slept with friends in another. Even a registered resident fully entitled to use his room could develop several uses for the foyer's rooms. In Claire Clouet's account of the ambiance at Foyer Argonne (nineteenth arrondissement), she mentions that one délégué would rarely receive visitors in his room but met them in his cousin's room, which he had turned into his "office."[21] To investigate the spatiotemporal arrangements that allowed for polyvalent uses of the same space, I focus on rooms that many visitors frequented and in which I spent most of my time.[22]

Any analysis should begin with the fact that these spaces are narrow and experienced as such. Newcomers speak of their first encounter with the foyer as a shock. At best, sharing a place with other men is a return to premarital practices where young men had a common living space in the village. Even this must be mitigated by the urban origin of many young migrants; several of my younger interlocutors had a room of their own in Dakar or Bamako before leaving. As a result, many features of the foyer are akin to descriptions of other confined spaces, with orderliness and regulations over the smallest surface being the rule. For instance, when I visited old Demba in his single room that hosted up to five men, I noticed that one of the other inhabitants always hung his cap on a nail on the wall when he came back from work—a glance at this nail was enough to know if he was around or not.

That this order was consciously maintained was apparent from the gestures and indications that accompanied my moves in the foyer: upon entering a room, I was always invited to sit in a specific place on a chair or on a bed. Someone would get up and move my coat if I left it in a place deemed inappropriate.

This attention directed toward an often-intimidated visitor was similar to the consideration given to each other by inhabitants. While I was chatting with Seydou, a délégué at Foyer D'Hautpoul, one of the other men present in the room got up from his chair to move Seydou's flip-flops, which he had left at the entrance to the room, closer to him. Such careful gestures betray the narrowness of spaces, where the sheer necessity of avoiding bumping into one other necessitates continual attention to one's environment. They further attest to a sense of physical and social positions, which translates into constant attention to the surrounding space.

At Foyer D'Hautpoul, I spent countless hours in the lively room of my friend Dramane, a man in his late thirties. He had arrived in France ten years earlier, secured a residence permit, and registered as the official occupant of his father's former bed.[23] He was from one of the key founding villages of Foyer D'Hautpoul, and more than fifty of his covillagers were living in the foyer. Dramane had a core position in his village youth association and regularly held meetings of the association in his room. Echoing textbook anthropological thinking, he once told me, "I'm not rich in things, but I'm rich in people."[24] I visited him in the afternoon on his days off, and the sun reflected off the glass of the building across the street, making the room so warm that the windows were often left open. I generally found several people in his room, and counted up to eleven visitors in one single afternoon. At that time of day, his roommate was at work, and the groups were often groups of peers, although sometimes younger or older residents also visited. Part of a "unité de vie" together with the adjacent one-bed room, his room shared a small entrance-cum-kitchenette where only one person could stand and cook on the stoves, leaving enough space for those exiting the rooms to access the shower (figure 4.1).

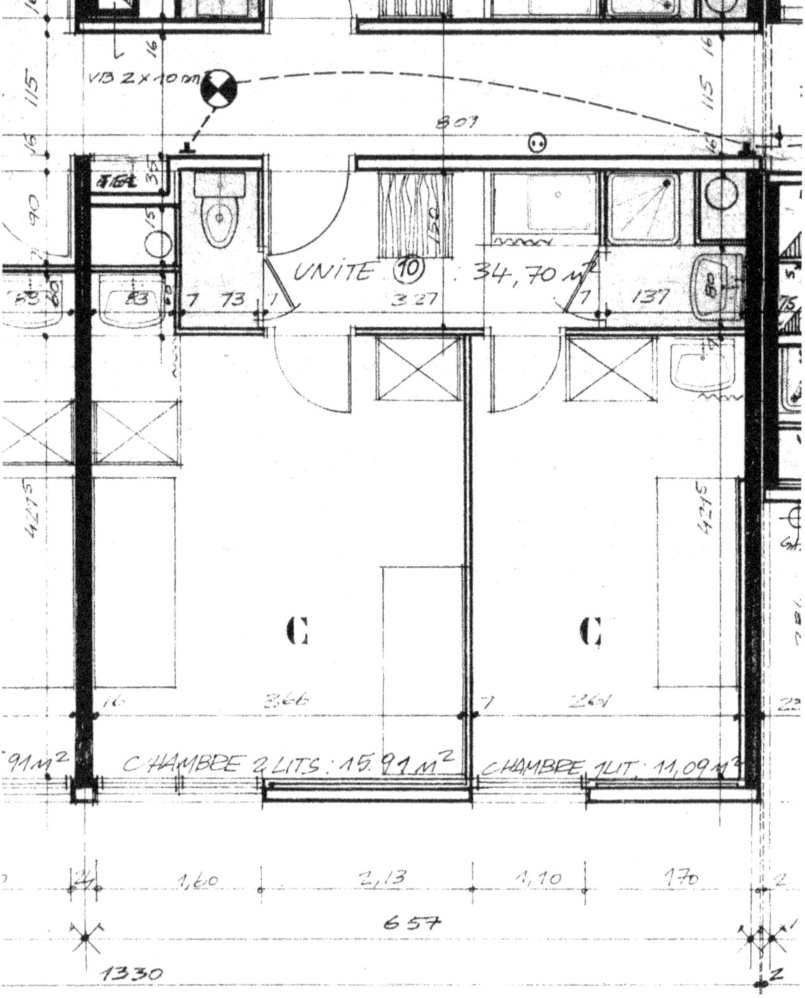

**FIGURE 4.1** Architectural drawing of a room, Foyer Lorraine.

*Source*: Archives de Paris 1178 W 2959.

Dramane's room status as a gathering place depended in part on his willingness to host such a crowd: a grouchy answer to a greeting sufficed to deter a would-be visitor. The respective positions of the door to his room and the door to the entrance could also indicate his availability, as I experienced one day when I found him alone. I had come in, sat down in my usual chair next to his bed where he was lying down, and thoughtlessly closed the door. Soon after, someone knocked and opened the door in the same movement; the visitor swiftly apologized upon seeing that Dramane was receiving a woman. This incident made Dramane get up to reopen the door inside the room while closing the entrance door that led into the corridor. In this way, we were not visible to people passing in the corridor, but anyone coming in the entrance would find the room door ajar, and thus not feel that he was interrupting.

Upon entering the room (less than 16 m²), visitors faced a large window, with the two beds positioned along the two walls, right and left; a TV set was placed at a right angle; and three chairs occupied various spaces depending on the activities going on and the number of visitors. Steadily employed, Dramane regularly funded the cooking of meals that all men present would eat, spreading out newspaper sheets in the space in the middle of the room and placing a common bowl down, with everyone sitting on either a chair or a bed. As soon as we had finished, one of the men would swiftly gather the newspaper sheets and throw them away. Tea was generally put on the stove in the entrance, with whomever was assigned this task standing there and occasionally joining in the discussion in the room. Spreading one's prayer mat was possible either in the corner next to the sink or in front of the window. Finally, in addition to the two registered roommates, two other men occupied the room, drawing their mattresses out from under the beds at night.

This overview of the room's main uses (as a place for discussions and visits, eating and drinking tea, sleeping, and performing individual prayers) demonstrates its changing functions. This ability builds on West African ways of using domestic space as described by Elodie Razy: "Cooking, eating, and sleeping are techniques of the body which require minimal tools in spaces that are not specifically dedicated to these activities."[25] The performance of the Islamic prayer also fits into such a pattern, with the mat sufficing to establish "a mobile space-time within the accommodation," as has been described in other French domestic spaces.[26]

As suggested by Assane's case, this lability occasioned possibilities for inclusion and exclusion. In the dynamics of verbal exchanges, for instance, there was both the possibility to develop private conversations (through code-switching) and a constant awareness of the presence of others; smartphones also served to abstract oneself from the copresent, be it by conversing with distant others or by immersing oneself in a digital activity.[27] I argue that foyers, with their multiple spaces (and the importance of intermediary spaces), provided architectural and material affordances for re-creating spheres of privacy within an environment characterized by social control. Second, I consider that specific social practices and uses of the space, which allowed forms of compartmentalizing, played a key role in setting provisional boundaries demarcating the time and space of one activity or a sphere of individual or shared intimacy.

## OF *MAFÉ, MARMITES,* AND RELUCTANT COOKS

In West African foyers, the smell of stews cooking for hours melts with the scent of strong green tea boiling on electric stoves. Food is conspicuous: copious plates of rice, macaroni, or French fries sold in the canteen; bowls of rice prepared in the kitchens and shared among large groups of men; bags of dried couscous made from millet brought from home and carefully distributed to their recipients. Prepping, sharing, and consuming food are crucial dimensions of daily life that depend on economic resources and domestic labor and convey key social and symbolic values; in transnational spaces, these dimensions take on new meanings.

Commercial kitchens or canteens existed in some foyers. Cooks, generally women, catered to inhabitants and outside customers for a modest price. Heading each team (generally, two teams alternated every week), an entrepreneur organized the work and managed the finances.[28] She paid the délégués a fixed amount corresponding to the expenses for electricity, gas, and water. Since 2000, associations and residents have attempted to certify these kitchens, providing training so foyer canteen workers comply with sanitation department and labor regulations.[29]

Foyer inhabitants were easy to spot in the canteens because they came down with a bowl into which several portions were served together, and they took this back to their rooms. This was a convenient expedient, but their most regular habit was to consume food prepared in their internal kitchens. Facing two robust electric stoves on the yellow wall of one Foyer D'Hautpoul cooking space, a white sheet of paper listed twenty-three names: these were the members of the "*tour de cuisine*," expected to cook (in pairs) approximately twice a month. Being a man and cooking is an experience linked to the migration context. In many instances, my interlocutors referred to the role of cook as a female task. As my friend Souley was accompanying me down Foyer Lorraine's staircase one day, we came across a friend of his who asked if he was going out. "No," he said, jokingly adding, "Today it is me who is your woman" (Wolof: *Teyi man maa seen jigéen*). Cooking in itself is associated with women, and the notion of taking turns is further reminiscent of the organization of domestic and sexual labor in polygynous households where cowives take turns. Indeed, the same metaphor of being one's woman or wife was a notion that Souley also rejected: on another day, when I asked him if someone else decided on the dish to be cooked, he replied, "No! I'm not someone else's wife" (Wolof: *Déedéet! Man duma jabaru kenn*) and explained that the cook of the day decided the dish that he would prepare on the basis of what was available.[30]

Souley's uneasiness with the gendered connotation of cooking reflected a wider understanding of cooking as a task to be performed by men of subaltern status. As previously indicated, this work initially came down to subordinate statutory groups, but this labor division was widely contested in the 1970s and generally abandoned at the level of the foyer.[31] All formalized cooking groups that I documented allocated this task to younger men, and more specifically relied on the labor of the unemployed. Those who took part in cooking were exempt from paying the monthly contribution, an amount that varied from €30 to €50 in the cases I documented.

Cooking groups varied greatly in size. At Foyer D'Hautpoul, villagers from Odobere, Senegal, and neighboring villages assembled almost one hundred men. The same cooking group (in terms of dues and the logistics of buying food) included three "*marmites*" (large cooking pots), which operated on three floors (the first floor was reserved for elderly men, and others were dispatched between the third and sixth floors). Other groups only numbered a dozen men. Cooking groups could include outsiders to the village community ready to contribute financially. The cooking groups that I observed offered one meal per day on weekdays and one or two during weekends. They systematically cooked rice-based West African dishes. The meal was served in one or several bowls. Men gathered around these communal platters, either seated, as is common in West Africa, or standing when space was insufficient (figure 4.2). My interlocutors described this way of eating as specific to the migratory context, as is the term "*tuuse*" used by Soninke migrants and occasionally by others.[32]

Together with this contribution to a village-based cooking group, or in place of it in cases where no such organization prevailed, smaller cooking organizations existed. Hence, Seydou, délégué at Foyer D'Hautpoul, regularly cooked for a smaller

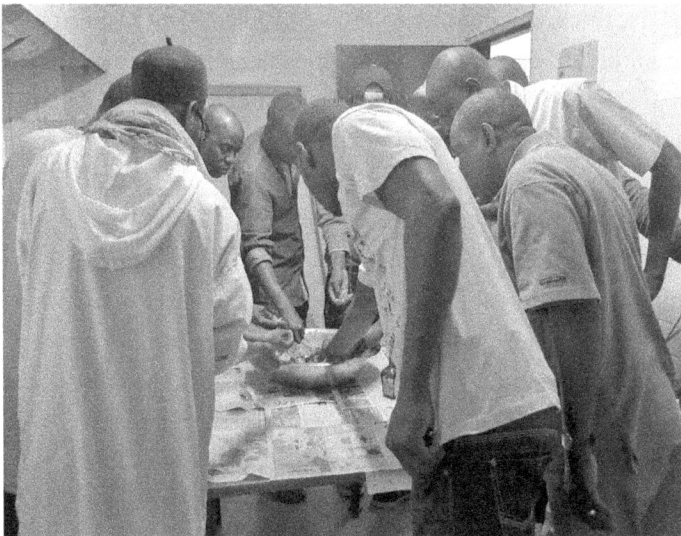

**FIGURE 4.2** Shared meal of a group of men organized for taking turns in collective cooking, Foyer D'Hautpoul, 2013.

*Source*: Photo by Anissa Michalon.

group and also contributed to the village's collective cooking group. His brother, a taxi driver, paid for most of the foodstuffs, buying rice, meat, and oil. Seydou's role was to buy vegetables and to cook; when the meal was ready, he shared it with the younger men living with them. Months into our relationship, he began to offer me food—served on an individual plate, I ate alone in a room facing a TV, whereas at Dramane's I shared the meal from the same bowl as the men. Through this practice of cooking, the brothers manifested their prodigality and supplemented the common dish.

Some of my interlocutors, especially younger ones, complained of the monotony of the food.[33] Indeed, that the infrastructure for such collective cooking was incorporated in the foyer's layout suggests that the possibility to feed oneself cheaply and copiously—which, to borrow from Marxist vocabulary, enables the reproduction of the labor force—had been part of the foyers' initial conception, inasmuch as it limited these possibilities to the production of basic collective food. French phrases surrounding collective food (such as "*la popote*") also borrow from working-class culture and even evoke military connotations.

Nonetheless, most of my interlocutors preferred to emphasize and value the continuity with West African practices. As the anthropologist Chelsie Yount-André notes about Senegalese migrant families in France, "eating around a communal dish functions as a metonym for solidarity, generosity, and hospitality."[34] The shared meal elicited many comments on the values that it promoted. First, residents highlighted the practical advantage of a daily gathering. As in West Africa, the rule was to eat more or less silently, or in any case not to engage in profound discussions, but the time immediately after the meal, before everybody went back to his place, was described as a moment when people could exchange news. Second, although hierarchies permeated ways of eating and sharing the meat or fish placed in the center of the bowl, sharing the common meal ensured that everyone ate the same food. Third, two of my interlocutors evoked a notion of "pity" (French: *pitié*), used to denote compassion and empathy. One referred to the fact of eating with their hands, stating that "symbolically, putting one's hand in the same bowl, this allows feelings of pity toward one another." The other mentioned it in reference to the village custom of sharing the same ladle to eat millet porridge: "It recalls the pity we feel toward each other, it's like sucking from the same breast."[35] The notion of commensality as kin-making was pervasive, attesting to the inclusive form of kinship that prevailed in the West African context, from which most of the foyer inhabitants had migrated.[36] In addition, although this comparison with breastfeeding was unique, it evoked uterine kinship as the product of commensality, building on ideals relating to matrilineal bonds characterized by cooperation and affection. However, turning to the core of the foyers' internal workings—the transference of beds—degrees of relatedness appear crucial and mitigate the relative openness observed at the level of meal-sharing.

## HERITAGE AND HOSPITALITY: DEGREES OF RELATEDNESS AND PRECARIOUS ARRANGEMENTS

The constitution of foyer populations followed two axes: synchronically, people were initially hosted by registered residents before being able to access this status; diachronically, beds were handed from one inhabitant to another.

The most common way to find a bed in the foyer was to join a relative, preferably through patrilineal ties, otherwise through matrilineal ties, or else through looser acquaintances from the same locality. Dramane described the logic of joining someone in the foyer in the following terms: "If [a newcomer] has no relatives, we look for someone from the same village, or who knows his family; we seek a solution, looking for his closest [relative]."[37] At any given time, most registered residents hosted at least one of their relatives. The all-male environment of the foyers was deemed a space where newcomers could be hosted, whereas relatives living with their family in an apartment generally objected to hosting a male relative because they sought to preserve conjugal intimacy.[38]

Hospitality, often described as a burden, is also a demonstration of (partial) success, of one's capacity and achievement. Hosting arrangements are caught in the wider logic of debt that undergirds the migratory project from its inception. Accommodating someone often follows from the migrant's relatives' involvement in the departure of another migrant: Dramane, who funded his younger brother's trip, was thus expected to provide him with a place to stay upon arrival. In a social context characterized by closer bonds with uterine siblings, and rivalry with agnatic ones, he insisted that he had to provide all the support that his brother (an agnatic one) needed: behaving otherwise would draw immediate criticism.

The newcomer was accommodated for free as long as he did not work, being expected to support part of the cost of the room once he was settled but without back payment for the time already spent. In normative discourses, my interlocutors emphasized this moral obligation, although they admitted to deviant cases. I heard both Soninke and Haalpulaar boast that they still complied with this rule, whereas other groups tended to calculate the newcomer's debt and have him reimburse them whenever he could. Seydou, a Haalpulaar, stated: "There is a basic difference in mentality: from the first day, Soninke keep count of all that you will owe; [among us] Haalpulaar, you arrive as undocumented, we lodge you freely, as long as needed. Then you find documents, a job, and you can send money home."[39] When I questioned my friend Dramane on this topic, he told me the reverse: "It's only when you get a job that you begin to contribute. Before that, you don't even accrue debts. But among Haalpulaar, I was told that, as soon as you arrive, you become indebted. This is their invention, among us [Soninke], solidarity prevails."[40] From these accounts, I conclude that expecting compensation for time spent "for free" is an existing albeit stigmatized practice in both groups.

Being hosted does not guarantee access to a bed, not even to a fixed mattress because there is a hierarchy of spaces: a bed, a mattress kept under a bed or along the wall during the daytime, and even more precarious installations. The case of Kandé, hosted at Foyer D'Hautpoul, is one such extreme case in terms of the number of men sharing a room.[41] Having arrived in France at age twenty-six, Kandé had first spent a week with a relative in a town in the east of France before joining another distant relative in the foyer. He had a closer connection (his father's cousin), but this man lived with his wife, so he only visited them on special occasions, such as Eid. At Foyer D'Hautpoul, there were eight living in a two-bed room. He spent most of the night in the living space of the unité de vie.[42] Since he could not sleep there, he had to wait until six o'clock in the morning to find a place in the room. The man paying the rent had his own bed, and two more shared the other bed. A big mattress hosted three to four men. Finally, Kandé had a roll-up mattress. At the time of our interview, he had left the foyer (as a consequence of a move detailed in chapter 6). He spoke of his headaches and red eyes caused by lack of sleep and stated that he could not imagine living in a foyer once he had secured his documents. As a close relative, he was never asked to pay, although he had a hard time securing even small amounts to buy toothpaste or other items. Occasionally, he borrowed money from the stall owners in the hall.

When an occupant obtained a job, he was expected to contribute to the payment of the bed or room. The usual understanding was that a mattress was cheaper than a proper bed. According to the figures I was given in Foyer Lorraine, generally speaking, the guest paid €100 a month, and the man sleeping on the bed paid €170. But I also heard guest residents complain that most of the burden of the rent fell to them, despite the uncomfortable nature of their accommodation. Exploitative arrangements occurred more easily when people were not related: one of my interlocutors explained how he shared a two-bed room with four other men, and altogether they paid the official rate of €460 to the registered resident; benefiting from subsidies, this resident paid less and thus pocketed a monthly profit; he concluded that hosting for free was something that "only kin could do" (Wolof: *Mbokk rekk a ko mën na def*).

Dovetailing such hosting practices was the need to have someone take the place of the host during long absences: for men whose families were far away, it was common to wait years to save enough money and accrue enough vacation days to spend several months in the home country. The substitute (French: *remplaçant*) was expected to pay the rent. Evidencing the de facto acceptance of such practices by the foyer director, the payment of rent by someone who was not the registered resident was generally accepted. Receipts then contained both the name of the registered resident and the name of the payer.

This logic of cohabitation intersected with the mode of transferring beds, which also followed kinship relations. "It's a matter of inheritance" (Wolof: *Afeeru ndono la*), Souley stated plainly when commenting on the probable transfer of one of his room's beds, which would go to a member of the registered resident's patrilineal kin following the general pattern. Although the space of the room is open to kin in a wider sense, when it comes to heritage, patrilineal ties prevail. This reflects the migration pattern from areas where households were formed from segments of a patrilineage and where migration strategies were generally devised at this level.

The preferred succession was when a son took over the bed when his father retired, ideally without actual cohabitation— which again brought up issues of shame. However, tightening migratory regulations made it difficult for families to determine such timings. Hence several of my interlocutors actually joined their fathers: Dramane, who slept alongside his migrant father for several years, recalled both tensions and moments of fondness. Those were the years, he said, when he got to know this man who had only been an occasional visitor in his childhood. When passing one's bed to the member of the owner's household was not possible, residents sometimes engaged in other practices, such as finding a long-term substitute, thus saving time, with the hope that they would eventually manage to have one of their sons or relatives migrate to France.

The designations given to a room or bed's registered occupant betray a sense of ownership—of being entitled to decide who can stay and who will inherit a bed. These phrases include the term used for "chief of" or "head of" in locutions such as "head of the household" (in the following phrases used for "head of the room": *konpogume* in Soninke; *joom suudu* in Pulaar). However, this semblance of control must be mitigated by two considerations. First, the two logics of kinship, the more inclusive one regarding cooking arrangements and hosting practices intersect with the withdrawal into a more limited sense of kinship when it comes to transferring one's bed. This can be a source of conflict, for instance, when a long-term occupant who had nurtured hope of inheriting the bed was ousted by a newcomer closer to the bed owner. Second, these practices could only function as long as managers agreed to reallocate a bed according to the registered resident's instructions. Such arrangements could benefit the managing structure: for instance, if a resident was heavily indebted, the transfer of a bed meant that the new owner had to accept paying the debt. Other measures included the acceptance of someone to act as a placeholder for a resident who had previously been evicted for reasons of debt.

## CONCLUSION: WHAT HOLDS THE FOYERS' INHABITANTS TOGETHER?

Contrary to the sociologist Abdelmalek Sayad's description of Maghrebis' experiences of the foyers as "a home without a family," in West African foyers, notions of kinship and relatedness were crucial to the bonds that tied coresidents together.[43] References to these notions played out differently depending on whether the synchronic dimension of copresence or the diachronic perspective of heritage was considered. A bed in the foyer, a key element of the material infrastructure in male labor migration, was an integral part of the family "migratory capital."[44] Foyers played a pivotal role in the reproduction of transnational families. They ensured emplacement in the sense of permanence in the foyer at the individual level and distributed at the family level through intergenerational replacement.

Foyers were places where newcomers were socialized to migration and subjected to forms of social control that have altered over time, from drastic measures such as controlling one's pay slip to the transnational circulation of information and the making and unmaking of reputations across borders, in a context of strong material dependence by newcomers on more established migrants. References to relatedness came with obligations and hierarchies, and in this respect, foyers were places where subaltern roles could be recalled and sometimes challenged, but not avoided.

This examination of the inner workings of the foyers demonstrates how these spaces, the products of segregated urban and housing policies, have also been sites where West African migrants have established original rules and ways of being together. How the renovation process has affected these collectives, which were rooted in long-term sociocultural arrangements but also rife with tensions, is the topic of the next two chapters.

# 5

## WHEN WILL THE FOYERS END?
### Contentious Renovations and Temporal Disjunctions

*The team from the managing structure [Coallia, new name for AFTAM] opens the floor for Q&A after presenting their plans to renovate a foyer. A resident asks the first question: "Did you remove the mosque?" Mr. Bonnet [from Coallia] refers to the principle of secularism (French: laïcité) and explains: "You are accustomed to calling the room a 'mosque.' We call it a 'multifunction room.' From now on, you will call it a 'multifunction room.' You will be able to pray there, but without calling it a mosque."*

Field notes, meeting at Foyer Lorraine,
nineteenth arrondissement, December 2014

*A délégué raises the issue of the "prayer room." A municipal officer interrupts him: "You mean the multifunction room." The délégué insists: "The social worker in charge of introducing the project called it a prayer room." The officer maintains: "It is a multifunction room—which, as we are well aware, will be fully dedicated to prayer."*

Field notes, meeting at the Mairie de Paris on the renovation
of a foyer in the thirteenth arrondissement, March 2017

Т he future of the foyer prayer rooms was only one contentious point among others raised in the renovation
process. These field note excerpts serve to introduce key
aspects of the renovation process. First, the residents were vocal.
They discussed topics they found important, either themselves
when given the occasion or through their representatives. In so
doing, they entered an unequal terrain: institutional and governmental stakeholders controlled the legitimate language and
held the power to make decisions. Nonetheless, in the second
verbal exchange quoted here, the délégué did not back down but
objected to renaming the prayer room and exposed the contradictions among the renovation's institutional agents, who were
far from consistent in their use of the presumed neutral phrase
"multifunction room." As I detail in this chapter, residents had
more leverage on some aspects than on others.

Second, the renovation was part of a moral and political project aimed at shaping residents' behavior according to values that
extended far beyond housing. References to laïcité and the "values of the Republic" were conspicuous in debates about the foyers. At the same time, the change concerning the prayer room
was semantic rather than factual (the new residences would
offer rooms exclusively used for the performance of collective
Islamic prayers), demonstrating the limits of such a project. The
two excerpts epitomize distinct stances toward such a situation:
Mr. Bonnet instructed his interlocutors to change their vocabulary while acknowledging that religious practice would endure,
whereas the municipal officer seemed annoyed and hinted that
such a situation was merely tolerated.

What played out about the prayer rooms and their modes of
designation extended to the outcome of the renovation process
itself: Was the semantic change from foyer to residence a decisive

break with the foyer system? Even though the renovation altered the legal structure of the foyers, their architecture, and their daily workings, both the residents and the institutions in charge of urban policies and migration management continued to deal with the foyers/residences as spaces with specific rules. Relying on a detailed study of the move from Foyer D'Hautpoul, in this chapter I explore the unfinished process of "ending" the foyers and its various understandings.

## THE LEGAL, POLITICAL, AND INSTITUTIONAL MACHINE OF THE RENOVATION

In the mid-1990s, a legal and institutional framework developed that shaped the transformation of the foyers for the following decades. Its two pillars were the legal category of *"résidence sociale"* (residence) and the institutional framework of the Plan de traitement des foyers de travailleurs migrants (PTFTM).[1] The residence appeared as a new housing type in 1994, and was formalized in a 1995 memorandum which was replaced by another in 2006.[2] The PTFTM was adopted in 1997 (hereafter the Plan). Created in 1998 as the successor to CNLI, the Commission interministérielle pour le logement des populations immigrées (CILPI), operated by the Ministry of Housing, was in charge of implementing the Plan.

In contrast to foyers dedicated to migrant workers, the residence was designed for "disadvantaged people." This catch-all category had gradually gained traction in French housing policies.[3] It encompassed individuals or families in a wide array of circumstances, such as "young workers, people in vocational training, women in difficult situations, immigrant workers."[4]

The residence belonged to the administrative category of "very social housing," explicitly defined as a lower form of social housing. Located between emergency housing, on one hand, and regular social housing, on the other, the residence was conceived as a temporary solution on a path toward standard social housing. The notion that public policies should promote the autonomy of their beneficiaries translated into the architectural choice of "autonomous lodgings," and each studio included a kitchenette and a private shower room and toilet.

Furnished and providing basic hotel services (mostly a change of sheets), a studio in a residence had a monthly fee. Legally distinct from rent, this fee could be alleviated by subsidies depending on individual circumstances. A migrant worker earning slightly more than the minimum wage did not qualify for these subsidies because he was considered being without dependents. The residence fee—between €450 and €600 per month for a studio—was slightly lower than private market rates for studios in the Paris urban area.

Most foyers did not meet the architectural requirements to be transformed into residences, and any transformation generally called for heavy building work, which took the form of either renovation or demolition and rebuilding (figure 5.1). Such work required substantial funding.

The Plan allowed renovation operators to obtain loans from the "1 percent," funded by employers, and from direct state subsidies, so the managing structures only funded a minor part of the operations.[5] As a consequence, each institution contributing financially to the renovation plan (the employers' association, the prefecture, the municipality) got to allocate its share of the studios in the final structure.

The Plan listed a number of foyers to be dealt with as priorities based on the following criteria: degraded buildings,

**FIGURE 5.1** Contemplating the building site of Foyer Lorraine, 2016.

*Source*: Photo by author.

dormitories or rooms smaller than 7.5 m², and an over-occupancy level above 30 percent. The Plan was presented as generic, without explicit mention of sub-Saharan residents, but this last criterion made it clear that it targeted the foyers where migrants lived. This was also apparent from expressions such as "over-occupied foyers developing phenomena of folding-in on communitarian ways of life."[6] The notion of "folding-in" (French: *repli*) is discursively tied to the semantics of communitarianism.

Implementation of the Plan in 1997–98 coincided with a moment of relative political openness and experimentation in terms of integration policies in France.[7] In the 2000s, the process became more rigid and left less room for negotiation. This resulted from both the internal dynamics of stabilization of practices and a wider political tightening that became perceptible in the 2000s and evident after the accession of the rightwinger Nicolas Sarkozy to the presidency in 2007. However, the initial ambition of normalization was only partially achieved, notably in terms of population. When a residence replaced a foyer, all former residents were allowed to reintegrate into the new structure; the rule that no one should stay more than two years in a residence was not applied; and the hybrid category of "ex-FTM residence" reflected the unfinished dimension of the process.

When the Plan began, there were 130,000 beds across approximately 680 foyers.[8] A significant number of facilities were concentrated in the Paris region: in 2010, 150 foyers/residences were scattered around the capital and the three surrounding departments.[9] West African residents were numerically dominant because their share within the foyer population had grown since 1990, particularly Malians.[10] Within Paris, 63 percent of residents were nationals from sub-Saharan countries, 18 percent had French citizenship, and 16 percent were from the Maghreb.[11]

Inaugurated as a five-year program, the Plan has been renewed several times since 1997. In 2018, twenty years after the effective beginning of the Plan, 64 percent of the 690 initially identified foyers had been transformed into residences. In 2020, government officers in charge of the Plan contended that the whole process was approaching its end.[12] However, some of their colleagues acknowledged that some early projects had been "failed renovations" (because West African residents had put back in place visible forms of collective organization), and a new list featured already transformed residences, suggesting that rather than a long process this might be an almost never-ending one.

## TABLE 5.1 SYNTHETIC VIEW ON THE CHANGES INDUCED BY THE TRANSFORMATION FROM FOYER TO RESIDENCE

| Structure/Aspect | *Foyer de travailleurs migrants (FTM)* | *Résidence sociale* | *"Ex-FTM" résidence sociale* |
| --- | --- | --- | --- |
| Architecture | Varying from single rooms to dormitories<br>Large collective spaces | Studios<br>Few collective spaces | Studios<br>Few collective spaces |
| Rules on stay | Long-term stay possible | Two years maximum | Long-term stay possible |
| Population | Male migrant workers | People facing housing difficulties | Male migrant workers |
| Rules on hosting practices | Tolerance on hosting practices | Strict rules as to whom a resident can legally host | Strict rules as to whom a resident can legally host |

Table 5.1 summarizes the main dimensions of the renovation process, and the following sections focus on changes in terms of architecture and rules. Chapter 6 scrutinizes the effects of this process in terms of population and hosting practices.

## AGENTS OF THE RENOVATIONS

As the opening field notes indicate, the renovation scheme brought together distinct stakeholders. In this section I briefly introduces them, from the residents' representatives and their allies to government and municipality officers, including the staff in charge of the renovation within the managing structures.

## Representatives of the Foyers' Residents: The Délégués

The foyers' populations had initially been represented by community leaders, and subsequently by délégués, a term akin to political forms of representation, as in unions, for example. These délégués were often politicized figures during the rent strikes and political movements of the 1970s and 1980s. In Paris in the 2000s, elections for "residents' committees" were formalized, and the new foyer representatives became known as "members of the residents' committee."[13] In keeping with ordinary usage, I retain the term "délégué" to designate all such representatives.

During my fieldwork, délégués were mostly men in their late fifties and early sixties who had arrived in France in the 1970s. In contrast to the first foyer leaders, who had been autodidacts at best, many of these délégués had some level of formal schooling, which equipped them with key literacy and linguistic skills. A few had previous political experience in their home countries, but most were socialized into political action in three areas. First, they had often taken part in the struggles of the 1970s and later, in the foyers and beyond; and many were trade unionists or had experience of workplace struggles. Second, they had played a key role in village-based associations and in the wider field of associative structures for the development of their home regions.[14] Third, several were involved in French politics primarily at the municipal level. For the minority who had French citizenship, this could translate into direct involvement through voting, but many who were not French citizens were still co-opted during political campaigns to influence voters with immigrant backgrounds.[15] In fact, these last two factors were tied together because transnational politics makes relationships with French municipal

politicians useful both in France and at home in the arena of
*"cooperation décentralisée."*[16]

This generation presented itself in sharp distinction to
how older délégués had acted as representatives of an ethnically or regionally defined community. However, the dynamics
of mobilization showed that the délégués were in fact caught
between these two conceptions of their role. Rather than a
switch from traditional authority to a legal-rational one, as
suggested by Hélène Béguin, I analyze their political repertoire as mixed, relying on a variety of resources both internal
to the foyers and constituted outside.[17] External resources were
acquired in the French political and associative field, and internal resources could be linguistic resources such as linguistic
ability in both Soninke and Pulaar. A few délégués performed
their identity as members of status groups associated with brokerage. Hence the eloquence of the délégués was rooted in ora-
tory abilities acquired in their youth, cultivated in migration in
internal arenas, and reinforced through their political experience in France.

In the 2010s, this generation was dominant but also was on
the verge of leaving given their age. Retirement often involved a
permanent or partial return to their home countries; even when
medical or other reasons kept a resident in France, they generally
withdrew from collective positions such as that of délégué. Most
of the délégués teams included younger men in their thirties or
forties, along with the prominent délégués of this generation,
but this generational transition was an uneasy one, with several
younger men co-opted but failing to find their place in the team.
In general, younger residents were even more educated than
their elders, but unlike in the previous transition, this capital
was not enough to guarantee them their turn running the foyers'
affairs. The few who successfully maintained their involvement

were often also engaged across several spheres, including activism in support of sans-papiers movements.

Ultimately, the ability of the délégués to mobilize depended on their relationships with other figures of authority. For instance, good relationships between the délégués and the imam meant that a call to go out for a demonstration would be communicated in the prayer room after the service, ensuring that the information was widely spread. Other key figures included elders, who as a group were formalized in some foyers as an "elders' council." Finally, dynamics with organized groups of sans-papiers were variable, but when good relations prevailed, they could be turned into useful allies.

## Associative and Political Allies

At the time of my research, the main support group working in the foyers—and among my key interlocutors—was the Collectif pour l'avenir des foyers (COPAF), created in 1996. COPAF included both foyer délégués, most but not exclusively West Africans, and a handful of white activists, approximately the same age as the délégués, in their late forties to early seventies.

COPAF activists had a background in militant actions in the foyers. For instance, Geneviève Petauton had been active in the Sonacotra movement.[18] With other COPAF cofounders, she was also part of the field of "codéveloppement," taking part in the activities of the Groupe de recherche et de réalisations pour le développement rural and of *Nouvelles d'ici et là-bas*, a journal highlighting migrants' involvement in development projects back home. When the group consolidated into an association and took the name COPAF in 1996, they contributed to Michel Fiévet's book *Le Livre blanc des travailleurs immigrés des foyers*.[19]

The book mobilized ethnological knowledge about the foyers, illustrating exchanges between academic and activist spheres that were intense in this transnational field of research and action about migrants and development.

COPAF's activities can be summarized along the following lines. First, they constituted a lobby dedicated to the defense and enhancement of the foyer residents' legal status and living conditions. Beginning in 1999, COPAF organized several fora at the National Assembly. The group claimed tenant status for the foyer residents, already a main demand of the Sonacotra movement in the 1970s, which had been taken up again in light of the existing legislation, notably Article 8 of the European Convention on Human Rights on the respect due to private and family life.[20]

Second, COPAF played an important role in providing information and legal assistance. It notably implemented training sessions for foyer délégués, for which it benefited from public subsidies. It offered a wealth of documentation and detailed information through its website. Assisted by lawyers, COPAF members also provided direct support in cases where collective mobilizations led to legal reprisals, or in individual or collective cases of eviction.

Finally, COPAF was influential in setting up organizations bringing together délégués from a given managing structure. A COPAF member was assigned to each such coordination, which convened monthly meetings. These occasions worked as spaces where information on different foyers could be shared and strategies devised for collective actions, such as demonstrations in front of the Ministry of Housing or negotiations with a managing structure. COPAF attempted to bridge the generational gap by inviting representatives of sans-papiers, who occasionally attended, but the personal ties between COPAF activists and the general tone of their interventions were more in line with the older délégués' stances.

As a result of their multiple roles and the several spheres in which they intervened, COPAF members both articulated a critical political discourse and were considered as useful mediators by government and municipality officers. This tension in COPAF's positioning explains in part their relationships with other groups. No other group specialized in the foyers in the same way as COPAF, but various groups supported the foyer residents. Groups specializing either in housing or in migrants' rights intervened. Droit au Logement (DAL) was present but mainly to back up COPAF actions.[21] Migrants' groups included Droit Devants!!, which tended to work with COPAF as did DAL. The Confédération nationale du logement (CNL), the main French tenants' association, was strongly involved in at least two foyers in the Paris region and tended to develop its own forms of support and mobilization outside COPAF networks. In addition, local dynamics and personal relationships resulted in the involvement of other groups. For instance, in the case of the renovation of Foyer David D'Angers (nineteenth arrondissement), (former) activists from the Organisation politique (OP) were involved and demanded the inclusion of undocumented migrants in the rehousing process, arguing that COPAF generally supported legalization in principle but did not tactically support this group during this struggle.[22] Finally, unions had played a significant role in earlier periods and were present when their support was requested (together with wider organizations such as the Ligue des droits de l'homme), as were some leaders of political parties (generally on the Left), who could occasionally be influential, depending on local configurations.

## Managing Structure Staff

I spent most of my fieldwork with the residents, and my encounters with the staff of managing structures were often mediated because of this position. However, over the years I set up research situations in which I detached myself from the residents to better observe the work of the staff and engage with them. I did not conduct biographical interviews and cannot offer a fully fleshed sociology of these workers, but I highlight the diversity of positions within this professional group, building on other more detailed accounts on immigration bureaucrats.[23]

A managing structure's staff was composed of several categories of worker. First, the foyer directors, who used to be appointed to the facility where they also lived, acted as janitors and watchmen for the managing structure. At Soundiata and AFTAM, they tended to be former residents, and their relationships with residents were not as tense as in many Sonacotra foyers, although their intermediary position left them open to suspicion on both sides. At Foyer D'Hautpoul and Foyer Lorraine in the 2010s, the directors were former Soundiata staff with this profile and of West African origin. The material working conditions of the directors had shifted in the wake of wider managerial changes: they no longer lived on site, and in a context of diminishing staff they were each allocated several foyers where they provided on-call services. Their job description had further evolved from cashing the rents and monitoring the site based on their intimate knowledge of the residents to forms of management oriented around quantitative objectives: an Adoma job description for this position thus read: "The director [*responsable de residence*] optimizes the management of the residence in terms of occupancy and turnover."[24] The directors were key figures in the daily workings of the foyers, but they were not centrally involved in the renovation plans. This task fell to other staff members.

Midlevel employees were crucial in the renovation process and were effectively in charge of its implementation. In ordinary times, they would only have meetings in the structure's headquarters, but they were regularly in the foyers during the process and personified the renovation in the eyes of the residents. Within managing structures, they worked in various departments specializing either in construction and real estate operations or in population management and social work. But because an architect working on the project management aspects might find herself admonishing residents about how lucky they were to be offered a new building, I focus here on their shared practices rather than their various backgrounds. In addition, many of these employees had careers within the association and occupied separate positions without any special training.

In his analysis of immigration bureaucrats, Alexis Spire offers a useful typology between three types of workers, characterized as "moral entrepreneurs," "defiant ones," and "pragmatic ones."[25] Illustrating the first category, some midlevel managers constantly based their exchanges with residents and the délégués on moral evaluations of individual and collective behaviors, from their ways of using the foyers (condemning over-occupancy) to criticizing how much money they transferred to their families back home. An example of such a stance was the way Julie, a middle manager who had a degree in sociology and a master's in urban studies, described a rehousing site: "It's chaotic, wildly overcrowded; we close our eyes, pretending not to see that, but personally I'm having a hard time with this situation."[26] Throughout our encounters, Julie seemed suspicious of my proximity to the residents and constantly provided me with examples of the residents' wrongdoings. Although this particular manager was a white woman, the moral entrepreneur profile was also epitomized in my fieldwork by staff members of immigrant origin, such as Nadia, another middle manager with a similar educational background, who was particularly prone to making references to the French Republic and principles such as secularism when addressing residents.[27]

These were the more vocal staff members, but many others adopted a "pragmatic" attitude toward the moral and political principles of the renovation. They presented the residents with the existing rules without accompanying these statements with justifications. They tended to find solutions to individual cases without considering that exceptions could jeopardize the whole process. Their stance toward the reforms that the renovation was meant to bring was not apparent from their work practices and discourses toward the residents.

Finally, I met a few overtly critical individuals in the managing structures and in the institutions in charge of the renovation. These young professionals were generally well educated (master's or PhD holders), and some had firsthand knowledge of African societies. They selectively adhered to the principles of the renovation scheme, cherry-picking the aspects of the plan with which they agreed. For instance, the general notion of despecifying immigrant housing appealed to this category of workers. They believed that public subsidization implied that the resulting residences should not be designated for those defined as an ethnic constituency or a historically constituted group. More or less autonomous depending on their position, they were particularly prone to elaborating these critiques in front of me as a researcher. They also tended to either leave their jobs after a few years' experience or align with the pragmatic way of dealing with the residents.

## Institutional Stakeholders

Government officers played a key role in implementation of the Plan at several levels. The inclusion of each renovation in a national policy meant that each foyer renovation was examined by the board of CILPI, as part of the Ministry of Housing. A CILPI officer regularly attended the steering committees organized before and during each foyer renovation.

The officers implementing the renovation worked for the prefecture or, in the capital, for the City of Paris (i.e., the municipality at city level, not at the level of the arrondissement).[28] Two municipal services were involved: the Housing Department (Direction Logement et Habitat) and the Integration Department, in charge of "non-EU immigration," whose name and scope of action were redefined during my fieldwork. The power balance clearly tilted in favor of the former: the Housing Department convened steering committees and conducted each renovation scheme (by securing its funding arrangements and financial guarantees), whereas the Integration Department monitored the inclusion of the residents' representatives in the process. Finally, the relevant Mairie d'arrondissement also intervened and could influence the process (notably as the authority in charge of granting construction permits). These municipal and government officers' attitudes also varied with more "pragmatic" or "moral entrepreneurs" stances.

## MOVING A FOYER

From planning the Foyer D'Hautpoul move to residents being settled into a new building took five years. First discussed in 2011, the move took effect in June 2014 when the residents left the foyer for provisional rehousing locations; in November 2016, the new residence opened. I focus here on the discussions that took place before the move from the old foyer because it is during this phase that both provisional arrangements and the shape of the future residence were debated.[29]

In late 2011, Coallia announced their intentions to renovate the foyer. At an initial steering committee meeting convened by the municipality, Coallia officers presented an outline of the project. In terms of construction work, the plan was to use some vacant space on the plot to erect a new building where some of the residents would be rehoused, with residents progressively vacating those parts of the old building being dealt with. This modus operandi was used in other renovation schemes and meant that the construction work lasted several years, at considerable inconvenience to the residents who lived on the building site throughout and faced strong constraints during the building process.

At that meeting, Coallia officers announced that they would transform the foyer with 124 beds organized in unités de vie, with shared kitchen and bathroom facilities for every two rooms. into a residence of 106 studios The studio prices would range from €420 to €547 per month, in lieu of beds ranging from €239 to €309 per month. In place of a collective kitchen and two vast meeting rooms, the new residence would include one much smaller meeting room. Délégués opposed the notion of including the bathing and toilet block inside the studio because thin dividing walls made every noise audible for others in the room. As for the kitchenette, the délégués pointed out that residents were used to preparing dishes that took a long time to cook; highlighting the inconvenience of a studio for such practices, they demanded a collective kitchen. They further objected to the fact that the meeting room was not a dedicated prayer room.

Finally, they inquired about the lot of over-occupants. Coallia officers dismissed the residents' remarks on the choice of studios and educated them about the semantics of the multifunction room, but the point about the kitchen appeared negotiable. As for the over-occupants, they informed the residents that a process of selection of those who could be rehoused would take place according to rules that had previously been established and were thus nonnegotiable (see chapter 6).

Urged to accept the beginning of the process, the délégués agreed to assist the social workers who were screening the foyer's population, the first concrete step in the renovation process. But then, due to what was framed as technical difficulties, Coallia halted the whole process for most of 2012. They then came up with a new plan that involved entirely rebuilding the site and thus displacing the residents to other locations during the construction work. When this plan was presented in a new steering committee meeting in late 2012, Coallia's operating manager for this sector, Mr. Bonnet, detailed the plans to provisionally rehouse residents across several residences, including some run by other organizations. This implied that residents would pay rent and sign a new contract with another managing structure.

This point elicited strong opposition among the residents: arguing that the decision to renovate had come from Coallia, the residents insisted that they were responsible for ensuring the same rent and conditions during the course of the move. The délégués took this opportunity to again voice all their previous grievances. In an internal meeting, they presented their list of demands: they requested the inclusion of a second meeting room and a collective kitchen in the plans; they rejected the most expensive studios above €500 per month; they announced that they had counted eighty-six over-occupants; and they insisted on being rehoused in Coallia foyers exclusively. A few weeks later, when the Coallia team came to present the project in the foyers, the délégués, accompanied by a COPAF activist and a handful of residents, announced that the meeting was boycotted. In a poetic flourish, the leading délégué, Harouna, challenged the representative of the municipality: "You are naming a tram station after Rosa Parks, but you don't even treat your own black population correctly!" At the end of his speech, they all left the room.

Disregarding this aborted meeting with the residents, the managing structure went on with its schedule. A few days later they convened a meeting in a local school to present the project to the neighbors. An impressive delegation—comprising the arrondissement mayor and two other arrondissement-level officers, a city officer in charge of the foyers, four members of Coallia, and a representative of the architect—met with the half-dozen neighbors who had responded to the invitation in the absence of the residents. During the Q&A session, neighbors' concerns revolved mainly around the practical disagreements caused by the development of a construction site in their street, but two questions were more specific. One asked if there would be "a janitor to remedy current troubles, such as garbage on the sidewalk and hawkers?" The Coallia officer could not provide a positive answer because, as we have seen, the idea of a dedicated building manager had been abandoned. However, he did reply: "Once the building has been refurbished, let's hope that habits will change." Second, in response to a question about the existence of a prayer room, he stated that there would be no place of worship but a multifunction room for meetings and events.

A tentative status quo lasted most of 2013. Coallia officers invited residents to visit several of the sites envisioned for their rehousing during the rebuilding process. Accompanying the residents on these visits, I observed how they would project themselves into the new apartment and, more often than not, try to figure out if one additional mattress could be laid out. One resident brought a compass to see how his prayer mat would fit into this new space. Used to sharing kitchen facilities set aside from their rooms, they also paid attention to the position of the hotplates and extractor hoods within each room, tending to prefer studios where this block stood apart, for instance, near the entrance to the room as opposed to in the middle of the living space. Individual opinions varied as to the quality of the residence, but the general refusal to move outside of Coallia stock was steadfastly maintained.

A new phase began in November 2013. Determined for the move to take effect, Coallia officers convened a meeting in the foyer with representatives of the Mairie of the nineteenth arrondissement. In a room packed with over sixty residents, they made some decisive announcements: they had included a collective kitchen in the new project; they offered the possibility of rehousing half of the foyer residents in Residence David D'Angers, located a street over, and the rest within their own residences; and they agreed to reconsider the case of the over-occupants listed by the délégués. A representative of the Mairie of the nineteenth arrondissement guaranteed that such commitments would be kept and presented the deal in a favorable light. There was palpable excitement among the residents, and the délégués felt that they had made sufficient gains to be able to collaborate on the project. The following day, they convened a general meeting in the foyers. Since the first talks about renovation, maintenance of the building had been kept to a minimum; as a result, the site was falling into disrepair, including a persistent leak in the entrance hall, which inclined residents to accept a move to a better place—ruination as an institutional tactic.

From this point onward, the process accelerated, with regular meetings conducted by Mr. Bonnet with a cooperative team of délégués. Mr. Bonnet sometimes admonished the residents (and the ethnographer) with moral arguments, but he mostly acted pragmatically. Frictions occasionally arose: for instance, regarding the practical issue of residents on long-term absence, the délégués asked that the key should be handed to someone else. Mr. Bonnet reluctantly accepted but warned: "We too have positions to keep, otherwise we are going to blow up the Plan." The main topic of discussion was the list of over-occupants: twenty-four had already been identified in the initial phase, and twenty-two more were later listed (see chapter 6). This figure of forty-six, over a third of the registered residents, was far less than the actual number of over-occupants, but it compared favorably with other renovation cases.

On the day of the move, new faces showed up: acting tough, a couple of Coallia employees who usually worked in other places joined the usual team to ensure that everything would go smoothly. Countering the possibility of squatters was the general obsession; several foyer closures had resulted in a number of inhabitants, left out of the process, refusing to leave the building and effectively squatting.[30] Although accompanied by this extra staff, Mr. Bonnet did not play tough. On the contrary, my interlocutors told me that he was so pleased with the happy ending that he let residents enter their new lodgings with loose mattresses (a clear indication that they planned to host unofficial residents because each studio was already furnished with a mattress on the bed). The day after the move, Harouna received a phone call from Mr. Bonnet, who congratulated him; in a conversation with me a few days later, standing behind his stall in the flea market, Harouna shared this impression of success in soberer terms. He dismissed the attitudes of some residents who had been left out of the process and were seeking help from him as délégué. Regarding one such individual who had pleaded with him to find a solution, claiming, "My life is ruined" (Wolof: *Suma àdduna yàqu na, suma àllaaxira yàqu na*). Harouna commented to me: "How can one act like this over just a room? I told him, 'Well, you are healthy, you can work, what are you complaining about?'" This aligned with the words of another senior resident who had told me on the day of the move: "You need to be a man" [Wolof: *góor*], before adding: "Well, even a woman too must get by [*góor-góorlu*]. Being a man means that, if you lose, you get by. But staying put [*toog di xaar*]?!" Délégués and senior men thus used the semantics of manhood and dignity to justify the way they had reached an agreement with the managing structure and the authorities to ensure a smooth closure of the foyer and to delegitimize the claims of younger, more precarious inhabitants.

Over the following two years, communication between Coallia and the délégués mainly addressed the conditions of provisional rehousing, and compared to other cases, these were generally acceptable.[31] Coallia officers reopened discussions with the délégués a few months before they planned to move the residents back into the residence. In principle, this second move was also a possible opportunity for negotiation because any impasse would be costly; in this case, however, negotiations only bore on organizational details.

The délégués, the activists, and the Coallia staff all hailed the renovation of Foyer D'Hautpoul a success. Tensions arose, but solutions were found through continuous exchange and with the intervention of arrondissement-level officers. Although the délégués maintained an adversarial rhetoric against the manager, always identified as a "boss" (French: *patron*), the process evidenced a back-and-forth between protesting and nonprotesting collective action. In a few other situations, deadlocks in negotiations led to collective actions in which residents drew on their long-established repertoire of contestation, from demonstrations to legal action; but in general, foyer renovations evidenced the search for compromise and the avoidance of outright opposition, with the délégués internalizing a large part of the Plan's constraints.

## MARGINAL GAINS

The 2010s was a period during which the renovation scheme became routinized. Earlier cases had helped the institutions iron out their doctrine: for instance, Residence Commanderie (nineteenth arrondissement) was unanimously upheld as an infamous counterexample because of its very small studios (13 m²). In contrast, off the back of fraught negotiations between the managing structure, the Mairie de Paris, and the residents, the solution reached during the renovation of Foyer Fontaine-au-Roi (eleventh arrondissement) to rehouse the foyer's over-occupants served as a template for later negotiations.

Routinization led to acceleration: Julie, the middle manager, indicated that between 2012 and 2015 the pace of operations had become "mad," insofar as they were expected to manage many more foyer renovations with the same number of staff.[32] The pressure also weighed on rehousing capacities, which meant that any delay could jeopardize other operations. In 2020, a CILPI policy officer acknowledged that the Plan was being conducted under higher constraints, resulting in less flexibility toward the residents' demands.[33]

In this respect, the specificity of the Parisian situation is twofold. On one hand, the municipality prided itself on introducing provisions in favor of the residents: for example, délégués were always invited to steering committees, which was not a legal obligation. On the other hand, the stabilization of practices meant that the scope of what could be negotiated shrunk. The choice to provide studios was not open to discussion, even though legal texts maintained the possibility of unités de vie.[34] Some renovations followed a different path. One exemplary case was the Foyer Centenaire in Montreuil.[35] Due to its history of long-term activism and its local context (a strong network of associations and ties with the municipality), the renovation was a participatory experiment in which residents collaborated in designing the spaces. The result was a residence arranged with a few rooms opening onto a shared space and kitchen; the opening of a restaurant to replace the former canteen; and the possibility for craftsmen to rent a few commercial spaces. In Le Blanc-Mesnil, the renovation of a foyer conducted by staff used to dealing with social housing tenants also led to attempts to include the residents in the building layout, which resulted in a number of floor kitchens being maintained. In contrast, in Paris the omission of a floor kitchen was presented as mandatory.

The most enduring point of dissent was the reduction of collective spaces, a position dictated by several types of consideration. First, technical and economic considerations ran counter to the inclusion of collective spaces in residences. The managing structures conducted the operations with a view to creating as many studios as possible, both because they needed to rehouse as many residents as possible and for reasons of profitability. Second, authorities and managing structures were against collective spaces for reasons of public order. A CILPI best practice document read that "their surface area should not be overestimated to avoid any risk of misuse (illegal activities, places of worship unmonitored by the managing structure)."[36]

Several foyer canteens had been closed in previous years, and only fifteen canteens were listed in Paris in 2010, of which ten were supposed to be certified. Due to the difficulty in putting together a successful application, only two such "social restaurants" were functioning in 2020.[37] To compensate for the drastic reduction in the ability to buy cheap food, the municipality launched the idea of meal deliveries, a solution that ultimately did not work.

Attracting worshipers from the neighborhood, the prayer rooms likewise concentrated several anxieties in a context of growing suspicion toward Muslims. The authorities' public stance was the impossibility to include a space dedicated to religious worship in a building funded by public funds, choosing one principle, secularism, over others, such as freedom of worship. As we have seen, this was accompanied by allusions according to which multifunction rooms could de facto be devoted to Islamic worship. This came with two conditions: any prayer apparatus was intended to be removable; and attendance by outsiders was to be prohibited or at least limited. To this end, the architects received instructions to carefully position the rooms and doors to impede easy access to these spaces from the outside.

## LIMITED "CONCERTATION"

The notion of concertation—a French word that can be translated as "dialogue"—appeared in the textual apparatus of the renovation as an echo to wider norms of including inhabitants in urban renewal processes.[38] The 2002 memorandum stated: "At a time conducive to efficient dialogue, representatives of the residents will be invited to the meetings of the steering committee." Thus determining the adequate timing for this inclusion of the representatives was left to the managing structure and government officers. The CILPI document was more explicit: "[The renovation process] must include a phase of information and dialogue with the residents and their representatives. . . . However, consideration of the residents' wishes must be secondary to the project's technical quality or adherence to legal rules on collective life."[39] At a time when urban renewal often went together with ambitions surrounding the participatory aspects of the processes, the foyer renovation process attested to the subaltern status of the residents. This was also apparent from the way institutions projected a future in which foyer residents would eventually merge into a larger and more diverse public. Working under the fiction of social mixing while dealing with well-established West African communities whose reinstallation in the residence was guaranteed, institutional and professional stakeholders were caught up in contradictory injunctions.

The renovation notably evidenced a deep ambiguity in the way the managing structure officers and institutional stakeholders still relied strongly on délégués, whose authority the whole process eroded. As an example of this complicated stance, Mr. Bonnet, in a meeting for another foyer's renovation, summoned "délégués and community leaders" to encourage the residents to transfer their beds when they were no longer spending most of their time in the foyers so residents who had left the foyer could let another person benefit from their bed.[40] However, three months later, faced with resistance, he lectured the audience in the following terms: "We live in a Republic. There is liberty and individual consciousness: each individual has the right to make his own decisions, and it is not a community that decides for him. It is difficult to be open to change, it can even be violent, so to speak."[41] On this occasion, he abandoned his usual pragmatic stance to align with the renovation's hard-line ideological project of emancipation. In another instance of the same twist, while she was preparing the ground for the renovation of a Parisian foyer, Nadia stated: "There is no sub-Saharan foyer without a village chief, a community leader: we know how you live." This assessment was rooted in her familiarity with the residents' ways of living as well as in the ethnological knowledge boasted by many long-term practitioners in this field; however, she concluded her sympathetic evocation of the foyer as a village abruptly: "But imagine an ordinary Frenchman landing from a helicopter in your foyer!"[42] The emphasis on insularity was used as a way to render the foyer residents ways of living out of place rather than trying to bridge existing practices with the future project.

Contrary to these rough encounters within the foyers, the steering committees provided more policed arenas, in which speech was more controlled but roles were even more sharply defined. Concessions could be made to the délégués, but these changes were generally minor compared to what residents could obtain by direct confrontation with the managing structure. Rather than level spaces where all groups would deliberate on an equal footing, these arenas were moments of performance for the municipality concerning their action and occasions for institutional and professional stakeholders to define desirable users of the residences.

During these meetings, shared knowledge about the populations in question circulated and consolidated. In one such committee, Julie, the program officer, announced: "We have no plan for a floor kitchen, nor *tuuse*, nor village kitchen." When one attendee on the municipality's side frowned, she explained: "At the start, there was only a North African population. It's only due to rehousing processes that we ended up lodging Africans. Our position is to avoid providing kitchens as much as possible."[43] From this exchange, it can be inferred, first, that she assumed participants in the committee would understand the term "*tuuse*," the Soninke word used to designate the collective organization of meals; second, that decisions were guided by a typified understanding of the needs of each foyer "population." The simple mention of the fact that West Africans were new-comers to this foyer sufficed to shrug the issue off.

Toward the residents, a pedagogical tone prevailed. An offi-cer in the Municipal Department of Housing explained: "The financial support from the City [of Paris] means that we need to formalize allocation rules," which he translated into "no more co-optation."[44] One of his colleagues, working directly for the cabinet, constantly depicted the entire renovation scheme as a huge "effort" on the part of the City of Paris. This emphasis went together with envious comments about the locations of the foyers, which found themselves in gentrified areas. This last type of remark elicited some connivance among the professionals and sought to shift the residents from individuals asserting their rights to beneficiaries of an enviable operation.

Délégués were unequally equipped for these encounters, often relying on activists to explain documents to them and draft written answers, but speech was their domain. Even if unable to strongly influence a process whose conception they did not participate in, they often opposed the renovation projects with a counterdiscourse based on their rights. During a discussion on the form of the studios, when a representative of the municipal-ity remarked that foyer residents were not the only ones having to cope with small living spaces, she stated: "Well, you are com-plaining that the hot plates are too close to your bed, but some Parisians have very tiny apartments where the kitchen is close to the room." The answer was immediate and calm: "But Madam, we are Parisians." The délégué went on to explain: "They want to rebuild our foyer" [thus attributing the initiative to the managing structure], but, he objected, "we live as a community, we did not ask for stoves in our rooms," and he concluded, "we are here to defend our rights."[45]

## CONCLUSION: HISTORICAL ARGUMENTS AND THEIR MISUNDERSTANDINGS

Misunderstandings are at the root of contemporary situations when the French state deals with migrants and racialized individuals and groups. Proposals for an "ethnography of misunderstanding" and conceptualizations of "working misunderstandings" have proven productive lines of thinking among anthropologists.[46] To this notion of a distance maintained by state and ordinary practices of relegation, I add the idea of asynchrony as the source of many tensions between the residents and the institutions.

Professional and institutional agents of the renovation were for the most part unaware of the foyers' past. In the meetings on Foyer Lorraine and Foyer D'Hautpoul, residents' references to 216 bis tended to pass by the professionals. Furthermore, they equated the renovation with progress—as Mr. Bonnet once put it: "It's the course of history." Already otherized (recall the helicopter metaphor), foyer inhabitants' ways of living were further disqualified as anachronistic, and the whole system was treated as a relic. During one steering committee, when one foyer resident tentatively argued for consideration of the past by stating "there is a history behind it," he was rebuffed by Nadia, who declared, "all foyers have a history." Nonetheless, the délégué team managed to pick the subject back up, with one mentioning the fact that they came from Foyer Sedaine, adding that "people are still traumatized by the [1977] fire." Rummaging in her notes, Nadia announced triumphantly: "Only 16 percent of residents came from Sedaine, that's almost nothing!" As the meeting went on, when one délégué insisted that "the residents said they want to remain in an AFTAM foyer" (a common request, as we have seen), a representative of the structure owning the foyer picked up the erroneous reference to AFTAM (which had been renamed Coallia ten years earlier) and sarcastically dropped to the person next to him: "Like the Département de la Seine!"[47]

History had different resonances for foyer residents. Given the stability of part of the foyer populations, many men confronted with the renovation had a longer memory of the foyers than the renovation officers who had come to this line of work in the late 1990s or the 2000s. Older residents often dismissed the authority of the managing structures by insisting that they had seen a lot of "bosses," turning them into transient organizations compared to their own permanence. The fact that the foyers were no longer reserved to immigrants, and more specifically the abandonment of references to shared Franco-African history claimed by institutions as normalization, was understood as dispossession. As one resident emphasized during a meeting at Foyer Lorraine: "We have been immigrants since Maréchal Pétain. When we left the 216 rue Saint Denis, the elders came with us, we were children at that time. Today, we are with our nephews, our sons, our grandsons."[48] This evocation of an intergenerational chain, and of the specific others he claimed the choice to live with, introduces the topic of the next chapter.

# 6

## ACKNOWLEDGING SOLIDARITY

### Bureaucratic Relatedness, Hosting Practices, and Exclusionary Dynamics

n September 2015, the activist group supporting foyer residents, Collectif pour l'avenir des foyers (COPAF), convened a rally in front of Adoma's headquarters to protest the eviction of three residents convicted of undeclared hosting practices. In a crowd of mostly West African foyer inhabitants, several men held placards that read: "Evictions of over-occupants: no. Right to host who you want, when you want: yes." One of the speakers captured the spirit of the day in this catchphrase: "We're victims of our solidarity." In another demonstration, a slogan asked for a "rehousing of all our 'surnuméraires'"; the use of the first person plural possessive pronoun gave an affectionate designation to an administrative and derogatory term that literally designates "persons in surplus" (figure 6.1). The defense of hosting practices was backed up by a series of arguments: the ethical imperative of hosting cohabitants redefined as kin; the economic necessity of having someone to pay for the bed during long absences; and the political denunciation of wider inequalities and injustices that trapped many migrants in undocumented status for years, leaving them no other options than to be hosted in the foyer.

These arguments elicited two types of response from the institutional and professional stakeholders. Adopting a simplistic

**FIGURE 6.1** A demonstration in front of the townhall, Paris, nineteenth arrondissement, 2015.

*Source*: Photo by Anissa Michalon.

view on the hosting arrangements prevailing in the foyers, and pointing to the financial compensation gained for hosting others, some portrayed foyer residents as "slumlords for one another," to quote an oft-heard phrase, suffused with moral judgments and the ordinary assumption that monetary practices and affective relations are antagonistic.[1] However, in the same institutional and professional spheres, and particularly during the renovation period, solidarity was also somewhat acknowledged. As an officer of the Housing Department at the municipality of Paris stated during a meeting: "The renovations are costly, with significant support from the municipality, this implies that lodgings are on a formal basis, but we don't disregard solidarity."[2]

Moving beyond these contentious and normative understandings of solidarity, here I focus on the fate of coresidence ties in the course of the renovation process. My empirical point of departure is the observation of a partial recognition by the institutions of the bonds between cohabitants of the foyer through a mechanism built into the renovation scheme, whose effects I trace on the coresident groups. Conversely, the renovation scheme, as a moment of social engineering, pervades internal decisions regarding who will be able to follow and who will not; as a result, the renovation process occasions a requalification of the ties between cohabitants and a reordering of their statuses. Such entangled dynamics evidence what I call "bureaucratic relatedness": how vernacular practices based on kinship found their way into the bureaucratic process, and how the renovation process affected forms of relatedness.

This study is grounded in an anthropological approach that investigates the junction between bureaucratic practices and individual and collective experiences. Migration contexts provide a fascinating area in which to investigate such themes because migrants and their families are confronted with invasive administrative demands, and studies have shown how deeply ingrained into the social fabric these requirements could be, in emigration contexts as well as in transit and migration locations.[3] Fake IDs, changes in name and age, and forged family relations are fascinating objects from which to reflect on relations to the state as well as on relatedness.[4] Building on sociohistorical and ethnographic studies of immigrants' encounters with state categories and services, my aim is to capture migrants' individual and collective experiences of bureaucratically defined worlds.

The foyers are ideal sites from which to conduct such an endeavor because these facilities were run by associations whose requirements reflected French migratory and urban policies; they were also spaces where robust collective and individual strategies were built to escape or reduce the effects of these demands. Examining the reconfigurations within groups of cohabitants in the foyers during the renovation period enables us to scrutinize the frictions between these two facets of the foyers. These dynamics further evidence a wider trend whereby foyers were devalued in administrative procedures. In this process, the exclusionary power of the address as a micro-technology of governance played a crucial role.[5]

## RENOVATION AS SOCIAL ENGINEERING

The ambition of the renovation was twofold: transforming the legal status and physical structure and reordering the modes of inhabiting the site. This second dimension was rooted in a notion of housing as an instrument of social reform that has a long history in France and beyond.[6] It operated by focusing on the foyer as a population. The process aimed at changing this population both quantitatively (by putting a halt to over-occupancy) and qualitatively (by developing new ways of controlling the makeup of this population, notably by changing the rules for allocating lodgings). This work fell to a specialized service: the Social and Urban Project Management (Maîtrise d'oeuvre urbaine et sociale [MOUS]).[7]

Studies of the effect of urban renewal on ordinary social housing demonstrate that rehousing is a crucial step in residential trajectories, and it is a privileged moment for observation.[8] This scholarship shows that rehousing is often experienced as a moment of "residential insecurity" and increased vulnerability. Research among other racialized groups in France, such as

Roma, also points to the role of MOUS as a form of social engineering that carries with it moral evaluations on individual and collective behaviors.[9]

During a foyer renovation, MOUS operated in two crucial phases. First, before the move they conducted a survey called "social diagnosis" (French: *diagnostic social*) aimed at providing an overview of the foyer's population before renovation and screening the individual situations and aspirations of the residents. Second, during the move MOUS allocated studios to the residents in the provisional relocation site as well as in the new residence after the renovation work.[10]

Social diagnosis was a key phase of the renovation. The MOUS team held individual appointments with each of the foyer residents. In the foyer where I conducted a close observation of this phase, the survey consisted of an impressive set of 175 questions on personal and family status; occupation, income, and monthly remittances; frequency and duration of trips abroad; history of arrival in France and housing trajectory; uses of local transport and facilities; and expectations in terms of rehousing. During this survey, the MOUS officers performed several tasks. First, they produced knowledge on two levels: aggregate data on the foyer residents (such statistical data as the distribution of employed, unemployed, and retired individuals among the residents; their average income, etc.) and individual data allowing each resident's personal file to be updated. This double mission caused some confusion among the residents, who were not always in a position to understand what would serve to produce aggregate data (typically a question on how much money they sent back home monthly served to produce statistics on the topic of remittances) and what would be consigned to their personal file and directly influence their future (for instance, the question of where they wanted to be rehoused).

Second, the survey was generally the first moment (after a few collective meetings) when each resident could ask specific questions on the rehousing process and the future residence. MOUS officers also provided information on the process, but they did not always provide clear indications as to which points were still open to negotiation and which were unlikely to change. A member of a MOUS team, Pauline, who had a background in associative work and invested her job with enthusiasm as an opportunity to learn more about West Africa, acknowledged such constraints: "It makes me uneasy that we ask them about their rehousing preferences, only to tell them afterwards: 'It's actually going to be that way.'"[11]

Third, MOUS officers suggested that some residents should seek other types of housing. This was the case for M. Sacko, who earned more than minimum wage. In this case, Damien, the MOUS officer, emphasized the difference between what he paid currently and what he would pay after the renovation: "Now you pay 211 €/month; in the new building, it will be around 500."[12] This practice attested to the tendency, which was observed by the sociologist Camille François in the rehousing processes for social housing schemes, whereby officers would adjust the expectations of residents with regard to the available stock of apartments.[13] Damien's attitude can be interpreted in two ways: first, as a pragmatic attempt to lower the number of residents to rehouse in the new residence (there is generally a diminished capacity, so reorienting some residents toward other types of housing is necessary), and second, as adherence to the political project of the renovation and compliance with the idea that the purpose of a residence was to house individuals in difficulty and on welfare.

In addition, MOUS provided social counseling and helped some residents claim benefits they were not aware of but to which they were entitled. This was explicitly thought of as a quid pro quo that could help get the residents on their side. In this capacity, MOUS officers guaranteed that they would not pass on sensitive information to other social services. However, I noticed that the survey included the following notation in red: "If an address elsewhere than the foyer is indicated on the documents presented by the resident, make a note of it here." When questioned on this point, Damien replied that several addresses could indicate the resident had obtained lodgings elsewhere and was subletting his bed in the foyer; although they would rarely take any legal action ("that would take too long"), it could be used to "put pressure on the resident," for instance, to ensure that he would accept being among the minority of residents who would be rehoused outside the foyer.

## COMBATING OVER-OCCUPANCY

As described in part 1, anxieties over the presence of unregistered inhabitants emerged in the early 1970s and were consolidated in the following decades. The existence of overcrowded lodgings had been observed previously, but it was at this point that the two following processes came together. First, the term "illegal" allowed an overlap between the condition of being undocumented in France and unregistered in the foyer; once limited to avoiding troubles and containing problems, control took on a new meaning and came to be understood a process for identifying and filtering out individuals. Second, over-occupancy began to be ascribed to West African hosting practices (and not, for instance, to dishonest landlords), with the term "solidarity" being part of a wider semantic field that tended to naturalize and racialize this phenomenon.

On the eve of the renovation plans, estimates of the number of over-occupants in West African foyers reached a head: the *Rapport Cuq* estimated "an over-occupancy rate of 11 percent, peaking at 200 percent and even 300 percent in some structures."[14] In 2010, over-occupancy in Parisian foyers was estimated at 58 percent, with three of them—including Foyer D'Hautpoul—above 100 percent.[15] Over-occupancy was associated with economic deficits in foyer management and security problems, both in terms of a numerically superior population than the building's capacity and the impossibility to correctly identify inhabitants.

Based on these assessments, one of the main aims of the renovation scheme was to "hinder and diminish over-occupancy."[16] This translated into precise instructions regarding the spatial layout: "In Adoma residences, the living space is designed to prevent the installation of additional bedding."[17] The first residence erected in Paris, Foyer Commanderie (nineteenth arrondissement), offered 13 m² studios with floor-fixed furniture. Departing from these extreme arrangements, later projects generally included studios of at least 15 m² and followed recommendations to provide lodgings of around 18 m².[18] Although floor-fixed furniture was broadly abandoned, other measures served the same aim: storage beds making it impossible to keep a mattress underneath; allocation of only one entry pass per room to the foyer building; and installation of individual water meters.

In parallel, the legal conditions related to hosting evolved. The right for a registered resident to host somebody was legally enshrined in 2007. However, it has been strictly delimited: a resident cannot host the same person for more than three months, and one hosted person cannot stay more than six months in the same structure. In addition, the managing structures charge a daily fee for this additional person (1 euro per day in Coallia residences), which can add up to a significant monthly amount.

Most important, the hosted person must present a valid ID and proof of his legal status in France. To make this point even clearer, internal rules in "residences" are expected to reproduce the legal provisions defining the fact of assisting an undocumented migrant as a legal offense.[19] Such provisions were designed to regulate the situation after the move, but during the move professional and institutional stakeholders were already attempting to monitor the population.

## SELECTING "REHOUSABLE OVER-OCCUPANTS"

As the Foyer D'Hautpoul move described in chapter 5 indicates, the fate of the over-occupants was a major concern for the residents. As a result of negotiations between the municipality of Paris, the managing structure (by then Sonacotra), and the residents' committee of Foyer Fontaine-au-Roi (eleventh arrondissement), an agreement made for this particular foyer laid the ground for subsequent processes.[20] The idea was to define a set of criteria according to which some over-occupants would be eligible for rehousing.

Often boasting knowledge of the foyers' inner workings, institutional and professional stakeholders relied on the distinction between "substitute" (French: *remplaçant*) and "over-occupant" (French: *surnuméraire*). As part of their aim to reduce the population to be handled, managers sought to convince residents with regular substitutes (for instance, those retired, who spent little time in France) to transfer the bed under the name of their substitute. As for over-occupants proper, they were guaranteed housing (though outside the foyer) as long as they met three criteria: legal residency in France; proof of at least three years' presence in the foyer at the date of the initial screening; and the sponsorship of a registered resident, with the restriction that they could only sponsor one person per room.

## Criterion 1: Legal Residency

Délégués generally did not dispute the necessity of possessing a valid residence permit in order to be included on the list. Sans-papiers organized at the level of a foyer sometimes conducted collective action, but in parallel with the negotiations concerning over-occupants. During the Foyer D'Hautpoul move, a group of sans-papiers from the foyers tried to appeal to the Mairie d'arrondissement, a venture not approved of by the délégués. In contrast, in the case of Foyer Lorraine, at one point in the rehousing process the residents issued a pamphlet asking that all inhabitants of the foyer be taken into account, regardless of their legal status.[21] Both attempts failed. Generally speaking, residents resorted to a collective tactic of avoiding the sans-papiers issue when discussing the renovation.

## Criterion 2: Proof of Residence in the Foyer

This criterion was less straightforward than that of legal status. To begin with, what could count as written evidence of one's residence in the foyer varied from one renovation to another; there was no fixed list of documents that could serve as proof.[22] In one instance (in an operation run by a managing structure with a large housing stock), I observed that MOUS workers accepted any document mentioning the foyer as proof of residence—even an X-ray with the sole stamp of an association that had conducted a screening program in the foyer. In other cases, a restrictive list of documents was set.

More important, the first two criteria tended to be mutually exclusive. Unregistered residents who were eligible because they had legal status were often former sans-papiers legalized in the 2000s. But since the early 2000s, accommodation in a foyer has not been recognized as a valid domicile by some prefectures, notably that of Paris. To provide an acceptable address, many of them who were physically living in the foyer had sought an address in ordinary housing, asking to use a relative or acquaintance's address, either as a favor or as a paid service. As Dramane, who arrived in France in 2001, recalled: "I have always lived here, but my address was elsewhere. Only when I got my ten-year residence permit did I transfer my address to Foyer Lorraine."[23] Referring to the French expression "*sous couvert de*" ("care of," or "c/o" in a postal address), he elaborated that sous couvert de in a foyer and sous couvert de in another lodging did not have the same value. This illustrates how the same hosting relation could transfer or not into administrative evidence—relatedness reconfigured by bureaucracy.

Most of the time, a change in one's official address required the systematic use of this other address in all instances (opening a bank account, receiving pay stubs, or filing taxes), with sans-papiers aware that any inconsistency in their file could jeopardize the entire process. Once granted a residence permit, few had amended their official address back to the foyer as swiftly as Dramane had done; thus they failed to meet the second criterion. At the time of my fieldwork, all professional and institutional stakeholders were aware of this problem, but no solution had been offered. Délégués often suggested that they could provide verbal guarantees that listed over-occupants had long lived with them, but this option was not considered.

## Criterion 3: Sponsorship of a Registered Resident

Contrary to the first two, this requirement involved not only the petitioner in the process but also a registered resident, at least, and often the délégués. Through the inclusion of a sponsorship (French: *parrainage*) criterion in the bureaucratic process, the authorities recognized the foyer's community dimension on two levels: first, they acknowledged the existence of specific ties between unregistered foyer inhabitants and one registered resident (the hosted/host pairing, perceived as kinlike and protective, given the connotation of the official French term);[24] and second, they limited the bounds of a foyer collective to those over-occupants recognized by registered residents. The obverse side of this inclusionary dynamic was the exclusion of those inhabitants who navigated from one host to another, and the condemnation of hosting practices beyond the scope of the one-to-one service.

In fact, although the initial definition of the sponsorship scheme suggested that all registered residents could sponsor one unregistered person, it also stipulated that, as a whole, the number of unregistered inhabitants acknowledged through the process could not exceed the number of rooms in the foyer.[25] During the 2010s, I observed a constant back-and-forth between these distinct understandings of the rule (either one unregistered person per registered resident or per bed, or one unregistered per room). The difference between the two versions of the rule could be numerically significant: at Foyer D'Hautpoul, there were 124 beds for 86 rooms; at Foyer Masséna (thirteenth arrondissement), there were 240 beds for 80 rooms. The stricter version generally prevailed, a point residents consistently opposed because it resulted in competition within the room to decide who could sponsor the person (or one of the persons) he accommodated. Délégués invariably asserted that "everyone has his over-occupant." One délégué, Boubacar, stated during a meeting at Foyer D'Hautpoul: "If you rehouse me without my clandestine, it's like kicking me out."[26] This notion of "one's" clandestine or over-occupant hinted at the complex bond of hospitality through which the host asserted his authority over the person, generally a younger kinsman, whom he accommodated. By focusing on this mutual and exclusive link, the délégués left aside other dilemmas: the choices those registered residents who hosted more than one person had to make; and the fate of those who acted as collective substitutes, finding a place to stay whenever a bed or a mattress became vacant; or of those who slept in the corridors or other spaces. This attested to a common assumption within the foyer that hosting one person could be defensible, but not more than one.

This notion of sponsorship resulted in forms of self-limitation in the number of unregistered residents, as well as considerable confusion as to its exact meaning. It served to reassure institutions, anxious about being overwhelmed by the number of over-occupants. It was, however, often loosely applied, as evidenced by the actual dynamics in play during the screenings.

## BATTLES OVER LISTS, DISCRETIONARY LOGICS, AND LIMITED RESULTS

Foyer D'Hautpoul hosted 124 registered residents, and a number of additional (unregistered) inhabitants estimated at 160.[27] A first screening as part of the "social diagnosis" resulted in a list of twenty-four unregistered men eligible for rehousing. In the course of the contentious dynamics detailed in chapter 5, the délégués earned the opportunity to reopen the process and provided their own list of eighty-six unregistered residents.

The list was established by the délégués, who were heavily solicited at this stage in the process, and in turn mobilized residents they trusted. As I observed while assisting a resident in charge of this task, the whole process was dealt with by families or "sectors" (village communities). Often, those who managed to get their names on the délégués' list were not aware that they would be subjected to a subsequent screening process by the managing structure.[28] Generally, the first criterion was easy to assess and this list only included individuals with legal status, but the notion of steady residence in the foyer was far more difficult to gauge. In addition to the aforementioned address conundrum, some men actually navigated between several lodgings. Occasionally, a resident would slip someone not living in the foyer onto the list, a practice frowned upon by the délégués. In Foyer D'Hautpoul, among the eighty-six names presented by the délégués, only twenty-two met the three criteria according to the social workers in charge of the screening; the final list included forty-six names.

To the individuals so identified, the managing structure was obliged to offer one proposal for a studio in a residence in the Paris region. This provision compared negatively to standard procedures in rehousing operations, which required three proposals to be made to a tenant. Managers often reiterated that this measure had been initiated by authorities and that they were in charge of finding housing for this surplus population. A Coallia officer admitted: "The decision to rehouse over-occupants is an ambition of the municipality. A noble one, but difficult to implement."[29] Even the municipality officers highlighted the exceptionality of the procedure: "The rule is already generous, it goes beyond the managing structure's obligations. We offer you the chance to include people who were not supposed to be there in the first place."[30] This general tone combined with the latitude afforded MOUS officers in making rehousing offers. Damien explained to me that "no one wants the over-occupants; they are perceived as bad payers. So one solution is to offer them lodgings in residences that stink, and have significant turnover." His stance was in line with his profile of "moral entrepreneur," but even pragmatic MOUS officers worked with heavy constraints because they often had no or very few lodgings to offer in Paris.

In the case of Foyer D'Hautpoul, two days before the day of the move Mr. Bonnet and one of the MOUS officers came to announce that they had fifteen studios in Paris for some of them, and that given the lack of suitable criteria by which to choose who would benefit from these enviable propositions, there would be a random draw—an occasion remembered as "Bonnet's tombola." Meanwhile, out of those who remained and were offered studios in "residences" far from Paris, most refused. The délégué Harouna told me about two young men who went on a daily basis to an interim agency in Paris that opened at 5 A.M. Having been offered studios in Sartrouville, they had calculated that there was no public transportation that would allow them to arrive that early at the agency. The end result was the rehousing of thirty over-occupants: twenty "rehousable over-occupants" successfully rehoused; and ten over-occupants whom former residents had transferred their beds to as part of the process of "substitution." As indicated, this figure fared favorably compared with other outcomes of such processes during this same period.[31] Compared to the estimate of over-occupants, the final number of unregistered inhabitants actually rehoused (here, in a "successful" operation, 30 out of 160) appeared very limited.

The selection of "rehousable over-occupants" lends itself to a cynical reading of the whole process as being a diversion in the sense that délégués put considerable time and energy into compiling lists, all for a modest result. As in other mobilizations, the initial acceptance of criteria, even if their implementation is debatable, resulted in many lists being drawn up, sometimes competing ones, a process that ran counter to the collective mobilization.[32] Beyond this effect of the lists on negotiations, I argue that this process led to gradual adjustments among the inhabitants regarding the possibility of maintaining, or not, their group of residence. I turn now to these dynamics at the level of one room.

## FIVE MEN IN A ROOM

Prior to the Foyer D'Hautpoul move, Demba, eighty years old, lived in a room with several other men, all coming from a Haalpulaar village located on the banks of the Senegal River. The room, with a surface area of 11 m$^2$, was officially a one-bed room; it had two beds, and four to six people slept there (figure 6.2).[33]

In 2012, the registered resident Abou was about seventy years old. He had been given the opportunity to put the bed in his name in the 1980s, after holding the room for a year when it was registered under one of his brothers, who had been joined in France by his wife. Then Abou's own wife joined him, and he had left the foyer, leaving Demba as his replacement. Demba was his friend but not related, and he belonged to a statutory group distinct from Abou's.[34]

Demba had arrived in France in 1974 and had been accommodated in another foyer before joining Abou's room, where he had resided from 1987 to 2011, the date of his retirement. Since then, Demba had alternated between one- to two-year stays in Senegal and returning to France for several months (for

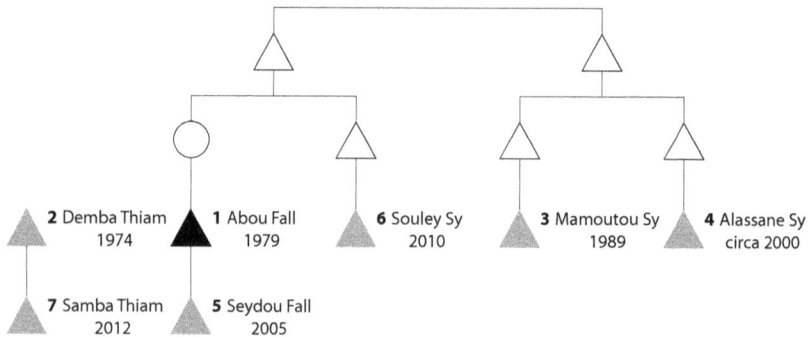

**FIGURE 6.2** Inhabitants of a room before the move, with their genealogical ties and arrival date in France. The registered resident, who did not live in the room, was Abou Fall (featured here in black). The room's inhabitants, regular or not, appear in gray: Demba, Abou's substitute, and Demba's son Samba; Abou's son and three of Abou's cousins, Souley Sy, Mamoutou Sy, and Alassane Sy."

*Source*: Diagram by the author.

administrative or health reasons). As Abou's first substitute, and regularly present in the room for more than twenty-four years, Demba had seen the arrival of Abou's maternal cousins, Souley, Mamoutou, and Alassane, as well as Abou's son, Seydou. Among the cousins, two were there continuously; and Alassane, who rented a studio in the suburbs acquired through work, which he sublet, only slept in the foyer occasionally. Finally, Demba's own son had recently arrived.

Over the years, the collective had grown denser in the absence of the owner but without any change in the allocation of the bed because Abou had not wanted to put the bed in Demba or one of his maternal cousins' names. Although agnatic lineage prevailed as the desired axis of inheritance (see chapter 4), the residence brought together Seydou and his maternal relatives (Souley,

Mamoutou and Alassane), on one hand, and people linked by friendship (Demba and Samba), on the other. The presence of Demba and his anchoring (because he was allowed to lodge his son) demonstrated that the basis for coresidence could be found in other ties than kinship in the strict sense—such as proximity or friendship—and it could be strengthened over time by one's status as a substitute ensuring or contributing to payment of the fee. This broadening of kinship, particularly in the uterine line, was also apparent from my observations of other rooms.

It is in this context that the move occurred. The twofold dynamics exposed here—the tightened transmission around the agnatic nucleus and the accommodation of a broader meaning of kinship—implied a plurality of potential principles in rehousing choices. Principles of proximity in terms of degrees of kinship and seniority within the room played a decisive role in the way residents seized the opportunity to regularize their status through the screening of over-occupants. At the time when the prospect of relocation became clearer, out of the six possible candidates for "rehousable over-occupant" status, one was ruled out from the outset: Samba, who had only arrived in France in 2012 and had no regular status. The other five all held residence permits and had been living in the foyer for more than three years. Among them, Seydou, Abou's son, did not submit an application on the assumption that he would remain the unregistered holder of the bed as long as his father did not decide to change his address, and he counted on the fact that transferring the studio under his name would remain possible after the renovation.

As for the cousins, both Mamoutou and Alassane managed to put together an application that was considered valid and were thus included on the list of "rehousable over-occupants," but both sought a sponsor outside the room, preferring to avoid asking the holder so as not to risk encroaching on his son's potential request. Souley did not have adequate proof of residence in the foyer. When the MOUS social worker received him, he asked him if the roommate was effectively present; when he answered in the negative, the social worker said that all he needed was an agreement with the holder to put the room in his name. This solution, given the configuration just described, was simply not feasible.

Finally, Demba did not complete his application in time; although he presented the required evidence, he initially did not find himself on any list. The move having coincided with one of his absences, he was not taken into account. He eventually obtained a bed on his return, several months after the move, because of his medical needs.

As the move approached, I was still only getting evasive answers to my questions about where they were going to go. Although they were on the list of "rehousable over-occupants," Mamoutou and Alassane only learned their fate a few days before the move: they were unsuccessful in the random draw, and they refused offers of relocation to the outer suburbs from where their daily commute to their workplaces would have been complicated. One week before the move, Seydou called a meeting with the room's occupants to tell them he had visited the planned relocation site (a smaller room where only one extra mattress could be laid out) and could not take everyone with him, and that he would be leaving with Samba. Alassane was forced to go back to his studio, and he decided to take Souley with him. Only Mamoutou remained, the most bitter, having been there for nearly twenty-five years and suddenly in need of an emergency solution. He eventually became an over-occupant in a foyer in Boulogne with a more distant relative (figure 6.3).[35]

This case demonstrates that the relocation resulted in the dislocation of the densest residential collectives because some

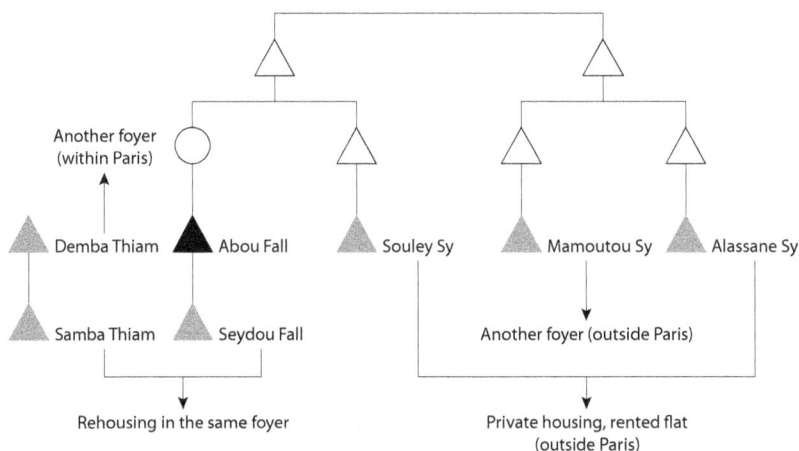

**FIGURE 6.3** Results of the rehousing process for the inhabitants of the room.

*Source*: Diagram by the author.

residents were unable to follow. This observation is important to underline because these individuals were omitted from rehousing reports and no social support measures were in place to target this group. Moreover, such an analysis conducted at the level of a room overlooks the most marginal over-occupants in relation to the foyers' residential collectives, those with no attachments to a room. Many of the unregistered inhabitants, and all the undocumented ones, were completely invisibilized.

In addition, of the two collectives that emerged from the move, one did not correspond to the closest degrees of kinship (Alassane favored Souley over Mamoutou) and the other bypassed kinship relations altogether (Seydou choosing Samba to the detriment of his uncles). The move gave the members of a collective formed over the years the opportunity to divide up according to lifestyle compatibility and reciprocity of services rendered. The two pairs that formed corresponded to the departure of a more economically secure migrant with a younger one who was less so, within the framework of an asymmetrical but mutually dependent relationship.[36] In the case of Samba, who did not contribute to the payment of the room because he only worked occasionally, it is possible that Seydou was instructed by his father to take care of his friend's son; or perhaps collectively the decision was taken not to leave the most vulnerable of them in trouble. The relocation also separated Samba from his father, which was a relief for him because he often expressed his discomfort living in such close quarters with his aging father, but it nonetheless resulted in him traveling almost daily between the two relatively distant foyers to help his father in his daily life. Finally, Demba—who obtained a bed out of consideration for his difficulties accessing medical care—fell within the definition of the residence according to the difficulties and needs of its population as part of a wider compassionate shift in attitudes toward migrants.[37]

Epitomizing the normalization-with-exception dimension of the renovation, the process of screening "rehousable over-occupants" could be read as a form of compromise with existing ways of inhabiting the foyer. In particular, the sponsorship of over-occupants seemed to be a tribute to local forms of organization. But this mechanism served more as a means of numerically limiting the population in the renovation scheme than one of maintaining actual ties. Mimicking existing bonds, it often resulted in their de facto breakup, either separating roommates or exacerbating tensions between several over-occupants and the registered resident. However, within such a constrained framework, foyer inhabitants still managed to safeguard reduced forms of solidarity that were understood as the ability to constitute economically and socially viable groups (here: pairs).

## UNCERTAIN DOMICILES

At various steps in the renovation process, several elements indicated that lower standards were applied to foyer residents than to ordinary tenants. This appeared notably in how prefectures, in the 2000s, began to reject applications with an address in a foyer for nonregistered residents. The renovation process took place in a context of administrative suspicion, which resulted in new degrees of constraint on the lives of foyer inhabitants.

The refusal to consider an address in a foyer as valid extended to tax services. Because a tax declaration rests precisely on a "declaration," it was an important part of the documentation of undocumented migrants and one normally deemed as solid proof of one's presence in France.[38] The new requirements affected not only sans-papiers but also migrants with a regular presence in France. On the basis of a 2006 note from the fiscal administration on "uncertain domiciles," the tax services have since rejected cases in which the declarant's address was given as "c/o" a foyer resident.[39] The recommendations given to fiscal workers were based on this notion: "If a person is domiciled in a foyer, he or she must produce a certificate of accommodation. A person in possession of a certificate of accommodation cannot, in turn, provide a certificate of accommodation for someone else."[40] As irrefutable as the argument was, it rested on the redefinition of residence in a foyer as mere accommodation. Some foyers' managing structures shared the list of their registered residents with the fiscal services, which only accepted tax declarations from registered residents, attesting to an alignment in the administration with the internal decision taken by the foyers' management to combat undeclared hosting practices.[41] Although sans-papiers collectives, trade unions within the fiscal administrations, and associations all contested this new interpretation of fiscal rules, it remained in place in the years that followed.[42]

As this example illustrates, the renovation scheme must be read against a wider trend of administrative reforms and tightened bureaucratic practices that weakened the status conferred by residence in a foyer. This came in addition to more diffused discriminatory attitudes and practices among social workers and civil servants toward foyer residents.[43]

## CONCLUSION: FRAGILE ADDRESSES

In stories of 216 bis, the address functioned mainly as a toponym, recalling a past location and conjuring times of collective identities and political action. Stories about addresses during the renovation process were much more dramatic. Previously, being hosted could be converted into an administrative relation of "c/o" status, both for the postal services and within the foyers. The later disconnect between the place where one could live and one's official address appeared to be a drastic change, as Dramane's uncle Boubou reflected:

> In our day, it wasn't like this [referring to the difficulty in applying for rehousable over-occupant status]. Your address was in the foyer, whatever your status. My address was 13 rue de Lorraine, that's it. The foyer director would know your face, and provide a certificate of accommodation. Nowadays . . . pff! You don't even own your address. You see, in this country, they always change their methods.

This bitter remark pointed to a past familiarity between the director and the residents, which was conspicuous in older

narratives, and an ambiguous stance toward arrangements perceived as paternalistic yet still recalled as having facilitated many
aspects of their lives. More important, Boubou captured a wider
feeling of dispossession, which was pervasive in many more general comments regarding the renovation process.

Tying together a person and an identified place is initially a
technology of control, in that the individual was obliged to provide an address. However, the conditions of this control (who
was allowed to claim an address in a foyer) had been laxer in
the past. Although some pressure could be put on unregistered
inhabitants (for instance, the threat that mail would only be
distributed to registered residents), no generalized mechanism
excluded them from claiming an address in the foyer where they
stayed. The tightening of the administrative requirements in
foyers, fueled by assumptions that foyers residents' hosting practices had reached an uncontrollable level, led to a new situation
in which the already precarious arrangements that had prevailed
until the early 2000s became untenable. A "distributed residence" (the dislocation between one's postal and administrative
address and one's actual dwelling place) came at the migrant's
cost, from owing multiple rents to potential loss of mail.

The trajectory of the foyer address across generations of foyer
inhabitants is thus revealing. For older men, these two dimensions of index and title had coincided. Subverting the disciplinary power of the address by using it in narratives of emplacement,
the migrants had transformed a token of identification into an
attribute of the city dweller status. This was rendered possible
by loose management practices in the foyers designed for West
Africans: bringing someone new to the foyer, finding a bed for
him, and having his mail distributed was generally possible.

In the era of migration irregularization, younger migrants
have been confronted with new rules: the foyer does not function

as an accepted domicile because an address in a foyer does not confer a solid basis for getting a resident permit. The whole renovation process drastically limits the possibility of hosting, and this administrative requirement is only one layer in the devaluation of the foyer as a migrant institution. Migrants' ties to a place go far beyond the right to call one's place of life a domicile. But even when migrants found tactics to circumvent the new requirements, actual choices regarding where to live were highly constrained through the political technology of address by wider administrative requests. Stuckness, marked with precarity, did not allow for emplacement.

# III

# AMBIVALENT ATTACHMENTS, CONTESTED BELONGING

F oyers and residences have sustained migratory networks and transnational projects for generations of men. They have played, and continue to play, a key role in transnational migratory networks. At the same time, they occupy a peculiar position within West African diasporas in France because they typify a seemingly outdated moment of migration to France. Nonetheless, old foyers and also some of the new residences draw visitors and occupy a significant place in French cities and in the nation's political imagination. The roles and positions of the foyers are at once both symbolic and material, hence the importance of approaching them as assemblages of beds and mattresses, kinship ties and diasporic networks, and legal titles and fragile addresses—that is, as infrastructures of migration.

The next two chapters take a broader look at the foyers in light of current debates on race, religion, and integration in France. In this endeavor, I use "belonging" to uncover a variety of attachments to both the city (and other relevant scales, such as the neighborhood) and to their places of origin. For migrants who have spent most of their adult life in France, but also for younger ones who have been stuck in Europe for years, the reference to home is a complex one. Ultimately, the notion of belonging is a way to reconsider and further historicize the dynamics of emplacement demonstrated in the part 1 at a time when irregularization processes made the issue of legal documents vital.

Part 3 draws on research conducted in a decade during which the renovation process unevenly affected Parisian foyers. I spent time in foyers and residences, and occasionally both in an old foyer and in the residence that replaced it, as in Lorraine and D'Hautpoul. This longitudinal perspective on the lives and engagements of my interlocutors with the city casts the changes induced by the renovation within wider transformations in French cities and society, as well as in the diasporic West African space.

Moving from the horizontal ties explored in part 2 to the verticality of individual and family projects, I begin by asking what kind of *lives* do the foyers allow. Chapter 7 situates the infrastructure of the foyers at the intersection between the lifelong trajectories of the men in the foyers, on one hand, and French policies and global mobility regimes, on the other. I explore the disentanglement of capitalism, male migration, and social reproduction and reflect on its consequences in the affective lives and masculinities of men in the foyers. This approach is sensitive to the various attitudes toward the foyers and the ambivalent attachments to these places, sometimes the topic of harsh internal critique.

I then turn to the ties formed through the foyers and that extend far beyond them. In chapter 8, I scrutinize the *urban* character of the foyers in two related ways. Asking what the foyers do to the city, I investigate the social and political meanings of old and new buildings in changing urban landscapes. Conversely, I delineate the dynamics of the urban emplacement of foyer inhabitants, and I ask what kind of politics of belonging developed thanks to or despite the foyers.

By way of conclusion, in chapter 9 I examine the way living in or passing through the foyer makes it possible to be—or not to be—part of a neighborhood, a city, and ultimately part of the French nation.

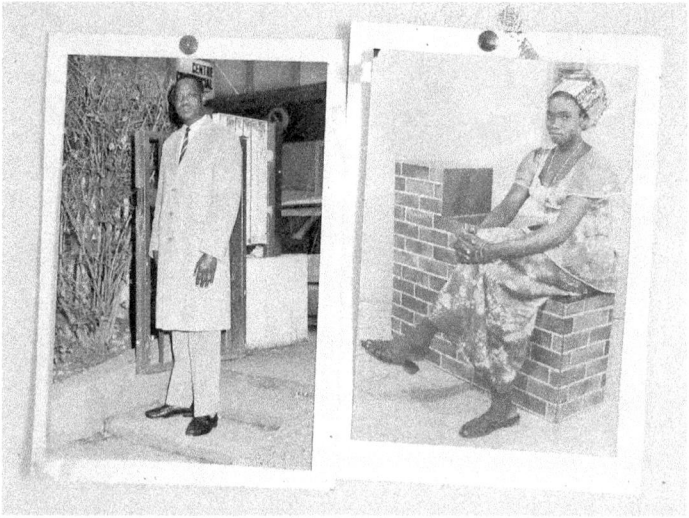

**FIGURE 7.1** Spouses apart.

*Source*: Photo by Anissa Michalon.

# 7

## FOYERMEN

### Class, Gender, and Race Across Generations

*Malick was twenty when he arrived in France from Kayes, Mali, in 2000. He joined his elder brother in a foyer in the south of Paris. On the understanding that Malick would take his turn in supporting their small homestead, his brother then went back to Mali. Malick only had a few years of formal schooling, after which he had taken Soninke literacy classes in Kayes. A sturdy and open-hearted man, he soon found a job as a handyman in a grocery store, but it still took him ten years to secure legal status: "I lost ten years here," he commented bitterly. Upon his first return visit, Malick married a cousin; five years later, having had no children despite several trips back home, he married a second wife, the younger sister of one of his friends. His younger brother arrived in 2018 and quickly found a job too, thus alleviating the financial burden of rent in the foyer. By 2020, being highly involved in both transnational associations and Malian politics, Malick was developing an agricultural project, hoping that one day he could earn a decent living in his home region.*

*Also hailing from the Kayes region, Dramane arrived in France in 2001 at age twenty-four. After high school, he had spent some time in Bamako, considering a career in the army, before moving to Dakar in search of his way to France. The eldest son of a polygynous family, he joined his father who lived at Foyer D'Hautpoul. After two years, Dramane managed to secure legal documents thanks to the help of his boss, and he got a permanent job in a restaurant. Shortly after obtaining legal status, he married a relative living in Dakar. When we met in 2013, he was separated from his wife but still supported her and their son. He later married a French citizen of Algerian background in France, a marriage that lasted barely two years; he never moved into his wife's apartment, keeping his room in the foyer instead. He also funded the arrival of a younger brother, who rapidly married a relative born in France and moved out of the foyer to live with her. Keeping his father's bed—then keeping a studio in his name—was essential to Dramane's pivotal status in an expected chain of migration involving several of his siblings. Known as a generous man, although with a carefully cultivated reputation as one always ready for a fight, he had an intense social life within the foyer but did not envision himself staying there all his life.*

*After reaching university level in Dakar, **Souley**, born in a Haalpulaar village in Senegal, arrived in France in 2013 at the age of thirty, having registered for an MA law program in a university town in the east of France. Without a scholarship, he did not manage to pursue his studies while working in parallel to earn a living. When he failed his exams, he slipped into undocumented status. He then moved to Paris and headed to Foyer Lorraine where his deceased father had once lived and where he still had maternal relatives. He was allowed to live in the foyer thanks to these kinship ties and his contribution to cooking. During the move, he was among the unregistered residents the official residents took with them throughout because* *of their vulnerable status. Witty and facetious, Souley had intellectual ambitions, but he found himself earning irregular money from short-term contracts in unskilled positions, such as a security guard. Neither his fleeting involvement in a sans-papiers collective nor his return to university were enough to build an application that he deemed worthy of submission to the prefecture. Although still married to a cousin back home, he was outspoken about his partners in France and contemplated marriage with a relative born in France as a way to secure legal documents.*

The trajectories of these men, who arrived in France between twenty and thirty years of age, epitomize distinct ways of living in a foyer at the beginning of the twenty-first century.

Malick symbolizes a lifestyle in which the form of the foyer is symbiotic with the migration project, with his wives back home, a strong insertion in transnational networks, and the prospect of return. Malick's trajectory should also be read as a lucid assessment of his slim opportunities in France. Given his limited literacy skills, I often assisted him in his administrative dealings, from the bank to the prefecture. While I was drafting a letter requesting that his one-year residence permit be upgraded to a ten-year one, he told me that he had already applied several times: once the immigration agent told him that he did not pay enough tax; another time the officer said that an address in the foyer was insufficient to obtain a ten-year residence permit. These experiences forged his understanding of French society as offering little chance for upward mobility.

In contrast to Malick's positive appreciation of the foyer, Dramane and Souley voiced ambivalent stances toward this place of living and highlighted the need to get out of the foyer to connect with other people. Dramane capitalized on the social networks provided by the foyer, providing services often in exchange for money, such as assisting with paperwork. But he also theorized that one should not stay in the foyer. Sitting in a café near the foyer, he once explained to me that he "needed air" and further complained about conversations in the foyer: "The guys only speak about which phone card is cheapest to call back home. Sometimes I come and sit here if I need to fit in this country" [French: *si j'ai besoin de m'intégrer*]. The eagerness with which he invited me to his place, as he did with other people passing through the foyer, from activists to the occasional anthropology student, attests to his longing for connections outside the foyer. Dramane's case suggests that living in the foyer could be a choice, sometimes provisional, for men whose lives extended far beyond and who had sufficient resources to move out.

Souley's claustrophobia in the foyer materialized in the fact that most of our conversations took place in other places outside because he did not feel comfortable enough to invite me into the crowded room where he slept: we spent time in a park near the foyer; sat on benches facing a playground near the university; and chatted during metro rides that he carefully studied to avoid police checks. Souley once told me that he was fed up with the older men in the rooms insisting that he shave his head (the common hairstyle of foyer residents) while he was trying to grow out dreadlocks. Like Dramane, he was bored with the foyer conversations revolving around either daily life in the foyer or news from the village back home. But he also acknowledged that, in the suspended life he lived, being with others had positive aspects: "You see Astou, you wake up and say your morning prayers because the others are around: that's a good thing, imagine if you were by yourself." Although no one could predict what Souley would do when an opportunity to leave the foyer presented itself, his marginalized position within the *chambrée* and his own aspirations converged on an exit trajectory further down the line.

From feeling at home in the foyer to feeling stuck there, with an intermediate stance of provisionally choosing this kind of accommodation, these distinct attitudes help unpack the figure of the *foyerman*. I approach the lives of these men through an intersectional perspective combining gender, class, race, and age.[1] These dimensions are both socially and culturally significant identities debated within and beyond the foyers and categories of immigration policies, some of them built into the foyer system. Tracing the marks of the foyers on men who spend limited periods or their entire active lives within their walls, I contribute to the understanding of the ways in which legal requirements shape migrants' lives, and crucially their temporal deployment.[2]

Extractive capitalism, migration policies, and gendered expectations of success in West African societies once converged to define the expected life course of foyer inhabitants as alternating between phases of continuous work in France and return visits to Africa. I call this the "sacrificial trope": although subordinate in terms of class and race in France, the migrant nonetheless fulfilled his breadwinner role and embodied masculine success back home. How this model, which functioned as a "hegemonic masculinity" in the transnational space of West African migration to France, has been challenged is the topic of this chapter.[3]

Focusing on the foyers' bearing on migrants' lives, the following pages reveal the changing meanings of the foyer in biographical trajectories. Exploring the affective lives and conjugal intentions of my interlocutors sheds light on the weight of gendered and racialized categories, recasting the foyers as one instance of a wider condition of being racialized as black in France.[4]

## COMPARING EXPERIENCES OF
## MIGRATION ACROSS GENERATIONS

Foyers not only host men from distinct generations but are places of comparisons. I pinpoint the changes in the masculine identities of foyermen across generations. Men like Malick, Dramane, and Souley, who migrated in the 2000s or early 2010s and were between thirty and forty during my fieldwork, belonged to the group of "young ones" (French: *les jeunes*) or even "kids" (Soninke: *lemunu*). They were set apart from two other categories: (1) older than them, residents ages fifty to sixty constituted the group of mature and generally still professionally active men, from among which the délégués mostly recruited; and (2) older still, the "elders" (French: *les anciens*) or "old ones" (French: *les vieux*) were a group characterized in principle by their withdrawal from collective responsibilities and longer phases of return to their countries of origin. Younger or later-arrived men constituted a group from which Malick and the others distanced themselves.

These categories were evolving, and access to mature age was delayed: eighty-year-old Demba said that when he arrived in the 1970s the foyer had been dominated by young men (Wolof: *waxambaane*, a term he glossed as designating a man aged twenty-five to forty); in contrast, during my fieldwork, men of this age were still considered "young" because older men were in charge of foyer affairs. Likewise, Stefan Le Courant notes that "those who arrived last remain the 'young ones' indefinitely until such time as new members of the village have arrived in sufficient numbers."[5]

In the 2000s and later, would-be migrants in West Africa faced much higher costs for the trip. Although Caroline Melly contends that in Dakar "migration is increasingly imagined as an individualized activity, as a matter of chance or luck, and as involving a personal engagement with risk," a focus on the foyers and the influx of arrivals that they still sustained attests to the endurance of more traditional mechanisms of support from kin, generally reduced to close kin.[6] In fact, uncertainty tended to enhance the importance of the community as a "security net" because migrants in the most precarious conditions tend to remit more.[7]

Migrants experienced extended periods of illegal status at a time of exclusionary migration policies against the backdrop of a rise in migration to France during the 2000s and 2010s, after a moment of stabilization in the 1990s. Several of my interlocutors who had arrived in the early 2010s still had no papers after seven, eight, or even ten years of being in France.[8] For these undocumented men living in a state of "deportability," each move in the city involved some measure of risk.[9]

Intersecting with the issue of documentation, migrants were often hired as workers in low-skilled and precarious jobs with temporary contracts.[10] For the most part, African migrants worked in three sectors: cleaning, construction, and catering.[11] Foreigners from outside the EU had an unemployment rate of 24 percent, compared to 9 percent for French nationals, and were harder hit by the 2008 economic crisis.[12] In addition, as often in migration contexts, many of them experienced downward mobility. Meanwhile, having a job had been increasingly tied to opportunities for regularization after a 2012 memorandum (the *Circulaire Valls*, named after Manuel Valls, by then Minister of the Interior) stated the possibility of acquiring a residence permit on presentation of a number of pay slips and a work contract.

Even the situation of men who arrived after the economic downturn of the 1970s compared favorably to the experience of more recent migrants.[13] At the turn of the twenty-first century,

West African migrants and French citizens of West African backgrounds belonged to the more stigmatized ethno-racial minorities of French society.[14] Their socioeconomic conditions remained much lower than those of other immigrant groups, despite demonstrating forms of cultural integration such as in their civic and associative engagement.[15] In particular, they remained highly discriminated against in access to social housing.[16]

In this context, I trace a shift in the foyers' role from dealing with spatial ruptures to temporal ones instead. In earlier decades, the social organization of the foyers had mitigated the geographical distance from one's country of origin. With new means of communication, on one hand, and the reduced size of the network funding the departure, on the other, more recent generations of migrants appear to be less collectively dependent on their elders. But at a time of dilated temporalities, the foyers regained a key role.

## BECOMING A MAN IN A FOYER

In 2015, during a group discussion in a newly opened residence in Créteil, an eastern suburb of Paris, a man took the floor and said: "I've been here for, say, twenty or forty years. My younger brother or son sleeps next to me. Then he becomes a man, he starts sorting out his own business: he should be given a room of his own."[17] That my interlocutor tied together "becoming a man" and "getting a room" exemplifies the importance of the foyer in a gendered socialization to migration, and it demonstrates how progress within the foyer was associated with the construction of a masculine identity in migration.

Narratives from younger migrants still portrayed the foyer as a place where knowledge was acquired. Hence, Bouba, a délégué of a Parisian foyer in his early thirties, recalled how upon arrival in the foyer he was instructed on how to behave in France. This education revolved around principles such as learning patience (Soninke: *muñu*, endurance) in the face of racism at work; or how to behave in mundane circumstances, for instance, the recommendation not to hurry over to help someone with a heavy bag for fear of being taken for a thief. Although these anecdotes had become stylized through countless renditions of the same story—bearing a similarity to the recounting of mishaps of newly arrived migrants—they pointed to the value of the foyer as a place where one followed in the steps of previous migrants.

Beyond this role in becoming socialized as migrants, key biographical turning points were built into the foyers' structure: marrying in France or being joined by a spouse generally translated into leaving the foyer, whereas keeping one's wife back home meant staying there; "returning" and transferring one's bed to someone else versus keeping one's bed and staying in France (or going back and forth) again crystallized distinct positions. As a result, the population of a foyer was made up of distinct groups with varying relationships to the place: sans-papiers stayed there for lack of a better choice, and some of them expected to leave the foyer as soon as possible; men married back home and in possession of documents formed the core group in terms of social norms, but were not necessarily the most numerous; retired men were not expected to stay too long in the foyer, and they rendered palpable the fact that returning home was not always a straightforward option or an attainable goal.

Obviously, migrants' trajectories sometimes blurred these clear-cut group definitions. Souley's situation as a student is absent from insiders' and outsiders' perspectives on the foyers, which are still envisioned as being for *working* men. Dramane's conjugal history complicates the view of marriage in France and at home as mutually exclusive. Malick's ambition to return before retirement displaces the temporality of this expected conclusion of a migrant's life. Rather than postulating a stable life course in which these turning points would occur, I remain attentive to the ways my interlocutors assessed their own, often uncertain paths through such a framework, notably around the key moments of marriage and return.[18]

## MARRIAGE "OPTIONS" AND REPRODUCTIVE ANXIETIES

Marriage opens up possibilities as much as it comes with constraints.[19] Possibilities offered by unions made in France included, notably, a route to obtaining documents and a way out of the foyer. Marrying back home constituted a path toward fulfilling expected family roles and attaining a social status in keeping with the hegemonic masculinity formed around the foyers. Decisions regarding marriage, from choice of a partner to the timing of the union, were tightly framed by a set of at times contradictory requirements, notably administrative constraints in France and religious and social rules determining acceptable marriage forms and possible partners.[20] The matrimonial value of a migrant in French society and in the transnational Franco-West African space, and his moral values and affective background, further determined this experience. Nonetheless, the moment of marriage could be experienced as one of regained agency, particularly when it coincided with the acquisition of legal status. Despite the significant limitations faced by migrants when it came to marriage, I retain the notion of "marriage options" because my interlocutors discussed them as such. I focus on the case of migrants arriving as unmarried, still a statistical majority.[21]

Relying on conversations with men, my account does not fully depict gender dynamics among West Africans in France.[22] Rather, it explores male subjectivities as forged in and against the foyers. Like Katharine Charsley's study of the situation of Pakistani men in Bristol, my aim is to portray my interlocutors as "people with comprehensible emotional lives."[23] Set within the foyers or among foyer inhabitants, discussions about marriage often took the form of cautionary tales, in which the personal experience of the orator was overshadowed by statements posited as general truths. Far from treating such "rumors" with suspicion, I consider them as serious responses to complex situations when migration crucially affects gender relations and norms.[24]

Throughout my fieldwork, I heard stories about marriage, but I also followed the relationships and conjugal plans of those among my interlocutors willing to touch on this aspect of their lives during our conversations. In their twenties to early forties, they were either unmarried or married back home but, for lack of documents, stuck in France and openly considering the possibility of contracting other unions. As for the sexual and affective experiences of older, generally married men, I occasionally heard anecdotes in this regard, but the topic was not explicitly discussed when I was around.[25]

## Family Reunion and Its Pitfalls

On a sunny afternoon in July, I join Souley and his friend Idy (age around forty, recently arrived and still sans-papiers) at the premises of a social center next to the foyer. Both come from the same Haalpulaar Senegalese village and only work occasionally. They suggest that we go to the Buttes Chaumont: it is the month of Ramadan, and being in the park seems a good way to kill time (Wolof: *dàq koor gi*). As we wander in search of a space on the lawns, we spot one of their covillagers and a friend from the foyer, Djibo, Idy's age-mate who has been in France longer and has a residence permit. Djibo is lying on the grass listening to music on his tablet, and we sit around him. While *L'amour a tous les droits*, by Senegalese singer Ismaël Lô, plays, the conversation turns to a common topic: women, marriage, and the lot of migrant men. Souley and Idy concur that in France women and children "have all the rights," and they single out the bad influence of female friends [French: *copines*] on women. Regarding family reunion, Idy states: "If you opt to have your wife join you, it means how much she means to you. See, you love her, but she drops you for just anybody." Souley adds that in Senegal it is rare for a woman to initiate a separation, but it is common in France. Djibo remains silent.[26]

The full plot of these oft-repeated stories portrayed a wife, whom a man "brings to France" through family reunion, who becomes aware of her rights and seeks a divorce and manages to kick her husband out of their flat, obtain legal custody of the children, and claim family allowance benefits. As a variant of the "copines" mentioned here, the villain is usually a social worker.[27] Often told as a general truth, the story was sometimes supported by specific known cases. During our discussion at the Buttes Chaumont, Souley and Idy, both sans-papiers for whom the issue was theoretical, were the ones discoursing on the topic, whereas Djibo, the only one who might actually have been weighing the pros and cons of family reunion, remained silent.

These stories must be heard as defensive stories. In another conversation on the same topic, Idy made his argument even more explicit by stating that women were taken care of as *"femmes isolées,"* but there was no help available to *"hommes isolés."*

This made explicit the way in which West African men felt that black African women in France could fit into a victim position, and their attempt to reverse this situation.[28] Obviously, the main narrative espoused patriarchal norms: the woman "brought to France" was expected to be grateful and the scandal laid in her regained agency. But these discourses on family reunion were also anchored in suspicion as to the possibilities of marital and family life in France. As previously indicated, the facilitation of family reunion met with some enthusiasm in the early years, but attitudes began to cool based on observations of their difficulties in family life.[29] Family reunion, practiced in the late 1970s or 1980s, coincided with the economic crisis, and many immigrant families moved into social housing projects at a time when these were deteriorating. The illegality of polygyny in France from 1993 further deterred family reunion ambitions for men involved in or planning such unions. Rather than a categorical refusal of changing gender roles, these stories are commentaries on the social and administrative complexities of having one's wife in France in a context of racial discrimination and limited options for upward social mobility.

## "*Mariage au pays*": A Challenged but Enduring Model

The first generations of migrants generally married back home, and many spent most of their adult life apart from their wives (figure 7.1). In approaching the endurance of this model, one needs to avoid two opposing normative pitfalls. First, it is important not to portray this long-distance conjugal lifestyle in a pitying perspective but to envision how it can be willingly adopted. Second, one must also pay attention to opposition to such a model, voiced by men who adhere to a globalizing companionate ideal of marriage.

Transnational couples living separately in France and West Africa are a common pattern; based on statistical data collected in the late 2000s, a study indicated that 60 percent of Senegalese migrants remained separate ten years after the initial geographical separation.[30] This study showed that men holding jobs in skilled occupations and with good financial situations were more likely to reunify in Europe. Factors negatively associated with reunification in Europe included origin from ethnic groups characterized by strong patrilineality (including Soninke) and variables such as "men whose father decided or paid for migration," which was taken as an indicator of "a strong vertical hierarchy in the family and subordination to the interests of the extended family." Although not a direct measure of the effect of life in a foyer on family reunion, this study enumerates social characteristics associated with lower odds of reunification in Europe that fully apply to migrants living in the foyer.

Marriage made sense as part of family dynamics and patterns of intergenerational reciprocity. Marrying back home reinserted the migrant into a position of deference toward his father and his paternal uncles who negotiated the marriage and ostensibly paid the bridewealth (even if the money was in fact sent by the migrant). It further ensured the availability of domestic work for his mother. By retaining a spouse, a family made sure a migrant maintained his role as a provider; as soon as he brought his wife to France, family obligations tended to weaken.

Marrying back home encompassed a wide range of configurations. A typical situation was when a newly legalized migrant sent word to his parents to find him a spouse, as Malick did. Such marriages tended to conform to marriage preferences among kin to an even greater degree proportionally than in the emigration society, a point also demonstrated in other migration contexts.[31] But, as Dramane's marriage in Dakar evidences, marrying "back home" could translate into supporting a wife separated from one's home by hundreds of kilometers and national borders, because the transnational space includes not only the home villages and towns but also the capital cities where many migrants invest in building houses.

My interlocutors often framed life plans and decisions, notably those concerning spousal reunion, as part of wider reflections, including their children's prospects. For instance, Harouna, a délégué in his fifties, proudly reported that one of his daughters was pursuing medical studies at the University of Dakar. In a way, his decision to maintain his family back home was akin to middle-class transnational Senegalese families sending their children home for schooling.[32]

However, this kind of marriage was also challenged by many of my interlocutors. The pitfalls of remote conjugality were all the more evident to men who had grown up with absent fathers. Having experienced marriage from afar, Dramane had developed critical thoughts on the matter:

> You can't get along with your wife when you're 6,000 km apart. She doesn't know what you're doing—and here, many men secretly mess around with girls in a way they shouldn't. Our wives are tired, they're unhappy. The way we live, do you think many people can still put up with that? Take my father: he lived that way until he retired. That's not a life. At the end of the day, we can't go on like that. In my son's time, "Your wife is there and you are here"—that won't exist anymore.[33]

Dramane expressed his ambition to share a steady conjugal life with his wife, a desire reinforced by his experiences with girlfriends in France. He also mentioned in this interview the importance of leading a fulfilling sexual life for him and for his wife.

Sexuality usually appeared in terms of calculations and anxieties surrounding reproduction. Several interlocutors timed their returns according to calculations of their wives' fertility, and other studies document the pressure on women to become pregnant during their husband's visits.[34] As summarized by Caroline Bledsoe and Papa Sow, "conducting a transnational existence means that a state to which a person does not belong can set the terms by which his or her reproductive life must transpire."[35] Finally, men also expressed concerns about women's faithfulness (along with a more pragmatic admission that a woman has sexual "needs"), framed in religious terms or otherwise. Stories of children born outside the time frame of a husband's visit are common, leading to divorces or to the social recognition of the child by the absent husband. One way out of this dilemma between undesirable remote marriage and risky family reunion was to marry in France, as Dramane did and as Souley considered.

## FOYERMEN AS BLÉDARDS: NAVIGATING RACIAL AND CLASS STIGMATIZATION

FSS [Frenchwomen of Soninke extraction] talk about "Foyerman" [in English in the text] to mock Soninke men who are uneducated and fundamentally blédards, whereas in fact in the foyer you find all types of people [head scratching emoticon].[36]

A prolific contributor to the Soninkara.com community website, Makalou, a migrant himself, framed the opposition between two groups of the same age—French second-generation Soninke migrants and newly arrived migrants—as gendered. In this section, I examine the wider racial and class assignations that weigh on the young men inhabiting the foyers.

## Multidimensional Assignations in France

*Blédard* is a depreciative term used to designate first-generation migrants. Derived from the Arabic word for "country," the phrase "*le bled*" was initially used by Algerians and their descendants to refer to their locality of origin, before becoming a common way for individuals of migrant background to refer to the birthplace of their parents—including children born of sub-Saharan African immigrants.[37] Among my interlocutors, some used it as a descriptive term; others, like Makalou, resorted to it in an ironic way; and others still highlighted the violence of the category, which they discovered after they arrived in France. Makan, a sociology student at the time we met, traced the origin of the term to a sketch one of his French cousins had shared on Facebook. Often used as an equivalent to blédard, the English-sounding "foyerman" was popularized in the 2000s through comedy shows circulating on social networks.[38] The word equated life in a foyer with a lifestyle: a dress code marked by cheap and ill-adjusted clothing; culinary habits imported from West Africa; low levels of education and French linguistic skills; and unskilled employment.

These stereotypes need to be recast in a multidimensional experience of stigma and the changing dynamics of racialization. The first generations of men in the foyers were racialized as blacks: the management of the foyers and their interactions at work relied on racist assumptions. Because Islam did not appear as a prominent characteristic of black migrants, Michèle Lamont suggests that for white working-class men "blacks [were] less salient than North Africans in French workers' definitions of 'us' and 'them.'"[39] Racial stigma coexisted with an interest toward them fueled by exoticism, as is evident from their stories about white French girlfriends. In the 1970s, some of them also took part in cultural and political movements building on references to Pan-Africanism and black internationalism. Their peers in the 2000s encountered a radically distinct context. Although demographic dynamics of West African migration offered young foyer inhabitants a new possibility of evolving within a diasporic space in France, it also inscribed them in more prescribed social spaces, generally subaltern ones. Finally, since the 1990s, the re-Islamization process of many West African communities made them easy targets of mounting Islamophobia. In the wake of the 2005 riots, media discourses further popularized an ethnicized reading of French immigrant groups whereby internal hierarchies were created among sub-Saharan migrants and their children. Populations with Soninke and Haalpulaar backgrounds were particularly targeted as symbolizing patrilineal, polygynous families incapable of raising their children properly.[40]

These assignations further brought to the fore internal lines of division within groups of African migrants sharing a common racial assignation. Processes of distinction, in Bourdieu's sense, were crucial among West African immigrants.[41] Ethnicized and often derogatory views of men living in foyers permeated the attitudes of other migrants from the same countries.[42] Finally, even within Pulaar-speaking and Soninke families and communities, the foyer occupied an ambiguous position. Men who had lived in the foyers but managed to leave it, as well as their wives, generally emphasized their ambition to move forward within French society. As Makalou's commentary evidences, stereotypes worked in pairs: the category blédard took its meaning from its opposition to the French children of migrants of the same origin—referred to as "those who are born here"—depicted at best as culturally uprooted, at worst as morally lost. At the same time, families outside the foyers maintained some ties with the foyer, and children were often part of family visits. Occasionally, some might be sent to the foyer for a form of cultural reeducation. In this tension between groups that were also construed as related, gender relations played a key role, notably practices of and debates over cross-marriage.

## The "Blédard Boom"

Do you know why Soninke parents here no longer want to give us their daughters [as brides]? It all began in 2000, when sans-papiers were marrying these girls just for the sake of papers; once they got legal status, they dumped them and went back to the *bled* to marry someone else. Parents here became cautious, and they no longer agreed to give away their daughters before you got documents. But now, when you get documents, they make offers of marriage. I myself had two or three proposals after [I got] my documents, and I said no; and then the girl remains unmarried.[43]

Marriage across borders within the same diasporic community is a regular pattern throughout Europe.[44] The prevalence of such unions, however, varies from one group and one national context to another. In France, African migrants from Sahelian countries were the second population group in which such unions were common, after migrants from Turkey. In the late 2000s, half of the French daughters of Sahelian immigrants were married to an immigrant from this region.[45] At the same time, 70 percent of Sahelian migrant men were married to an immigrant from the same region, 22 percent formed "mixed couples" with French women from the "majority" population, and only 5 percent married a French woman from a Sahelian background.[46]

In light of this statistical evidence, the apologue told by Dramane can be read as reflecting an existing configuration, with French Soninke or Haapulaar young women tending to marry their migrant counterparts. Even though in the static view of men's conjugal status provided by the statistics these marriages represented a small minority of their unions, this configuration increased as young women of the second generation entered the matrimonial field. Furthermore, as a new possibility and conjugal experience, it elicited much attention and commentary. Conversely, reasons for the prevalence of this form of union among French women from West African backgrounds range from the easiness with which such unions were accepted by their families to the will of these French women to conduct their own conjugal and family life as part of a religiously and culturally homogeneous couple—in a context in which migrants could be ascribed greater moral qualities than young men from the same background born in France.[47] Such unions appeared all the more comfortable because these women were looked down on as potential marriage partners in many families, including Muslim families from other ethnic backgrounds.[48]

Although seriously envisioned by some of my sans-papiers interlocutors, these unions were understood as an alliance between two individuals with distinct apprehensions of gender roles. They were further fraught with the suspicion that the man's only motivation was in gaining legal status. As "anisogamic relations," to quote from Ghassan Hage's exploration of transnational Lebanese couples, they required effort.[49] From their male perspective, my interlocutors placed the burden of this work on the woman, emphasizing that when a man gained regular status through marriage his wife should be tactful enough never to give any impression of taking advantage of this situation. The possibility of finding a balance in this asymmetric situation emerged from a few ethnographic cases. In contrast, Dramane dismissed this option, and the final reversal story, in which the once humiliated sans-papiers could in turn offer a swaggering refusal, restored a gendered social order conceived as immutable.

## "Mixed" Unions

When using the phrase "mixed marriage," my interlocutors generally designated marriages involving a white French (or European) woman. This acceptation excluded cases of marriages with other migrants from Africa or elsewhere, or with French women from the West Indies. In the following text, I focus on relations with white women inscribed for foyer men in a historical continuity.

> Those who came between 1970 and 1976, they had a lot of *metis* kids compared to our generation. Sometimes we debate this topic in the foyer . . . , let me take the example of my father: he told me that he used to leave the foyer on Friday night and be back on Monday. With his friends, they spent the weekend out dancing like that, and many married white women.[50]

During my fieldwork, I encountered very few instances of marriages with white French women, a situation that contrasted with the accounts of previous generations of migrants, where such unions figured prominently (see chapter 2), and which was corroborated by my interlocutors—such as Moussa, whom I quote here, himself married to a French woman of West African background. Quantitative studies suggest that foyer inhabitants had fewer chances to marry white French women than the general figure of 22 percent of Sahelian migrants in such unions.[51] The pattern of "mixed union" was more widespread among highly qualified immigrants and among those who arrived with a solid knowledge of the French language; these characteristics applied only to a minority among the foyer inhabitants (although it may apply, for instance, to the few students who live in foyers).[52]

At the same time, the topic of French girlfriends was widely discussed among my interlocutors, and several of them either had a white French partner or had had one at some point during their years in France. They engaged in relationships with women of various social backgrounds, and for many men this space constituted the occasions of their most socially diverse interactions, in stark contrast, for instance, to the more socially homogeneous sociability developed around work.

In addition to the demographic element of the advent of a diasporic conjugal space, the decline of mixed marriages can be explained by internal as well as external factors. My interlocutors often mentioned cultural gaps as obstacles to mixed unions, a stance also noted by other scholars.[53] Even I, a daughter of such a union, was not spared from negative comments on the durability and even the desirability of mixed marriages. The increased importance of religion among West Africans in France also accounts for the limited interest in such unions, not in terms of religious feasibility (a Muslim man can religiously marry a Christian or Jewish woman) but in terms of ideals of religious homogeneity within one's family.

However, these professed attitudes must be set against a wider context of racism and discrimination and of shrinking conjugal opportunities, which led them to favor unions with women of African backgrounds even beyond the culturally endogamous marriages described in the previous section.[54] For a white French woman in the 1960s and 1970s, having a black partner brought to the fore notions of racial and cultural alterity, but four decades later it also came with assumptions of subaltern status in French society. Reciprocal curiosity could render social and cultural distance attractive at the stage of nonformalized relationships but led less easily to unions. In addition, suspicion of marriages of convenience, or of an undocumented man's interest in marriage as a path to legalization, weighed heavily on such marriages.[55]

Marriage projects entailed temporal projections at distinct scales: when unlocking the possibility of regularization, it accelerated chances to regain one's ability to move across borders and improve one's situation; in the dominant heteronormative frame, forming a couple generally went together with expectations of having children, which introduced reflections on the future, with evaluations of the right place to raise them; ultimately, marriage choices came with expectations regarding one's old age. One argument against family reunion was that women were likely to refuse to move back to the country of emigration when their husbands reached retirement age because they themselves were generally much younger and still working at that time. Pursuing the analysis of how the foyers molded their inhabitants' lives, I now turn to this last phase of a migrant's existence, another key moment when the dilemma of transnational lives are acute.

## GROWING OLD IN A FOYER: SENIORITY, EXPECTATIONS OF RETURN, AND AGING BODIES

The figure of the old man in a foyer is problematic on several fronts. First, within the institutions in charge of the foyers, aging had been a concern since the early 1990s, and a series of reports examined this topic.[56] It has since fueled a steady flux of academic publications.[57] For a long time, this focus on aging developed along a racial divide, according to which aging was the main concern among North African migrants, whereas West Africans posed other problems, such as illegal arrivals and over-occupation. However, in gray literature as in scholarly work, aging has since emerged as an issue for migrants of all origins.[58]

Second, return (or failure to perform it) is a widespread concern within the foyer. At the beginning of my fieldwork, one of my interlocutors in Montreuil told me that I should address this question: "Why do old men stay in the foyer rather than retire?" Being in his thirties, he himself found this question highly worthy of investigation but could not ask the elders about it directly. The figure of the old man haunted younger residents as living proof that their own return plans might not materialize.[59] This highlights the fact that return is a politically, socially, and morally loaded expectation combined. Here I focus on men who expressed their will to return to their country, a common stance among my interlocutors. Nonetheless, I met a few men who did not adopt this position, even one old man who had never been back to Mali, the country he had migrated from, since his arrival in the 1960s. Existing studies demonstrate that return is a process full of pitfalls, notably because of the lifelong migrant's lack of familiarity with his family.[60] Still, many men approaching retirement age contemplated this prospect with excitement.

Although the pioneers of migration assumed that another family member would eventually take their place, today's retired men are both disadvantaged—because the prevailing harsh conditions make it difficult for younger individuals to take their turn—and privileged because most have acquired pension rights. In principle, pension rights were independent of one's place of residence. Legally, it was possible to receive one's pension in one's country of origin. However, many older foyer inhabitants had experienced disjointed careers and received not only pensions but also benefits that were generally tied to conditions of residence. Furthermore, health insurance (French: *sécurité sociale*) depended on where one lived. Finally, the tightening of migratory regulations also affected older migrants: notably the ten-year residence permit required that the holder not stay abroad more than three years.[61] And bureaucratic practices further impeded the mobility of older migrants: for example, the renewal of a residence permit could take several months, more than six in some cases that I followed. Therefore, older residents who came back for this purpose could end up getting stuck for half a year. Those who had managed to secure French nationality (a difficult achievement for foyer inhabitants) were an exception.

Health issues, and the rational choice of being cared for in France rather than in countries with less well-equipped health systems, also conditioned the timing and duration of sojourns in France, at times making it altogether impossible for the migrant to envision long-term stays in his home country. These considerations sometimes included the question of the right place to die. When a délégué of Foyer Lorraine died in Senegal, where he had rushed back to in the terminal phases of a long-term illness, I heard many young and old men praising him for his gesture. Considering that repatriating a body is expensive (a cost absorbed not by an individual's insurance but by a village-association fund), successfully getting back in time was deemed wise.[62]

In contrast to "definitive" return, "back and forth" configurations (French: *faire la navette*) seemed more acceptable in terms of administrative requirements. These arrangements were rendered complicated by foyer regulations, however, because no provision for such mobility was made. Men spending several months back home either kept their bed/studio under their name, thus barring other occupants from acquiring accommodation under their own names, or relied on substitution arrangements frowned upon by the managers.

Ultimately, the foyer served to frame the no-longer-working migrant as out of place. An understanding of migration as the exploitation of able bodies pervaded rumors around the mistreatment of retired migrants. A délégué in a foyer in Stains told me that old men feared injections because they had seen many die only two or three years after an injection.[63] As I pressed old Demba to visit a doctor upon his return to France after more than one year in Senegal, aware (from having accompanied him to the hospital) of the treatments he needed, he objected that the nurses had taken too much blood on his previous visit. Such distrust took on full meaning in light of low life expectancy among industrial and service workers; the difficulties in obtaining one's pension rights; and the wider suspicion toward the lasting presence of guest workers no longer being welcome in French society.[64]

## CONCLUSION: FOYERS AND THE MANAGEMENT OF UNCERTAINTY

Younger migrants with distinct historical experiences from their predecessors challenged the expected path for attaining seniority in the foyers. The balance that the "sacrificial trope" was premised upon—a relative acceptance of subaltern positions in terms of class and race in France, compensated by social success back home—often appeared as unbearable, with extended delays preceding regularization and uncertainties surrounding the rhythm of family visits, as well as an erosion of this model based on observed difficulties in both emigrant and immigrant locations. Companionate marriage tended to be the ideal, further undermining the figure of the foyerman as a success. The presence of older residents incapable of return inverted the value of the foyer from a place of fulfillment to a trap. Although stories of social success and conjugal happiness could be told about couples in France, no single clear-cut path stands out, as reflected in internal debates.

> DIADIÉ: It's the end of immigration. We need to find something else.
>
> BOUBA: At any rate, I'd like to see my children grow up.
>
> DIADIÉ: You won't see that, for those of us who are here, it's over! Even for you![65]

In this exchange between Bouba, previously introduced, who was thirty, and another délégué of Foyer Mûriers in his fifties, a now banal statement that immigration was coming to an end arose. Having already been shaken by the 2008 economic crisis, migratory projects will undoubtedly evolve in the postpandemic era of global uncertainty, in terms of both economic conditions and mobility. Not only did Diadié open up the possibility of a postmigration era, but he also abruptly denied Bouba the option of family reunion, despite this being all the more attainable as he had French citizenship. This tension between projections over a future in which migration would not be determined by the constraints of the foyers and an impossibility to escape this form at an individual level was often expressed. To reiterate Dramane's stance, he portrayed himself as caught between his father's existence—personifying the sacrificial trope—and his son's existence that he envisioned as being free of the foyer model. In between, like Bouba, he expressed a wish to be living with his wife.

Although the end of the foyers aligned with the personal wishes of some of the foyers' inhabitants, the way in which the renovation imposed such a timing was problematic for most of my interlocutors. The residents were not bound to the foyer because each of them would adhere to the fixed pathway that it implied. On the contrary, bifurcations were numerous. But the model of the foyer as refashioned by West African migrants had turned them into spaces of possibilities. The renovation was presented as a path toward normalization, but it did not provide the necessary openings in terms of carrying out family reunion in material and social conditions perceived to be safe. This deprived migrants, collectively and individually, of certain resources, such as the ability to design migration strategies at the level of the family and the flexibility to keep a room and return in case of setbacks.

# 8

## ERODED EMPLACEMENT

Urban Incorporation, Containment Policies,
and the Politics of Belonging

n February 2014, I met Dramane at the restaurant where he
worked as a kitchen porter. We got off the bus several stops
before reaching Foyer D'Hautpoul and began a 1 kilometer
walk along avenue Jean-Jaurès to the foyer. Halfway to our destination, we met another man from the foyer; shortly after that
we bumped into an acquaintance of Dramane's, a black woman
living nearby; arriving at a small square near the metro station
where old foyer men often sat on public benches, we began to
cross paths with many more inhabitants of the foyer, occasionally engaging in short conversations.

Places that accommodated around three hundred individuals created a flux of human traffic in the neighborhood, which
was particularly visible along the axis between the foyer and
its surrounding public transportation stops. As we move from
one foyer to another in the course of this chapter, the distinct
ambiance, changing from one city to another, from one neighborhood to another, is palpable. The uses of a neighborhood
varied greatly from one foyer resident to another according to
their age, occupation, and legal status. Even so, foyer dwellers' attachment to their neighborhood, apparent from previous

descriptions of the move, attests to their incorporation into their urban environment far from the imagined insulation of the foyer.[1]

Pursuing this line of thought, in this chapter I move from daily urban practices in the city to a broader reflection on the foyers and their contribution to Paris as a "global city."[2] Through these explorations of the urban dynamics from and around the foyers, I return to the notion of emplacement to discuss the ongoing yet limited value of the foyer/residence in terms of conferring the right to be in the city and the nation, with consideration to how the foyers were shaped by as much as they have transformed wider "politics of belonging."[3] This chapter navigates across distinct scales—neighborhood, municipality, city, and nation—without ever positing that these scales interlock coherently and contributing to "a multiscalar analysis that situates urban actors within various networks of power."[4]

## BEING EMPLACED IN CHANGING NEIGHBORHOODS

The foyer case enriches our understanding of the "varied roles that transmigrants have been playing in relationship to the neoliberal restructuring and rescaling of localities."[5] Paris was notably different from North American cities in the relative dispersion of migrants across its territory, as evidenced by Caroline Brettell's study of Portuguese populations in the capital in the 1970s.[6] Since then, as in many of the world's metropolises, poor and often racialized minorities have progressively left the rehabilitated urban center.[7] In the 2000s and 2010s, as income inequalities continued to increase, public policies tended to reinforce the dynamics of gentrification.[8]

Against this general pattern, the endurance of foyers or of the residences stemming from older foyers is remarkable. They are still scattered within Paris according to the same 1970s and 1980s geography of the city, in which the northern, eastern, and part of the southern peripheries of the metropolis were working-class areas. Their sites do not overlap with the localization of the few areas identified as "black African"—there are no foyers in Château-d'Eau, nor in Château-Rouge, two African hubs in terms of commercial, cultural, and religious activities. A striking outcome of the renovation scheme was the stability across time of the foyers/residences on their initial building sites. In Paris, of the forty-nine foyers involved in the renovation plan, forty-one dated from before 1985.[9] Rebuilt on the same spot, each residence represented a degree of stability in the city for a significant part of the population of immigrant background (figure 8.1).

This was the result of several constraints. The lack of empty land in Paris made it difficult to find other sites, and it was easier for the authorities to deal with neighbors already accustomed to the presence of a foyer than to negotiate the introduction of a foyer in a new block. Furthermore, as the districts comprising foyers were often in the process of gentrifying, the municipality could congratulate themselves on preserving the "social mix."[10] Far from merely symbolic, this translated into actual political gain, allowing the municipality to attain quantitative goals in terms of percentage of social housing.[11]

A broader look at other municipalities in the Paris region indicates that foyer relocation did occasionally occur, with new residences being erected on different sites in the same commune, but the general pattern was to rebuild the residence on the site of the old foyer. This produced highly diverse situations. From the 1960s to the 1980s, foyers were erected in sites that could often be characterized as interstitial. But precisely because of

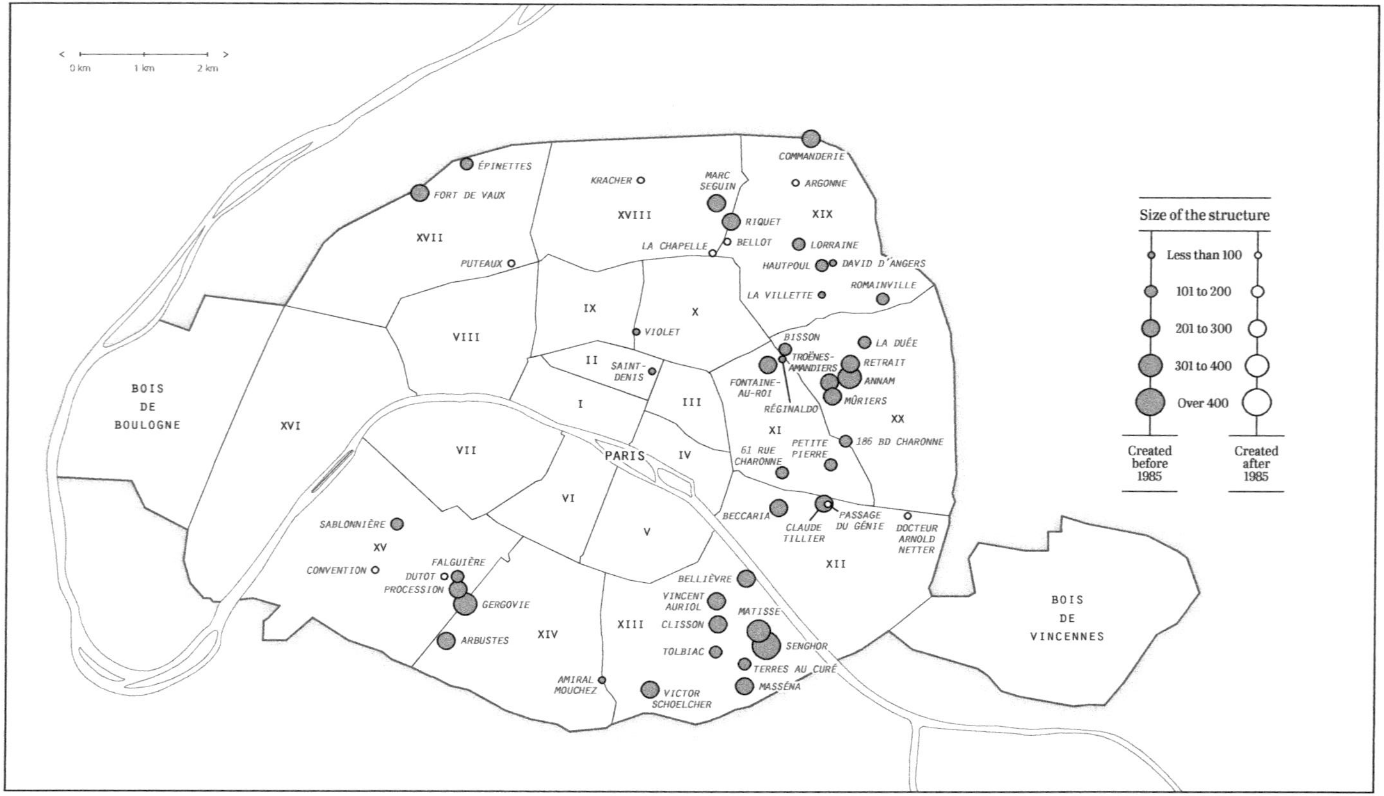

**FIGURE 8.1** The long-term stability of foyer/residences locations (1970 to 2010).

*Source:* Atelier Parisien d'Urbanisme, *Les foyers de travailleurs migrants à Paris. État des lieux en 2010 et inventaires des interventions sanitaires et culturelles*, 2011.

this negative characterization, the evolution of these spaces has been uneven. In some places, the initial location of the foyer in a peripheral area still roughly corresponded to the characterization of the site; for instance, in the northern city of Le Blanc-Mesnil, the only foyer in the locality was still situated in one of the cheapest areas of the municipal territory at the time of the renovation and perpetuating the foyer on the same building site was not an issue. However, municipalities bordering Paris such as Montreuil, Saint-Ouen, and Boulogne-Billancourt were undergoing much more drastic changes when the foyer renovation was discussed.

Boulogne-Billancourt, west of Paris, is the region's second-largest city after Paris. It offered the most dramatic example of foyers remaining in neighborhoods that in a few decades have gone from working-class to upper-class status. The car firm Renault, established in 1898, opened its first factory in 1929 and occupied a vast area along the River Seine and on Seguin Island. In the 1960s, the company prospered and preserved its industrial sites in the southern part of the city in Billancourt, but the rest of Boulogne followed a distinct path of deindustrialization, attracting more upper-class households because of its proximity to the bourgeois arrondissements of Paris.[12] Since the 1950s, Renault had relied heavily on postcolonial workers, mostly Algerians, but in the 1970s, Senegalese were recruited in numbers.[13] At that time, two foyers were opened in the vicinity of the Billancourt factory: a facility constructed on rue Nationale in 1974 and a former hotel turned foyer on Quai de Stalingrad in 1977, Assane's foyer (see chapter 4). These foyers mainly hosted Senegalese and Moroccans in a working-class area.[14] As industrial activity came to an end in 1992 with the closure of the Billancourt firm, the more stable workers benefited from redeployment schemes; at the time I was doing fieldwork in the foyer in the late 2010s, a few still worked for Renault at its other installation in Flins, thirty-six kilometers further west.

As the departure of Renault and other industrial firms freed up vast amounts of space, the area around the foyers (known as the Trapèze) became the site of construction programs mixing offices and upscale apartment buildings.[15] My fieldwork took place just as Foyer Nationale was becoming surrounded by brand new buildings, and apartments were selling at prices comparable to those of Inner Paris (figure 8.2). I also witnessed the shrinking of collective spaces within the foyer. The collective kitchen had been closed down by the police (an event to which I return later), but there was still a wide room on the ground floor with a cafeteria where I could sip green tea before a meeting or a visit,

FIGURE 8.2 Foyer Nationale, in the back, surrounded by new constructions, Boulogne-Billancourt, 2020.

Source: Photo by author.

chatting about Senegalese politics with the friendly manager. In the following months this cafeteria was also closed, in a neighborhood where residents lamented the loss of spaces for sociability around the foyer, such as affordable cafés.

In contrast to a foyer becoming out of place as a result of sudden changes in its environment, going from abandoned to hip, the case of the nineteenth arrondissement evidenced a more complex urban evolution, which still allowed emplacement dynamics to take place. Foyer Lorraine residents experienced a shock similar to that of the Boulogne-Billancourt foyers' residents when they spent two years living in a chic part of the seventeenth arrondissement in their provisional housing site. Souley commented: "[in contrast to the seventeenth], Foyer Lorraine is well located" [*bien placé*]. I asked what he meant by this, and he mentioned the shops, the cafés, as well as the proximity of the canal where younger foyer inhabitants had their spot called *Maayel* (Pulaar: *the little river*).

In Paris, although inequalities have increased with rich ghettos, on one hand, and pockets of poverty, on the other, a large proportion of intermediate neighborhoods composed of a range of social categories still prevailed.[16] This categorization applied to the area of the nineteenth arrondissement where Foyer Lorraine and Foyer D'Hautpoul were located, and it allowed the residents of these two foyers to still feel at home even as they observed the transformation of their environment. This was due to the characteristics of the foyers' immediate surroundings, as well as to their location within reach of other significant places. The location of the nineteenth arrondissement within the wider northeast of Paris notably meant that the residents were only a two-station metro ride from African commodities in Stalingrad and close to the temporary work agencies of Gare du Nord and Gare de l'Est. These elements contributed to the perpetuation of the dynamics of emplacement that were limited in Boulogne-Billancourt.

Even though they remained on the same urban site, the residences were very differently integrated into the urban fabric than the old foyers. A common feature of the new residences was their inward-looking character, as the appearance of the building that replaced Foyer Lorraine evidenced.[17] Although the lamps and flowers whose images had traveled back to the home villages of the residents had long disappeared, Foyer Lorraine in the early 2010s was open onto the eponym street. Behind the trees, passers-by could get a glimpse of groups of residents having a chat in the alley or sitting on benches in the entrance. The whole space could also receive larger crowds when a giant screen occupied the façade during the foyers' film festival. The renovated residence, in contrast, enclosed the small space devoted to social life by adding a smaller building along the street. This architectural choice shielded the residence from the public space (figure 8.3). Such practices of enclosure were tied to the aim of controlling the fluxes of visitors, which were often due to the foyers' roles as Islamic centers (see chapter 5).

## UNACKNOWLEDGED ISLAMIC CENTERS: CIRCULATION, CONTAINMENT, AND SURVEILLANCE

Scholarship on global cities has reassessed the constitutive dimension of religion in shaping urban realities, and the transnational approach has been fruitfully adopted by scholars of religions.[18] In Europe, the way in which African Pentecostalists engage in place-making processes is the topic of fine-grained studies.[19] Dynamics of Islamic practices are shaped by a different

**FIGURE 8.3** Street view of Résidence Lorraine, 2017.

*Source:* Photo by author.

context of growing anxieties toward migrants of Islamic back-ground, notably in France.[20] Studies of Muslim uses of urban space in French cities detail the contentious dynamics surrounding the construction of mosques and analyze how "street prayers" were construed as public problems in the early 2010s.[21] The foyers were sites where these two issues—dedicated places of worship and the extension of collective prayers into the public space—were raised and discussed in the 2000s and 2010s.[22]

In terms of urban incorporation, a foyer offering a prayer room open to outsiders (and sometimes other religious activities, such as Quranic lessons) invited streams of traffic from around the whole neighborhood. An order to close the prayer room at Foyer Riquet (nineteenth arrondissement) in January 2017 was issued on the basis of a bailiff's report counting more than one thousand people joining in the Friday prayer service.[23] At Foyer Lorraine, I observed intensified back and forth during prayer hours. On these occasions, I regularly bumped into the father of a girl who was at the same school as my daughters, a Senegalese man who often attended the prayer service there. I also got to know through personal acquaintances a Malian woman in her sixties who told me how she attended every Friday service in the room set aside for female attendees. Mixed crowds of West African residents, as well as their peers living outside the foyers, together with French of West African but also Maghrebi or Comorian origin, gathered for these occasions. Previously mentioned lines of divisions across Muslim communities of West African origin, and between these groups and Muslims of other origins, regularly surfaced. A key point was the language of the sermon; Imam Fofana at Foyer Gergovie (fourteenth arrondissement) emphasized that he was cautious to translate his sermon from Soninke to French and even Pulaar, but in other places I heard non-Soninke worshipers complain that they were not offered a multilingual service.

Beyond these fluxes toward the foyers, collective religious practices created complex traffic within their walls. Not all residents joined in collective prayers, and the possibility to go and pray in the collective room or to stay in one's room contributed to the many options that rendered these spaces livable for their inhabitants. It also created occasional encounters within the foyer because the prayer rooms acted as places of internal sociability. Several of my interlocutors indicated that not seeing an older resident at prayer time meant that they had to check on him.

These dynamics testify to forms of social mix and intergenerational encounters, with young French men of West African origin notably coming to pray in the foyer. However, the institutions disqualified these religious practices as out-of-place and offered two types of responses. An emphasis on "dignity," part of the renovation project, led to an insistence on the fact that foyer prayer rooms did not provide acceptable conditions of worship. This went along with conflation of the concrete site often occupied (the basements) with the notion of underground status, resulting in the widespread condemnation of "basement Islam" (French: *l'islam des caves*). Hence, "doing away with the more obscure prayer spaces" appeared to be a means to "combat Islamic extremism."[24] In some instances, the institutions allied with foyers' imams. These men assumed the roles of "honorable" Muslim leaders promoting a form of Islam "compatible with French secularism," in a kind of public management of Islam that characterizes many local level interactions with religious representatives.[25]

The second type of response was driven by concerns over security—the semantics of security encompassing a wide range of issues, from individual security to public order. Nonetheless, the precarious conditions of worship were not enough to prompt public action. It was the visibility of such conditions, notably the "outpouring" of worshipers outside of dedicated sites, that led to the building of a mosque (figure 8.4). In the nineteenth arrondissement, the number of worshipers attending Foyer Lorraine Friday prayer service attracted the attention of the authorities when the space outside the foyer began to be used and some neighbors called for action .[26]

In many cases, the closure of a prayer room did not coincide with the opening of a dedicated worship site. Although the number of sites dedicated to Islamic worship increased between

**FIGURE 8.4** Collective prayer in front of Foyer Riquet, 2017.

*Source*: Photo by Hugo Aymar.

1999 and 2012 (from 1,500 to over 2,000 nationwide), Muslims still remain less equipped in terms of religious spaces than other congregations such as Catholics.[27] When the renovations began, almost all West African foyers offered a prayer room. The combined effects of the renovation process and the administrative closures of foyer prayer rooms led to a slow decrease in such spaces in the 2000s and 2010s.[28]

It was in this context that the Paris terror attacks of January 7–9, 2015, occurred, targeting the magazine *Charlie Hebdo*, police officers, and a kosher supermarket.[29] Killing seventeen, it was the worst attack on French soil in more than fifty years. In the aftermath, authorities declared a "state of emergency" that lasted almost two years. In the days following the attacks, TV sets in the foyers' rooms were tuned to French news rather than African channels, and my interlocutors commented on the ongoing events. Besides the shock of such violent events taking place in familiar and nearby locations, many expressed their anticipation of growing suspicion toward all Muslims in France in the wake of the attacks. With one of the perpetrators (Amedy Coulibaly, the assailant on the Kosher supermarket) being of Soninke origin, some comments took an introspective turn—often to fuel the usual criticism on family life in France. At Dramane's, a lively discussion developed, and one of his relatives in his forties reflected on Coulibaly's trajectory, bitterly concluding that "you cannot raise a child properly here."[30]

The events also resonated with the fate of prayer rooms. In an informal discussion in May 2015, Idy, cynical as ever, observed, "They want to destroy our mosques [speaking about the foyer prayer rooms] because they think that those who come and pray are terrorists." Among my interlocutors, others voiced a fear that would-be terrorists might be present at the prayer services in the foyers. As the Kouachi brothers, the perpetrators of the *Charlie Hebdo* killings, had lived in the part of the nineteenth arrondissement where Foyer D'Hautpoul and Foyer Lorraine were located, Yero expressed the need to control who was coming to the foyer prayer service: "Folks need to understand that the country is not what it used to be," he said. Thus the events encouraged residents, délégués, and imams to reinforce their own surveillance practices.[31] This internal policing was, however, disputed. Hence, at an internal meeting immediately after the Foyer Riquet prayer room had been shut down, a man argued the impossibility, in terms of religious legality, of banning another Muslim from attending a prayer service, an argument I have heard on other occasions. However, a respected délégué of a nearby foyer stated that such a religious requirement did not apply to the foyer prayer rooms because the residents did not own these places, and in any event they were not "proper mosques."

## TARGETS FOR INTERVENTION, SITES OF MOBILIZATION

The issue of Islamic practices brings to the fore the dimension of control in the management of foyer populations, and beyond to segments of West African communities tied to the foyer. The material fact of the concentration of migrants in the same location, together with the existence of managing structures with employees who interacted on a daily basis with the inhabitants, made the foyers ideal sites for intervention. They were targets for administrative surveillance and occasional police operations. Such interventions punctuated the history of the foyers; notably from the mid-1970s, when launching police searches for undocumented migrants became a way of managing these places (see chapter 3). As Marc Bernardot observed in reference to police roundups conducted in two foyers located in Paris and Montreuil in 2008 that resulted in over one hundred sans-papiers being detained, such operations endured if not intensified in the 2000s.[32]

Two dramatic events at Foyer Nationale in Boulogne-Billancourt illustrate the availability of the foyer as a site of intervention, and the intertwined processes of the renovation and policing. On May 23, 2016, an antifraud operation took place in the foyer: early that morning a team of officers arrived, unannounced and accompanied by police officers, tasked with verifying compliance with labor laws, among other social frauds. After inspecting the collective kitchen, they decided to shut it down that same day on suspicion of illegal labor and on the grounds that health and safety measures were not being respected. They brought the cooks to the police station and charged them with working illegally. Turning to the residents, the officers carried out several checks, targeting retired migrants suspected of not adhering to certain residence requirements.

Joint antifraud operations such as that one were part of a nationwide antifraud scheme.[33] These practices endured even after a national antidiscrimination agency declared such actions discriminatory because the focus on the foyers amounted to targeting foreigners.[34] They epitomized a wider trend to inscribe in French law and administrative practices a coercive version of the welfare state. As elsewhere in Europe, campaigns against "benefit fraud" stigmatized immigrants who were portrayed as profiteers and were made responsible for the shortcomings of the welfare system.[35]

Foyer inhabitants experienced this event as particularly violent. Beyond the commotion caused by the raid, the fact that the officers destroyed the kitchen's 700 kilogram stock of meat by pouring detergent on it, shocked several of my interlocutors. More generally, the kitchen's informal status, with cooks working without formal contracts, was a well-known fact. One délégué presented me with press clippings showing that municipal officers had attended the opening of the kitchen in the 1990s.

Boulogne-Billancourt's right-wing mayor, Pierre-Christophe Baguet, publicly took credit for the operation, which he stated had been "long requested by [himself], and then prepared in secret by judicial and police authorities."[36] His handling of the foyer situation elicited criticism from all sides. One of his local political opponents, another right-wing leader, Pierre-Mathieu Duhamel, emphasized the disappointment of the new neighbors at the way in which the foyers' inhabitants "took possession of their surroundings." Sliding into in a well-used register, he went on to state that "locals feel that they live in a neighborhood that is exempt from common rules, where street businesses develop recklessly, from selling grilled corn to repairing cars." In contrast, local socialists observed that "new structures have been let to surround the dilapidated foyer" and demanded that "it be reconstructed on the same spot, so as to house those who have done so much and continue to work for the prosperity or our city."[37]

In the wake of the closure of the collective kitchen, foyer residents engaged in a rent strike, reactivating an old mode of political action. Some of the délégués had already been part of a protest twenty years earlier, in 1995–96, when they had conducted a sustained rent strike to oppose one of the earliest attempts at foyer renovation. The managing structure (then AFTAM) had planned to carry out minimal renovation work, consisting mainly in introducing sanitary blocks to already small rooms, so as to transform the foyer into a residence without engaging in heavy renovation work. Besides the rent strike, residents, supported by the Confédération Nationale des Locataires, had successfully engaged in legal action. They had also resorted to older forms of their repertoire of action by occupying the foyer director's office for several hours and preventing him from leaving. Ultimately, the project was abandoned.[38]

The 2016 strike appeared to be well followed, at a time when other foyers' délégués were having trouble uniting their residents in collective action. Several factors can account for the relative strength of the Boulogne-Billancourt foyers. First, among their team of délégués, several had been trained as worker delegates at Renault or other firms. Furthermore, the two foyers of Stalingrad and Nationale were still operating with a shared team of délégués. Finally, the strength of transnational ties with Senegal materialized in strong support from the Senegalese authorities, these foyers constituting important meeting places during electoral campaigns.[39] After the residents went on strike, the Senegalese consul visited the residents, followed in September by the former Minister of Foreign Affairs, Cheikh Tidiane Gadio. In addition to these personalities, ties to the wider socially diverse

Senegalese community also resulted in support from intellectuals involved in the foyers' affairs as well as in the hometown-based associations active in these foyers.

In December 2016, while the rent strike was going on and negotiations were stagnating, a criminal fire occurred, resulting in one dead and fourteen wounded. The fire started in the entrance hall during the night, and several inhabitants of the building block located along the street panicked and jumped out from several floors up. A fire in a foyer is far from anecdotal. Among those taking the floor during a large support meeting two days after the incident, one former foyer resident indicated that he had previously lived at Foyer Sedaine (eleventh arrondissement) when an act of arson had caused three deaths in 1977—an event whose memory remained vivid for many foyer residents. More generally, deadly fires in foyers, as well as in other precarious lodgings such as hotels, have been recurrent.[40]

As the police promptly discovered material evidence of the fire's criminal nature (in the form of traces of fire accelerant), the first press release on the event pointed to internal tensions in the foyer, quoting a source at the Ministry of Interior who dismissed the possibility of a racist act; the accusation that the perpetrator was among the residents was, however, soon dropped.[41] Meanwhile, the mayor's first response was to demand the foyer's closure.[42] Disaster as a mode of managing the foyer was again part of the history of these places.

Already mobilized in the context of the rent strike, the well-connected délégués rallied widely, within the network of activists focused on the foyers (COPAF and long-term local allies of the foyer) and far beyond to human rights, antiracism organizations, as well as left-wing parties. On January 10, 2017, around five hundred people demonstrated in Boulogne-Billancourt, heading toward City Hall and asking that the municipality act as a mediator in the tense relationship with the managing structure. As the early winter night settled in, we walked through the streets chanting "Free the foyer," along with other more obscure slogans such as "Free *mafé*." Drummers led the convoy, and a few men danced. The demonstration elicited the support not only of many activists but of some neighbors too. Although a formal request for a meeting had previously been addressed to the mayor, no one from the City Council came out to receive the residents on this occasion. Bakary Cissokho, one of the délégués, commented bitterly: "As citizens of Boulogne, we should be received by the mayor."

Recent work on urban citizenship emphasizes that the "claim to have rights is associated with membership in a city rather than a nation."[43] The characterization of the city as the space reclaimed by the migrant is adequate for both past and present-day situations. Indeed, as most of the foyer residents are African nationals and not French citizens, the emphasis on belonging to the city has been a way to assert the rights that mere presence confers, without entering the disputed field of national citizenship. In contrast, more radical claims made by sans-papiers elicited troubled reactions from the foyer communities.

## SANS-PAPIERS AND THE FOYERS' RESIDENTS: DISTINCTION AND SUPPORT

The relationship between sans-papiers and délégués intersected with intergenerational tensions. The attitudes of the délégués combined support—in terms of their own hosting practices and understanding of undocumented status as a shared step in a migrant trajectory—with an expectation of deference: sans-papiers claims should be channeled through them, the only legitimate authorities in the foyers. Toward outsiders, in public discourses, their support for sans-papiers was often mitigated by their own concerns with respectability: they emphasized their own legal status as documented foreigners, workers, and taxpayers. Their suspicions that organized groups of sans-papiers could bring trouble to the foyer materialized in two aspects. First, the fate of sans-papiers in the renovation process was generally not openly dealt with (see chapter 6): the residents fought for their own ability to host whomever they wanted but rarely took the occasion of the renovation as a chance to push for the legalization of their fellow inhabitants. Second, the possibility for the sans-papiers collectives to hold their meetings within the walls of the foyer was often contested. In this respect, investigating the counterexample of Foyer Saint-Just (seventeenth arrondissement) makes it possible to fully understand the conditions in which the logic of support could prevail over that of distinction.

At Foyer Saint-Just, strong ties were maintained between the Collectif des sans-papiers du 17e and the foyer, as I witnessed during the years 2014 to 2017. Although not unique (Boulogne-Billancourt was another case where the sans-papiers group worked together with the team of foyer representatives), this was among the few cases where such a relationship existed. Conducting some of its meetings in the large foyer meeting rooms, the Collectif was also influential in turning Foyer Saint-Just into a key site for cultural and political events. A film festival in the foyers, created by the Attention Chantier association, was launched at Foyer Saint-Just in 2009 with the support of the Collectif. Likewise, when collective action was initiated to provide legal advice to sans-papiers regarding their tax declarations, Foyer Saint-Just was among the few sites in Paris where day-long sessions were held, again with the help of the Collectif. When I volunteered in May 2016 to participate in one such session, we installed improvised desks in the foyer's hall, and residents from the foyers and other places arrived throughout the day, transforming the hall into a lively space.

The story of the sans-papiers mobilization, as recounted by Soumana, a cofounder of the collective, provides an apt lens through which to examine the series of social, political, and organizational conditions that made such a convergence possible. In 2008, a mobilization of sans-papiers took place in Les Mureaux, a city northwest of Paris, as part of a larger wave of strikes and workplace occupations by sans-papiers asking for regularization on the basis of their status as workers.[44] At some point, the mayor of the city indicated that only sans-papiers living in Les Mureaux would be considered in the regularization process. Among this group, a number lived in Parisian foyers, and at least one in Foyer Saint-Just. That night, back in the foyer, that man took the floor in the prayer room after the evening service, inviting interested people to gather in the foyer. Later that night, Soumana got news of this declaration in the prayer room, and he joined the meeting. As he had been active in Islamic organizations in Bamako before migrating at the age of forty, the others acknowledged his organizational skills as well as his linguistic skills in Soninke and Bamanan, thus complementing the initial group of mainly Senegalese Pulaar-speaking men. Soumana proposed a structure of mobilization: each of the foyer's six floors would designate one representative, who would deal with the situation of sans-papiers on his respective floor, before consolidating with the group. From the outset, Soumana also sought to mobilize people he had met outside the foyers: migrants of diverse origins and levels of education, including women.

Another key feature of the Collectif was the ability of founding members to connect with other organizations. During a demonstration, they met railway trade unionists who provided much needed help, notably the provision of an office in their premises located next to the foyer; and they also connected to Réseau éducation sans frontières, a network initially devoted to supporting pupils with undocumented family members. After a couple of years of mobilization together—though not to be conflated—with the more important Collectif des sans-papiers 75 (which encompassed the whole of Paris), the Collectif had the opportunity to participate in meetings at the prefecture where they presented their members' applications.[45] Eventually, Soumana acquired his documents and retired from the Collectif, only to enter the foyers' representative committee as a délégué, an indication of the legitimacy that the sans-papiers' mobilization had in this foyer and of the enduring ties between the two committees.

In this case, the Collectif succeeded in bringing home a mobilization of sans-papiers by combining key associative resources with a local insertion within the foyer, which relied on a detailed understanding of the functioning of the foyer; on the social skills of its leaders able to provide elders with guarantees that the sans-papiers' activities would not disturb the workings of the foyers; but also on the use of the prayer room as a daily space from which to spread political messages; and finally on the existence of vast meeting rooms.

Beyond sans-papiers, the dynamics of (limited) solidarity, distinction, and occasional competition played out throughout the 2010s with other groups of African migrants. To begin with, as of 2012, Malians fleeing the war in Libya began to arrive in Paris, generally after transiting through Italian camps.[46] Probably due to the fame of Foyer Bara in Montreuil as a Malian centrality, many of those who arrived sought refuge in this foyer. This occurred at a moment when the renovation process of this foyer had slowly begun. Also highly symbolic for local and national authorities, Foyer Bara, with its 410 beds in dormitories of four to eight bunk beds, was one of the oldest foyers still standing, a dormitory opened in 1968 in an industrial building.[47] The newly arrived migrants were able to use some of the foyer's facilities, buying a meal in the canteen or having an occasional shower, but they were not, as a group, hosted there. This should not come as a surprise given their heterogeneity in terms of the region they originated from within Mali and in the absence of the family ties that generally supported hosting practices. Notwithstanding individual acts of solidarity, the public stance of several Malian associations distancing themselves from their fate in an open letter in March 2013 made such tensions palpable.[48] The migrants outside the foyer, who camped for months, moving from one location to another, still took the name of the street and the foyer and became known as "Les Baras."

In 2015, the foyer residents witnessed the arrival of more than twenty thousand migrants in Paris.[49] As any other Parisians, foyer residents were confronted with the visibility of camps, notably in the east and north of Paris. In a few instances, and because the main managing structures of the foyers such as Coallia and Adoma were also in charge of lodging refugees and asylum seekers, migrants with other administrative statuses and geographical origins were housed in foyers. At Foyer Victor Hugo in Clichy, one of my interlocutors explained how they had cohabited with Sudanese migrants. He did not emphasize tensions and merely told anecdotes of mutual incomprehension together with stories of shared meals, but the situation was nonetheless complicated. Rooms had been vacated in this foyer on the grounds of over-occupation, and these rooms had been closed, even though some long-time foyer inhabitants had made demands, because of an impending renovation process; then all of a sudden Adoma reopened these same rooms to offer accommodation to asylum seekers as part of an emergency scheme.

I did not meet the East African migrants, who had left the foyer by the time this conversation took place, but I can imagine their disappointment at being lodged in a poorly maintained building awaiting renovation.[50] Beyond such limited cases of cohabitation, the arrival of new migrants, in a context in which media coverage and political discourses tended to focus on the economic and social burden they represented, elicited anxious reactions among my interlocutors.

Most the activists supporting the foyers were still sympathetic to a wider "migrant cause." During a meeting at Foyer Claude Tillier, I met one activist from La Chapelle debout!, a group recently constituted by and in support of migrants who had been camping in Paris since the summer of 2015. As this young white man took the floor to indicate that they supported the foyer residents, attendants politely listened and thanked him. In the following years, this *"jonction"*—to borrow from activist semantics—materialized in occasional joint actions. In 2018, a group called the "Gilets Noirs" emerged, claiming to be based within the foyers, and launched several coordinated actions borrowing from the long-term repertoire of sans-papiers political actions, such as the occupation of symbolic places.[51] How far such a group can revitalize the political struggles of the sans-papiers and infuse into the political life of the foyers is an empirical question I cannot answer, but their endurance will depend on their ability to grapple with the complex social and material dynamics exposed in this chapter.

## COVID: ABANDONMENT AND CONTAINMENT

In France, as in many countries, studies have demonstrated that migrants as well as racial minorities have been harder hit by the pandemic.[52] Explanations for such a situation combine their overexposure to the virus (as workers who could not work from home), their housing and living conditions, the higher prevalence of preexisting conditions, and degraded access to health care. Foyer residents combined several of these characteristics, notably their precarious access to health care.[53] In the media report, dramatic accounts sometimes only rendered visible already precarious situations, such as the fact that the provisional housing for residents of an Adoma-run foyer in Marseille consisted of shipping containers.[54] Others chose an alarming register, such as several media reports calling one improvised foyer in Montreuil a "sanitary time bomb."[55]

The pandemic is still ongoing as I write these lines, so the following remarks are provisional. First, no evidence of a higher death toll in the foyers has been gathered, although in April 2020 some délégués expressed alarm at the deaths of aging residents.[56] Likewise, startling figures on the rate of exposure to the virus circulated, but they did not seem representative of the situation in the foyers.[57] On the basis of phone exchanges with my long-term interlocutors throughout 2020, and of visits I was able to conduct between the several lockdowns, I interpret the unfinished moment of the crisis as offering a prism exemplifying and amplifying the dynamics already at work in the foyers; and as opening an era in which new questions emerge whose potential developments are still unpredictable.

The pandemic context confirmed key aspects of the foyers' governance, notably the (micro-)technologies of control of space as enforced by the managing structures and disputed by the inhabitants.[58] The context of emergency, associated with a nationally imposed quarantine and a semantics of "war" in statements by President Emmanuel Macron, made firm governance of the foyers by the managing structures, as well as their status as sites of targeted interventions by public authorities, particularly salient. However, authoritarian measures were sometimes contested, and the délégués appeared, notably in Paris, as key interlocutors, whose authority the pandemic may well have reasserted, at least toward external interlocutors.

Among the first measures taken by management structures was the closing of collective spaces within foyers and residences. In some instances, délégués anticipated such measures: closing the collective rooms themselves was also a means of ensuring that they could keep the keys, otherwise the employees of the managing structure could put a new lock on the doors. In parallel, public health authorities attempted to monitor the situation in the foyers as sites where the development of infectious clusters seemed inevitable.[59] In Montreuil, where long-term foyer support networks were well established, general practitioners were among the first to visit the foyers and alert the authorities.[60] In line with the status of the foyer as sites of intervention, and echoing earlier hygienist concerns for such places, the Regional Health Agency (Agence Régionale de Santé [ARS]) launched a testing campaign in the foyers in early April 2020. Several attempts to organize such tests within African foyers provoked outright opposition. According to accounts collected by COPAF, at Foyer Commanderie (nineteenth arrondissement) on April 8, 2020, and Foyer Marc Séguin (eighteenth arrondissement) on April 27, 2020, medical teams entered the foyer, accompanied by an officer from the managing structure, knocking on room doors in search of aging residents. These methods were deemed intrusive by délégués. Furthermore, in some instances, an individual volunteering for a test had to provide his room number in addition to other identification tokens. This elicited a widespread fear that data collected during the testing campaign would serve to measure over-occupation and expel unofficial inhabitants.

In a series of online meetings with top-ranking Paris municipality officers, délégués and COPAF voiced their concerns and
secured oral guarantees that the tests would not result in a transfer of information to the managers, and that délégués would be
involved at all stages. From this point on, the medical teams only
required a phone number in addition to the person's name and
his social security number, if any. This process was the occasion
to reestablish the délégués as key actors able to restore trust in a
volatile situation where rumors spread widely, as I noticed from
messages sent via social networks about these testing operations.
Although contentious moments seemed to pitch the institutions
managing the foyer against unified collectives of residents, my
study has amply demonstrated the ambiguous relationship of
institutions toward the foyers/residences as unruly but practical
places of interventions where the presence of délégués guarantees a form of internal governance.

In addition to the health situation, the lockdown phases
induced by the pandemic had severe consequences in the foyers.[61] This was the first time I had heard of foyer inhabitants
eager to receive food aid packages. Among them, many worked
in restaurants, facilities that were closed for a large part of 2020;
those who worked legally benefited from state subsidies and were
paid 84 percent of their salary (the loss of wages being severe for
minimal earners); undocumented individuals simply often lost
all avenues of income. In addition, restrictions on daily mobility,
requiring self-certification, made the sans-papiers' movements
in the city even riskier because certification checks amounted to
presenting an ID and could thus result in deportation.[62] When
I questioned Souley in June on his experience during the first
lockdown, he philosophized that being under "house arrest" had
been his ordinary experience since setting foot in France in 2013,
as an undocumented migrant. The way in which the present-day

crisis, deemed unprecedented by many of us, was lived by men whose intimate knowledge of uncertainty and constraint is far deeper than is usual remains to be explored.[63]

## CONCLUSION: THE POLITICAL DIMENSION OF EMPLACEMENT

Rather than outward relegation, the foyers reflect the fact that some level of concentration of migrants appeared useful to the authorities, notably, but not only, at the municipal level: the foyer system allows for knowing where to find migrants in times of crisis and for having identifiable interlocutors. In this light, the renovation is a specific form of intervention on the foyers that sustains this logic of targeting a population, containing it, but also maintaining possibilities of public action toward it. But a side effect of the maintenance of the foyer system is that it perpetuates situations in which migrants were directly confronted with state or para-state (in the form of the associations managing the foyers) actors. In a comparative study, Nicolas Jounin has hypothesized that such specific situations of subordination, also experienced at work, explain the overrepresentation of West Africans, notably Malians, in the struggles of the sans-papiers.[64] Indeed, for older foyer inhabitants, the adversarial semantics of the patron traveled from the workplace to the housing structure; and, as we have seen, younger ones also articulated claims in the foyers in terms of rights they had.

Earlier chapters demonstrate that the ability, to which the foyer had contributed, to convert urban attachments into an acknowledged status, and urban dwellers into citizens, has diminished. Emplacement rested on expectations of social stability, on the relative control a migrant had over his migratory and life path, and on the perpetuation of such dynamics via the foyer system. With mounting uncertainties regarding the legal status of migrants and heightened administrative suspicion toward foyer residents, younger inhabitants developed much more ambivalent relationships to these places. The close consideration of urban dynamics and of contentious politics in the foyers nuances and enriches this depiction on two plans. First, the dynamics of urban emplacement greatly vary from one foyer to another, sensitive as they are to the immediate urban environment but also to the dynamics at the neighborhood and city level. Second, resources for political mobilization still existed in the foyers, even if struggles for documents and for the foyer do not always align in terms of objectives and tactics.

# 9

## FOCAL POINTS

### Reflections from the Foyers

*[At the time of the move from 216 bis in 1979,] journalists were
waiting for us to go out with our bundles, but we did not want
to appear on TV, so we moved in small groups.*

Interview with Alassane Ba, Foyer Lorraine, May 2013

n the ordinary and political imagination of contemporary
France, the foyers have been construed as epitomizing a form
of alterity. Even though many foyers were located in the central parts of French cities, public discourses on these places share
some features with those on the banlieues, notably the semantics of the ghetto.[1] I do not contrast these images of the foyers
as self-segregated places in the city with a mere view of these
places as open. Rather, I put the ascribed closure of the foyers under scrutiny, demonstrating how foyer inhabitants have
been subjected to contrasting demands in terms of visibility and
discretion, openness and closure, and analyzing how they have
navigated these shifting demands.

The foyers have been subjected to a form of media overexposure, reinforced or challenged by documentary and artistic projects. This conclusion offers some exploratory considerations on the iconic status of the foyers. Because artistic and documentary projects on the foyers often tackle the foyers as sites of memory, I also briefly reflect on the politics of the heritage of these sites, another topic deserving further research. The final section comes back to the core argument of this book: the heuristic interest of scrutinizing the intricacies between state and administrative practices and migrants' communities across generations. This stance has proved illuminating at distinct scales, from a detailed study of the micropolitics of the address to a broader view of the foyer as being located at such a junction—as both a housing system and a migrant institution. This perspective highlights how the social and material shape of the foyers has espoused changing ways of dealing with postcolonial migrants—and how they have been at the heart rather than insulated from the cultural, social, and political dynamics of French cities.

## ICONIC PLACES AND POLARIZED IMAGES

The regimes of visibility of black communities in the foyers have been construed by media and scholarly as well as by artistic interventions.[2] To this frenzy of images, foyer inhabitants responded by devising their own tactics of visibility shaped by their visual culture and suffused by ideas of honor and shame, as Alassane Ba's opening quotation recalls. Speaking more broadly about African diasporas in Europe, Tyler Stovall has also pointed to this "paradox between a small demographic presence and a significant cultural impact."[3]

This book owes a lot to my incursions in various fields of discursive and visual production about postcolonial migrants in Paris. Between 2010 and 2016, as part of a collective research project, I collaborated with photographer Anissa Michalon on a section of an art and academic exhibition and on a photographic album. With Daniela Swarowsky, curator and filmmaker, we entered in conversations about the representation of migrants in various settings, attended projections and debates within the foyers, and worked on a short film at Foyer Lorraine.[4] Academic productions, such as this book, are part of a wider field of production and circulation of knowledge and images, and many genres blur a clear-cut distinction between documentary and creative productions.[5]

Such projects intervene in a longer history of the visualization of black migrants that is closely associated with the foyers. In the 1960s and 1970s, black workers became a figure of blackness in France. West African migrants erupted on the screen in 1964 as a topic of documentary films in France.[6] Reporters reached out to black Africans primarily in dilapidated foyers: in his book on audiovisual representations of immigrants in France, Edouard Mills-Affif lists nine documents with at least one sequence within the foyers.[7] Together with the *bidonville*, the foyer stood out as epitomizing the dire condition of postcolonial workers. As Jean-Philippe Dedieu recalls, West Africans were active in determining what could or could not be shown; they had migrated with their own photographic visual culture and developed a strong interest in television in France; they often refused to be filmed or photographed because they wanted to control the public image that would be given of their living conditions; Malian and Senegalese authorities also protested after the broadcast of the first documentaries and took measures to prevent other films being shot in the foyer.[8]

After 1968, amplifying the denunciation by outsiders of dire living conditions, the figure of the African activist emerged as part of wider transformations in militant film productions.[9] Competing with outsider views, African activists and artists produced their own views, such as the Mauritanian filmmaker Sidney Sokhona. In 1975, an *animateur* in Parisian foyers received instructions not to show *Nationalité Immigré*, the first film by Sokhona, which followed a rent strike at Foyer Riquet (nineteenth arrondissement).[10]

In parallel, the 1970s were also a moment when policy makers developed a cultural dimension for immigration policies, notably by setting up specific TV programs.[11] The account by Jacques Barou of an attempt to film within Foyer Commanderie (nineteenth arrondissement) in 1984 is telling in several respects.[12] First, the producer of a series for French national TV reached out to Barou to provide expertise, testifying to the dominance of the ethnological reading of these places in the late 1970s and early 1980s. Second, this case demonstrated the agency of the foyers residents in shaping the visual production about them. Barou reports that the délégués, young and politicized and whose election had challenged traditional authorities within the foyer, wanted to put forward their struggle with the managing structure. They resented the appearance in the film of a "griot" as contrary to the modern image they wanted to cast of their community, and possibly reinforcing the traditional social order they were fighting. The result was that the film was not shot within the foyer; instead, it was shot among families of immigrants from the same region, as well as in Senegal.

In a distinct vein but in the same years, a fiction typified the connection between a Parisian foyer and "the village" through another paradigmatic figure, the marabout: the comedy *Black mic mac* (1986) attracted more than 800,000 spectators.[13] The film told the story of a hygiene inspector dealing with the inhabitants of an African foyer who have a marabout travel from a West African village to help them out. Born in Côte d'Ivoire, Isaac de Bankolé was the first black actor to win the highest French distinction for his role in this film (César du meilleur espoir masculin, 1987). Part of a series of films tackling the condition of blacks in France, it "has been criticized as deeply compromised by its cliché-ridden construction of the black community."[14] In contrast, writers Alain Mabanckou and Abdourahman Waberi retrospectively praised the film for offering a first questioning of the condition of blacks in France.[15] In fact, although set in a foyer, the film echoed the changes within the sub-Saharan presence in Paris with the appearance of Congolese migrants.

A minority type of housing, the foyers have garnered a place of choice in the public imagination, eliciting both fascination and stigmatization. Visions of the foyers have oscillated between the folkloric image of the foyer-village, fueled by ethnological studies, and the threatening view of the foyer-ghetto, publicized by media and official reports, which aligns the foyers with the banlieues as "lost territories of the Republic."[16] After the eruption of sans-papiers on the media and political stage in 1996, images of black Africans also regained some political agency.[17] Beyond such common tropes, a series of metonymies has reinforced their spatial alterity; as villages within the city, they stand for "bits of Africa" in French cities; among the foyers, Foyer Bara alone stands out as describing the foyers, and more specifically the Malian presence in France as being "a Malian oasis."[18] Bara was featured on a "cartography of Paris's Afropean sites" by Francophone black writers, as well as on specialized tourist guides.[19] To these images of spatial and politico-moral alterity, the present-day situation of renovation adds another layer of temporal alterity—obsolete and antique, the foyers appear as relics.

## A VANISHING HERITAGE AND THE QUESTION OF MEMORY

Foyer Lorraine and Foyer D'Hautpoul, the twin foyers whose history I have followed, were built by the same architect, Anthony Béchu, and their facades exhibited straight lines that provided them with a certain amount of similarity. As they entered separately into the process of renovation, distinct architectural teams worked on the new residences. Evidencing the two possible fates of such buildings, Foyer D'Hautpoul was razed to the ground, whereas the material structure of Foyer Lorraine was kept as the underlying structure of the new residence once the asbestos fiber was removed. That once-related buildings would follow distinct architectural paths went unnoticed by all of my interlocutors, from foyers' inhabitants to the management structure staff, and an architectural trace of a shared history was lost in the process.

Although a foyer is occasionally inventoried as part of the built heritage, in the renovation processes I have followed, the preservation of the built structure was never an objective.[20] Memory projects in the foyers generally rely on photographic and discursive evidence and do not emphasize the value of their architecture. Similar in this respect to the other, more transient housing types devoted to migrants (such as *bidonvilles* and *cités de transit*), they are tokens of the working-class city that disappear much more easily than other parts of the urban fabric.[21]

Emerging reflections around heritage practices with respect to immigration have pinpointed the ambiguities of the processes.[22] The French landscape has evolved tremendously in this respect: these issues were first imposed by associative actors, notably the association *Génériques* founded in 1987, but in 2006 the state became the leading actor in the process leading to the opening of the National Museum of Immigration History (CNHI), which coincided with intense public debates around race and postcolonial immigration. As landmarks in the history of North and West African migrants, the foyers obviously featured in the collections and exhibitions of the museum, both through evocation of the social issues of housing, the iconic political struggles around the foyers in the 1970s, and in artworks that generally took the form of memory work.[23] This wider context loomed large, even on projects conceived outside public institutions.

The collaborative project that I developed with Anissa Michalon did not emanate from a public commission but rather from reflections among academics on the productivity and tensions of collaborations with artists. After getting to know Anissa Michalon's work, a long-term collaboration with another photographer, Claire Soton, among inhabitants of a foyer in Montreuil and back in their Malian village, I was curious to present her to my fieldwork interlocutors.[24] We had planned that she would take photographs at Foyer D'Hautpoul, a project that at least one of the délégués was enthusiastic about, saying that "[something of the foyer] should remain so that we can teach our children born here what African life is like."[25]

We did not seek funding from the managing structure, but we felt that we ought to seek a formal authorization. As I presented the project to a Coallia officer in April 2013, she nodded: "It's almost mandatory for renovation programs to include a memory-oriented or artistic project,"—much to my dismay, as I had never thought of our project as a routinized step in a renovation process I had critically observed. Our project of collecting memories of a foyer before its closure was ambiguous: it seemed to consecrate the status of the foyer as from the past, and it ran the risk of aligning with the presentation of the renovation plan by institutional actors as progress-oriented. Fostering the political dimension of nostalgic accounts, we attempted to document past practices of conviviality with a view to opening up wider debates about these places and their future. We made a conscious choice to combine photographs inside and outside the foyer, offering a view of migrants as Parisians, a dimension we also put forward discursively by using our interlocutors' narratives from 216 bis to the new residence as the narrative thread of the publication.

Funded by public funds or only indirectly benefiting from such funds through public subsidies, each project navigated the institutional demands differently. Some commissioned work was from the outset designed and conducted by the managing structure as part of their communication, and it aimed at foregrounding the positive aspects of the renovation.[26] Other projects emanated from family history or personal encounters.[27] African artists could be sent to a foyer with the notion that they would build on some kind of familiarity, with various results.[28] Some projects elicited controversial reactions among experts and activists.[29] Activist and independent productions contributed to heritage processes as they found their way into associative collections.[30] Some projects included foyer inhabitants' own pictures, at a time when the association Attention Chantier! organized film workshops among foyer inhabitants and a yearly film festival within the foyers.[31]

Heroic pictures of the migrants as contributors to French society rehabilitating the figure of the worker, on one hand, and pictures of the foyers as pathways to the African locales of emigration, featuring migrants as travelers and adventurers, on the other hand, dominated the cultural/artistic productions of the time.[32] Attention to foyers as places of moorings, probably visually less evident, guided a few projects.[33] It is with images of the foyer as an urban place that I feel more comfortable because they dismantle the image of the foyer-village.

# HOW A HOUSING SYSTEM HAS SHAPED MIGRANTS' LIVES

The foyers emerged as a response to the need for a cheap, temporary, male workforce in (post)colonial France and as an administrative system of managing postcolonial migrants. West African migrants swiftly made this type of housing a social model and have incorporated it in their family projections and their migratory paths, notably because the celibacy imposed by the foyer system aligned with the patriarchal social organization resting on the migration of young men. My main argument is that the endurance of the foyers owes much to the convergence of these projects, but also that their instability, and their ulterior disjunction, explain the historical trajectory of this singular housing system.

Examining how the lives of migrants have been molded by a housing system requires attention to the infrastructure of the foyers: from the built space, the architectural layout, and the urban location of each structure; to the bureaucratic requirements, administrative rules, and social regulations dictating who could get a bed and stay there, under which status, and with which social prospects. Furthermore, the foyer system and the foyer model both stabilized under specific socioeconomic and political circumstances and regimes of mobility— hence my exploration has focused on, but never limited itself to, these places.

The birth of black foyers illuminates African migrants' agency in the making of the foyers in the 1960s. Not only did these migrants bring modes of organization elaborated in African cities to France, they also created alliances, albeit fleeting, with African intellectuals and students, mobilizing their national authorities, and putting direct pressure on the associations and the state to secure living spaces and improve their material conditions in French cities. Sure, this was not a bargain among equals. The design of "black African foyers," which consciously encouraged the community-like character by architectural and managerial choices, rested on racialized categorizations distinguishing between postcolonial migrants and often on racist assumptions that endured; the reinforcement of internal hierarchies also had lasting consequences.

In the 1960s and 1970s, the foyers allowed forms of emplacement within French cities: by this term, I encompass visible moments of collective action and political subjectivation and more ordinary processes of urban incorporation. In 1974, the decision to halt labor migration resulted in two related dynamics that could have meant the end of the foyer as an institution in migratory paths: first, the tendency of migrants to stay for longer periods, and second, the timid encouragement to family reunion. However, the main effect of these changes was to create more complex situations of arrival as irregular migrants, and a bed in a foyer became an even more coveted asset in sustaining family migratory projects at a time when such projects were rendered even more complicated by new legal requirements. As for family reunion, departures from the foyer to form couples and families in France did occur, but this option was progressively viewed by the migrants as entailing its own difficulties—here the context of economic crisis, the subaltern position of West African migrants, the urban relegation and racial discrimination against black families, and their limited prospects of upward social mobility are crucial to understanding the endurance of the foyers.

At that point, the coherence between the migratory projects of West African migrants and the administrative system of the foyer began to crack. For the migrants, the dilated temporalities between arrival and access to jobs and legal residence transformed the foyers from convenient, if not ideal, places from which to conduct transnational lives into what made possible less-desired but better-than-nothing configurations. These precarious circumstances have further engrained the foyer into family dynamics and kinship relations and key life-shaping events: departure in migration (as the expected, often negotiated in advance, point of arrival of many migrants); marriage and the option of staying in the foyer or leaving it; and retirement and the expected return of old men after a life of labor in France.

These social dynamics form the backdrop against which the French authorities designed a nationwide renovation plan of the foyers, inaugurated in 1997. The issue of irregular migration had come to the fore in discussions about the foyers and practices of surveillance were intensified; the problem of Islam in the 1980s added a layer to the ambition to control these places. As a result, the community-oriented features of the foyers, such as their roles as religious centers and the level of grouping of some ethnolinguistic groups within their walls—all products of historical processes—were naturalized as attributes of the black foyers and of their inhabitants, and the use of racial categories were decisive in such processes, as crucially demonstrated by Hélène Béguin.[34] The renovation plan translated political concerns with "communitaurianism" into architectural design, management practices, and technological devices. However, the outward rejection of "communities" as meaningful actors in French society went together with much more pragmatic ways of dealing with groups with immigrant backgrounds. The renovation of the foyers involved myriad state actors, and a close-up examination of this process reveals the endurance of the old idea that groups of migrants of the same origin could develop some forms of self-organization contributed to maintaining some order in these places. As management of COVID-19 has demonstrated, national and municipal authorities still make use of the foyers as convenient places to convey messages to these segments of the immigrant population (and beyond, to the immigrant communities of which they are a part).

Besides this ambiguity in the way the French state deals with communities, the half-finished dimension of the renovation can be explained by the persistence of migration by mostly young, West African men in search of work. As places of accumulated experience with the condition of migrants and changing bureaucratic demands, they have provided places for exchanges and intergenerational comparisons. This explains the endurance of the foyers, despite the fact that the end of this system has been announced for more than two decades and that many of their inhabitants judge this model obsolete. Fraught with friction and conflicts, the foyers have nonetheless shielded many migrants from the more drastic effects of irregular processes and marginalization dynamics. Focused on how former foyers residents use the space in the new residences, Laura Guérin's work brings to the fore the tactics used by the inhabitants to circumvent the effects of the renovation.[35]

By asking what kind of lives the foyers allow, I delineate the normative expectations and social forces that frame individual paths. In so doing, I detail how life in a foyer takes on distinct meanings depending on each migrant's position in wider family projects around migration, as well as on his work, conjugal, and residential aspirations and opportunities, forged prior and during migration. This fine-grained exploration also reveals general trends. It notably allows grasping the changing meanings of the foyers: while they used to allow a style of life epitomizing what I call the "sacrificial trope," they have mainly become a way to manage uncertainty and to keep options open at several key moments of a migrant's trajectory.

Tracing a shift in the foyers' role from mitigating spatial distance to dealing with temporalities, I suggest that this reflects a wider turn in transnational migration. At individual level, new forms of copresence have been made possible in the digital age, but irregular processes have rendered temporal projections both longer and more uncertain. At the group level, the foyer collectives can only be understood by considering the work of comparison across generations of migrants that constantly takes place among their inhabitants. All this makes time, the way it is managed collectively and individually, a key entry to understanding migration.

# ACKNOWLEDGMENTS

This book exists because inhabitants of the foyers generously shared with me stories about these buildings and their lives within their walls. Among the many délégués with whom I crossed paths, I warmly thank Alassane Ba, Mamadou Baradji, Silly Diabira, Boubacar Diallo, Bakary Cissokho, and the much missed Samba Sylla and Adama Sow. For their trust and friendship, I am most grateful to Demba Gaye, Abba Sall, Abderhamane Cissokho, Abdoulaye Bathily, and Moustapha Bathily. Special thanks to Adama Saounera for introducing me to a room full of laughter in a Parisian foyer, and later to his family in Mali.

My thanks to the members of the Collectif pour l'avenir des foyers (COPAF), and especially to Jacqueline Geering, for welcoming me in their meetings and sharing their deep knowledge of the foyers. Collaboration with Attention Chantier! on the 2013 edition of their film festival was a great opportunity to engage differently with residents and visitors of the foyers. At the Mairie de Paris, I thank Benoît Harent and Pascaline Dolo for granting me permission to sit at the steering committees between 2012 and 2017, and Magali Robert for her interest in my research and collaboration on a visual production. I am grateful to Isabelle Backouche for guidance within the Archives de Paris. I also thank archivists Elsa Quétel and Guillaume Normand for introducing me to the archives of the CASVP before their transfer to the Archives de Paris.

This book originated while I was a postdoctoral researcher at Zentrum Moderner Orient in Berlin. I am grateful to Samuli Schielke for inviting me to join *In Search of Europe*, a memorable research project, which included an art exhibition curated by Daniela Swarowsky. I am most saddened that Daniela, who encouraged me to enrich my research practice with many other kinds of collaborations, will not be able to read these pages; I hope that some of her enthusiasm and curiosity resonate in them. Daniela astutely paired me with photographer Anissa Michalon who was much more knowledgeable about the region of Kayes than I was. In turn, introducing Anissa to my interlocutors proved challenging but productive, and her images and our discussions pushed me to rethink many of my previous interpretations of the foyers.

This book took shape in joint rides to the archives and smoky conversations with Jean-Philippe Dedieu. It has been a privilege to work on several copublications with Jean-Philippe, who generously shared his books and erudition. I am incredibly grateful for his tireless readings of versions of this manuscript, invaluable comments, and continuous encouragement.

I had the good fortune of crossing paths with colleagues involved in fieldwork projects in and around the foyers at the same time as my research, notably, Amélie Grysole, Laura Guérin, and Stefan Le Courant—with whom we productively experimented cross interviews with our respective interlocutors. For rich discussions on research and art projects in and around the foyers, I thank Hélène Béguin, Claire Clouet, Tiphaine Bernard, Lucie Revilla, Sara Domenach, and Pierre-Marie Aubert.

Presenting parts of the manuscript to various audiences helped me better shape my ideas, and I wish to thank Anne-Christine Trémon for inviting me to the University of Lausanne, and Lorena Rizzo for inviting me to the University of Basel. Previous publications helped me sharpen my arguments, notably my 2016 *American Ethnologist* paper, of which substantial sections appear throughout the book. My thanks to Niko Besnier for fruitful exchanges on this paper. A discussant in an early presentation in Berlin, Charles Piot has since been a kind and supportive interlocutor. My gratitude to Jennifer Cole for her encouragement throughout this project and for our ongoing exchanges on postcolonial migrations in France. Gregory Mann and Bruce Whitehouse both kindly shared useful documents.

I feel extremely lucky that my institution, the CNRS, allowed me to pursue for ten years what was initially a *détour*, and that my colleagues made room for my Parisian fieldwork in our discussions, notably, Caterina Guenzi, Guillaume Lachenal, Marianne Lemaire, and Camille Lefebvre. My interest in the street address grew out of research previously conducted with Cécile Van den Avenne on urban toponymic and addressing practices in Mopti, stirred by insightful suggestions by Béatrice Fraenkel.

In 2015–16, I joined an inspiring seminar dedicated to ethnographic writing, organized by Michel Naepels at EHESS, where I experimented with some writing formats that found their way into this book. Navigating the Anglophone editing world proved a challenge, and I thank Benjamin Lawrance and Hélène Neveu Kringelbach for useful tips, as well as Eric Schwartz and all the team at Columbia University Press for welcoming my project and bringing it into the world. As always, Dominic Horsfall provided a careful and rigorous linguistic edit. Many thanks to Kristin Vold Lexander for correcting my quotations in Wolof.

In Paris and Dakar, my father Babacar and my uncle Modou shared their memories of their visits to the foyers as students in Paris in the 1970s. Far from the foyers, in her flat in Brittany, my mother Anne also crucially contributed to this book by providing ideal writing retreats. Spending time with men whose families were afar made me even more aware of the immense luck I have to come back daily to a place I call home; my deepest thanks go to my husband Badara, and to our daughters Ndèye-Anne and Oumy, for their unwavering support and joyful presence.

# NOTES

## INTRODUCTION

1. Gauz, *Black Manoo* (Paris: Le Nouvel Attila, 2020).
2. Mali and Senegal gained independence in June 1960 as the unified but ephemeral Mali Federation, whose demise led to separate independence for each country, proclaimed in August (for Senegal) and September (for Mali). Mauritania became independent in November 1960. In the foyers, the presence of men from other sub-Saharan African countries is occasionally reported, notably from Côte d'Ivoire, The Gambia, Niger, Guinea, and Haute-Volta (present-day Burkina Faso).
3. Alain Dubresson, "Les travailleurs Soninké et Toucouleur dans l'Ouest parisien," *Cahiers ORSTOM Série Sciences Humaines* 12, no. 2 (1975): 190.
4. Bruce Whitehouse, *Migrants and Strangers in an African City: Exile, Dignity, Belonging* (Bloomington: Indiana University Press, 2012); Sylvie Bredeloup, *La Diams'pora du fleuve Sénégal: sociologie des migrations africaines* (Toulouse: Presses Universitaires du Mirail, 2007), 186.
5. Sylvain Pattieu, "The BUMIDOM in Paris and Its Suburbs: Contradictions in a State Migration Policy, 1960s–1970s," *African and Black Diaspora: An International Journal* 10, no. 1 (2017): 12–24.
6. These figures are calculated from INSEE, *Atlas des populations immigrées en Ile-de-France: regards sur l'immigration* (Paris: INSEE, 2004), 27. For the whole country, 22 percent of Malians and 8 percent of Senegalese lived in foyers in 2006 according to Secrétariat général à l'immigration et à l'intégration, "Atlas national des populations immigrées," March 20,

2013, 22. https://www.immigration.interieur.gouv.fr/Archives/Les-archives -du-site/Archives-Statistiques-etudes-et-publications/Atlas-national -des-populations-immigree

7. Khalid Koser, ed., *New African Diasporas* (London: Routledge, 2003).

8. Tiffany Ruby Patterson and Robin D. G. Kelley, "Unfinished Migrations: Reflections on the African Diaspora and the Making of the Modern World," *African Studies Review* 43, no. 1 (2000): 20.

9. Félix F. Germain, *Decolonizing the Republic: African and Caribbean Migrants in Postwar Paris, 1946–1974* (East Lansing: Michigan State University Press, 2016).

10. The postwar French state inherited a centralized system in which the capital did not elect a representative. Before 1968, Paris was part of a larger subdivision, the Department of the Seine, and was ruled by appointed officers (French: *préfets*). In 1968 (as a result of a 1964 law), a department was created for Paris; surrounded by three other departments (Hauts-de-Seine, Seine-Saint-Denis, and Val-de-Marne), it was part of the wider *"région parisienne,"* renamed *"région Île-de-France"* in 1977. A 1975 law reinstated the position of Mayor of Paris.

11. Nadia Boussad, Nathalie Couleaud, and Mariette Sagot, "Une population immigrée aujourd'hui plus répartie sur le territoire régional," *INSEE Analyses Ile-de-France*, October 17, 2017. Demographers distinguish between "foreigners," individuals residing in France who do not have French citizenship, and "immigrants," individuals born abroad (and not French) who came to live in France. A person who has acquired French citizenship is no longer a foreigner but is still counted as an immigrant. In line with ordinary usage in migration studies, I generally use the term "migrant" because it captures the double nature of the migrant, as an emigrant (from the point of view of his society of origin) and immigrant (from the point of view of his place of arrival). When discussing statistics or specific situations when emigrant or immigrant status matters, I switch to one of these terms.

12. Catherine Borrel, Gérard Bouvier, and Bertrand Lhommeau, *Immigrés et descendants d'immigrés en France* (Paris: INSEE, 2012).

13. Abdelmalek Sayad, "Le foyer des sans-famille," *Actes de la recherche en sciences sociales* 32, no. 1 (1980): 89–103.

14. Stephen Castles and Godula Kosack, *Immigrant Workers and Class Structure in Western Europe* (London: Oxford University Press, Institute of Race Relations, 1973).

15. Samir Amin, ed., *Modern Migrations in Western Africa* (London: Oxford University Press, 1974); UGTSF, *Le livre des travailleurs africains en France* (Paris: Maspero, 1970); Émile Le Bris, Pierre-Philippe Rey, and Michel Samuel, *Capitalisme négrier: la marche des paysans vers le prolétariat* (Paris: Maspro, 1976); Claude Meillassoux, *Maidens, Meal, and Money: Capitalism and the Domestic Community* (Cambridge: Cambridge University Press, 1981); Michel Samuel, *Le prolétariat africain noir en France* (Paris: Maspero, 1978).

16. Adrian Adams, *Le long voyage des gens du fleuve* (Paris: Maspero, 1977); Samuel, *Le prolétariat africain noir en France*; Julien Condé and Pap Syr Diagne, *Les Migrations internationales Sud-Nord: une étude de cas* (Paris: OCDE, 1986); Catherine Quiminal, *Gens d'ici, gens d'ailleurs: migrations Soninké et transformations villageoises* (Paris: C. Bourgois, 1991).

17. François Manchuelle, "Background to Black African Emigration to France: The Labor Migrations of the Soninke, 1848–1987" (PhD diss., University of California, Santa Barbara, 1987); François Manchuelle, *Willing Migrants: Soninke Labor Diasporas, 1848–1960* (Athens: Ohio University Press, 1997).

18. Jacques Barou, *Travailleurs africains en France: rôle des cultures d'origine*, Collection Actualités-recherche (Grenoble: Presses Universitaires de Grenoble, 1978).

19. An overview of these studies appears in Véronique De Rudder, "Notes à propos de l'évolution des recherches françaises sur 'l'étranger dans la ville,'" in *Les étrangers dans la ville: le regard des sciences sociales*, ed. Simon-Barouh Ida and Simon Pierre-Jean (Paris: L'Harmattan, 1990), 60–80. On the delayed interest in race in French urban studies, see Élise Palomares, "Le racisme: un hors-champ de la sociologie urbaine française?," *Métropolitiques*, September 11, 2013.

20. Patrick Weil and John Crowley, "Integration in Theory and Practice: A Comparison of France and Britain," *West European Politics* 17, no. 2 (1994): 110–26.

21. Mahamet Timera, *Les Soninké en France: d'une histoire à l'autre* (Paris: Karthala, 1996).

22. Christophe Daum, *Les associations de Maliens en France: migrations, développement et citoyenneté* (Paris: Karthala, 1998).

23. Liliane Kuczynski and Élodie Razy, "Anthropologie et migrations africaines en France: une généalogie des recherches," *Revue européenne des migrations internationales* 25, no. 3 (2010): 79–100.

24. Transnationalism was popularized in Linda Green Basch, Nina Glick Schiller, and Cristina Szanton Blanc, *Nations Unbound: Transnational Projects, Postcolonial Predicaments, and Deterritorialized Nation-States* (London: Gordon and Breach, 1994). Transnational perspectives on the foyers include Abdoulaye Kane, *Tontines, caisses de solidarité et banquiers ambulants: univers des pratiques financières informelles en Afrique* (Paris: L'Harmattan, 2010); and Hamidou Dia, *Trajectoires et pratiques migratoires des Haalpulaaren du Sénégal: socio-anthropologie d'un "village multisitué"* (Paris: L'Harmattan, 2015).

25. Marie-France Moulin, *Machines à dormir: les foyers neufs de la sonacotra, de l'a.d.e.f et quelques autres* (Paris: Maspero, 1976); Mireille Ginésy-Galano, *Les Immigrés hors la cité: le système d'encadrement dans les foyers 1973–1982* (Paris: L'Harmattan, 1984).

26. Choukri Hmed, "Loger les étrangers 'isolés' en France: socio-histoire d'une institution d'État" (PhD diss., Université Panthéon-Sorbonne, Paris, 2006); Marc Bernardot, *Loger les immigrés: la Sonacotra* (Bellecombe-en-Bauges, France: Editions du Croquant, 2008).

27. Jean-Philippe Dedieu, *La parole immigrée: les migrants africains dans l'espace public en France (1960–1995)* (Paris: Klincksieck, 2012); Gregory Mann, *From Empires to NGOs in the West African Sahel. The Road to Nongovernmentality* (Cambridge: Cambridge University Press, 2014); Jean-Philippe Dedieu and Aïssatou Mbodj-Pouye, "The Fabric of Transnational Political Activism: 'Révolution Afrique' and West African Radical Militants in France in the 1970s," *Comparative Studies in Society and History* 60, no. 4 (2018): 1172–1208; Gillian Glaes, *African Political Activism in Postcolonial France* (London: Routledge, 2019).

28. Johanna Siméant, *La cause des sans-papiers* (Paris: Presses de Sciences po, 1998).

29. Tyler Stovall, "Race and the Making of the Nation. Blacks in Modern France," in *Diasporic Africa: A Reader*, ed. Michael A. Gomez (New York: NYU Press, 2006), 201.

30. Pap Ndiaye, *La condition noire: essai sur une minorité française* (Paris: Calmann-Lévy, 2008); Audrey Célestine and Sarah Fila-Bakabadio, "Introduction to the Special Issue 'Black Paris and the Lived Experiences of Black Subjects,'" *African and Black Diaspora: An International Journal* 10, no. 1 (2017): 1–11.

31. I use the word "inhabitant" to refer to any person living in the foyer regardless of his status; I adopt the term "resident" when issues of entitlement come to the fore; I refer to outsiders who regularly visit the foyer (to pray, to attend literacy classes, to work or eat in the canteen, to sell items door-to-door, etc.) as "users" of the foyers.

32. Paul Stoller, *Money Has No Smell: The Africanization of New York City* (Chicago: University of Chicago Press, 2002); Kristen Sarah Biehl, "A Dwelling Lens: Migration, Diversity and Boundary-Making in an Istanbul Neighbourhood," *Ethnic and Racial Studies* 43, no. 12 (2020): 2236–54.

33. Marc Bernardot, "Invisibiliser par le logement. De Sonacotra à Adoma," in *Les nouvelles frontières de la société française* (Paris: La Découverte, 2012), 79–100.

34. On how "migrant institutions" operate a junction between national and international institutions and allow labor migration to take place by the routinization of social practices of migration, see Thomas Lacroix, "Conceptualizing Transnational Engagements: A Structure and Agency Perspective on (Hometown) Transnationalism," *International Migration Review* 48, no. 3 (2014): 643–79.

35. Biao Xiang and Johan Lindquist, "Migration Infrastructure," *International Migration Review* 48, no. S1 (2014): S122–48. For recent reflections on this notion in the context of migration, see Julie Kleinman, *Adventure Capital: Migration and the Making of an African Hub in Paris* (Oakland: University of California Press, 2019); and Bruno Meeus, Karel Arnaut, and Bas Van Heur, eds., *Arrival Infrastructures:Migration and Urban Social Mobilities* (London: Palgrave Macmillan, 2019).

36. Nikhil Anand, Akhil Gupta, and Hannah Appel, eds., "Introduction: Temporality, Politics, and the Promise of Infrastructure," in *The Promise of Infrastructure* (Durham, NC: Duke University Press, 2018), 11.

37. Roland Lovatt, Christine Whitehead, and Claire Lévy-Vroelant, "Foyers in the UK and France—Comparisons and Contrasts," *International Journal of Housing Policy* 6, no. 2 (2006): 153.

38. Never assuming a shared "desire to live in tightly knit immigrant communities," my analysis emphasizes the "diversity of migrants' relationships to their place of settlement." Ayşe Çağlar and Nina Glick Schiller, *Migrants and City-Making: Dispossession, Displacement, and Urban Regeneration* (Durham, NC: Duke University Press, 2018), 4.

39. Paolo Boccagni, *Migration and the Search for Home* (New York: Palgrave Macmillan, 2017).

40. Meillassoux, *Maidens, Meal, and Money*.

41. Mirjana Morokvasic, "Birds of Passage Are Also Women . . . ," *International Migration Review* 18, no. 4 (1984): 886–907; Caroline B. Brettell, *We Have Already Cried Many Tears: Portuguese Women and Migration* (Cambridge, MA: Schenkman, 1982); Sarah J. Mahler and Patricia R. Pessar, "Gender Matters: Ethnographers Bring Gender from the Periphery Toward the Core of Migration Studies," *International Migration Review* 40, no. 1 (2006): 27–63.

42. Katharine Charsley and Helena Wray, "Introduction: The Invisible (Migrant) Man," *Men and Masculinities*, 18, no. 4 (2015), 403–23; Ester Gallo, "Italy Is Not a Good Place for Men: Narratives of Places, Marriage and Masculinity Among Malayali Migrants," *Global Networks* 6, no. 4 (2006): 357–72.

43. Recent studies on West African women in France include Nehara Feldman, *Migrantes: du bassin du fleuve Sénégal aux rives de la Seine* (Paris: La Dispute, 2018). On Senegalese men in France and Italy, see Liu Mao-Mei, "Becoming a Man: Legal Status, Networks and Male Migration Between Senegal and Europe," MAFE Working Paper 38 (Paris: INED, 2015); and Giulia Sinatti, "Masculinities and Intersectionality in Migration: Transnational Wolof Migrants Negotiating Manhood and Gendered Family Roles," in *Migration, Gender and Social Justice: Perspectives on Human Insecurity*, ed. Thanh-Dam Truong, Des Gasper, Jeff Handmaker, and Sylvia I. Bergh (Berlin: Springer, 2014), 215–26.

44. For the United States, see Mary E. Pattillo, *Black on the Block: The Politics of Race and Class in the City* (Chicago: University of Chicago Press, 2007); and Edward Glenn Goetz, *New Deal Ruins: Race, Economic Justice, and Public Housing Policy* (Ithaca, NY: Cornell University Press, 2013). For France, see Renaud Epstein, "La rénovation urbaine: démolition-reconstruction de l'État" (Paris: Presses de Sciences po, 2013).

45. Andrew Newman, *Landscape of Discontent: Urban Sustainability in Immigrant Paris* (Minneapolis: University of Minnesota Press, 2015).

46. Frederick Cooper, *Citizenship Between Empire and Nation: Remaking France and French Africa, 1945–1960* (Princeton, NJ: Princeton University Press, 2014).

47. Gregory Mann, "Immigrants and Arguments in France and West Africa," *Comparative Studies in Society and History* 45, no. 2 (2003): 362–85.

48. Germain, *Decolonizing the Republic*; Glaes, *African Political Activism*.

49. Ann Laura Stoler, ed., "Introduction. 'The Rot Remains': From Ruins to Ruination," in *Imperial Debris: On Ruins and Ruination* (Durham, NC: Duke University Press, 2013), 8.

50. Didier Fassin and Estelle d'halluin, "The Truth from the Body: Medical Certificates as Ultimate Evidence for Asylum Seekers," *American Anthropologist* 107, no. 4 (2005): 597–608; Miriam Iris Ticktin, *Casualties of Care: Immigration and the Politics of Humanitarianism in France* (Berkeley: University of California Press, 2011).

51. Pierre Baron, Anne Bory, Sébastien Chauvin, Nicolas Jounin, and Lucie Tourette, *"On bosse ici, on reste ici !": la grève des sans-papiers, une aventure inédite* (Paris: La Découverte, 2011).

52. In 2013, 3.4 percent of the residence permits issued by French authorities were delivered on health grounds. See Nicolas Klausser, "La régularisation pour soins des étrangers: symptômes d'une pathologisation d'un droit de l'homme," *La Revue des droits de l'homme* 11 (2017), https://doi.org/10.4000/revdh.2890.

53. Henri Cuq, "Mission parlementaire sur la situation et le devenir des foyers de travailleurs migrants," Mission parlementaire auprès ministre chargé de l'intégration et de la lutte contre l'exclusion (Paris: 1996).

54. Véronique De Rudder, François Vourc'h, and Christian Poiret, *L'inégalité raciste: l'universalité républicaine à l'épreuve* (Paris: Presses universitaires de France, 2000); Didier Fassin and Éric Fassin, *De la question sociale à la question raciale?: représenter la société française* (Paris: La Découverte, 2006); Sarah Mazouz, *La République et ses autres: politiques de l'altérité dans la France des années 2000* (Lyon: ENS Éditions, 2017).

55. Mayanthi L. Fernando, *The Republic Unsettled: Muslim French and the Contradictions of Secularism* (Durham, NC: Duke University Press, 2014), 6.

56. Steven Feld and Keith Hamilton Basso, eds., *Senses of Place* (Santa Fe, NM: School of American Research Press, 1996).

57. Cressida Jervis Read, "A Place in the City: Narratives of 'Emplacement' in a Delhi Resettlement Neighbourhood," *Ethnography* 13, no. 1 (2012): 87–101.

58. Harri Englund, "Ethnography After Globalism: Migration and Emplacement in Malawi," *American Ethnologist* 29, no. 2 (2002): 261–86.

59. My understanding of emplacement partly coincides with Ayşe Çağlar and Nina Glick Schiller's definition of the notion as "the relationship between, on the one hand, the continuing restructuring of place within multiscalar networks of power and, on the other, a person's efforts, within the barriers and opportunities that contingencies of local place-making offer, to build a life within networks of local, national, supranational, and global interconnections." Çağlar and Glick Schiller, *Migrants and City-Making*, 20–21. In addition to their emphasis on power relations at distinct scales, I take as a starting point the way in which time and space are experienced, and from there I explore the consequences of national contexts and mobility regimes. See Aïssatou Mbodj-Pouye, "Fixed Abodes: Urban Emplacement, Bureaucratic Requirements, and the Politics of Belonging Among West African Migrants in Paris," *American Ethnologist* 43, no. 2 (2016): 295–310. As Henrik Vigh and Jesper Bjarnesen state, "emplacement implies a conceptual move away from place as location toward place as a process of socio-affective attachment, as a point of valued or tenable being." Henrik Vigh and Jesper Bjarnesen, "Introduction: The Dialectics of Displacement and Emplacement," *Conflict and Society* 2, no. 1 (2016): 13.

60. Nina Glick Schiller, Linda Basch, and Cristina Szanton Blanc, "From Immigrant to Transmigrant: Theorizing Transnational Migration," *Anthropological Quarterly* 68, no. 1 (1995): 48.

61. Scholars of West African societies have pointed to the experience of immobility in emigration places, see, for instance, Gunvor Jónsson, "Migration, Identity and Immobility in a Malian Soninke Village," in *The Global Horizon. Expectations of Migration in Africa and the Middle East*, ed. Knut Graw and Samuli Schielke (Leuven, Belgium: Leuven University Press, 2012), 105–20. Immobility, or "stucknesss," is also a fundamental part of the migrant experience in present-day Europe. See Andrew Jefferson, Simon Turner, and Steffen Jensen, "Introduction: On Stuckness and Sites of Confinement," *Ethnos* 84, no. 1 (2019): 1–13.

62. Michel Agier, *Esquisses d'une anthropologie de la ville: lieux, situations, mouvements* (Louvain-la-Neuve: Academia-Bruylant, 2009), 94.

63. Annika Lems and Jelena Tošić, "Preface: Stuck in Motion?," *Suomen Antropologi: Journal of the Finnish Anthropological Society* 44, no. 2 (2019):

3–19. On place-making, see Leslie Fesenmyer, "Bringing the Kingdom to the City: Mission as Placemaking Practice Amongst Kenyan Pentecostals in London," *City & Society* 31, no. 1 (2019): 34–54.

64. Reuben Rose-Redwood and Anton Tantner, "Introduction: Governmentality, House Numbering and the Spatial History of the Modern City," *Urban History* 39, no. 4 (2012): 607–13. Parts of this section have already been published in Mbodj-Pouye "Fixed Abodes."

65. A key reference in the renewal of anthropological approaches on bureaucracy is Matthew S. Hull, *Government of Paper: The Materiality of Bureaucracy in Urban Pakistan* (Berkeley: University of California Press, 2012).

66. In the French street address system, when a new structure is built between consecutively numbered buildings, it is given the neighboring house number followed by *bis* (literally "twice").

67. During a stay in Mali (2017–2019), I maintained contact with my key foyer interlocutors via social networks or during return visits; I also met some of them in Bamako, Kayes, and their home villages. While completing this book in 2019–2020, I conducted follow-up research in Paris, often over the phone and via social networks due to the several lockdown phases induced by the COVID-19 pandemic.

68. I never took an active role in the negotiations on the future of these two foyers; the residents themselves and other activists were far more expert than I was.

69. The old foyers had mostly collective rooms that were occupied at all hours of the day, making it complicated to receive visits from sex workers, and my interlocutors described sexual and affective encounters as generally taking place outside the foyers.

70. This last example is borrowed from Anne Monjaret's reflection on her presence in male working environments. See Anne Monjaret, *La pin-up à l'atelier: ethnographie d'un rapport de genre* (Grâne: Créaphis éditions, 2020). Reflections on the situation of female ethnographers in all-male spaces have accompanied the reflexive turn in the social sciences and are part and parcel of feminist anthropology. See Henrietta L. Moore, *Feminism and Anthropology* (Cambridge, UK: Polity Press, 1988). Inspiring reflections include Sandra Meike Bucerius, "Becoming a 'Trusted Outsider': Gender, Ethnicity, and Inequality in Ethnographic Research," *Journal of Contemporary Ethnography* 42, no. 6 (2013): 690–721; and Anne

Monjaret and Catherine Pugeault, *Le sexe de l'enquête: Approches sociologiques et anthropologiques* (Lyon: ENS Éditions, 2015).

71. I borrow the term "halfie" from Lila Abu-Lughod, who made a forceful case to consider the epistemic challenges of the position of scholars of mixed background. See Lila Abu-Lughod, "Writing Against Culture," in *Recapturing Anthropology*, ed. Richard Fox (Santa Fe, NM: School of American Research Press, 1991), 137–62. Following Kirin Narayan, who emphasizes the "many strands of identification available" to anyone, I understand this "halfie" identity in a nonessentialist way. See Kirin Narayan, "How Native Is a 'Native' Anthropologist?," *American Anthropologist* 95, no. 3 (1993): 673. Born in Paris, I never lived in Senegal as a child, but I spent most of my teenage holidays in Dakar, struggling to improve my Wolof amid the playful banter of my cousins.

72. Except for historical interviews in Part 1, all names are pseudonyms.

73. I conducted formal interviews in French but occasionally used Wolof or Bamanan during informal discussions, which constituted second languages for Soninke and Pulaar speakers.

74. *Sukk* is associated with age and gender (typically, women sukk when greeting senior men). It is deemed backward in present-day urban middle-class milieus.

75. Lila Abu-Lughod, "Fieldwork of a Dutiful Daughter," in *Arab Women in the Field: Studying Your Own Society*, ed. Soraya Altorki and Camillia Fawzi El-Solh (Syracuse, NY: Syracuse University Press, 1988).

# 1. IMPROVISING THE FOYERS: FRANCO-AFRICAN INSTITUTIONS OF MIGRATION (1958–1967)

1. Interview with Bakary Traoré, June 2013. In quotes from historical interviews, my interlocutors appear under their real names. This is done with their permission and reflects the status of some of them as public figures. In subsequent chapters, when pseudonyms are used, individuals appear under their first name only.

2. Interviews with Samba Sylla, July 2013 and September 2015. For biographical accounts of Samba Sylla (1948–2019), see Carine Eff, "Mémoire d'un homme au foyer," *Vacarme*, no. 30 (2005): 90–93; and Dennis D. Cordell and Carolyn F. Sargent, "Samba Sylla (1948), Doulo

Fofanna (b, 1947 or 1948), and Djenébou Traoré (b. 1972): The Colonies Come to France," in *The Human Tradition in Modern Africa*, ed. Dennis D. Cordell (Lanham, MD: Rowman and Littlefield, 2012), 249–66.

3. Interviews with Moussa Kanté, October 2013 and May 2015.

4. The lodgings at 32 rue Petit were also identified as the "first foyer" in France by Bakary Gandega, who arrived in August 1958 and lived in Saint-Denis. Interview with Gandega, October 2015. Other narratives point to alternative sites: for Yatera, from Diaguily, Mauritania, who arrived in 1960, the first African foyer is also located in the nineteenth arrondissement but at 4 rue du Rhin. Interview with Yatera, February 2014.

5. Haalpulaar translates as "those who speak Pulaar." Originating from the middle valley of the Senegal River, they are a subgroup of the wider ethnolinguistic group known as "Fulbe." In Mali, they generally identify as Fulbe but not Haalpulaar. I do not pluralize ethnonyms.

6. Douglas S. Massey, "Social Structure, Household Strategies, and the Cumulative Causation of Migration," *Population Index* 56, no. 1 (1990): 7.

7. Sue Peabody, *"There Are No Slaves in France": The Political Culture of Race and Slavery in the Ancien Régime* (Oxford: Oxford University Press, 2002).

8. Brigitte Bertoncello and Sylvie Bredeloup, *Colporteurs africains à Marseille: un siècle d'aventures* (Paris: Autrement, 2004); François Manchuelle, *Willing Migrants: Soninke Labor Diasporas, 1848–1960* (Athens: Ohio University Press, 1997); and Sylvain Pattieu, "Souteneurs noirs à Marseille, 1918–1921: Contribution à l'histoire de la minorité noire en France," *Annales. Histoire, Sciences Sociales* 64, no. 6 (2009): 1361–86.

9. Philippe Dewitte, *Les mouvements nègres en France, 1919–1939* (Paris: L'Harmattan, 1985); Brent Hayes Edwards, *The Practice of Diaspora* (Cambridge, MA: Harvard University Press, 2003); Gary Wilder, *The French Imperial Nation-State: Negritude and Colonial Humanism Between the Two World Wars* (Chicago: University of Chicago Press, 2005); Michael Goebel, *Anti-Imperial Metropolis: Interwar Paris and the Seeds of Third-World Nationalism* (Cambridge: Cambridge University Press, 2015); and Tyler Stovall, *Paris Noir: African Americans in the City of Light* (Boston: Houghton Mifflin, 1996).

10. Dewitte, *Les mouvements nègres en France, 1919–1939*, 25.

11. Myron Echenberg, *Les Tirailleurs sénégalais en Afrique occidentale française (1857–1960)* (Paris: Karthala, 2009), 143.

12. See the fourteen newspaper articles and four special issues published between December 1962 and the summer of 1963, cited in the bibliography of "Etude sur les travailleurs d'Afrique noire à Paris et dans le Département de la Seine," 1963, p. 83, a report by Jacques Legru, a sociologist apointed by the Préfecture de la Seine, kept in Archives Nationales: 5AGF art. 3385. A shorter version of this report appeared as "Main d'oeuvre noire dans la Seine," *Cahiers Nords-Africains*, no. 102 (1964).

13. Note, March 15, 1967, Archives Nationales: 5AGF art. 3384. This note dates the arrivals in Seine-Maritime from 1957 on a national scale from 1959.

14. Gérard Espéret, *Problèmes posés par l'immigration des travailleurs africains en France*, Rapport au Conseil économique et social, 1964, 547.

15. Jacques Legru, "Main d'oeuvre," 10.

16. Muriel Cohen, *Des familles invisibles: Les Algériens de France entre intégrations et discriminations (1945–1985)* (Paris: Editions de la Sorbonne, 2020), 380.

17. Of these, 40 percent came from Mali, 35 percent from Mauritania, and 25 percent from Senegal. Note by the Direction de la population et des migrations, January 1968. Archives Nationales: 5AGF art. 3385.

18. Maryse Tripier, *L'immigration dans la classe ouvrière en France* (Paris: L'Harmattan, 1990); and Gérard Noiriel, *Les ouvriers dans la société française: XIXe-XXe siècle* (Paris: Le Seuil, 1986).

19. Georges Tapinos, *L'Immigration étrangère en France: 1946–1973* (Paris: Presses Universitaires de France, 1975), chap. 3.

20. Gregory Mann, *From Empires to NGOs in the West African Sahel. The Road to Nongovernmentality* (Cambridge: Cambridge University Press, 2014), 153.

21. Manchuelle quotes several testimonials, most from press articles. See François Manchuelle, "Background to Black African Emigration to France: The Labor Migrations of the Soninke, 1848–1987" (PhD diss., University of California, Santa Barbara, 1987), 496n7.

22. Tapinos, *L'Immigration étrangère en France*, 63–64. These policies remained "relatively permissive through the 1960s." Mann, *From Empires to NGOs*, 131.

23. The Soninke constituted 72 percent of black Africans. Souleymane Diarra, "Les travailleurs africains noirs en France," *Bulletin de l'Institut*

*fondamental d'Afrique noire* 30, no. 3 (July 1968): 902. Khassonke, Bamanan, Wolof, and Haalpulaar were also represented.

24. As early as the 1940s, Manjak migration involved whole families; therefore, Manjak men were seldom lodged in foyers. See Amadou Diop, "Tradition et adaptation dans un réseau de migration sénégalais: la communauté manjak de France" (PhD diss., EHESS, Marseille, 1981).

25. Jacob Paskins, *Paris Under Construction: Building Sites and Urban Transformation in the 1960s* (New York: Routledge, 2016); Danièle Voldman, *La reconstruction des villes françaises de 1940 à 1954: histoire d'une politique* (Paris: L'Harmattan, 1997).

26. The presence of West Africans was occasionally reported in the *bidonvilles*: in the one at Pleyel in Saint-Denis, there were approximately two hundred unmarried black African male workers. See Note by the city of Saint-Denis on *bidonvilles*, November 30, 1965. Archives Municipales, Saint-Denis: 18 ACW art. 22.

27. Alain Faure and Claire Lévy-Voelant, *Une chambre en ville: hôtels meublés et garnis de Paris 1860–1990* (Grâne: Créaphis, 2007); and Rosemary Wakeman, *The Heroic City: Paris, 1945–1958* (Chicago: University of Chicago Press, 2009).

28. Diarra, "Les travailleurs africains noirs en France," 972.

29. Note by the Préfet de Police, December 1965. Archives Nationales: 19770391 art. 9.

30. Diarra, "Les travailleurs africains noirs en France," 896.

31. In West African contexts, a traveler finds a "host" in each destination: a *jatigi* (Bamanan), *jaatigi* (Soninke) or *njatigi* (Pulaar). The relation between a jatigi and his guest is reciprocal and asymmetrical (the host is responsible to provide lodging, and sometimes a job, to his guest; the guest is expected to show respect to his host, and often to offer some kind of compensation such as participation in domestic labor) and exclusive (one has one jatigi in one locality). The institution is unstable, all the more so as it develops in transit and migration contexts where social control may not be strong, and stories about exploitative hosts abound. My interlocutors did not refer to their initial contact in the foyer as a "jatigi" because, even if they found lodging through personal acquaintance, they knew they were in either private or semipublic facilities. Rather than a replication of jatigi-guest relations, I find echoes of

the expectations around hospitality at the level of interpersonal relations as well as in the collective ties of a community toward a lodger.

32. Manchuelle suggests that the name "*chambres*" was borrowed from the "*chambrées*" organized by sailors in French coastal cities in the nineteenth century; see Manchuelle, *Willing Migrants*, 274. On "*suudu*" as a social formation emerging from the migration setting of Dakar, based on the provisional cohabitation of male migrants, see Abdoulaye-Bara Diop, *Société toucouleur et migration: (enquête sur l'immigration toucouleur à Dakar)* (Dakar: IFAN, 1965), 155–56.

33. "Nombre et implantation dans le département de la Seine des travailleurs originaires des Etats d'Afrique Noire," September 5, 1963. Archives Nationales: 5AGF art. 3384, p. 5.

34. See, for instance, a testimonial in Ahmed Diop, "Une nouvelle vie pour les travailleurs africains en France grâce à des centres d'accueil," *Bingo. Le mensuel du monde noir*, May 1967, 13. My thanks to Hélène Neveu for sharing this reference with me.

35. See Letter by the Préfet to the Ministry of Interior, July 1963. Archives Nationales: 5AGF art. 3384; press clippings in Archives Municipales, Saint-Denis: 18 ACW 23; and Gillian Glaes, *African Political Activism in Postcolonial France* (London: Routledge, 2019). For other instances of less violent incidents, see Diarra. "Les travailleurs africains noirs en France," 976–77.

36. Interview with M'Pama Siby, June 2015.

37. The list notably omits rue Polonceau, described by Sylla as being kept by a Malian.

38. Garba Traoré, for instance, a war veteran, was in charge at Ivry. See Mann, *From Empires to NGOs*, 152–55. Chikou Fofana managed a facility hosting 292 black African workers at 4 rue Caillé in the eighteenth arrondissement. See *Logement collectif à caractère non lucratif des travailleurs à Paris et dans les trois départements limitrophes*, Préfecture de Paris, October 1968. Archives Nationales: 19682005150 art. 61; hereafter: *Logement collectif*, 1968. Along Garba Traoré, one woman is mentioned as comanager for Ivry's foyer, Mme N'Diaye Nafissatou. See note by the Renseignements Généraux, June 13, 1965. Archives Nationales: AGF5 art. 3384. The distinction between owners and managers is often unclear in the record.

39. See note, August 22, 1962. Archives de la Préfecture de Police de Paris: GA A7; and interview with Yatera.

40. Mann, *From Empires to NGOs*, 153.

41. On this category, see Laure Pitti, "Les 'Nord-Africains' à Renault: un cas d'école de gestion coloniale de la main-d'œuvre en métropole," *Bulletins de l'Institut d'Histoire du Temps Présent* 83, no. 1 (2004): 128–43.

42. Marc Bernardot, *Loger les immigrés: la Sonacotra* (Bellecombe-en-Bauges, France: Edition du Croquant, 2008), 10. "Foyer" conveys military and colonial resonances, as in the foyers for "Africans and Malagasy soldiers" opened in Paris in the aftermath of World War I. See Dewitte, *Les mouvements nègres en France, 1919–1939*, 28. It could, however, have positive notes, as demonstrated by the envisioned—but unrealized—plans for a "West African student *foyer*" in Paris discussed by black activists in 1933. See Edwards, *The Practice of Diaspora*, 265.

43. Run by an Agency for North African Workers' Foyers (Régie des foyers ouvriers nord-africains) created in 1931, almost all of these foyers closed in the following years as a result of mismanagement. See Clifford D. Rosenberg, *Policing Paris: The Origins of Modern Immigration Control Between the Wars* (Ithaca, NY: Cornell University Press, 2006), chap. 7.

44. On the Association of North African Foyers in the Parisian Region (Association des Foyers Nord-Africains de la Région Parisienne, AFNARP) created in 1949, see Fathia Lounici, "Les foyers de travailleurs nord-africains en banlieue parisienne: une politique de logement social d'exception (1945–1962)," *Cahiers d'histoire. Revue d'histoire critique*, no. 98 (2006): 43–63. On the creation in 1948 of the "Foyer du Marin Sénégalais," under the impulse of West African sailors in Marseille, see Manchuelle "Background to Black African Emigration to France," 473.

45. Choukri Hmed, "Loger les étrangers 'isolés' en France: socio-histoire d'une institution d'État" (PhD diss., Université Panthéon-Sorbonne, Paris, 2006); Bernardot, *Loger les immigrés*.

46. Vincent Viet, *La France immigrée: construction d'une politique, 1914–1997* (Paris: Fayard, 1998); and Amelia H. Lyons, "Social Welfare, French Muslims and Decolonization in France: The Case of the Fonds d'action Sociale," *Patterns of Prejudice* 43, no. 1 (2009): 65–89.

47. Bernardot, *Loger les immigrés*, 81.

48. *Logement collectif*, 1968, 48.

49. On the fear of frictions, see note, July 18, 1964. Archives de la Préfecture de Police de Paris: GA A7.

50. Pattieu, "The BUMIDOM in Paris and Its Suburbs: Contradictions in a State Migration Policy, 1960s–1970s," *African and Black Diaspora: An International Journal* 10, no. 1 (2017): 19.

51. In contrast to Sonacotra, these associations have not been the focus of detailed studies, with the exception of the valuable PhD thesis by Hélène Béguin on AFTAM. Hélène Béguin, "Héberger des migrants ou gérer des logements? L'Aftam et ses 'foyers d'Africains noirs' (1962–2012)," (PhD diss., University of Paris Est, 2015).

52. At that time, Stéphane Hessel was in charge of international cooperation at the Ministry of National Education. The Central Economic Cooperation Fund (Caisse Centrale de Coopération Economique), the institution in charge of distributing aid to former French colonies, supported the creation of AFTAM. See Sylvain Laurens, *Une politisation feutrée: les hauts fonctionnaires et l'immigration en France, 1962–1981* (Paris: Belin, 2009), 100–107.

53. File Associations de travailleurs. Archives Nationales: 19850087 art. 158.

54. Espéret, *Problèmes posés par l'immigration des travailleurs africains en France*, 557.

55. "Travailleurs africains en France," AFTAM, undated (1966 ?). Archives Nationales: 19850087 art. 158, p. 13.

56. File Associations de travailleurs. Archives Nationales: 19850087 art. 158; and Demande de subvention, F1a art. 5106. On the White Fathers' interest in Algerians in France from 1945, see Angéline Escafré-Dublet, "Aid, Activism and the State in Post-War France: AMANA, a Charity Organisation for Colonial Migrants, 1945–1962," *Journal of Modern European History* 12, no. 2 (2014): 247–61.

57. Report by Mamadou Niambele, *Immigration des travailleurs maliens en France*, Archives Nationales du Mali, fonds documentaire, n.d. (December 1963?), 609, p. 38. My thanks to Greg Mann for sharing his copy of this document.

58. Note by Monique Hervo, October 1973, IHTP 313, Hervo papers. Among them features Sally N'Dongo, to be discussed later.

59. My reading departs from Mann's encompassing approach of the associations as all more or less fictive, see Mann, *From Empires to NGOs*, 161; as well as from Germain's emphasis on the derogatory views held by AFTAM's initiators on Africans, see Germain, *Decolonizing the Republic*, 3–38.

60. The main employers' association involved in housing is the Association pour le Développement des Foyers du Bâtiment et des Métaux (ADEF), created in 1955. Mireille Ginésy-Galano, *Les Immigrés hors la cité: le système d'encadrement dans les foyers 1973–1982* (Paris: L'Harmattan, 1984), 42. Housing provided by employers often took the form of barracks, planned as provisional lodging but that sometimes became permanent.

61. Agence France Presse, "Bulletin d'Afrique," December 20, 1967, File Associations de travailleurs. Archives Nationales: 19850087 art. 158.

62. AFRP took over from the aforementioned AFNARP. See Ginésy-Galano, *Les Immigrés hors la cité*, 46.

63. Note, FAS, April 1, 1968. Archives Nationales: 5AGF art. 3385.

64. In general, foyers were named after the street on which they were located. I follow this usage for all foyers within Paris except for "216 bis," for which this rule would be confusing because Saint-Denis is also a city. For foyers outside Paris, when there was only one facility, I use the name of the locality, as in "Ivry's foyer"; when there were several of them, I specify the name and street, as in "Foyer Pinel (Saint-Denis)."

65. Letter by the Préfet de Police to the Ministry of Interior, November 16 (?), 1963. Archives Nationales: 5AGF art. 3384.

66. Programme pluriannuel de résorption et de réhabilitation, 1975. Archives Nationales: 19870056 art. 3. The building had been part of a lace factory. In 1947, the building was renovated to make it suitable for housing, notably by installing an oil tank for heating. See Dossier de ravalement, Etablissements Henri Caen et frères, 1961. Archives de Paris: VO 13 art. 261.

67. Espéret, *Problèmes posés par l'immigration des travailleurs africains en France*, 558.

68. As in other neighboring societies, Soninke society is composed of status groups organized into three categories: (former) slaves, "free persons" of unmarked status, and several endogamous groups tied to specific crafts whose members act as social brokers (sing. *ɲaxamala*, pl. *ɲaxamalo*). *Sakko* (sing. *sakke*) are a *ɲaxamala* group historically devoted to wood carving but who define themselves as keepers of oral traditions in Sobokou.

69. Fieldnotes, Sobokou, November 2017. Born in Congo-Brazzaville to migrants from Sobokou, she had never been to France.

70. Interview with M'Pama Siby, June 2015.

71. Haalpulaar inhabitants of 216 bis organized themselves at the level of the Nguenar region. Papa Demba Fall, "Migration internationale et développement local dans le Nguènar sénégalais," in *Le Sénégal des migrations. Mobilités, identités et sociétés*, ed. Momar-Coumba Diop (Paris: Karthala, 2008), 201.

72. Note on Pierre Landemaine, November 27, 1962. Archives Nationales: 19940023 art. 20.

73. Born in 1926 in Senegal, N'Dongo had come to France in 1956 as a domestic servant before being employed in Paris as a chauffeur. On his trajectory and activism, see Jean-Philippe Dedieu, *La parole immigrée: les migrants africains dans l'espace public en France (1960–1995)* (Paris: Klincksieck, 2012); and Glaes, *African Political Activism*.

74. UGTSF, *Le livre des travailleurs africains en France* (Paris: Maspero, 1970), 78.

75. Note by Renseignements Généraux, January 28, 1965. Archives Nationales: 19940023 art. 20.

76. UGTSF, *Le livre des travailleurs africains en France*, 80.

77. See the case of the Saint-Denis fire in 1963, when the municipality called on the African authorities: "Note succincte sur la situation des travailleurs d'Afrique Noire à Saint-Denis," March 26, 1963. Archives Municipales, Saint-Denis: 18 ACW art. 23.

78. Daouda Gary-Tounkara, "Quand les migrants demandent la route, Modibo Keïta rétorque: 'retournez à la terre!' Les Baragnini et la désertion du 'chantier national' (1958–1968)," *Mande Studies* 5 (2003): 49–64.

79. Note dated October 13, 1965. Archives de la Préfecture de Police de Paris: GA A10.

80. Note dated September 29, 1966. Archives de la Préfecture de Police de Paris: GA A7.

81. Report for the year 1967, Technical Assistance Service. Archives Nationales: AGF5 art. 3385. See also Dedieu, *La parole immigrée*, 91–92.

82. Letter from the Minister of Interior to the Prime Minister, March 23, 1964. Archives Nationales: AGF5 art. 3385. The author compared the situation of West Africans with that of the Algerians, among whom a newly created Association des Algériens de France was active.

83. Thanks to the contacts provided by these students, Sylla enrolled in literacy classes organized by French teachers at a nearby school on Avenue

Max Dormoy at rue Polonceau (interview with Sylla, May 2015). The federation had been active since the 1950s in support of decolonization movements in their home countries, as well as in struggles in France, such as rent strikes in university housing facilities. See Françoise Blum, "Trajectoires militantes et reconversions," *Genèses* 107, no. 2 (2017): 106–30.

84. On the debates among students on the stance to adopt toward fellow migrant workers, see Burleigh J. Hendrickson, *Decolonizing 1968: Transnational Student Activism in Tunis, Paris, and Dakar* (Ithaca, NY: Cornell University Press, 2022), 153–55. Bridging the gap between worker and intellectual was a concern for black activists as early as the 1920s as Jennifer Boittin points out; see Jennifer Boittin, "The Militant Black Men of Marseille and Paris, 1927–1937," in *Black France/France Noire*, ed. Trica Danielle Keaton, T. Denean Sharpley-Whiting, and Tyler Stovall (Durham, NC: Duke University Press, 2012), 223.

85. Jean-Pierre Ndiaye, J. Bassene, and D. Germain, *Les travailleurs noirs en France: pourquoi les migrations?* (Paris: Bureau d'études des réalités africaines, 1963), 13.

86. Glaes, *African Political Activism*, chap. 6.

87. Created in 1958 for the surveillance of Algerians, SAT was staffed by former colonial military. Alexis Spire, *Étrangers à la carte: l'administration de l'immigration en France (1945–1975)* (Paris: Bernard Grasset, 2005), 202–5; Viet, *La France immigrée*, 188. In 1963, SAT's mandate was extended to other migrants, notably West Africans. Jim House, "Contrôle, encadrement, surveillance et répression des migrations coloniales: une décolonisation difficile (1956–1970)," *Bulletin de l'Institut d'Histoire du Temps Présent* 83 (2004): 144–56.

88. Note by the Direction de la population et des migrations, January 1968. Archives Nationales: 5AGF art. 3385. Health officials' fears, often based on racist arguments, abound in the archival record (as emphasized by Germain, *Decolonizing the Republic*); they went along community-based approaches, such as the Centre Médico-Social Bossuet, an institution devoted to providing medical care and social assistance to West Africans, see Glaes, *African Political Activism*.

89. From October 1964 to October 1965, out of 1,772 Africans examined, "420 were previously living in basements and were presented to doctors upon admission to FAS-subsidized foyers." Conférence sur l'état

sanitaire chez les travailleurs originaires d'Afrique Noire, November 19, 1965. Archives de Paris: 3873 W art. 18.

90. Note, May 22, 1963. Archives Nationales: 19850087 art. 158.

91. Leaflet by the *Comité du 13e arrondissement de défense des expulsés*, and Notes by the Renseignements Généraux, November 1963. Archives Nationales: 5AGF art. 3384.

92. For historical background on the complex relationship between communists and black organizations in the interwar period, see Edwards, *The Practice of Diaspora*, chap. 5; and Boittin, "The Militant Black Men of Marseille and Paris."

93. Dedieu, *La parole immigrée*, 53–56.

94. N'Dongo notably supported the 164 residents of a *garni* located at 3 bis rue Riquet (nineteenth arrondissement). Refusing to pay a rent increase, the residents had a bailiff visit the place and report on their dire living conditions. UGTSF, *Le livre des travailleurs africains en France*, 39–41, and Note by Renseignements Généraux, April 14, 1965. Archives de la Préfecture de Police de Paris: GA A7.

95. UGTSF, *Le livre des travailleurs africains en France*, 169–70.

96. Letter from the Préfet de Police to the Secrétaire Général de la Présidence de la République pour la Communauté et les Affaires Africaines et Malgaches, December 13, 1967. Archives Nationales: AG5 art. 3385.

97. For example, the area between the Foyer Pinel in Saint-Denis and Paris is described by Bakary Gandega as "covered by trees like in Africa." Interview with Gandega, October 2015. Other narratives resort to imagery of the "bush" to describe the environment into which they moved.

98. See testimonials from migrants in Diarra, "Les travailleurs africains noirs en France," 941; Juliette Minces, *Les travailleurs étrangers en France: enquête* (Paris: Le Seuil, 1973), 363; Nianguiry Kanté, "Contribution à la connaissance de la migration Soninké en France" (PhD diss., University of Paris 8, 1986), 358; and Catherine Quiminal, *Gens d'ici, gens d'ailleurs: migrations Soninké et transformations villageoises* (Paris: C. Bourgois, 1991), 42–43.

99. Laura Bear, "Ruins and Ghosts: The Domestic Uncanny and the Materialization of Anglo-Indian Genealogies in Kharagpur," in *Ghosts of Memory: Essays on Remembrance and Relatedness*, ed. Janet Carsten (Hoboken, NJ: Blackwell, 2008), 37.

## 2. MODERN BUILDINGS: POLITICAL CHALLENGES, ADMINISTRATIVE ANXIETIES, AND THE CONSOLIDATION OF THE FOYER SYSTEM (1968–1979)

1. Note, July 8, 1969. Archives de la Préfecture de Police de Paris: GA A7; and Programme pluriannuel de résorption et de réhabilitation des foyers, 1975. Archives Nationales: 19870056 art. 3.

2. Daniel A. Gordon, *Immigrants & Intellectuals: May '68 & the Rise of Anti-Racism in France* (London: Merlin Press, 2012); Xavier Vigna, "Une émancipation des invisibles? Les ouvriers immigrés dans les grèves de mai-juin 68," in *Histoire politique des immigrations (post)coloniales, France, 1920–2008*, ed. Abdellali Hajjat and Ahmed Boubeker (Paris: Editions Amsterdam, 2008), 85–94.

3. Interview with Samba Sylla, November 2015. For another example, see Archived interview with Djiby Sy, 2014, Association Génériques, Oral history campaign, "History and memory of immigration, mobilization and fight for equality, 1968–1988." Archives Nationales: 20160153 art. 24.

4. Jean-Philippe Dedieu and Aïssatou Mbodj-Pouye, "The Fabric of Transnational Political Activism: 'Révolution Afrique' and West African Radical Militants in France in the 1970s." *Comparative Studies in Society and History* 60, no. 4 (2018): 1172–1208; and Burleigh J. Hendrickson, *Decolonizing 1968: Transnational Student Activism in Tunis, Paris, and Dakar*. Ithaca, NY: Cornell University Press, 2022.

5. See the list of these distinct movements in Centre d'étude des mouvements sociaux, *Sociologie des mouvements sociaux urbains: enquête sur la région parisienne*, Vol. 1 (Paris: EHESS, 1974), 94–95. They could occasionally intersect: hence, Geneviève Petauton, a key figure in foyer activism, was originally involved in a student facility struggle. Interview with Geneviève Petauton, October 2013.

6. Laure Pitti, "'Travailleurs de France, voilà notre nom.' Les mobilisations des ouvriers étrangers dans les usines et les foyers dans les années 1970," in *Histoire politique des immigrations (post)coloniales, France, 1920–2008*, ed. Abdellali Hajjat and Ahmed Boubeker (Paris: Editions Amsterdam, 2008), 95–111. The opportunity to become a trade union representative was opened to foreigners in 1972.

7. On the CGT's hesitancy surrounding immigrants, see François Platone, "'Prolétaires de tous les pays.' Le Parti communiste français et les immigrés," in *Les étrangers dans la cité: expériences européennes*, ed. Catherine Wihtol de Wenden and Olivier Le Cour Grandmaison (Paris: La Découverte, 1993), 64–80; and Jean-Philippe Dedieu, "L'internationalisme ouvrier à l'épreuve des migrations africaines en France," *Critique internationale* 50, no. 1 (2011): 145–67.

8. Annie Fourcaut, *Bobigny, banlieue rouge* (Paris: Éditions ouvrières: Presses de la Fondation nationale des sciences politiques, 1986); Tyler Stovall, *The Rise of the Paris Red Belt* (Berkeley: University of California Press, 1990); and Olivier Masclet, "Du 'bastion' au 'ghetto.' Le communisme municipal en butte à l'immigration," *Actes de la recherche en sciences sociales* 159, no. 4 (2005): 10–25.

9. Marie-Claude Blanc-Chaléard, *En finir avec les bidonvilles: immigration et politique du logement dans la France des Trente Glorieuses* (Paris: Publications de la Sorbonne, 2016), 283–86. On the necessity of considering immigration policies at a municipal level, see Françoise de Barros, "Les acteurs municipaux et 'leurs' étrangers (1919–1984): gains et contraintes d'un détour communal pour l'analyse d'un travail de catégorisation étatique," *Genèses* 72, no. 3 (2008): 42–62. For detailed studies, see Olivier Masclet, "Une municipalité communiste face à l'immigration algérienne et marocaine," *Genèses. Sciences sociales et histoire* 45, no. 4 (2001): 150–63; Melissa K. Byrnes, "French Like Us? Municipal Policies and North African Migrants in the Parisian Banlieues, 1945–1975" (PhD diss., Georgetown University, Washington, D.C., 2008); and Cédric David, "Logement social des immigrants et politique municipale en banlieue ouvrière (Saint-Denis, 1944–1995). Histoire d'une improbable citoyenneté urbaine" (PhD diss., University of Paris Ouest Nanterre, 2016).

10. Used in a 1964 report on the rehousing of a bidonville, the notion of a *"seuil de tolérance"*—referring to an immigrant threshold, generally set at 15 to 20 percent of the general population, over which integration becomes problematic—was formalized in the early 1970s. See Maryse Tripier, *L'immigration dans la classe ouvrière en France* (Paris: L'Harmattan, 1990), 277. Communist mayors adopted various stances toward immigrant populations in general, and the implantation of foyers in particular. A widely publicized episode took place in December 1980 in the communist town of Vitry. Opposing the reinstallation of 320 Malian workers from the

nearby city of Saint-Maur, members of the local communist section backed by the mayor brought a bulldozer on-site to make the building uninhabitable. See Yvan Gastaut, *L'opinion française et l'immigration sous la Vème République* (Paris: Le Seuil, 2000), 243–51.

11. Note, July 12, 1975. Archives de la Préfecture de Police de Paris: GA A10.

12. The ASTI had existed since 1962, an initiative of Catholic activists. See Johanna Siméant, *La cause des sans-papiers* (Paris: Presses de Sciences po), 360.

13. The Parti Social Unifié was created in 1960 among anticolonial activists disappointed by the compromises made by all left-wing parties. On the loss of credibility of the French Communist Party during the Algerian War of Independence, see Frédérique Matonti and Bernard Pudal, "L'UEC ou l'autonomie confisquée (1956–1968)," in *Mai–Juin 68*, ed. Bernard Pudal, Boris Gobille, Frédérique Matonti, and Dominique Damamme (Paris: Editions de l'Atelier, 2008), 130–43.

14. Gilles de Staal, *Mamadou m'a dit: les luttes des foyers, révolution Afrique, Africa fête* (Paris: Syllepse, 2008); and Dedieu and Mbodj-Pouye, "The Fabric of Transnational Political Activism."

15. Among many accounts, see Jacques Frémontier, *La forteresse ouvrière: Renault: une enquête à Boulogne-Billancourt chez les ouvriers de la Régie* (Paris: Fayard, 1971), 101–6; and the documents published in UGTSF, *Le livre des travailleurs africains en France* (Paris: Maspero, 1970), 44–47.

16. Agence France Press Release, July 7, 1969. Archives Nationales: 19940023 art. 20.

17. For a contemporary account including residents' testimonies, see Juliette Minces, *Les travailleurs étrangers en France: enquête* (Paris: Le Seuil, 1973), 356–67. Detailed analyses can be found in Jean-Philippe Dedieu, *La parole immigrée: les migrants africains dans l'espace public en France (1960–1995)* (Paris: Klincksieck, 2012); and Gillian Glaes, *African Political Activism in Postcolonial France* (London: Routledge, 2019), chap. 2.

18. Note, June 19, 1969. Archives Nationales: 5AGF art. 3386; and UGTSF, *Le livre des travailleurs africains en France*, 49.

19. SAT Report, first trimester 1969. Archives Nationales: 5AGF art. 3385.

20. Note, July 8, 1969. Archives de la Préfecture de Police de Paris: GA A7 (despite a misspelling of the address).

21. Report, August 22, 1969, from the Préfet to the Minister of Interior. Archives Nationales: 5AGF art. 3385.

22. Note, February 2, 1970. Archives de la Préfecture de Police de Paris: A10.

23. See, e.g., Jacques Legru, "Main d'oeuvre noire dans la Seine", *Cahiers Nords-Africains*, no. 102 (1964)., p. 27.

24. Gastaut, *L'opinion française et l'immigration sous la Vème République*, 52–66; and Tangui Perron, ed., *Histoire d'un film, mémoire d'une lutte* (Paris: Scope & Périphéries, 2009), 71–79.

25. Note, January 15, 1970. Archives de la Préfecture de Police de Paris: GA A7. Ivry's foyer was closed in November 1970 and residents were rehoused in existing facilities.

26. The *circulaires* occasioned a strong political response and the first hunger strikes by undocumented workers, most by Turkish and Maghrebi. See Siméant, *La cause des sans-papiers*; they were finally abrogated in July 1973, although the decision to suspend economic immigration followed in 1974.

27. Vincent Viet, *La France immigrée: construction d'une politique, 1914–1997* (Paris: Fayard, 1998), 159.

28. Informal conversation with Michael Hoare.

29. Key studies include Marie-France Moulin, *Machines à dormir: les foyers neufs de la sonacotra, de l'a.d.e.f et quelques autres* (Paris: Maspero, 1976); Mireille Ginésy-Galano, *Les Immigrés hors la cité: le système d'encadrement dans les foyers 1973–1982* (Paris: L'Harmattan, 1984); and Choukri Hmed, "Loger les étrangers 'isolés' en France: socio-histoire d'une institution d'État" (PhD diss., Université Panthéon-Sorbonne, Paris, 2006).

30. Jean-Philippe Dedieu and Aïssatou Mbodj-Pouye, "The First Collective Protest of Black African Migrants in Postcolonial France (1960–1975): A Struggle for Housing and Rights," *Ethnic and Racial Studies* 39, no. 6 (2016): 958–75. Abdoulaye Gueye also argued for a better consideration of these early struggles, but what he called the "protest of 1972" must be set in a wider chronology. See Abdoulaye Gueye, "The Colony Strikes Back: African Protest Movements in Postcolonial France," *Comparative Studies of South Asia, Africa and the Middle East* 26, no. 2 (2006): 225–42.

31. Letter from the representatives of the main managing structures to the Secrétaire d'Etat auprès du Ministre du Travail chargé des travailleurs immigrés, February 21, 1975. Archives Nationales: 19870056 art. 12. Early fears that North Africans would join the movement appear in a Letter

from the Préfet de la Seine-Saint-Denis to M. Le Ministre du Travail, de l'Emploi et de la Population, February 1974. Archives Nationales: 19870056 art. 7.

32. Hmed, "Loger les étrangers 'isolés' en France," 400. Stark differences existed among national groups from the Maghreb. In 1975, only a minority of Algerians lived in foyers, either because they preferred private, even precarious housing or because they had accessed social housing. In contrast, Moroccans, in particular, more recently arrived, still often lived in these facilities. Brigitte Jousselin and Michèle Tallard, *Les conditions de logement des travailleurs migrants en France* (Paris: Centre de Recherches et de Documentation sur la Consommation, 1975), 205.

33. Printed Sonacotra leaflet. Archives Nationales: 19870056 art. 12.

34. "Point de la situation à la date du 26 novembre 1974." Archives Nationales: 19870056 art. 7 (Foyer David Siqueiros also appears as Foyer Allende or Les Tartres). On the strike at Foyer Gaston Philippe in 1971–72, see Archives Départmentales de la Seine-Saint-Denis 1801 W 430. The same dynamics took place at Foyer Romain Rolland in Saint-Denis, where the West African residents coming from a *garni* rue Fontaine were the driving force behind the dispute; and in Villejuif among former residents of the Ivry foyer, see Note by Marc Roberrini to Monsieur le Préfet de la Seine-Saint-Denis, "Agitation maoïste et comportement des Africains dans un foyer de la SONACOTRA à St-Denis," May 19, 1971. Archives Nationales: 19770317 art. 1.

35. Assane Ba, a Senegalese student lodged at Foyer La Noue in Montreuil, took part in the mobilization and cooperated with prominent leaders of the Sonacotra rent strike, such as Mustapha Cherchari. See Stany Grelet, Philippe Mangeot, Victoire Patouillard, and Isabelle Saint-Saëns, "Vingt ans après," *Vacarme* 16, no. 3 (2001): 4–14; and his archived interview, 2014, Génériques oral history campaign. Archives Nationales: 20160153 art. 22.

36. Another committee initiated by the PCF and the CGT in the Seine-Saint-Denis department negotiated a separate compromise with Sonacotra in 1975. This political alliance might be ascribed to Foyer Siqueiros West African residents' long-lasting ties with the municipality as ex-residents of Gaston Philippe. Interview with Jean Bellanger, June 2015.

37. Blanc-Chaléard, *En finir avec les bidonvilles*. The Vivien Law did not specifically target immigrant housing but rather aimed at suppressing

unsanitary housing in general. Once a lodging was declared unfit, it allowed the prefecture to take over the property after paying the owner a legally fixed financial compensation. It also prohibited the renting of spaces deemed unfit for accommodation, such as basements or windowless rooms.

38. Viet, *La France immigrée*, 288.

39. Michelle Guillon, "Ouvriers étrangers et français des usines Renault. Pratiques de mobilisation de la main-d'œuvre," *Espace Populations Sociétés* 6, no. 3 (1988): 455–66.

40. Barbara Prost, "Les 'saisonniers' immigrés dans le collectif de travail. Paris, fin des années 1950-début des années 1980," in *Les travailleurs des déchets*, ed. Delphine Corteel and Stéphane Lelay (Paris: ERES, 2011).

41. Hélène Béguin, "Héberger des migrants ou gérer des logements? L'Aftam et ses 'foyers d'Africains noirs' (1962–2012)." (PhD diss., University of Paris Est, 2015), 198; Hmed, "Loger les étrangers 'isolés' en France," 197.

42. Letter from the Préfet de la Seine-Saint-Denis to the Minister of Labor, undated. Archives Nationales: 19870056 art. 7.

43. Sylvain Laurens, *Une politisation feutrée: les hauts fonctionnaires et l'immigration en France, 1962–1981* (Paris: Belin, 2009); Béguin, "Héberger des migrants."

44. "Le problème du logement des ouvriers étrangers. Le cas des ouvriers étrangers 'isolés,'" September 17, 1971. Archives Nationales: 5AGF art. 3386.

45. Viet, *La France immigrée*, 367.

46. Note sur l'APL, les problèmes de gestion des foyers, 1977. Archives Nationales: 19870056 art. 1.

47. A new institution, the Commission Nationale du Logement Immigré (CNLI), brought together representatives from several ministries and institutions, with a view toward coordinating actions in the area of immigrant housing.

48. Valérie Sala Pala, "Politique du logement social et construction des frontières ethniques: une comparaison franco-britannique" (PhD diss., University of Rennes 1, 2005), 117–18; and Béguin, "Héberger des migrants," 53–54.

49. These norms set better standards for students than migrants: for instance, the minimal surface area for a room in a youth hostel was

12 m², compared to the 9 m² authorized in foyers. See Béguin, "Héberger des migrants," 53. Furthermore, exempt structures still existed (such as provisional "foyers d'accueil" during the period 1971–1974). To expedite things, a subsidy called "Aide transitoire au logement" (ATL) was also introduced to enable residents living in (thus far) unrenovated foyers to receive the APL. Funded directly by FAS as a provisional measure, it was to last into the 1990s.

50. "Note sur les problèmes soulevés par la gestion des foyers d'hébergement de travailleurs africains dans la région parisienne," April 1973. Archives Nationales: 19870056 art. 1.

51. Bernardot, *Loger les immigrés: la Sonacotra* (Bellecombe-en-Bauges, France: Edition du Croquant, 2008), 113; and Hmed, "Loger les étrangers 'isolés' en France," 404.

52. After serving in colonial Algeria, he held several positions, notably director of the Service de liaison et de promotion des migrants, a division created in 1965 and attached to the prefecture. Blanc-Chaléard, *En finir avec les bidonvilles*, 210.

53. Minutes of meeting, December 4, 1969. Archives Nationales: 19770317 art. 1.

54. Memo on Foyer Charonne, 1975, IHTP Fonds Hervo, ARC 3019 (12).

55. Note by Roberrini, October 14, 1970. Archives Nationales: 19870056 art. 7.

56. Note by Roberrini, May 19, 1971. Archives Nationales: 19770317 art. 1.

57. Letter from the Directeur Départemental de l'équipement, June 13, 1975. Report by Roberrini, "La situation des travailleurs africains et de leurs familles à Paris," June 11, 1976. Archives de Paris: Pérotin/101/77/7 art. 63, file n° 8023.

58. For a contribution by Samuel, see "Note concernant le problème de l'exercice de certaines activités artisanales à l'intérieur des foyers habités par des travailleurs originaires d'Afrique Noire," December 1976, Archives Départementales de la Seine-Saint-Denis 1150W art. 13.

59. Barou's inclination to offer ethnic readings of housing populations appears in other contexts, such as the 1984 renovation of a housing project where Harkis lived in Marseille, as quoted in Minayo Nasiali, *Native to the Republic: Empire, Social Citizenship, and Everyday Life in Marseille since 1945* (Ithaca, NY: Cornell University Press, 2016), chap. 5.

60. Jacques Barou, "Rapport intérimaire. Note concernant le programme de relogement des Africains noirs vivant sur Paris et la proche banlieue," 1977. Archives Nationales: 19870056 art. 1.

61. Note, July 16, 1975. Archives de la Préfecture de Police de Paris: GA A7.

62. Note "Des risques d'incidents demeurent entre africains noirs et maghrébins après les incidents de Villejuif," July 28, 1975. Archives Nationales: 19870056 art. 87, p. 2.

63. Report by Roberrini, "La situation des travailleurs africains et de leurs familles à Paris," June 11, 1976. Archives de Paris: Box 62, no. 8023. His main alarm was the situation of African families, of which 1,500 had "suddenly" appeared in the capital.

64. Activists denounced it as a racist crime and blamed AFTAM and the authorities for the lack of security (see press clippings in Archives Nationales: 20050150 art. 103). Authorities attributed the toll to residents panicking in an "over-occupied foyer." Letter by J.-N. Chapulut, October 14, 1977. Archives Nationales: 20050150 art. 103.

65. Note, September 23, 1977. Archives Nationales: 19870056 art. 3.

66. Note by Renseignements Généraux, September 15, 1977. Archives Nationales: 20050150 art. 103.

67. Souleymane Diarra, "Les Travailleurs africains noirs en France," *Bulletin de l'Institut fondamental d'Afrique noire* 30, no. 3 (July 1968): 926.

68. Francine Kane and André Lericollais, "L'émigration en pays Soninké," *Cahiers ORSTOM. Série Sciences Humaines* 12, no. 2 (1975): 180.

69. Michel Samuel, *Le prolétariat africain noir en France* (Paris: Maspero, 1978), 231.

70. Diarra, "Les Travailleurs africains noirs en France," 928; and Samuel, *Le prolétariat africain noir en France*, 232.

71. Note by Renseignements Généraux, October 21, 1963, reporting on the situation in the Department of Oise. An attempt at conjugal life within the foyer is documented, in Legru, "Main d'oeuvre", 31. See also Bilan d'activité, Service d'assistance technique, 1968. Archives Nationales: 5AGF art. 3385. This point should be further explored because gendered biases may have made such arrivals invisible; for the Algerian case, Muriel Cohen demonstrates how the presence of Algerian women and family has been underestimated in administrative and scholarly accounts. Muriel Cohen, *Des familles invisibles: Les Algériens de France entre intégrations et discriminations (1945–1985)* (Paris: Editions de la Sorbonne, 2020).

72. Ginésy-Galano, *Les Immigrés hors la cité*, 155. As late as 1978, the director of Foyer Mûriers, run by the Parisian Bureau of social aid, monitored visits by women. Archives de Paris: 2024 W art. 1.

73. After visiting the AFTAM Foyer in Méru, the sous-préfet observed: "A spirit of healthy camaraderie prevails, which excludes any promiscuity," Letter from the Sous-préfet de Beauvais to the Préfet de l'Oise, May 19, 1970. Archives Départementales de l'Oise, 1005 W 77. Ginésy-Galano also notes that, for fear of homosexual relationships, some foyer directors prohibited visits between rooms. Ginésy-Galano, *Les Immigrés hors la cité*, 155. Such restrictions could not be applied to dormitories.

74. See, for example, Legru, "Main d'oeuvre" 32.

75. In 1963, 63 percent of French were against interracial marriage between an African and a white French woman. See Ministère de la Coopération, *Dix réponses sur l'Afrique: Opinions sur la coopération entre l'Afrique et la France*, Paris, 1963; quoted in Félix F. Germain, *Decolonizing the Republic: African and Caribbean Migrants in Postwar Paris, 1946-1974* (East Lansing: Michigan State University Press, 2016), 47. Hélène Neveu Kringelbach studies interracial unions in elite and student milieus. Hélène Neveu Kringelbach, "Gendered Educational Trajectories and Transnational Marriage Among West African Students in France," *Identities* 22, no. 3 (2015): 288–302; and Hamidou Dia among Haalpulaar labor migrants, mostly in the 1960s. Hamidou Dia, *Trajectoires et pratiques migratoires des Haalpulaaren du Sénégal: socio-anthropologie d'un "village multi-situé"* (Paris: L'Harmattan, 2015), 60–64.

76. "Le problème du logement des ouvriers étrangers. Le cas des ouvriers étrangers 'isolés,'" September 17, 1971. Archives Nationales: 5AGF art. 3386.

77. Alain Dubresson, "Les travailleurs Soninké et Toucouleur dans l'Ouest parisien," *Cahiers ORSTOM Série Sciences Humaines* 12, no. 2 (1975): 190.

78. Meillassoux addresses the situation of migrant workers by tying the rural homelands and the industrial cities of Europe and South Africa into the same analytical frame. This requires a crucial modification of Marxist thought in order to conceptualize the "articulation" of capitalist and domestic modes of production rather than the destruction of previous economic and social relations by the advent of capitalism. See Claude Meillassoux, *Maidens, Meal, and Money: Capitalism and the Domestic Community* (Cambridge: Cambridge University Press,1981), 97.

79. François Manchuelle, "The 'Patriarchal Ideal' of Soninke Labor Migrants: From Slave Owners to Employers of Free Labor," *Canadian Journal of African Studies* 23, no. 1 (1989): 108.

80. Charles S. Bird and Martha B. Kendall, "The Mande Hero: Text and Context," in *Explorations in African Systems of Thought*, ed. Ivan Karp and Charles S. Bird (Bloomington: Indiana University Press, 1980), 13–26.

81. In the West African societies under consideration, notions of work/labor encompass reproductive and productive fields (under the following terms: *golle*, in Soninke and Pulaar; *baara* in Bamanan; *liggéey* in Wolof). From this common matrix, highly gendered notions of work/labor are elaborated. On notions of labor across Mande societies (Soninke, Haalpulaar and Bamanan), see Mamadou Diawara, "Ce que travailler veut dire dans le monde mandé," in *Le Travail en Afrique*, ed. Hélène d'Almeida-Topor, Monique Lakroum, and Gerd Spittler (Paris: Karthala, 2004), 67–80.

82. Meillassoux, *Maidens, Meal, and Money*, 129.

83. For instance, in 1974, some residents had been expelled by Soundiata for using their room for tailoring, but they won their case and eventually returned to the building, Lucien Angevin, "L'usine dortoir de la rue Pinel" *Droit et Liberté*, May–June 1974, p. 13.

84. Interview with Samba Sylla, July 2013. When, in 1985, a smaller foyer opened at the 216 bis address, the bulk of the former residents remained in the nineteenth arrondissement, and only a couple moved back to the old location.

85. Letter dated October 1, 1977, from the Cabinet du Préfet to the Directeur de l'urbanisme et du logement. Archives de Paris: 1178 W art. 2959. For reasons that I have been unable to trace, the options suggested by Barou in the Rapport intérimaire did not materialize.

86. Anthony Lucien Béchu had designed accommodations for workers of the Banque de l'Afrique Occidentale in Abidjan, Yaoundé, and Niamey in the 1950s, as well as large social housing schemes in Algeria.

87. Interview with Jean-Jack Baron, June 2013.

88. The Sonacotra model of the "*unité de vie*" brought together a much larger number of rooms, and the individual rooms were extremely small (9 m², often divided into two bedrooms), as part of architectural choices made in the 1950s, later abandoned in favor of a more standard layout of 7.5 m² rooms along one corridor. See Hmed, "Loger les étrangers 'isolés' en France," 185–96. At Foyer Lorraine and Foyer D'Hautpoul, one-bed rooms provided an area of 11 m²; two-bed rooms, 15 m²; three-bed rooms, 22 m².

89. This case stands as an inversion of the ordinary logic whereby the architectural style of the "*unité de vie*" was conceived as facilitating the later conversion of foyers into family apartments. For a later example, see the *Paris Projet* special issue: "Politiques nouvelles de la rénovation urbaine," *Paris Projet* 21–22 (1982): 21.

90. Manuscript addition by the Sous-directeur de la construction to the Secrétaire général de la Ville de Paris, October 18, 1977. Archives de Paris: 1178 W art. 2959. "In lieu of an ordinary project [the epithet is circled and added] of 56 lodgings, surreptitiously and by means of a modification to the construction, leaving the municipality with no choice, construction works having been pursued under cover of the previously granted authorization for a completely different purpose."

91. Mémoire au Tribunal administratif de 3 syndicats de co-propriétaires contre le Préfet de Paris et la Société anonyme d'HLM Le Nouveau Logis. Archives de Paris: 1178 W art. 4235.

92. As we have seen, the nineteenth arrondissement was the hub of West African settlement in the 1960s (including a small Malian dormitory at 8 rue d'Hautpoul listed in Jaques Legru, "Etude sur les travailleurs d'Afrique noire à Paris et dans le Département de la Seine," 1963, p. 94, Archives Nationales: 5AGF art. 3385.

93. Blocages de construction de foyers de travailleurs migrants, 1978. Archives Nationales: 19870056 art. 1.

94. Interview with Alassane Ba, May 2013.

95. Part of the population of Foyer David D'Angers was later relocated in the thirteenth arrondissement, but Foyer David D'Angers remained a dormitory until 2009.

96. Interviews with Samba Sylla, July 2013 and April 2014.

97. Tract by a Permanences Anti-Expulsion French activist "Sundiata [sic] rue St Denis: une victoire," shared by Samba Sylla.

98. On this law proposed in September 1979 by Minister d'Ornano, see Ginésy-Galano, *Les Immigrés hors la cité*. On the protest at Foyer D'Hautpoul, see interview with Petauton, October 2013.

99. Interview with Bakary Traoré, June 2013.

100. As late as 1988, a discussion among Soundiata administrators about a rent increase differentiated between "foyers dortoirs" and "foyers modernes." Minutes of the Conseil d'administration, November 24, 1988. Archives Nationales: 20050150 art. 115.

101. The team building Lorraine and D'Hautpoul seems to have only modestly taken into account the specificities of the end users, but other examples reflect a deeper interest in the residents' ways of inhabiting the space. See notably the facility opened at 61 rue de Charonne (Paris eleventh arrondissement) in 1984, designed by the architects Estelle and Alain Schmied, who had previously contributed to post-1968 reflections on architectural projects, notably in relation to psychiatric facilities around the Centre d'Etudes de Recherches et de Formation Institutionnelle. They designed the project in close dialogue with its future West African occupants. Interview with Estelle and Alain Schmied, March 2017. My thanks to Adeline Gonin for organizing this meeting.

102. "Les nouvelles mises en service en 1979 et 1980," Report from the "Delmon" committee. Archives Nationales: 20050150 art. 96.

## 3. PERMANENCE AND DECAY: AFRICAN FOYERS, FROM SOLUTION TO PROBLEM (1980s–1990s)

1. Patrick Weil, "Immigration and the Rise of Racism in France: The Contradictions in Mitterrand's Policies," *French Politics and Society* 9, no. 3–4 (1991): 82–100.

2. Christian Poiret, *Familles africaines en France: ethnicisation, ségrégation et communalisation* (Paris: L'Harmattan, 1997), 68.

3. "Le logement des travailleurs immigrés isolés et les foyers en Ile de France," AFICIL Ile de France, May 1984. Archives de Paris: 3873 W art. 6.

4. Abdelmalek Sayad, *L'illusion du provisoire, L'immigration ou Les paradoxes de l'altérité 1* (Paris: Raisons d'agir, 2006).

5. The association first changed its name to Soundiata Nouvelle in 2001, and eventually ceased its activities in 2006, with its foyers being transferred to AFTAM.

6. Mahamet Timera, *Les Soninké en France: d'une histoire à l'autre* (Paris: Karthala, 1996), 99.

7. Poiret, *Familles africaines en France*, 67.

8. Until the 1993 ban on polygamy, family reunion was also opted for by men with several spouses, either in rotation (having one wife in France while the other(s) remained in the country of origin) or by bringing

several to France at once. Sylvie Fainzang and Odile Journet, *La femme de mon mari: étude ethnologique du mariage polygamique en Afrique et en France* (Paris: L'Harmattan, 1989).

9. In 1991, Sonacotra, an organization that by then hosted 20 percent of West African residents in the Paris region, included more than three hundred families. Poiret, *Familles africaines en France*, 149; see also Marc Bernardot, *Loger les immigrés: la Sonacotra* (Bellecombe-en-Bauges, France: Edition du Croquant, 2008), 248.

10. In her research among Khassonke families from the region of Kayes, Nehara Feldman demonstrates how considerations of domestic work weigh in family decisions around the mobility of women. Nehara Feldman, *Migrantes: du bassin du fleuve Sénégal aux rives de la Seine* (Paris: La Dispute, 2018).

11. Hamidou Dia, *Trajectoires et pratiques migratoires des Haalpulaaren du Sénégal: socio-anthropologie d'un "village multi-situé"* (Paris: L'Harmattan, 2015), 102–3.

12. Timera, *Les Soninké en France*, 94.

13. On the basis of research among South Asian migrants in Britain, Roger Ballard demonstrates how cultural dynamics are tied to economic and social circumstances; he notably explains a defensive moral attitude toward the imigrant society by the fact that family reunions coincide with economic crisis. Roger Ballard, "Migration and Kinship: The Differential Effect of Marriage Rules on the Process of Punjabi Migration to Britain," in *South Asians Overseas: Contexts and Communities*, ed. C. Clarke, C. Peach, and S. Vertovec (Cambridge: Cambridge University Press, 1990), 219–49.

14. Based on 1990s data, one study demonstrated a sharp discrimination against families from immigrant backgrounds (the general rate of acceptance of social housing after six months was 75 percent, but these families fared less at only 58 percent) and noted that families from sub-Saharan Africa were even more disadvantaged. Thomas Kirszbaum and Patrick Simon, "Les Discriminations raciales et ethniques dans l'accès au logement social," Note de synthèse no.3 du Groupe d'étude et de lutte contre les discriminations, May 2001, 33.

15. Scrutinizing administrative rehousing practices, David demonstrates the existence of racial discrimination against non-European families by the municipality of Saint-Denis. See Cédric David, "Logement social

des immigrants et politique municipale en banlieue ouvrière (Saint-Denis, 1944–1995). Histoire d'une improbable citoyenneté urbaine" (PhD diss., University of Paris Ouest Nanterre, 2016); as does Nasiali in Marseille. Minayo Nasiali, *Native to the Republic: Empire, Social Citizenship, and Everyday Life in Marseille Since 1945* (Ithaca, NY: Cornell University Press, 2016), chap. 5.

16. Christian Poiret, "L'inclusion des familles africaines en Ile-de-France: de la catégorie 'ethnique' aux groupes 'africains,'" *Espace Populations Sociétés* 14, no. 2 (1996): 335–46.

17. Jean-Philippe Dedieu, "The Rise of the Migration-Development Nexus in Francophone Sub-Saharan Africa, 1960–2010," *African Studies Review* 61, no. 1 (2018): 83. See also Christophe Daum, *Les associations de Maliens en France: migrations, développement et citoyenneté* (Paris: Karthala, 1998).

18. Agathe Petit, "L'ultime retour des gens du fleuve Sénégal," *Hommes & Migrations* 1236, no. 1 (2002): 44–52. Detailed studies of "caisses," from transnational financial streams to wider forms of transnational community organization, are featured in Abdoulaye Kane, *Tontines, caisses de solidarité et banquiers ambulants: univers des pratiques financières informelles en Afrique* (Paris: L'Harmattan, 2010); and Amélie Grysole and Aïssatou Mbodj-Pouye, "Bons, fax et sacs de riz. Tenir et maintenir un circuit économique transnational (France, Sénégal)," *Cahiers d'études africaines*, no. 225 (2017): 121–50.

19. Abdoulaye Gueye, *Les intellectuels africains en France* (Paris: L'Harmattan, 2001), 92–96.

20. On the persistence of slavery in West Africa, see Benedetta Rossi, ed., *Reconfiguring Slavery: West African Trajectories* (Liverpool: Liverpool University Press, 2009).

21. François Manchuelle, *Willing Migrants: Soninke Labor Diasporas, 1848–1960* (Athens: Ohio University Press, 1997); and Jean Schmitz, "Islamic Patronage and Republican Emancipation: The Slaves of the Almaami in the Senegal River Valley," in *Reconfiguring Slavery: West African Trajectories*, ed. Benedetta Rossi (Liverpool: Liverpool University Press, 2009), 85–115.

22. Michel Samuel, *Le prolétariat africain noir en France* (Paris: Maspero, 1978), 246–50. Unfortunately, the latter figures do not offer a basis for comparison because they are not supported by the group distribution in the villages of origin.

23. A counterexample, with a village chief controlling recruitment in the laundry services of Boulogne-Billancourt is cited by Daum, *Les associations de Maliens en France*, 107–8.

24. Francine Kane and André Lericollais, "L'émigration en pays Soninké," *Cahiers ORSTOM. Série Sciences Humaines* 12, no. 2 (1975): 186.

25. Jean-Luc Demonsant, "Family Prestige as Old-Age Security: Evidence from Rural Senegal," Department of Economics and Finance Working Papers EC200802, Universidad de Guanajuato, 2007.

26. Paolo Gaibazzi, "The Rank Effect: Post-Emancipation Immobility in a Soninke Village," *The Journal of African History* 53, no. 2 (2012): 215–34.

27. This fits into Lotte Pelckmans' typology of mobility of individuals of slave descent as "moving with." Lotte Pelckmans, "Moving Memories of Slavery Among West African Migrants in Urban Contexts (Bamako, Paris)," *Revue européenne des migrations internationales* 29, no. 1 (2016): 45–67.

28. As Samuel cautiously described in the 1970s, "in foyers, a frequent but not generalized, aspect of former slaves towards their former masters, is that 'sons of slaves' cook, meaning that they prepare the collective dinner, for the entire community." Émile Le Bris, Pierre-Philippe Rey, and Michel Samuel, *Capitalisme négrier: la marche des paysans vers le prolétariat* (Paris: Maspero, 1976), 111–12.

29. Moussa Konaté even evokes the case of groups funding the trip of a man of slave descent for the purpose of having him there to cook for them. Moussa Konaté, "Tunga: A Study of Malian Soninke Labor Migration to France" (PhD diss., University of California, Los Angeles, 1997), 78.

30. Le Bris, Rey, and Samuel, *Capitalisme négrier*, 83; and Timera, *Les Soninké en France*, 116.

31. Plans, Archives de Paris: 1178 W art. 2959 (Foyer Lorraine) and 1178 W art. 4235 (Foyer D'Hautpoul).

32. Fiches documentaires, November-December 1983, Soundiata. Archives Nationales: 2005150 art. 61.

33. Marcel Maussen, "Islamic Presence and Mosque Establishment in France: Colonialism, Arrangements for Guestworkers and Citizenship," *Journal of Ethnic & Migration Studies* 33, no. 6 (2007): 981–1002; Naomi Davidson, *Only Muslim: Embodying Islam in Twentieth-Century France* (Ithaca, NY: Cornell University Press, 2012).

34. Archives Nationales: 19850087 art. 158.

35. A prayer room was established at Foyer Charonne (Paris, eleventh arrondissement), according to Barou. See Centre national de la recherche scientifique and Régie nationale des usines Renault, *Les O.S. dans l'industrie automobile: recherche documentaire et bibliographique, 02: Analyse documentaire* (Paris: CNRS, 1986), 139; and another was established at Foyer Commanderie (Paris, nineteenth arrondissement). See Moustapha Diop and Laurence Michalak, "'Refuge' and 'Prison': Islam, Ethnicity, and the Adaptation of Space in Workers' Housing in France," in *Making Muslim Space in North America and Europe*, ed. B. D. Metcalf (Berkeley: University of California Press, 1996).

36. On Rouen, see "La Maison de la Mauritanie-Sénégal et la mosquée de la rue Moïse inaugurées par M. Moktar Ould Daddah," *Paris-Normandie*, September 30, 1968.

37. AFTAM annual report, 1969, p. 21, quoted in Hélène Béguin, "Héberger des migrants ou gérer des logements? L'Aftam et ses 'foyers d'Africains noirs' (1962–2012)" (PhD diss., University of Paris Est, 2015), 203. Among its planned improvements, the association listed the conversion of some spaces into prayer rooms.

38. For example, Liste des revendications des foyers en grève, October 13, 1975. Archives Nationales: 19870056 art. 7.

39. Choukri Hmed, "Loger les étrangers 'isolés' en France: socio-histoire d'une institution d'État" (PhD diss., Université Panthéon-Sorbonne, Paris, 2006), 453.

40. Hmed's account usefully mitigates Barou's overemphasis on this demand. Jacques Barou, "L'Islam, facteur de régulation sociale," *Esprit* 102, no. 6 (1985): 209.

41. Mahamet Timera, "Trajectoires du fondamentalisme parmi les communautés soninké musulmanes immigrées en France," in *Islam et villes en Afrique au sud du Sahara: entre soufisme et fondamentalisme*, ed. Adriana Piga (Paris: Karthala, 2003), 293.

42. Timera, *Les Soninké en France*, 165–67.

43. Subhi retraces the opening of a mosque in a factory in 1968. Toma Subhi, "Musulmans dans l'entreprise," *Esprit* 102, no. 6 (1985): 219. Hamès dates the revival in Islamic practices to 1975. Constant Hamès, "Islam et structures sociales chez les immigrés soninké en France," *Social Compass* 26, no. 1 (1979): 87–98. Cordell and Sargent quote the interview

of Imam Baradji at Foyer Claude Tillier (Paris, twelfth arrondissement) who came in 1979 "not to work but as a man of religion." Dennis D. Cordell and Carolyn F. Sargent, "Islam, Identity and Gender in Daily Life Among Malians in Paris: The Burdens Are Easier to Bear," in *L'islam politique au sud du Sahara. identité, discours et enjeux*, ed. Muriel Gomez-Perez (Paris: Karthala, 2009), 187.

44. Timera, "Trajectoires du fondamentalisme," 293.

45. Diop and Michalak, "'Refuge' and 'Prison,'" 88.

46. Such differentiation is tied to distinct politico-religious historical backgrounds between Haalpulaar and Soninke that I cannot expand on here. It is important to note that these societies offered distinct political roles for religious leaders: in Soninke regions, religious families tended not to have political power, whereas Haalpulaar clerics inherited the exercise of power from the theocratic period. I leave aside the case of the Murid brotherhood, who constitute a major group in Wolof international migration but are not well represented in the foyers. During their early phase of development in France in the 1980s, they did reach out to Senegalese in student hostels and foyers. See Moustapha Diop, "L'émigration murid en Europe," *Hommes & Migrations* 1132, no. 1 (1990): 23.

47. Moustapha Diop, "Structuration d'un réseau: la Jamaat Tabligh (Société pour la Propagation de la Foi)," *Revue européenne des migrations internationales* 10, no. 1 (1994): 150–51.

48. Interview with Imam Fofana, February 10, 2017. My thanks to Pierre-Marie Aubert for introducing me to Imam Fofana.

49. Benjamin F. Soares, "An African Muslim Saint and His Followers in France," *Journal of Ethnic and Migration Studies* 30, no. 5 (2004): 913–27.

50. Interview with Ba Mody Sow, Boulogne-Billancourt, March 1, 2017. A prayer room opened in 1976 at Renault Billancourt as a demand stemming from Senegalese workers. Jacques Barou, Moustapha Diop, and Toma Subhi, "Des musulmans dans l'usine," in *Ouvriers spécialisés à Billancourt: les derniers témoins*, ed. Renaud Sainsaulieu and Ahsène Zehraoui (Paris: L'Harmattan, 1995), 131–61.

51. This foyer is cited by Abdoulaye Kane in his exploration of transnational links between Senegal, Morocco, and France. Abdoulaye Kane, "Les pèlerins sénégalais au Maroc: la sociabilité autour de la Tijaniyya," in *Les nouveaux urbains dans l'espace Sahara-Sahel. Un cosmopolitisme par*

*le bas*, ed. Elisabeth Boesen and Laurence Marfaing (Paris: Karthala-ZMO, 2007), 192.

52. Ousmane Kane, *The Homeland Is the Arena: Religion, Transnationalism, and the Integration of Senegalese Immigrants in America* (Oxford: Oxford University Press, 2011), 147.

53. Jean-François Legrain, "Islam en France, Islam de France," *Esprit* 119, no. 10 (1986): 20.

54. Legrain, "Islam en France, Islam de France," 18.

55. Sylvain Laurens, "De la 'Promotion culturelle des immigrés' à 'l'interculturel' (1974–1980): Discours d'État sur une catégorie d'État," *Cultures & Conflits*, no. 107 (2017): 15–41.

56. For AFTAM, see Béguin, "Héberger des migrants," 214. On animation as part of the social engineering dimension of social housing in postwar France, see Kenny Cupers, *The Social Project: Housing Postwar France* (Minneapolis: University of Minnesota Press, 2014).

57. Interview with Seydou, June 2012.

58. Vincent Gay, "Grèves saintes ou grèves ouvrières?," *Genèses* 98, no. 1 (2015): 110–30.

59. Surveillance particularly targeted Maghrebi foyers, see, for example, a 1987 note on the presence of fundamentalists (French: *intégristes*) in a foyer in Asnières. Archives Départementales des Hauts-de-Seine: 2124W art. 89.

60. Diop and Michalak, "'Refuge' and 'Prison,'" 81–82.

61. Report by Association Soundiata for the year 1991, p. 10. Archives Nationales: 20050150 art. 115.

62. Béguin, "Héberger des migrants," 223; and Bernardot, *Loger les immigrés*, 193.

63. Hmed, "Loger les étrangers 'isolés' en France," 520. Leaflet from the Soundiata Nouvelle, 2004 (communicated by Francis Lacroix, former president of the association). Internal document, Soundiata association, 1989. Archives Nationales: 2005150 art. 61.

64. See, for instance, the "Rapport remis à Georgina Dufoix, Secrétaire d'État à la Famille, à la Population et aux Travailleurs immigrés, sur les conditions de logements des travailleurs migrants isolés et notamment les africains du sud du Sahara," 1984. Archives Nationales: 20050150 art. 61.

65. Hmed, "Loger les étrangers 'isolés' en France," 529; and Johanna Siméant, *La cause des sans-papiers* (Paris: Presses de Sciences po, 1998), 203.

66. Letter from Pierre Bolotte, Préfet of Seine-Saint-Denis, to the Minister of Interior, January 19, 1972, Archives Départementales de la Seine-Saint-Denis: 1150W art. 13; letter from Pierre Bolotte, Préfet of Seine-Saint-Denis, to the Minister of Work, Employment and Population, February 14, 1974 Archives Nationales: 19870056 art. 7.

68. Correspondence between the Préfet de Seine-Saint-Denis and the Directeur Départemental des Polices urbaines, February 1975. Archives Départementales de la Seine-Saint-Denis, 1150W art. 13.

69. Bernardot, *Loger les immigrés*, 247–48.

70. Audit de gestion, Soundiata, 1986. Archives Nationales: 20050150 art. 115, p. 17.

71. In 1986, BAS managed eleven structures, comprising 2,567 beds, of which 1,663 were occupied by sub-Saharan Africans. See "Situation of the foyers de travailleurs migrants," September 30, 1985. Archives de Paris: 3873 W art. 8.

72. Circular note, undated, EATM director to the directors of the foyers. Archives de Paris: 2024 W art. 1.

73. Letter from Robert Pandrau, Cabinet du Maire de Paris, to the director of the BAS, August 23, 1983. Archives de Paris: 3873 W art. 8.

74. Letter July 8, 1987, from the director of the BAS to the Préfet de Paris. Archives de Paris: 3873 W art. 8.

75. Circular note dated November 26, 1980, from director of the EATM to the directors of the foyers. Archives de Paris: 2024 W art. 1.

76. Béguin, "Héberger des migrants," 213.

77. CASVP [new name of the BAS] steering committee, October 16, 1995. Archives de Paris: 3873 W art. 8.

78. Pauline Gaullier, "La décohabitation et le relogement des familles polygames," *Revue des politiques sociales et familiales* 94, no. 1 (2008): 59–69; Cécile Péchu, "Black African Immigrants in France and Claims for Housing," *Journal of Ethnic and Migration Studies* 25, no. 4 (1999): 727–44.

79. Julien Beaugé and Abdellali Hajjat, "Élites françaises et construction du 'problème musulman.' Le cas du Haut Conseil à l'intégration (1989–2012)," *Sociologie* 5, no. 1 (2014): 31–59.

80. Henri Cuq, "Mission parlementaire sur la situation et le devenir des foyers de travailleurs migrants," Mission parlementaire auprès ministre chargé de l'intégration et de la lutte contre l'exclusion (Paris: 1996), 17.

81. Cuq, "Mission parlementaire," 23.

82. Cuq, "Mission parlementaire, 31.

83. Stéphane Dufoix, "Nommer l'autre. L'émergence du terme communautarisme dans le débat français," *Socio. La nouvelle revue des sciences sociales*, no. 7 (2016): 163–86; and Fabrice Dhume-Sonzogni, *Communautarisme: enquête sur une chimère du nationalisme français* (Paris: Demopolis, 2016). "Communautarisme" is sometimes translated into English as "communalism," but I favor the more common term "communitarianism." See John R. Bowen, *Why the French Don't Like Headscarves: Islam, the State, and Public Space* (Princeton, NJ: Princeton University Press, 2008).

84. For a wider presentation of the context in which French social studies developed around issues such as race, see Valérie Amiraux and Patrick Simon, "There Are No Minorities Here: Cultures of Scholarship and Public Debate on Immigrants and Integration in France," *International Journal of Comparative Sociology* 47, no. 3–4 (2006): 191–215; and Sarah Mazouz, *La République et ses autres: politiques de l'altérité dans la France des années 2000* (Lyon: ENS Éditions, 2017).

85. Pierre Pascal as quoted in Béguin, "Héberger des migrants," 104.

86. Michel Fiévet, *Le livre blanc des travailleurs immigrés des foyers: du non-droit au droit* (Paris: L'Harmattan, 1999).

## 4. TOLERATED BONDS: LIVING TOGETHER IN THE FOYERS

1. Field notes, Foyer Stalingrad, Boulogne-Billancourt, July 2016 to January 2017.

2. Catherine Quiminal, *Gens d'ici, gens d'ailleurs: migrations Soninké et transformations villageoises* (Paris: C. Bourgois, 1991), 87.

3. On greetings as key markers of distinct forms of sociability and on migrants' reflections on the topic, see Tilmann Heil, "Conviviality. (Re)negotiating Minimal Consensus," in *Routledge International Handbook of Diversity Studies*, ed. Steven Vertovec (Abingdon: Routledge, 2015), 321–22.

4. When originating from the same country, speakers from distinct ethnolinguistic groups generally have a vernacular language in common (Wolof in Senegal, Bamanan in Mali); but when, for instance, Malian

Soninke and Senegalese Haalpulaar meet, they generally use French to communicate.

5. For a critique of such statements, see Quiminal, *Gens d'ici, gens d'ailleurs*, 48.

6. The foyers where I conducted most of my fieldwork hosted only West Africans (such is the case for Foyer Lorraine and Foyer D'Hautpoul and for Foyer Nationale and Foyer Stalingrad, both located in Boulogne-Billancourt). When I spent some time in mixed foyers, such as Foyer Masséna (thirteenth arrondissement), I always entered these foyers through West African networks, so my interactions with Moroccans and Algerians were generally limited. On this topic, see Mahamadou Cissoko, "Les relations afro-maghrébines du foyer au quartier. La fraternité islamique à l'épreuve du quotidien" (PhD diss., Université Paris 8, 2019); Alistair Hunter compares the two groups and offers comments on coexistence. Alistair Hunter, *Retirement Home? Ageing Migrant Workers in France and the Question of Return* (New York: Springer, 2018).

7. Interview with Makan Koné, president of the Association de ressortissants Mauritaniens pour l'éradication des pratiques de l'esclavage et ses séquelles (ARMEPES), June 2016. See also Sidi N'Diaye, "Des 'restes' résistants en milieu soninké: esclavage, sens de l'honneur et mécanismes d'émancipation," *Critique internationale* 72, no. 3 (2016): 113–25. Most of my fieldwork preceded the emergence of the Ganbane movement in 2017, a period during which such issues became hotly debated in Mali, Senegal, and Mauritania, as well as in the diasporic space.

8. Mahamet Timera, *Les Soninké en France: d'une histoire à l'autre* (Paris: Karthala, 1996), 79–80; Yaya Sy, "L'esclavage chez les Soninkés: du village à Paris," *Journal des Africanistes* 70, no. 1 (2000): 43–69; and Moustapha Diop and Laurence Michalak, "'Refuge' and 'Prison': Islam, Ethnicity, and the Adaptation of Space in Workers' Housing in France," in *Making Muslim Space in North America and Europe*, ed. B. D. Metcalf (Berkeley: University of California Press, 1996), 79.

9. Original Wolof: "*Fii mom, ñepp ay travailleurs lañu, amul jamm, amul ger.*" Informal conversation with Demba, June 2013. Demba is of "freeman" origin (from the *cuballo* group). In the Haalpulaar environments where I spent time, I did not find the persistence of status-based distinctions in daily actions as conspicuous as among Soninke. This might be due to my lesser knowledge of the codes of this society, or it might

be the effect of more egalitarian practices. In New York, Ousmane Kane observed that "within the *galle wuro* or *suudu wuro* . . . , egalitarianism is the norm, and everyone takes his turn to cook, wash, and clean." Ousmane Kane, *The Homeland Is the Arena: Religion, Transnationalism, and the Integration of Senegalese Immigrants in America* (Oxford: Oxford University Press, 2011), 75.

10. Obviously, an interjection referring to one's status made in what seems to be a joking tone can be received as harmful, as recalled notably by Olivier Leservoisier, "Les héritages de l'esclavage dans la société haalpulaar de Mauritanie," *Journal des africanistes* 78, no. 1–2 (2008): 247–67.

11. I thus nuance Lotte Pelckmans' characterization of the foyers as places where migrants would systematically "move with" or "move back into" their slave status. Lotte Pelckmans, "Moving Memories of Slavery Among West African Migrants in Urban Contexts (Bamako, Paris)," *Revue Européenne Des Migrations Internationales* 29, no. 1 (2016): 45–67.

12. On the situation in his village, he alternated between acknowledging that being of slave descent had blocked him in his political career and the general statement that such issues had been settled "long ago" (in the 1980s).

13. Interview with Diaguily, November 2016, conducted with Stefan Le Courant. An even more dramatic example is provided in the testimony of Henoune ould Oumar ould Mbareck, a Mauritanian antislavery activist who had been forced to sleep in the foyer's kitchen and whose refusal had led him to leave the Paris region. "Interview of Henoune ould Oumar ould Mbareck (aka Diko)," AHME, March 2012, http:// www.haratine.com/Site/ancien/interview8.htm.

14. Sy, "L'esclavage chez les Soninkés."

15. "Règlement intérieur du foyer Lorraine," January 1994 (personal archive of Samba Sylla).

16. "Des règles à respecter pour une meilleure cohabitation," 2017 (personal communication by a délégué). This document regulates life in a former foyer recently turned into a residence (Résidence Mûriers, twentieth arrondissement).

17. Hamidou Dia, "Villages multi-situés du Fouta-Toro en France: le défi de la transition entre générations de caissiers, lettrés et citadins," *Revue Asylon(s)*, no. 3 (2008).

18. Field notes, January 2020.

19. In other accounts, the prayer room was a place where distinctions (of ethnicity or religious affiliation) did play a role.

20. Amélie Grysole and Aïssatou Mbodj-Pouye, "Bons, fax et sacs de riz. Tenir et maintenir un circuit économique transnational (France, Sénégal)," *Cahiers d'études africaines*, no. 225 (2017): 121–50.

21. Claire Clouet, *La Diaspora de la chambre 107. Ethnographies musicales dans la diaspora soninké* (Paris: Editions MF, 2021): 48.

22. Laura Guérin noted a vernacular terminology with such rooms named *"chambres-mères"*; I did not encounter this, but it is consistent with the practices I observed (personal communication).

23. The other bed in the room was occupied by a man from the same village, in his late forties, who used to live with Dramane's father; Dramane addressed him as his "older brother." Dramane is from a *naxamala* family, but his roommate is from a family identified as being of slave descent. Dramane could directly refer to some of his peers as slaves, but in this case the age difference prevailed and he adopted an attitude of deference toward his roommate.

24. On the concept of "wealth in people," see Jane I. Guyer and Samuel M. Eno Belinga, "Wealth in People as Wealth in Knowledge: Accumulation and Composition in Equatorial Africa," *Journal of African History* 36, no. 1 (1995): 91–120.

25. Elodie Razy, "Les migrants ont-ils des manières particulières d'habiter?," *Hommes & Migrations* 1264, no. 1 (2006): 81–82.

26. Marie-Laure Boursin, "À l'heure de la prière: entre pratiques et expérimentations," *Ethnologie francaise* 168, no. 4 (2017): 631.

27. Laura Guérin, "Le portable comme 'chez-soi' dans un contexte de précarité résidentielle. Le cas des habitants de résidences sociales issues de foyers de travailleurs migrants," *Socio-anthropologie*, no. 40 (2019): 97–113.

28. Natacha Calandre and Evelyne Ribert, "Les pratiques alimentaires d'hommes ouest-africains vivant en Île-de-France. Entre perpétuation de la culture alimentaire d'origine et aspiration à la modernité," *Hommes & migrations*, no. 1286–87 (2010): 162–73.

29. Potential profits were supposed to feed into the foyers' caisses, inducing money circuits that often raised suspicions of misappropriation. Kitchen managers were potentially successful businesswomen, but working conditions in informal kitchens could be harsh. One former foyer kitchen

employee I met detailed her personal dependency on her boss and mentioned physical abuse.

30. The term "wife" and, more generally, the association between cooking and sexuality could evoke institutionalized practices of homosexuality associated with domestic services similar to what has been described in South African migrant compounds. See T. Dunbar Moodie, Vivienne Ndatshe, and British Sibuyi, "Migrancy and Male Sexuality on the South African Gold Mines," *Journal of Southern African Studies* 14, no. 2 (1988): 228–56; and Patrick Harries, "Symbols and Sexuality: Culture and Identity on the Early Witwatersrand Gold Mines," *Gender & History* 2, no. 3 (1990): 318–36. Such vernacular institutions do not exist in the foyers. This leaves open the issue of homosexual practices, a topic that the few of my interlocutors who talked about their sex lives did not touch upon. Bernardot affirms that, alongside recourse to female sex workers, they are in fact part of life in the foyers. Marc Bernardot, "Le Grand âge dans les foyers, nouveau public, nouveaux enjeux," Paper presented at the Congrès de l'AFS, RT 7 (Vieillesse, Vieillissement, Parcours de Vie). Bordeaux, 2006, http://www.copaf.ouvaton.org/vieux/vieux_bernardot.pdf. Descriptions of these all-male environments should be read while keeping in mind that physical proximity between men is common in West African contexts, as Broqua reminds us about Bamako. Christophe Broqua, "La socialisation du désir homosexuel masculin à Bamako," *Civilisations. Revue internationale d'anthropologie et de sciences humaines*, 59, no. 1 (2010): 44.

31. Pelckmans signals two cases in the 2010s. See Pelckmans, "Moving Memories of Slavery," 58–59. Her account does not specify which type of kitchen was considered (an internal village-based cooking organization or a foyer kitchen).

32. "*Tuuse*" is not part of the Soninke language lexicon as used in West Africa. Born out of migration, it might have been derived from the French verb "*toucher*" (to touch).

33. For those who did not eat outside the foyer (for instance, during work hours), the common meal of rice was only supplemented by the cheapest breakfast (white bread and butter) and occasional snacks. Several men and a neighborhood doctor mentioned health issues associated with this diet.

34. Chelsie Yount-André, "Empire's Leftovers: Eating to Integrate in Secular Paris," *Food and Foodways* 26, no. 2 (2018): 131.

35. Interview with Bouba, Résidence Mûriers (twelfth arrondissement), October 2016; informal conversation with Tahirou, Résidence Bachir Souni (Saint-Denis), March 2017.

36. Approaching kinship as processual, I consider migration as an occasion for the "reconfiguring of relatedness." See Janet Carsten, "Introduction: Cultures of Relatedness," in *Cultures of Relatedness: New Approaches to the Study of Kinship* (Cambridge: Cambridge University Press, 2000), 1–36; and Leslie Fesenmyer, "'Assistance but Not Support': Pentecostalism and the Reconfiguring of Relatedness Between Kenya and the United Kingdom," in *Affective Circuits: African Migrations to Europe and the Pursuit of Social Regeneration*, ed. Jennifer Cole and Christian Groes (Chicago: Chicago University Press, 2016), 125. Rather than positing the existence of ties to which people would adjust during the migratory experience, the notion of relatedness suggests that an active effort to define and select meaningful kinship ties—already occurring in ordinary settings—takes on new meaning in a transnational context.

37. Field notes, October 2014.

38. Mahamet Timera, "Hospitalité et hébergement dans un réseau migratoire d'Afrique de l'Ouest," in *Logements de passage: formes, normes, expériences*, ed. Claire Lévy-Vroelant (Paris: L'Harmattan, 2000), 63.

39. Informal conversation with Seydou, June 2014.

40. Field notes, October 2014.

41. Interview with Kandé, February 2015.

42. Contrary to Foyer Lorraine, this space allowed for the installation of seats and had the area of a small room.

43. Abdelmalek Sayad, "Le foyer des sans-famille," *Actes de la recherche en sciences sociales* 32, no. 1 (1980): 89–103.

44. Pierre-Joseph Laurent, *Amours pragmatiques: familles, migrations et sexualité au Cap-Vert aujourd'hui* (Paris: Karthala, 2018).

## 5. WHEN WILL THE FOYERS END?
## CONTENTIOUS RENOVATIONS AND
## TEMPORAL DISJUNCTIONS

1. For a detailed analysis of the PTFTM, see Hélène Béguin, "Héberger des migrants ou gérer des logements? L'Aftam et ses 'foyers d'Africains noirs' (1962–2012)" (PhD diss., University of Paris Est, 2015) chap. 1. This

PhD thesis, defended while I was conducting fieldwork, is a crucial reference on the plan and its implementation. See also Hélène Béguin, "Des 'Africains noirs' à la 'mixité sociale': Usages paradoxaux des catégorisations ethniques dans les foyers de travailleurs migrants AFTAM (1962-2010)," in *Le peuplement comme politiques*, ed. Fabien Desage, Christelle Morel Journel, and Valérie Sala Pala (Rennes: Presses Universitaires de Rennes, 2014), 15573, and Hélène Béguin, "Un dispositif spatial à la rencontre ou à l'encontre des usages? L'introduction du 'logement individuel autonome' dans les foyers de travailleurs migrants," in *Transformations des horizons urbains. Savoirs, imaginaires, usages et conflits*, ed. Frédéric Coninck and José-Frédéric Deroubaix, L'oeil d'or. Paris, 2012.

2. Circulaire 95-33, April 19, 1995, creating "résidences sociales"; Circulaire 2006-45, July 4, 2006, related to "résidences sociales" (hereafter: Circulaire 1995 and Circulaire 2006). Later versions were published in 2014 and 2020, but during my fieldwork Circulaire 2006 prevailed.

3. The 1990 Besson law enshrined the shift from targeting specific demographics to an approach considering all vulnerable persons at a territorial scale. See René Ballain and Elisabeth Maurel, *Le logement très social: extension ou fragilisation du droit au logement?* (La Tour d'Aigues: Éditions de l'Aube, 2002).

4. Circulaire 2006.

5. Haut Comité Pour le Logement des Personnes Défavorisées, *16e Rapport: Du Foyer de Travailleurs Migrants à la résidence sociale: mener à bien la mutation*, 2010, 64.

6. Circulaire 2002-515, October 3, 2002, related to the prorogation of the Plan (hereafter Circulaire 2002). For a more general argument on how African residents of the foyers were targeted in the Plan, see Béguin, "Héberger des migrants," 115–16.

7. The ambivalence of the 1997–98 political climate is captured by Sarah Mazouz in her analysis of the political take on the issue of racial discrimination. Sarah Mazouz, *La République et ses autres: politiques de l'altérité dans la France des années 2000* (Lyon: ENS Éditions, 2017).

8. Haut Comité Pour le Logement des Personnes Défavorisées, *16e Rapport*, 12.

9. For figures in Paris, see APUR, *Les foyers de travailleurs migrants à Paris—Etat des lieux en 2010 et inventaires des interventions sanitaires et*

*culturelles* (Paris: APUR, 2011), 5. The neighboring departments offered 37,000 beds: 13,960 in Seine-Saint-Denis; 9,179 beds in Paris; 8,170 in Val-de-Marne; and 5,650 in Hauts-de-Seine. See Jean-Jacques Guillouet and Philippe Pauget, "Les structures d'hébergement et de logements adaptés en Île-de-France en 2012," *Institut d'aménagement et d'urbanisme,* July 31, 2013, 9.

10. Rémi Gallou, "Les immigrés isolés: la spécificité des résidants en foyer," *Retraite et société* 44, no. 1 (2005): 106–47.

11. APUR, *Les foyers de travailleurs migrants à Paris. Etat des lieux en 2010 et inventaires des interventions sanitaires et culturelles* (Paris: APUR, 2011) , 19. Given that some West Africans have French citizenship (despite the difficulties in accessing this status) and hosting practices were strong among West Africans, the ratio of West Africans was in fact greater.

12. CILPI, "Rapport d'activité 2018," 2019, 4.

13. The 2000 Solidarité et renouvellement urbains law instituted a "concertation council" consisting of representatives of both the managing structure and of the residents. In 2014 (a change applied in 2016), the existence of "residents' committees," distinct bodies from the aforementioned council, was acknowledged. See http://www.copaf.ouvaton.org /electionlien.html, accessed April 19, 2022.

14. Compared to migrants from other backgrounds, migrants from sub-Saharan Africa are particularly active in the associative field. See Vincent Tiberj and Patrick Simon, *La fabrique du citoyen: origines et rapport au politique en France* (INED Working Paper 175, 2016).

15. I heard such statements in left-wing municipalities (Paris nineteenth arrondissement) as well as right-wing ones (Boulogne-Billancourt). However, communist municipalities seemed to have built stronger ties within the foyers.

16. Sadio Soukouna, "Migrants maliens et paradiplomatie," *Monde commun* 3, no. 2 (2019): 72–85.

17. Béguin, "Héberger des migrants," 326.

18. On her trajectory, see Geneviève Petauton's archived interview, 2014, Génériques oral history campaign. Archives Nationales: 20160153 art. 11.

19. Michel Fiévet, *Le livre blanc des travailleurs immigrés des foyers: du non-droit au droit* (Paris: L'Harmattan, 1999). Fiévet had previously been "chargé de mission" at AFTAM. Michel Fiévet, "Le foyer, lieu de vie économique pour les Africains," *Hommes et migrations* 1202, no. 1 (1996): 23–27.

20. Public meeting on the foyers organized by the Mairie of the nineteenth arrondissement, November 15, 2014.

21. Meetings convened by COPAF were held at the premises of DAL.

22. Founded by philosopher Alain Badiou, another ex-member of UCF(ml), the Organisation Politique, also called "les noyaux," operated in foyers with a view to asserting migrants' rights. This activist field did not appear to be structured along ideological lines, and activists from the same organization could end up in competing ones, in contrast to earlier periods. See Cécile Péchu, *Droit au logement, genèse et sociologie d'une mobilisation* (Paris: Dalloz, 2006).

23. Alexis Spire, *Accueillir ou reconduire: enquête sur les guichets de l'immigration* (Paris: Raisons d'agir, 2008).

24. Adoma, "Les métiers de l'exploitation," accessed March 24, 2021, https://www.adoma.cdc-habitat.fr/adoma/Travailler-avec-Adoma /Espace-recrutement/Nos-metiers/Nos-metiers/p-522-Les-metiers -de-l-exploitation.htm.

25. Spire, *Accueillir ou reconduire*. The first category is coined after Howard S. Becker, *Outsiders: Studies in the Sociology of Deviance* (New York: Free Press, 1963).

26. Field notes, April 6, 2016.

27. On the dilemma facing staff of postcolonial immigrant background in charge of implementing "republican" policies, see Mazouz, *La République et ses autres*.

28. In 2005, the City of Paris, under the lead of the socialist Bertrand Delanoë, took responsibility for the Plan as a result of a national reform that allowed local authorities to request the management of state construction subsidies.

29. The following account is based on my observations during meetings and interviews. Except for a few internal meetings that I recorded (making my recording device apparent to those in attendance), I generally relied on intensive note-taking.

30. This was notably the case of Foyer David D'Angers (nineteenth arrondissement), whose replacement residence was about to open. In addition to the sixty-one official residents, a local committee supported by OP activists listed 116 unofficial residents who had not been considered and who occupied the foyer for months after the official residents had moved. It was closed in 2009 after a police intervention, with some

of the protesters camping in front of the foyer. The memory of this situation translated into an obsessive fear of squatting. On the use of squatting as a political mode of action by migrants, see Péchu, *Droit au logement*; and Florence Bouillon, "Des migrants et des squats: précarités et résistances aux marges de la ville," *Revue européenne des migrations internationales* 19, no. 2 (2003): 23–46.

31. In contrast, some of Foyer Lorraine's residents ended up in a former hospital hastily converted into a housing facility with up to eight-bed rooms and dire living conditions.

32. Informal conversation with Julie, July 2015. During the 2008 to 2013 municipal mandate, twice as many renovations were launched compared to the previous five years. See APUR, *Les foyers de travailleurs migrants à Paris—Etat des lieux en 2010*, 14.

33. Interview at CILPI, January 2020, conducted with Laura Guérin.

34. Circulaire 2002.

35. Tiphaine Bernard, "Habiter le foyer: approche anthropologique de la résidentialisation des foyers à travers l''exception' Centenaire, une résidence sociale en co-gestion à Montreuil-Sous-Bois," (PhD diss., University of Paris 8, 2017).

36. CILPI, "Document cadre. Orientations pour la mise en œuvre du plan de traitement des foyers de travailleurs migrants," 2018, 13, https://www.gouvernement.fr/sites/default/files/contenu/piece-jointe/2018/12/document_cadre_cilpi.pdf.

37. The two social restaurants were at Foyer Mûriers (twentieth arrondissement) and Foyer Arbustes (fifteenth arrondissement).

38. A wealth of studies have tackled the ambiguities of such a norm; see Marie-Hélène Bacqué and Claire Carriou, "Participation et politiques du logement en France. Un débat qui traverse le XXe siècle," in *La démocratie participative. Histoire et généalogie*, ed. Marie-Hélène Bacqué (Paris: La Découverte, 2011), 155–73.

39. CILPI, "Document cadre. Orientations," 14.

40. Field notes, December 2014.

41. Field notes, February 2015.

42. Field notes, April 2016.

43. Field notes, September 2014.

44. Field notes, October 2012.

45. Field notes, October 2012.

46. Alexandra Clavé-Mercier and Martin Olivera, "Une résistance non résistante? Ethnographie du malentendu dans les dispositifs d'"intégration' pour des migrants roms," *L'Homme. Revue française d'anthropologie* 219–220 (November 2016): 175–207; and Jennifer Cole, "Working Mis/Understandings: The Tangled Relationship Between Kinship, Franco-Malagasy Binational Marriages, and the French State," *Cultural Anthropology* 29, no. 3 (2014): 527–51.

47. An administrative division that disappeared in 1968.

48. Field notes, December 2015. I do not know why the speaker mentioned Marshal Philippe Pétain, the head of the French state who collaborated with Nazi Germany during World War II, but this illustrates the variety of historical references mobilized by foyer residents.

## 6. ACKNOWLEDGING SOLIDARITY: BUREAUCRATIC RELATEDNESS, HOSTING PRACTICES, AND EXCLUSIONARY DYNAMICS

1. I heard this phrase from local managers as well as from higher-ranked members of the managing structures and the institutions. For a classic counterargument, see Viviana A. Zelizer, *The Purchase of Intimacy* (Princeton, NJ: Princeton University Press, 2005).

2. Field notes, October 2012.

3. Paolo Gaibazzi, "Visa Problem: Certification, Kinship, and the Production of 'Ineligibility' in The Gambia," *Journal of the Royal Anthropological Institute* 20, no. 1 (2014): 38–55; Geoffrion Karine and Viviane Cretton, "Introduction: Bureaucratic Routes to Migration: Migrants' Lived Experience of Paperwork, Clerks, and Other Immigration Intermediaries," *Anthropologica* 63, no. 1 (2021).

4. Stefan Le Courant, *Vivre sous la menace. Les sans-papiers et l'Etat* (Paris: Le Seuil, 2022); and Charles Piot, *The Fixer: Visa Lottery Chronicles* (Durham, NC: Duke University Press, 2019).

5. Sections of this chapter have appeared in French in Aïssatou Mbodj-Pouye "'On n'ignore pas la solidarité.' Transformation des foyers de travailleurs migrants et recompositions des liens de cohabitation," *Genèses* 104, no. 3 (2016): 51–72.

6. Susanna Magri and Christian Topalov, "De la cité-jardin à la ville rationalisée: Un tournant du projet réformateur, 1905–1925: Etude comparative

France, Grande-Bretagne, Italie, Etats-Unis," *Revue Française de Sociologie* 28, no. 3 (1987): 417–51.

7. Established in 1995, the same year as the "residence sociale," MOUS is devoted to the "most dramatic and marginalized situations." Circulaire du 2 août, 1995, "relative aux MOUS pour l'accès au logement des personnes défavorisées."

8. Pascale Dietrich-Ragon and Yankel Fijalkow, "'On les aide à partir.' Le relogement comme révélateur des contradictions du développement social dans le cadre de la rénovation urbaine," *Espaces et sociétés* 155, no. 4 (2013): 113–28; Camille François, "Disperser les ménages," *Actes de la recherche en sciences sociales* 204, no. 4 (2014): 102–17; and Agnès Deboulet and Claudette Lafaye, "La rénovation urbaine, entre délogement et relogement. Les effets sociaux de l'éviction," *L'Année sociologique* 68, no. 1 (2018): 155–84.

9. Alexandra Clavé-Mercier and Martin Olivera, "Une résistance non résistante? Ethnographie du malentendu dans les dispositifs d'"intégration' pour des migrants roms," *L'Homme, Revue française d'anthropologie* 219–220 (November 2016): 175–207.

10. The work of MOUS could be conducted by the managing structure (e.g., in 2013, Adoma recruited a team who would perform both the diagnosis and the accompanying social work) or partly outsourced (Coallia out sourced the social diagnosis but dealt internally with the social work surrounding the moves with a team of dedicated employees). Although performing social work, not all MOUS officers were trained social workers, representing instead a number of heterogeneous profiles, as is the case in other rehousing processes. See Christine Lelévrier, "La rénovation urbaine, un re-peuplement des 'grands ensembles'?," in *Le Peuplement comme politiques*, ed. Fabien Desage, Christelle Morel Journel, and Valérie Sala Pala (Rennes: Presses universitaires de Rennes, 2019), 175–94.

11. Field notes, August 3, 2017.

12. In this project, the studios were designed to cost between €420 and €450 per month. Damien, who held a master's degree in urban studies, had already worked on this MOUS team for six years.

13. Camille François, "Au mépris des locataires," *Genèses* 96, no. 3 (2014): 86–109.

14. Henri Cuq, "Mission parlementaire sur la situation et le devenir des foyers de travailleurs migrants," Mission parlementaire auprès ministre chargé de l'intégration et de la lutte contre l'exclusion (Paris: 1996), 18.

15. APUR, *Les foyers de travailleurs migrants à Paris—Etat des lieux en 2010 et inventaires des interventions sanitaires et culturelles* (Paris: APUR, 2011),19.

16. CILPI, "Document cadre relatif au plan de traitement des foyers de travailleurs migrants, Cilpi, DGUHC, UESL et Anpeec," 2007, 6.

17. Cour des comptes, Rapport public annuel, Tome 1, 2ème partie, Chapitre IV, section 3 "La transformation des foyers de travailleurs migrants en résidences sociales: une politique à refonder" (Paris: 2014), 359.

18. CILPI, "Document cadre. Orientations pour la mise en œuvre du plan de traitement des Foyers de Travailleurs Migrants," 2018, https://www.gouvernement.fr/sites/default/files/contenu/piece-jointe/2018/12/document_cadre_cilpi.pdf, 12.

19. "The internal rules . . . reproduce in their entirety articles L. 622–1 to L. 622–7 of the Code de l'entrée et de séjour des étrangers et du droit d'asile," Code de la Construction et de l'Habitat, article R633-9.

20. Interview with Geneviève Petauton, January 2014. Negotiations were conducted by Khédidja Bourcart, a member of the Green Party and deputy mayor of Paris in charge of integration and non-EU foreigners at that time.

21. I hypothesize that distinct configurations in terms of support account for the divergence in the two foyers: Foyer Lorraine, with its canteen open to outsiders, had strong ties with a neighborhood social center where many young and often undocumented foyer inhabitants attended literacy classes. The social center was among the support committees and pushed for the inclusion of sans-papiers. In contrast, Foyer D'Hautpoul had fewer apparent ties with the neighborhood. In addition, a few years before the renovation, an attempt to create a sans-papiers collective had failed after the délégués had objected to meetings involving outsiders being organized in the building's collective rooms.

22. The Fontaine-au-Roi agreement listed a number of official documents, but this list did not serve as a template for subsequent cases.

23. In the years when Dramane had this arrangement, he paid around €120 a year to the relative who purported to be his landlord; this was understood as compensation for the increase in local residence tax, which increases according to the number of occupants.

24. *"Parrainage"* evokes the notion of godfather (*parrain*). At the time when the criteria were negotiated, activists organized ceremonies of *"parrainage républicain"* to protect sans-papiers.

25. This occurred in spite of the position of Khédidja Bourcart (initiator of the agreement), who stated that this criterion did not mean that "only one unregistered resident per room could be rehoused," simply that "each unregistered resident ha[d] to be sponsored, so to speak, by a registered resident acting as guarantor." Minutes of the debate, Examen du projet de délibération DLH 269, November 2007.

26. Field notes, April 14, 2013. Use of "clandestine" was a consistent choice of term by Boubacar, a former resident of 216 bis, who emphasized historical continuities between the 1979 and 2014 moves.

27. An association that conducted a prevention campaign against sexually transmitted diseases interacted with 317 men in the foyer; although this intervention also included some regular visitors, this suggests that the population inhabiting the foyer ranged between two hundred and three hundred men, thus concurring with the managing structure's estimate.

28. The bureaucratic culture of foyer residents builds on their familiarity with documentation in urban and rural West Africa, reconfigured in the migratory context where documents become even more vital. On lists and the importance of having one's name written down, see Aïssatou Mbodj-Pouye, *Le fil de l'écrit: une anthropologie de l'alphabétisation au Mali* (Lyon, France: ENS éditions, 2013).

29. Field notes, April 6, 2016, meeting at the Mairie of the nineteenth arrondissement.

30. Field notes, May 10, 2016, and February 18, 2016.

31. Figures I could obtain for earlier Parisian cases (such as Foyer Fort-de-Vaux, seventeenth arrondissement; Foyer Commanderie, nineteenth arrondissement; Foyer Fontaine-au-Roi, eleventh arrondissement) tended to be even better, with the number of rehousable over-occupants ranging from a fifth to half of the total residents. Formalization of the procedure led to a decrease in this number: an officer of a managing structure told me that the number of "rehousable over-occupants" should be around 20 percent of the foyer capacity, and a 2012 guideline suggested a figure of 10 percent. Délégation interministérielle à l'hébergement et à l'accès au logement (DIHAL), "Étude visant à mieux connaître et valoriser le champ du logement accompagné dit 'tiers secteur,'" *Tome 2: Monographies*, June 2012, 129. Outside Paris, situations varied greatly, and in some cases over-occupants were not considered at all (such as in Foyer Saint-Ouen in 2021).

32. Such a dilemma between divisible and indivisible goods has been high-lighted in the mobilizations of sans-papiers and poorly housed people. See Johanna Siméant, *La cause des sans-papiers* (Paris: Presses de Sciences po, 1998), 139–46; and Cécile Péchu, *Droit au logement, genèse et sociologie d'une mobilisation* (Paris: Dalloz, 2006), 147–54.

33. It was a room that the other foyer residents considered particularly overcrowded. Out of a dozen rooms whose fates I documented (of which only two reached such a degree of over-occupancy), I chose to focus on this one for the lens that it offers on more general dynamics.

34. Abou and his cousins were *sebbe*, and Demba was *cuballo*: both are social categories of "free" status in Haalpulaar societies, but the latter, without falling under the status of casted artisans, is a distinct endogamous group.

35. In this case, the decisions made at the time of the provisional move endured after the other move to the new foyer. In other cases, a room's group of cohabitants was refashioned twice: at this stage of the provisional move, and at the moment of moving into to the residence.

36. This concurs with the observation made at the level of the foyer: in one case, when the loss of capacity meant that only some of the former residents would be rehoused together, I observed délégués putting forward a criterion of anteriority within the foyer. A municipality officer attending the meeting argued that vulnerability was a morally superior principle. What she overlooked was that the residents were trying to maintain sustainable groups (in terms of mutual services such as cooking, even in much smaller groups than before), which an aggregation of more vulnerable individuals would not allow. Field notes, February 18, 2016.

37. Didier Fassin, "Compassion and Repression: The Moral Economy of Immigration Policies in France," *Cultural Anthropology* 20, no. 3 (2005): 362–87.

38. Scholars have highlighted how "illegality does not typically function as an absolute marker of illegitimacy, but rather as a handicap within a continuum of probationary citizenship." Chauvin and Garcés-Mascareñas 2012, 243.

39. "Traitement des déclarations de revenus déposées par les personnes dont la domiciliation fiscale est incertaine", internal note by the Direction

générale des impôts, April 24, 2006, https://www.gisti.org/IMG/pdf
/instruction-impots_2006-04-26.pdf.

40. Note for the 2017 campaign, internal recommendations for fiscal officers,
published by GISTI, https://www.gisti.org/IMG/pdf/_8_le_traitement
_des_declarations_.pdf_.pdf, accessed May 19, 2023. In 2017, the practice
seems to have been widespread, but earlier rejections are documented by
COPAF. See letter from COPAF to the fiscal administration, September
16, 2013, http://www.copaf.ouvaton.org/impots/130916copaf_declaration
.html.

41. GISTI and Solidaires Finances Publiques, *Sans-papiers et impôts: Pourquoi et comment déclarer ses revenus*, Les notes pratiques du GISTI,
October 2015, 17, http://www.gisti.org/spip.php?article5070.

42. Associations and unions had politicized the issue of sans-papiers' taxes
since 2008 through a campaign called "anti-racket," but the systematic
rejection by the fiscal services of addresses in foyers occasioned new
actions.

43. Camille François has demonstrated that the legal decisions leading to
the expulsion of residents behind on their payments were statistically
harsher than for residents of social housing, Camille François, "Une
discrimination au délogement," *Terrains travaux* 29, no. 2 (2016): 113.

## 7. *FOYERMEN*: CLASS, GENDER, AND RACE ACROSS GENERATIONS

1. Inspiring studies of migrant men using an intersectional approach
include Giulia Sinatti, "Masculinities and Intersectionality in Migration: Transnational Wolof Migrants Negotiating Manhood and Gendered Family Roles," in *Migration, Gender and Social Justice: Perspectives
on Human Insecurity*, ed. Thanh-Dam Truong, Des Gasper, Jeff Handmaker, and Sylvia I. Bergh (Berlin: Springer, 2014), 215–26; and Ali Nobil
Ahmad, "Gender and Generation in Pakistani Migration: A Critical
Study of Masculinity," in *Gendering Migration Masculinity, Femininity
and Ethnicity in Post-War Britain*, ed. Wendy Webster and Louise Ryan
(London: Routledge, 2016), 167–82. On the gendered identities and emotional experiences of migrant men as husbands, see Katharine Charsley, "Unhappy Husbands: Masculinity and Migration in Transnational
Pakistani Marriages," *Journal of the Royal Anthropological Institute* 11,

no. 1 (2005): 85–105. On the potential for life histories to illuminate the complex dynamics at work in migration processes, see Ben Rogaly, "Disrupting Migration Stories: Reading Life Histories Through the Lens of Mobility and Fixity," *Environment and Planning D: Society and Space* 33, no. 3 (2015): 528–44.

2. Nauja Kleist and Dorte Thorsen, eds., *Hope and Uncertainty in Contemporary African Migration* (New York: Routledge, 2017).

3. R. W. Connell and James W. Messerschmidt, "Hegemonic Masculinity: Rethinking the Concept," *Gender and Society* 19, no. 6 (2005): 829–59.

4. On blackness in France, see Pap Ndiaye, *La condition noire: essai sur une minorité française* (Paris: Calmann-Lévy, 2008); Christian Poiret, "Les processus d'ethnicisation et de raci(ali)sation dans la France contemporaine: Africains, Ultramarins et 'Noirs,'" *Revue européenne des migrations internationales* 27, no. 1 (2011): 107–27; Tyler Stovall, Trica Danielle Keaton, and T. Denean Sharpley-Whiting, *Black France/France Noire* (Durham, NC: Duke University Press, 2012); and Audrey Célestine and Sarah Fila-Bakabadio, "Introduction to the Special Issue: 'Black Paris and the Lived Experiences of Black Subjects,'" *African and Black Diaspora: An International Journal* 10, no. 1 (2017): 1–11.

5. Stefan Le Courant, "'Être le dernier jeune,' *Terrain. Revue d'ethnologie de l'Europe* 63 (2014): 43. Beyond the foyers, Julie Kleinman offers a finegrained study of the social trajectories of West African men in Paris, see Julie Kleinman, *Adventure Capital: Migration and the Making of an African Hub in Paris* (Oakland: University of California Press, 2019).

6. Caroline M. Melly, "Titanic Tales of Missing Men: Reconfigurations of National Identity and Gendered Presence in Dakar, Senegal," *American Ethnologist* 38, no. 2 (2011): 368.

7. Isabelle Chort, Flore Gubert, and Jean-Noël Senne, "Migrant Networks as a Basis for Social Control: Remittance Incentives Among Senegalese in France and Italy," *Regional Science and Urban Economics* 42, no. 5 (2012): 858–74.

8. For men who arrived before 1996, the average time needed to obtain a one-year residence permit was four years; for those who arrived between 1996 and 2004, it was five years; for those who arrived between 2005 and 2011, it was six years. Anne Gosselin, "Les délais pour obtenir un titre de séjour s'allongent," *De facto* [on line] 14 (December 2019), https://www.icmigrations.cnrs.fr/2019/12/09/defacto-014-04/. See also

Anne Gosselin, Annabel Desgrées du Loû, Éva Lelièvre, France Lert, Rosemary Dray-Spira, and Nathalie Lydié, "Migrants subsahariens: combien de temps leur faut-il pour s'installer en France?," *Population Sociétés* 533, no. 5 (2016): 1–4.

9. Nicholas De Genova, "Migrant 'Illegality' and Deportability in Everyday Life," *Annual Review of Anthropology* 31 (2002): 419–47; and Stefan Le Courant, *Vivre sous la menace. Les sans-papiers et l'Etat* (Paris: Le Seuil, 2022).

10. Alain Morice and Swanie Potot, *De l'ouvrier immigré au travailleur sans papiers: les étrangers dans la modernisation du salariat* (Paris: Karthala, 2010).

11. Margot Annequin, Anne Gosselin, and Rosemary Dray-Spira, *Trajectoires et mobilités professionnelles autour de la migration, Parcours* (Paris: La Découverte, 2017). Within these sectors, they further occupied low-level roles because the occupational hierarchy intersected with racial and ethnic lines, as demonstrated by Nicolas Jounin's research among construction workers. Nicolas Jounin, *Chantier interdit au public* (Paris: La Découverte, 2009).

12. INSEE, "Tableaux de l'économie Française, Edition 2019", (Paris: 2019), 36; and Cédric Jolly, Frédéric Lainé, and Yves Breem, *L'emploi et les métiers des immigrés* (Paris: Centre d'analyse stratégique, 2012).

13. Comparing the experiences of migrants of all backgrounds over two generations who arrived in France in the 1980s as opposed to those who migrated in the 2000s, Annalisa Lendaro exposes a sharp worsening of opportunities and the emergence of more precarious trajectories. Annalisa Lendaro, "Inégalités sur le marché du travail entre deux générations d'immigré-e-s," *Revue francaise de sociologie* 54, no. 4 (2013): 779–806.

14. Evidence of high levels of racial profiling in the public space is provided by a survey funded by the Open Society Justice Initiative in 2009: in distinct sites observed within Paris, "blacks [were] between 3.3 and 11.5 times more likely to be subjected to a police check than whites; and Maghrebis between 1.8 and 14.8 times." Fabien Jobard and René Lévy, "Les contrôles au faciès à Paris," *Plein droit* 82, no. 3 (2009): 13.

15. Mirna Safi, "Le processus d'intégration des immigrés en France: inégalités et segmentation," *Revue francaise de sociologie* 47, no. 1 (2006): 3–48.

16. Yael Brinbaum, Mirna Safi, and Patrick Simon, "Les discriminations en France: entre perception et expérience," Working Paper (Paris: INED, 2012).

17. Field notes, May 2015. This statement took place after I had invited the assembly to comment on life in the newly opened residence.

18. Focused on what happened after the renovation, Laura Guérin's study also highlights the various trajectories of (former) foyer inhabitants and their contrasted stances toward the foyer/residence. See Laura Guérin, "L'appropriation spatiale comme résistance habitante. Ethnographie de résidences sociales issues de Foyers de Travailleurs Migrants" (PhD diss., University of Paris 8, 2021), chap. 5.

19. In the following sections, I supplement my ethnographic material with recorded interviews conducted with Stefan Le Courant on marriage among West African migrants, which form the basis of Aïssatou Mbodj-Pouye and Stefan Le Courant, "Living Away from Family Is Not Good but Living with It Is Worse: Debating Conjugality Across Generations of West African Migrants in France," *Mande Studies* 19 (2017): 109–30.

20. Endogamous prescriptions persist in migration. Some of my interlocutors said that French youth of West African background tended to disregard such considerations, but I observed that young people were nonetheless inclined to frame such references as unfashionable but unavoidable requirements from their parents.

21. Twenty-four percent of Sahelian migrants arrived in France already married. Christelle Hamel, Bertrand Lhommeau, Ariane Pailhe, and Emmanuelle Santelli, "Rencontrer son conjoint dans un espace multiculturel et international," Working Paper (Paris: INED, 2012), 5. The quantitative studies I refer to in this chapter use the survey "Trajectoires et Origines," conducted by INED and INSEE in 2008, which relies on the category of "Sahelians." In addition to migrants from Mali, Senegal, and Mauritania, this group also includes migrants from The Gambia, Guinea Bissau, Guinea, Burkina Faso, Niger, and Chad.

22. I occasionally met the girlfriends of my interlocutors in Paris, and I visited several of my interlocutors' wives in Senegal and Mali. These encounters, framed by my longer acquaintance with the men in question, do not offer a solid enough view on women's perspectives to balance out those of men. For studies of West African women in France, see Jeanne Semin, "L'argent, la famille, les amies: ethnographie contemporaine des

tontines africaines en contexte migratoire," *Civilisations. Revue internationale d'anthropologie et de sciences humaines* 56 (2007): 183–99; and Nehara Feldman, *Migrantes: du bassin du fleuve Sénégal aux rives de la Seine* (Paris: La Dispute, 2018). For investigations of gender relations among Senegalese in the U.S. context, see Ousmane Kane, *The Homeland Is the Arena: Religion, Transnationalism, and the Integration of Senegalese Immigrants in America* (Oxford: Oxford University Press, 2011), chap. 6; and Cheikh Anta Babou, "Migration as a Factor of Cultural Change Abroad and at Home: Senegalese Female Hair Braiders in the United States," in *African Migrations. Patterns and Perspectives*, ed. Abdoulaye Kane and Todd H. Leedy (Bloomington: Indiana University Press, 2013), 230–47.

23. Charsley, "Unhappy Husbands," 101–2.

24. Muriel Azoulay and Catherine Quiminal argue that the foyers "act as safeguards in order to preserve masculine domination." Muriel Azoulay and Catherine Quiminal, "Reconstruction des rapports de genre en situation migratoire. Femmes 'réveillées,' hommes menacés en milieu soninké," *VEI enjeux: Migrants Formation* 128 (2002): 99. My account is more attentive to the plurality of men's perspectives.

25. Insights into the residents' extramarital sexuality in France is featured in URACA, "Annual Report 2006," http://uraca-basiliade.org/wp-content/uploads/2016/12/URACA_RapportActivites2006.pdf.

26. Field notes, July 2015.

27. On social workers, see Carolyn F. Sargent, "Reproductive Strategies and Islamic Discourse," *Medical Anthropology Quarterly* 20, no. 1 (2006): 44. On the copines, see Jennifer Cole, "The *téléphone malgache*: Transnational Gossip and Social Transformation Among Malagasy Marriage Migrants in France," *American Ethnologist* 41, no. 2 (2014): 276–89.

28. See also El Hadji Abdou Aziz Faty, "Quand les hommes haalpulaar se plaignent de la migration: La question de la précarité masculine au cœur des problématiques migratoires dans la vallée du fleuve Sénégal," in *La Migration prise aux mots*, ed. Cécile Canut and Catherine Mazauric (Paris: Le cavalier bleu, 2014), 209–24.

29. Mahamet Timera, *Les Soninké en France: d'une histoire à l'autre* (Paris: Karthala, 1996).

30. Pau Baizán, Cris Beauchemin, and Amparo González-Ferrer, "An Origin and Destination Perspective on Family Reunification: The Case of

Senegalese Couples," *European Journal of Population* 30, no. 1 (2014): 79. This figure refers to data collected among Senegalese migrants.

31. Roger Ballard, "Migration and Kinship: The Differential Effect of Marriage Rules on the Process of Punjabi Migration to Britain," in *South Asians Overseas: Contexts and Communities*, ed. C. Clarke, C. Peach, and S. Vertovec (Cambridge: Cambridge University Press, 1990), 219–49; and Charsley, "Unhappy Husbands." As Razy notes with regard to the Soninke context, union with a member of the kin group is ideal although not predominant (a third of her small sample of marriages), with a professed preference for marriage with a matrilineal cross-cousin and a de facto preponderance of marriage with a patrilineal parallel-cousin. Elodie Razy, *Naître et devenir: anthropologie de la petite enfance en pays soninké (Mali)* (Nanterre: Société d'ethnologie, 2007), 88.

32. Amélie Grysole, "De bonnes fréquentations," *Actes de la recherche en sciences sociales* 225, no. 5 (2018): 28–41.

33. Recorded interview, November 2016.

34. Feldman, *Migrantes*.

35. Caroline Bledsoe and Papa Sow, "Family Reunification Ideals and the Practice of Transnational Reproductive Life Among Africans in Europe," MPDIR Working Paper, February 2008, 4.

36. Post on http://www.soninkara.com, March 29, 2011, http://www.soninkara.com/forums/sujets-divers/bal-des-google-page-rankingejuges-entre-soninkes-de-divers-horizons-bledards-fss-etc-6808.html.

37. Chantal Tetreault, " Cultural Citizenship in France and *le Bled* Among Teens of Pan-Southern Immigrant Heritage," *Language & Communication* 33, no. 4 (2013): 532–43; and Lila Belkacem, "Dire, penser et vivre les frontières: catégorisations et présentations de soi des enfants d'immigrés maliens en France," *Migrations Société* 128, no. 2 (2010): 177–92.

38. The trio *Los Bledos*, formed in 2001 by three young actors born in Rosny (a town in the suburbs of Paris), notably performed a sketch called *Foyerman* that gained some popularity in 2010, when Franco-Senegalese producer Samba Kanté included it in his "Samba show": *Foyerman*, accessed August 12, 2020, https://youtu.be/z6TYCOOPeZc.

39. Michèle Lamont, *The Dignity of Working Men: Morality and the Boundaries of Race, Class, and Immigration* (New York: Russell Sage Foundation, 2000), 150.

40. Hugues Lagrange, *Le déni des cultures* (Paris: Le Seuil, 2010) contributed to popularizing such views in public debates; for a critique, see Didier Fassin, "Qu'il ne suffit pas d'être politiquement incorrect pour être scientifiquement fondé," *Revue française de sociologie* 52, no. 4 (2011): 777–86.

41. Pierre Bourdieu *La distinction: critique sociale du jugement* (Paris: Les Editions de minuit, 1979).

42. Among Malians in Marseille, Cécile Van den Avenne has noted the deterrent character of the Soninke foyer inhabitant for Malian migrants from other ethnic backgrounds. Cécile Van den Avenne, *Changer de vie, changer de langues: paroles de migrants entre le Mali et Marseille* (Paris: L'Harmattan, 2004). Likewise, Chelsie Yount-André has pinpointed the importance of such distinctions among middle-class families of Senegalese migrants in France. Chelsie Yount-André, "Empire's Leftovers: Eating to Integrate in Secular Paris," *Food and Foodways* 26, no. 2 (2018): 13.

43. Recorded interview with Dramane, November 2016.

44. Elisabeth Beck-Gernsheim, "Transnational Lives, Transnational Marriages: A Review of the Evidence from Migrant Communities in Europe," *Global Networks* 7, no. 3 (2007): 271–88; and Katharine Charsley, Marta Bolognani, Evelyn Ersanilli, and Sarah Spencer, "Marriage Migration and Integration: Unpacking the Arguments and Evidence," in *Marriage Migration and Integration* (New York: Palgrave Macmillan, 2020), 57–81.

45. Hamel et al., "Rencontrer son conjoint," 26. They were less prone to union with French sons of Sahelian immigrants (24%); the remaining 26% married French from the "majority" population.

46. Hamel et al., "Rencontrer son conjoint," 14.

47. On this "elective endogamy," see Emmanuelle Santelli and Béate Colet, "De l'endogamie à l'homogamie socio-ethnique: réinterprétations normatives et réalités conjugales des descendants d'immigrés maghrébins, turcs et africains sahéliens," *Sociologie et sociétés* 43, no. 2 (2011): 329–54.

48. Leyla Arslan, "Union halal: sexualité et mariage chez le couple 'musulman' dans les quartiers populaires," in *Les Sens du halal: une norme dans un marché mondial*, ed. Florence Bergeaud-Blackler (Paris: CNRS Éditions, 2019), 147.

49. Ghassan Hage, *The Diasporic Condition: Ethnographic Explorations of the Lebanese in the World* (Chicago: University of Chicago Press, 2021), 52.

50. Recorded interview, February 2017.

51. Hamel et al., "Rencontrer son conjoint," 14.

52. For sub-Saharan Africans, the aggregate number of mixed marriages celebrated in France increased until 2003 (reaching 7,643) before sharply decreasing (4,879) in 2015, probably due to the increased level of checks and constraints. Vanessa Bellamy, "236,300 mariages célébrés en france en 2015, dont 33,800 mariages mixtes," *Insee Première*, 2017.

53. Santelli and Collet, "De l'endogamie à l'homogamie socio-ethnique," 350.

54. Élise Marsicano, "Mixité, inégalité, hétéroconjugalité. La formation des couples chez les migrant·e·s d'Afrique subsaharienne en France," *Nouvelles Questions Féministes* 38, no. 2 (2019): 86–106.

55. Hélène Neveu Kringelbach, "'Mixed Marriage,' Citizenship and the Policing of Intimacy in Contemporary France," IMI Working Paper no. 77 (2013): 19.

56. Gérard Noiriel, Eric Guichard, and Marie-Hélène Lechien, eds., *Le vieillissement des immigrés en région parisienne* (Paris: Rapport au FAS, 1992); and UNAFO, *Le vieillissement des résidants dans les foyers de travailleurs migrants. Constats et propositions* (Paris: UNAFO, 1996).

57. Marc Bernardot, "Le vieux, le fou et l'autre, qui habite encore dans les foyers?," *Revue Européenne de Migrations Internationales* 17, no. 1 (2001): 151–64; and Rémi Gallou, "Les immigrés isolés: la spécificité des résidants en foyer," *Retraite et société* 44, no. 1 (2005): 106–47.

58. A key work on this topic is Alistair Hunter, *Retirement Home? Ageing Migrant Workers in France and the Question of Return* (New York: Springer, 2018).

59. Le Courant, "'Être le dernier jeune,'" 14.

60. Chantal Crenn, "Les retraités sénégalais entre Bordeaux et Dakar: 'bien vieillir' en restant cosmobiles," *Gérontologie et société* 41, no. 158 (2019): 125–38.

61. Cases of old men detained when coming back after more than three years of absence have made front-page news and prompted the Senegalese Consulate, notably, to conduct information campaigns: https://www.seneweb.com/news/Immigration/carte-de-sejour-laquo-retraite-raquo-le-_n_147983.html, accessed August 13, 2020. On the intricacies of the law, see Sophie Bobbé, Evelyne Ribert, and Emmanuel Terray, "Droits des travailleurs migrants: le cas des retraites," ENSANS, Environnement, santé et société, March 2013.

62. The principle of repatriation of bodies was not debated during my fieldwork, in contrast to observations made by Olivier Leservoisier among Haalpulaar in the United States. Olivier Leservoisier, "L'association Pulaar Speaking à la croisée des chemins. Dynamiques migratoires et débats autour du sens à donner à l'action communautaire au sein du collectif migrant haalpulaaren (Mauritanie, Sénégal) aux États-Unis," *Revue européenne des migrations internationales* 35, no. 1 (2019): 125–47.

63. Such rumors were rooted in a wider context of critical interpretations of biomedicine in colonial and postcolonial Africa. See Luise White, *Speaking with Vampires: Rumor and History in Colonial Africa* (Berkeley: California University Press, 2000).

64. In France in the 2000s, blue-collar men reaching retirement age had a life expectancy of seventy, compared to over seventy-six for white-collar workers. Nathalie Blanpain, "L'espérance de vie s'accroît, les inégalités sociales face à la mort demeurent," *INSEE Première* 1372 (2011).

65. Recorded interview with Bouba and Diadié, January 2017.

## 8. ERODED EMPLACEMENT: URBAN INCORPORATION, CONTAINMENT POLICIES, AND THE POLITICS OF BELONGING

1. The notion of "urban incorporation" is more specific and less normative than the idea of integration. See Monika Salzbrunn, "The Place-Making of Communities in Urban Spaces: The Invention of the 'Village Saint Louis Sainte-Marthe,'" in *Between Imagined Communities and Communities of Practice. Participation, Territory and the Making of Heritage* (Göttingen: Göttingen University Press, 2015), 185.

2. Saskia Sassen, *The Global City: New York, London, Tokyo* (Princeton, NJ: Princeton University Press, 1991).

3. Nira Yuval-Davis, "Belonging and the Politics of Belonging," *Patterns of Prejudice* 40, no. 3 (2006): 197–214.

4. Ayşe Çağlar and Nina Glick Schiller, *Migrants and City-Making: Dispossession, Displacement, and Urban Regeneration* (Durham, NC: Duke University Press, 2018), 11.

5. Nina Glick Schiller, "A Global Perspective on Transnational Migration: Theorising Migration Without Methodological Nationalism," in

*Diaspora and Transnationalism*, ed. Rainer Bauböck and Thomas Faist (Amsterdam: Amsterdam University Press, 2010), 126.

6. Caroline B. Brettell, *Anthropology and Migration: Essays on Transnationalism, Ethnicity, and Identity* (Walnut Creek, CA: Altamira Press, 2003), chap. 5.

7. On the dynamics in the 1960s, see Groupe de sociologie urbaine de Nanterre, "Paris 1970: reconquête urbaine et rénovation-déportation," *Sociologie du travail* 12, no. 4 (1970): 488–514; and more recently, Janoé Vulbeau, "Les 'Nord-Africains' dans la rénovation urbaine des années 1960," *Métropolitiques*, May 31, 2018.

8. Anne Clerval, *Paris sans le peuple: la gentrification de la capitale* (Paris: La Découverte, 2013); and Anne Clerval and Yoan Miot, "Inégalités et habitat en Île-de-France: quelles conséquences des politiques de renouvellement urbain sur le peuplement?," *Espaces et sociétés* 170, no. 3 (2017): 51–72.

9. Forty-one of the still existing facilities were opened between 1963 and 1984 (most of the construction dates are concentrated in the 1970s and early 1980s). The others opened as part of renovation plans: in the 1990s to support the (planned but largely ineffective) move from Foyer Nouvelle-France in Montreuil three small foyers opened in 1994–95 and one in order to renovate Foyer David D'Angers in 1999 (again, the facility opened and hosted some residents, but the planned renovation did not occur); and in the 2000s, in order to provisionally host residents whose foyers were undergoing renovation.

10. On "social mix" in France, see Marie-Hélène Bacqué, Yankel Fijalkow, Lydie Launay, and Stéphanie Vermeersch, "Social Mix Policies in Paris: Discourses, Policies and Social Effects," *International Journal of Urban and Regional Research* 35, no. 2 (2011): 256–73. For a discussion of the effects of voluntary public programs aimed at social diversity in the United States, see Robert J. Chaskin and Mark L. Joseph, *Integrating the Inner City: The Promise and Perils of Mixed-Income Public Housing Transformation* (Chicago: University of Chicago Press, 2015). I occasionally met neighbors of the foyers I was researching but did not engage in a systematic study of their attitudes toward the foyer. For homeowners, the proximity of a foyer often occasioned a fear of devaluing one's property. On how a neighborhood association put pressure on the municipality to control the circulation engendered by Friday prayers

in a residence, see Laura Guérin, "L'appropriation spatiale comme résistance habitante. Ethnographie de résidences sociales issues de Foyers de Travailleurs Migrants" (PhD diss., University of Paris 8, 2021), chap. 8.

11. A renovation grants the municipality a new contingent of social housing, each studio in a residence counting as one social housing unit. Social housing quotas are set by the "Solidarité et renouvellement urbains" law of 2000. The foyers' fate concurs with the observation that social housing projects managed by the municipality have allowed some working-class households to stay in the capital. See Guillaume Le Roux, Christophe Imbert, Arnaud Bringé, and Catherine Bonvalet, "Transformations sociales de l'agglomération parisienne au cours du XXe siècle: une approche longitudinale et générationnelle des inégalités d'accès à la ville," *Population* 75, no. 1 (2020): 84.

12. Eun-Gi Eun, "Une gestion socialiste en matière de logement: Boulogne-Billancourt (1947–1965)," *Le Mouvement Social* 213, no. 4 (2005): 31–51.

13. Michelle Guillon, "Ouvriers étrangers et français des usines Renault. Pratiques de mobilisation de la main-d'œuvre," *Espace Populations Sociétés* 6, no. 3 (1988): 455–66.

14. Alistair Hunter, *Retirement Home? Ageing Migrant Workers in France and the Question of Return* (New York: Springer, 2018).

15. In 2003, the municipality created a Zone d'Aménagement Concerté (ZAC), including the Seguin Island and the Trapèze.

16. Edmond Préteceille, "La ségrégation sociale a-t-elle augmenté?," *Sociétés contemporaines* 62, no. 2 (2006): 69–93.

17. I owe this epithet to Cristina Rossi, a scholar in urban studies, who kindly took me on a tour of a few foyers/residences in Montreuil. Studying operations combining social housing and a residence offered the opportunity for more fine-grained observations; beyond the foyers, the study of architectural projects combining private housing and social housing suggests that such projects result in the social housing project becoming a "closed space, in rupture with the rest of urban fabric." Matthieu Gimat and Julie Pollard, "Un tournant discret: la production de logements sociaux par les promoteurs immobiliers," *Géographie, économie, société* 18, no. 2 (2016): 275.

18. David Garbin and Anna Strhan, *Religion and the Global City* (New York: Bloomsbury, 2017). On transnational approaches to migration,

see, e.g., Sophie Bava and Stefania Capone, "Religions transnationales et migrations: regards croisés sur un champ en mouvement," *Autrepart* 56, no. 4 (2010): 3–15.

19. Luce Beeckmans, "Migrants, Mobile Worlding and City-Making: Exploring the Trans-Urban Circulation and Interconnectedness of Diasporic World-Making Practices," *African Diaspora* 11, no. 1–2 (2019): 87–100; and Leslie Fesenmyer, "Bringing the Kingdom to the City: Mission as Placemaking Practice Amongst Kenyan Pentecostals in London," *City & Society* 31, no. 1 (2019): 34–54.

20. In the 1980s, public anxieties over Islam emerged around concerns about the influence of Islam in factories, followed by controversies around cases of schoolgirls wearing the hijab in public schools. Since the 1990s, Islamophobic discourses have consolidated across the French public sphere. See Julien Beaugé and Abdellali Hajjat, "Élites françaises et construction du 'problème musulman.' Le cas du Haut Conseil à l'intégration (1989–2012)," *Sociologie* 5, no. 1 (2014): 31–59.

21. Claire de Galembert, "De l'inscription de l'islam dans l'espace urbain," *Les annales de la recherche urbaine* 68, no. 1 (1995): 178–88; Marcel Maussen, "Islamic Presence and Mosque Establishment in France: Colonialism, Arrangements for Guestworkers and Citizenship," *Journal of Ethnic & Migration Studies* 33, no. 6 (2007): 981–1002; and Aude-Claire Fourot, "Instruments d'action publique et régulation municipale de l'islam. Le cas de la mosquée de Créteil," *Gouvernement et action publique* 3, no. 3 (2015): 81–102. On "street prayers," see Mayanthi L. Fernando, *The Republic Unsettled: Muslim French and the Contradictions of Secularism* (Durham, NC: Duke University Press, 2014); and Fatima Khemilat, "La construction des prières de rue comme problème public," *Confluences Méditerranée* 106, no. 3 (2018): 81–94.

22. During my fieldwork, I rarely entered the prayer rooms and never attended a religious service. I witnessed ordinary performances of Islamic prayer in rooms or corridors, occasionally discussed religion with my interlocutors, and noted the multifaceted role that piety played in their lives, but the foyers' prayer rooms do not feature prominently in my ethnographic record. The following section relies on informal conversations on the topic, on two interviews with foyer imams, and on informal discussions with outsiders using the foyers' prayer rooms.

23. Arrêté n°2017-00082 portant fermeture administrative immédiate du local collectif du foyer Riquet situé 80/82 rue d'Aubervilliers, Préfecture de Police, January 27, 2017.

24. Marcel Maussen, *Constructing Mosques: The Governance of Islam in France and the Netherlands* (Amsterdam: Amsterdam School for Social Science Research, 2009), 170.

25. Solenne Jouanneau, "Faire émerger un 'islam français': paradoxes d'une action publique sous contrainte (1970–2010)," *Sociologie* 8, no. 3 (2017): 247–64; and Margot Dazey, "Les conditions de production locale d'un Islam respectable," *Genèses* 117, no. 4 (2019): 74–93.

26. There was an increase in attendance at the Friday prayer service after the neighboring mosque Adda'wa on rue de Tanger closed for renovation in 2006; this closure occurred with the prospect of a renovation that has not yet materialized. On the history of this mosque and the role of the municipal authorities, see Andrew Newman, *Landscape of Discontent: Urban Sustainability in Immigrant Paris* (Minneapolis: University of Minnesota Press, 2015), 8–9. For a detailed discussion of a contentious case of use of collective spaces in a residence for Islamic worship, see Guérin, "L'appropriation spatiale comme résistance habitante," chap. 8.

27. Hervé Vieillard-Baron, "L'islam en France: dynamiques, fragmentation et perspectives," *L'Information géographique* 80, no. 1 (2016): 22–53.

28. APUR, *Les foyers de travailleurs migrants à paris. Diagnostic et préconisations* (Paris: APUR, 2002), 13. In the 1990s, the Union professionnelle du logement accompagné (UNAFO) indicated that 119 of its 126 black foyers in the Paris region offered a prayer room. See Moustapha Diop and Laurence Michalak, "'Refuge' and 'Prison': Islam, Ethnicity, and the Adaptation of Space in Workers' Housing in France," in *Making Muslim Space in North America and Europe*, ed. B. D. Metcalf (Berkeley: University of California Press, 1996), 82. Administrative action resulted in many foyer prayer rooms being shut down in the 2010s.

29. "L'attentat le plus meurtrier depuis 1961," *Le Monde*, January 7, 2015. Coming after an attack in March 2012 in Toulouse, the events of January 2015 were followed by deadlier attacks in Paris in November 2015, in Nice in July 2016, and similar events every year until the end of the decade.

30. Field notes, February 2015.

31. Samba Sidibé, responsible for the prayer room at Foyer Bisson (twentieth arrondissement), indicated that they knew all the outsiders attending the service and were able to prevent individuals who would "go
wrong" access to the place. Quoted in collectif Sans A, "Dans les foyers,
la prière au tapis," February 2, 2007, https://jeromeleboursicot730001978
.wordpress.com/2017/02/07/dans-les-foyers-la-priere-au-tapis.

32. Marc Bernardot, "Une tempête sous un CRA. Violences et protestations dans les centres de rétention administrative français en 2008"
*Multitudes*, 35, no. 4 (2008), 219.

33. Department-level antifraud coordinations (Coordinations Départementales des Affaires Frauduleuses [CODAF]) were set up in 2010. For
another example, see "Plaisir. Opération coup de poing au foyer des travailleurs migrants," Le Parisien, June 10, 2016; the Director of the Family
Allowance Fund (Caisse d'allocations familiales [CAF]) of the Department of Yvelines, where this intervention took place, boasted six similar
operations over two years.

34. Ruling by the Haute autorité de lutte contre les discriminations et pour
l'égalité (HALDE), April 6, 2009, https://www.gisti.org/IMG/pdf/delib
_halde_2009-04-06_2009-148.pdf,

35. Vincent Dubois and Marion Lieutaud, "La 'fraude sociale' en questions," *Revue francaise de science politique* 70, no. 3 (2020): 341–71.

36. BBI, Municipal bulletin, Summer 2016, no. 447, p. 39.

37. BBI, Municipal bulletin, Summer 2016, no. 447, p. 38.

38. "Boulogne: un foyer à réhabiliter," *L'Humanité*, March 26, 1996; and "Le
foyer de Billancourt s'insurge," *Libération*, March 28, 1996. Press clippings kept by the délégués.

39. With the granting of voting rights to their emigrants, Senegalese
and Malian authorities have turned the foyers into sites of electoral
competition. See Jean-Philippe Dedieu, Lisa Chauvet, Flore Gubert,
Sandrine Mesplé-Somps, and Étienne Smith, "Les 'batailles' de Paris
et de New York," *Revue francaise de science politique* 63, no. 5 (2013):
865–92.

40. In 2005, around fifty individuals, mostly from African backgrounds,
including many children, died in several fires in the capital. On the
Paris-Opera hotel case, see Claire Lévy-Vroelant, *L'incendie de l'hôtel
Paris-Opéra. Enquête sur un drame social* (Grâne: Créaphis, 2018).

41. "Un Malien mort dans l'incendie d'un foyer d'immigrés," Agence France Press release, December 16, 2016. As of 2020, the investigation had not established any responsibility.

42. "Incendie mortel dans un foyer COALLIA de Boulogne-Billancourt: Le Maire Pierre-Christophe BAGUET demande sa fermeture immédiate," press release issued by the Municipality, December 16, 2016.

43. Michael Peter Smith and Michael MacQuarrie, *Remaking Urban Citizenship: Organizations, Institutions, and the Right to the City* (New York: Routledge, 2012), 3. Beyond a conventional understanding of citizenship emphasizing the "(legal) relation between the individual subject and the (nation-) state," recent scholarship has broadened the meaning of the notion to better "capture the current practices of claim making, participation, and membership." See Ayşe Çağlar, "Citizenship, Anthropology Of," *International Encyclopedia of the Social & Behavioral Sciences*, 2nd ed., Vol. 3 (Amsterdam: Elsevier, 2015), 637.

44. In April 2008, three hundred sans-papiers occupied their workplaces, demanding legalization. From this date to 2010, thousands of them mobilized, and an estimated two thousand gained legal status. Pierre Baron, Anne Bory, Sébastien Chauvin, Nicolas Jounin, and Lucie Tourette, "*On bosse ici, on reste ici !*": *la grève des sans-papiers, une aventure inédite* (Paris: La Découverte, 2011).

45. On this delegation to associations of the bureaucratic work regarding migrants' rights to residence, see Mathilde Pette, "Associations: les nouveaux guichets de l'immigration? Du travail militant en préfecture, Are non-profit organizations the new offices of immigration services? Activists' work in a local administration," *Sociologie* 5, no. 4 (2014): 405–21.

46. They belonged to the tens of thousands of sub-Saharan African foreign workers accused of having fought as mercenaries for Gaddafi. See Human Rights Watch, "World Report 2012: Libya," https://www.hrw.org/world-report/2012/country-chapters/libya.

47. A CILPI officer labeled it "the mythic Bara," Interview at CILPI, January 28, 2020. An agreement between the authorities and the residents' committee had been signed with great ceremony in February 2013, in the presence of the Minister of Housing, Cécile Duflot, member of the Green Party. Due to delays in the process, in September 2018, in a widely reported gesture, the communist mayor, Patrice Bessac, spent a

night at Foyer Bara to shed light on the dilapidated status of the place. The municipality then requisitioned an empty building and had Foyer Bara evacuated in November 2018. Official residents were provisionally lodged there and were to be rehoused in several residences sociales within Montreuil. Although the municipality boasted their management of Bara as a success, grassroots organizations and local observers highlighted that unofficial residents were not sufficiently considered.

48. Letter quoted in Pierre Benetti, "A Montreuil, les rescapés de la guerre de Libye," *Le Monde diplomatique*, November 2013.

49. Mireille Eberhard, Erwan Le Méner, and Emilie Segol, *Qui sont les migrants mis à l'abri? Île-De-France (Juin 2015-Novembre 2016)*, Rapport pour la Direction régionale et interdépartementale de l'hébergement et du logement d'Île-de-France (2018). On the wider context of migrants arriving in 2015, see Annalisa Lendaro, Claire Rodier, and Youri Lou Vertongen, *La crise de l'accueil: frontières, droits, résistances* (Paris: Éditions la Découverte, 2019).

50. For a similar case in Paris, see "Crise migratoire: dans un foyer du centre de Paris, l'inquiétude des "anciens" face aux 'nouveaux,'" *Le Monde*, September 11, 2015.

51. Anonymous, "'Gilets Noirs, pour rester en colère et puissants!,'" *Vacarme* 88, no. 3 (2019): 68–79.

52. In the Global North, studies demonstrating a higher proportion of deaths from COVID-19 among racial minorities include, for the UK, The OpenSAFELY Collaborative et al., "OpenSAFELY: Factors Associated with COVID-19-Related Hospital Death in the Linked Electronic Health Records of 17 Million Adult NHS Patients," *MedRxiv*, May 7, 2020, 2020.05.06.20092999; and for the United States, Uma V. Mahajan and Margaret Larkins-Pettigrew, "Racial Demographics and COVID-19 Confirmed Cases and Deaths: A Correlational Analysis of 2886 US Counties," *Journal of Public Health* 42, no. 3 (2020): 445–47; for UK public debates, notably on the possible role of discrimination in access to public health services in this situation, see Gareth Iacobucci, "Covid-19: Increased Risk Among Ethnic Minorities Is Largely Due to Poverty and Social Disparities, Review Finds," *BMJ*, October 22, 2020. In France, in the absence of statistics based on ethno-racial categories, studies have focused on geographical areas known for the preponderance of individuals of immigrant backgrounds, such as

the Department of Seine-Saint-Denis. See Solène Brun and Patrick Simon, "L'invisibilité des minorités dans les chiffres du Coronavirus: le détour par la Seine-Saint-Denis," *De facto* [on line] 19 (2020).

53. Although the provision of health services to undocumented migrants has existed since 2000, only 51 percent of potential beneficiaries are registered. Florence Jusot, Paul Dourgnon, Jérôme Wittwer, and Jawhar Sarhiri, "Le recours à l'Aide médicale de l'État des personnes en situation irrégulière en France: premiers enseignements de l'enquête Premiers pas," *Questions d'économie de la santé* 245 (November 2019): 8.

54. "Covid-19: des migrants oubliés dans des conteneurs d'Adoma," *La Marseillaise*, March 25, 2020.

55. "Coronavirus: le 138 rue de Stalingrad à Montreuil, 'une bombe sanitaire à retardement'," TV report, France 3, Paris Ile-de-France, April 3, 2020.

56. Press release from the residents' committee of Foyer Romain Rolland (Saint-Denis) and other organizations, April 23, 2020, http://blogs .mediapart.fr/fini-de-rire/blog/250420/vivre-et-mourir-dans-un-foyer -de-travailleurs-migrants.

57. Based on tests conducted in fourteen facilities for vulnerable populations, among which were two foyers in Seine-Saint-Denis, one study measured a far greater exposure to the coronavirus for foyer residents, with a level of SARS-CoV2 antibody seropositivity of 88.7 percent compared to an estimate of 10 to 12 percent in the general population of the Paris region, Thomas Roederer, Bastien Mollo, Charline Vincent, Birgit Nikolay, Augusto Llosa, Robin Nesbitt, Jessica Vanhomwegen, et al. "High Seroprevalence of SARS-CoV-2 Antibodies among People Living in Precarious Situations in Ile de France." *MedRxiv*, October 9, 2020, medRxiv 2020.10.07.20207795 . It found overcrowding to be the most important factor associated with such high prevalence. This striking figure was widely spread, even though, for the same period, tests conducted within Parisian foyers found a 10 percent level of exposure to the virus, similar to the general population (results communicated by Ian Brossat, Deputy Mayor of Paris in Charge of Housing, quoted in Minutes from the November 9, 2020, meeting between the délégués and municipal officers in charge of the foyers, COPAF).

58. Guérin, "L'appropriation spatiale."

59. "Coronavirus: la crainte d'une contamination rapide dans les squats et foyers de travailleurs," *Le Monde*, April 11, 2020.

60. "Coronavirus: la situation des migrants en foyers préoccupe les généralistes de Montreuil," *Lemedecingeneraliste.fr*, April 1, 2020.

61. A first lockdown was implemented from March 17, 2020, to May 10, 2020; a second one from October 29 to December 15, 2020; new restrictive measures were enforced on March 19, 2021. Restaurants resumed their activities slowly after the first lockdown, with strong constraints, and also suffered from curfews between the two lockdown phases.

62. Claire Lévy-Vroelant, "Les sans-papiers au risque du Covid-19. Entre 'protocole compassionnel' et déni de droits," *Métropolitiques*, May 1, 2020.

63. For an exploration of the nuanced reactions of Senegalese migrants to the 2008 economic in Spain, see María Hernández-Carretero, "Hope and Uncertainty in Senegalese Migration to Spain: Taking Chances on Emigration but Not Upon Return," in *Hope and Uncertainty in Contemporary African Migration*, ed. Nauja Kleist and Dorte Thorsen (New York: Routledge, 2017), 113–33.

64. Nicolas Jounin, "Aux origines des 'travailleurs sans papiers.' Les spécificités d'un groupe au service d'une identification généraliste," *Revue européenne des migrations internationales* 30, no 1 (2014): 131–52.

## 9. FOCAL POINTS:
## REFLECTIONS FROM THE FOYERS

1. For a critique of the analytical use of the term "ghetto" for French banlieues, see Loïc Wacquant, *Urban Outcasts: A Comparative Sociology of Advanced Marginality* (London: Polity, 2008). For comparative reflections on the term, see Ray Hutchison and Bruce D. Haynes, eds., *The Ghetto: Contemporary Global Issues and Controversies* (New York: Routledge, 2019).

2. Far from being exhaustive, the list of projects quoted here focuses on productions of the late 2000s and early 2010s. For earlier projects, see Rémi Gallou, "Le vieillissement des immigrés en France," *Politix* 72, no. 4 (2005): 70n24.

3. Tyler Stovall, "Race and the Making of the Nation. Blacks in Modern France," in *Diasporic Africa: A Reader*, ed. Michael A. Gomez (New York: NYU Press, 2006), 202.

4. The research project was "In Search of Europe: Considering the Possible in Africa and the Middle East," funded by the German Federal

Ministry of Education and Research (BMBF), based at the Zentrum Moderner Orient (ZMO, now the Leibniz-Zentrum Moderner Orient) in Berlin. The exhibition was titled *In Search of Europe? Art and Research in Collaboration*, Kunstraum Kreuzberg/Bethanien, Berlin, November 2013–January 2014, curated by Daniela Swarowsky. See Aïssatou Mbodj-Pouye and Anissa Michalon, "Locating Migration. Narratives, Memories, and Places of West African Migration in Paris," in *In Search of Europe?: Art and Research in Collaboration*, by Daniela Swarowsky et al., ed. Kunstraum Kreuzberg (Heijningen, Pays-Bas: Jap Sam Books, 2013), 80–93. The album: Aïssatou Mbodj-Pouye and Anissa Michalon, *On est les mêmes depuis le 216 bis. Une mémoire parisienne de l'immigration africaine* (Paris, 2015). The film: *How to Talk About the Experience of Migration Back Home?*, December 18, 2013, with Leila Morouche and Daniela Swarowsky.

5. Beyond visual productions, literary accounts of the foyers feature notably in biographical and fictionalized childhood memories by French individuals of West African descent. See, for instance, Hadama Bathily's contribution to Franklin Anzite, Hadama Bathily, Fabrice Dyndo, Endy Eboma, Gamal Hamada, Samba Kanouté, Mara Keïta, Yassine Mohammed, Mossi Traoré, and Yann Dagba, *Les Gars de Villiers* (Paris: Ginkgo, 2012); and Yancouba Diémé, *Boy Diola* (Paris: Flammarion, 2019).

6. Jean-Philippe Dedieu, "S'engager dans l'image. Migrants ouest-africains et journalistes français dans les années 1960," *Ethnologie française* 42, no. 4 (2012): 811–22.

7. Édouard Mills-Affif, *Filmer les immigrés: les représentations audiovisuelles de l'immigration à la télévision française, 1960–1986* (Bruxelles: De Boeck, 2004), 59.

8. Dedieu, "S'engager dans l'image."

9. Tangui Perron, ed. *Histoire d'un film, mémoire d'une lutte* (Paris: Scope & Périphéries, 2009).

10. Instruction given by the director of EATM to one "animateur" not to show the film by Sidney Sokhona in the EATM foyers. Letter dated November 17, 1975. Archives de Paris: 2024 W art. 2.

11. The office national de promotion culturelle des immigrés was inaugurated in February 1976. Angéline Escafré-Dublet, "L'Etat et la culture des immigrés, 1974–1984," *Histoire@Politique* 4, no. 1 (2008): 15.

12. Jacques Barou, "Immigrés africains devant la caméra," *Journal des africanistes* 60, no. 1 (1990): 141–51.

13. Blandine Stefanson and Sheila Petty, *Directory of World Cinema: Africa* (Bristol: Intellect Books, 2014), 134.

14. Carrie Tarr, "French Cinema and Post-Colonial Minorities," in *Post-Colonial Cultures in France*, ed. Alec G. Hargreaves and Mark McKinney (London: Routledge, 1997), 68; Sheila Petty, "Black Mic-Mac and Colonial Discourse," *CineAction* 18 (1989): 51–55.

15. Alain Mabanckou and Abdourahman Waberi, *Dictionnaire enjoué des cultures africaines* (Paris: Fayard, 2019).

16. Mamadou Diouf, "The Lost Territories of the Republic. Historical Narratives and the Recomposition of French Citizenship," in *Black France/France Noire*, ed. Tyler Stovall, Trica Danielle Keaton, and T. Denean Sharpley-Whiting (Durham, NC: Duke University Press, 2012), 32–56.

17. Mireille Rosello, "Representing Illegal Immigrants in France: From *clandestins* to l'affaire des sans-papiers de Saint-Bernard," *Journal of European Studies* 28, no. 109–110 (1998): 137–51.

18. "Foyer Bara à Montreuil, une oasis malienne à préserver," ZiKetZinC (blog), February 7, 2016, http://ziketzink.over-blog.com/2016/02/foyer-bara-a-montreuil-une-oasis-malienne-a-preserver.html.

19. Dominic Thomas, "Afropeanism and Francophone Sub-Saharan African Writing," in *Francophone Afropean Literatures*, ed. Dominic Thomas and Nicki Hitchcott (Liverpool: Liverpool University Press, 2014), 28; and Jean-Luc Porquet, *Guide actuel du Paris mondial* (Paris: Le Seuil, 1992).

20. A systematic photographic documentation of a foyer prior to renovation occurred in Guyancourt (Yvelines), accessed March 26, 2021, https://inventaire.iledefrance.fr/dossier/foyer-hotel-pour-travailleurs-celibataires-et-migrants-du-pont-du-routoir/36b65b36-d5a0-4b52-8f81-a63baf33d18b#interet.

21. Margot Delon, "Faire mémoire(s) de lieux disparus. Le cas des bidonvilles et cités de transit de Nanterre," *Ethnologie française* 44, no. 2 (2014): 341–53.

22. Michèle Baussant, Marina Chauliac, Irène Dos Santos, Evelyne Ribert, and Nancy Venel, "Introduction," *Communications* 100, no. 1 (2017): 7–20.

23. At the opening of the CNHI, foyers were represented by a photographic series, Hamid Debarrah, *Faciès inventaire. Chronique du foyer*

*de la rue Très Cloître*, 2002. It has since been replaced by another photographic series by Karim Kal, *Les Miroirs*, on a foyer in Evry.

24. Claire Soton and Anissa Michalon, "Natif de Bada. Vit à Montreuil (Foyer Rochebrune)," *Communications* 79, no. 1 (2006): 225–45; Anissa Michalon and Claire Soton, *Natifs de Bada. Récits d'une émigration Malienne* (Cherbourg: Le Point du Jour, 2014).

25. Funding for the exhibition came from the research project budget. For the publication, we sought additional funding from my research center and from the municipal service in charge of urban policies and integration, thanks to one interlocutor in this service with whom I had built a relation of trust; they did not review the publication before print.

26. As an example of a promotional object, see the short film about the renovation of a foyer in Bobigny https://www.dailymotion.com/video /xj5mho, accessed March 26, 2021. Another instance is the photographic series by photographers Willy Vainqueur and Coallia worker Malika Yahia Mayo, offering portraits of resident from the residence Barbusse in Aubervilliers in 2009. https://aftamgram.wordpress.com/2009/06/15/, accessed March 26, 2021.

27. The journalist Moïse Gomis, the son of a foyer director in Rouen, developed the web documentary "Grand écart" with portraits of the inhabitants of the foyer mirrored by interviews with their family members in Senegal. http://www.grandecartdocumentaire.com/, first released in 2012, accessed March 26, 2021.

28. See the testimony by the Ivoirian photographer Ananias Leki Dago recounting how penetrating Foyer Manouchian (Le Blanc-Mesnil) required time and patience. Hélène Lebon, "Blanc-Mesnil Noirs. Exposition Forum," *Hommes et Migrations* 1266, no. 1 (2007): 164–67. I met the Malian photographer Fatoumata Diabaté when the Musée du Quai Branly had assigned her to take photographs of Malians in Montreuil as part of outreach activities associated with the Dogon exhibition. She likewise emphasized how the foyers were far from easy to approach for her, a young woman.

29. See Vincent Leroux's photographic series documenting the construction of the first residence sociale in Paris, a work funded among others by Adoma and the municipality of Paris. Vincent Leroux, *Commanderie* (Paris: Temps Machine, 2011). Olivier Aubert, a photographer and a COPAF member, offered a fierce critique. Olivier Aubert,

"'Commanderie.' À propos d'Afrique, d'Africains, de foyers et de photographie," *Les Mots Sont Importants*, May 4, 2011. On this debate, see Caroline Trouillet, "(Dé)peindre les travailleurs migrants en photographie," *Africultures* (blog), February 17, 2013.

30. Several COPAF activists' collections were part of *Génériques* collection: posters kept by Geneviève Petauton and Jacqueline Geering's photographic documentation of the foyers.

31. Guglielmo Scafirimuto, "Les films associatifs autobiographiques des migrant-e-s et l'espace de réception des foyers parisiens," in *Images et réceptions croisées entre l'Algérie et la France* (Paris: Éditions science et bien commun, 2020)

32. Olivier Pasquiers, *Merci aux travailleurs venus de loin* (Grâne: Créaphis éditions, 2012). In addition to Soton and Michalon's work, a powerful case of a photographer following her interlocutors to their home villages is Anaïs Pachabezian's long-term photographic project between France and Mali, "Un migrant entre Paris et Monéa," on which see https://www.histoire-immigration.fr/agenda/2010-11/rencontre-avec-anais-pachabezian, accessed May 17, 2023.

33. Dalila Mahdjoub and Martine Derain, *D'un seuil à l'autre: perspective sur une chambre avec ses habitants* (Marseille: Editions Transit, 2007).

34. Hélène Béguin, "Héberger des migrants ou gérer des logements? L'Aftam et ses 'foyers d'Africains noirs' (1962–2012)" (PhD diss., University of Paris Est, 2015).

35. Laura Guérin, "L'appropriation spatiale comme résistance habitante. Ethnographie de résidences sociales issues de Foyers de Travailleurs Migrants" (PhD diss., University of Paris 8, 2021), and "Cohabiter dans un studio de travailleurs migrants: contraintes gestionnaires et 'arts de faire,'" *Espaces et sociétés*, vol. 186-187, no. 3-4 (2022): 35–50.

# BIBLIOGRAPHY

## 1. ARCHIVAL SERIES

Archives Départementales de la Seine-Saint-Denis, Bobigny
Archives Départementales des Hauts-de-Seine, Nanterre
Archives Municipales, Saint-Denis
Archives Nationales, Pierrefitte
Archives de Paris, Paris
Archives de la Préfecture de Police de Paris, Paris
Institut d'Histoire du Temps Présent, Paris—*Fonds Monique Hervo*

## 2. BOOKS, REPORTS, AND ARTICLES

Abu-Lughod, Lila. "Fieldwork of a Dutiful Daughter." In *Arab Women in the Field: Studying Your Own Society*, ed. Soraya Altorki and Camillia Fawzi El-Solh. Syracuse, NY: Syracuse University Press, 1988.

——. "Writing Against Culture." In *Recapturing Anthropology*, ed. Richard Fox, 137–62. Santa Fe, NM: School of American Research Press, 1991.

Adams, Adrian. *Le long voyage des gens du fleuve*. Paris: Maspero, 1977.

Agier, Michel. *Esquisses d'une anthropologie de la ville: lieux, situations, mouvements*. Louvain-la-Neuve: Academia-Bruylant, 2009.

Ahmad, Ali Nobil. "Gender and Generation in Pakistani Migration: A Critical Study of Masculinity." In *Gendering Migration Masculinity, Femininity and Ethnicity in Post-War Britain*, ed. Wendy Webster and Louise Ryan, 167–82. London: Routledge, 2016.

Amin, Samir, ed. *Modern Migrations in Western Africa*. London: Oxford University Press, 1974.

Amiraux, Valérie, and Patrick Simon. "There Are No Minorities Here: Cultures of Scholarship and Public Debate on Immigrants and Integration in France." *International Journal of Comparative Sociology* 47, no. 3–4 (2006): 191–215.

Anand, Nikhil, Akhil Gupta, and Hannah Appel. eds. "Introduction: Temporality, Politics, and the Promise of Infrastructure." In *The Promise of Infrastructure*, 1–38. Durham, NC: Duke University Press, 2018.

Annequin, Margot, Anne Gosselin, and Rosemary Dray-Spira. *Trajectoires et mobilités professionnelles autour de la migration. Parcours*. Paris: La Découverte, 2017.

Anonymous. "'Gilets Noirs, pour rester en colère et puissants!'" *Vacarme* 88, no. 3 (2019): 68–79.

Anzite, Franklin, Hadama Bathily, Fabrice Dyndo, Endy Eboma, Gamal Hamada, Samba Kanouté, Mara Keïta, Yassine Mohammed, Mossi Traoré, and Yann Dagba. *Les Gars de Villiers*. Paris: Ginkgo, 2012.

APUR. *Les foyers de travailleurs migrants à Paris. Diagnostic et préconisations*. Paris: APUR, 2002.

——. *Les foyers de travailleurs migrants à Paris—Etat des lieux en 2010 et inventaires des interventions sanitaires et culturelles*. Paris: APUR, 2011.

Arslan, Leyla. "Union halal: sexualité et mariage chez le couple 'musulman' dans les quartiers populaires." In *Les sens du Halal: une norme dans un marché mondial*, ed. Florence Bergeaud-Blackler, 137–52. Paris: CNRS Éditions, 2019.

Aubert, Olivier. "'Commanderie.' À propos d'Afrique, d'Africains, de foyers et de photographie." *Les Mots Sont Importants*, May 4, 2011.

Azoulay, Muriel, and Catherine Quiminal. "Reconstruction des rapports de genre en situation migratoire. Femmes 'réveillées,' hommes menacés en milieu soninké." *VEI enjeux: Migrants Formation* 128 (2002): 87–101.

Babou, Cheikh Anta. "Migration as a Factor of Cultural Change Abroad and at Home: Senegalese Female Hair Braiders in the United States." In *African Migrations. Patterns and Perspectives*, ed. Abdoulaye Kane and Todd H. Leedy, 230–47. Bloomington: Indiana University Press, 2013.

Bacqué, Marie-Hélène, and Claire Carriou. "Participation et politiques du logement en France. Un débat qui traverse le XXe siècle." In *La démocratie participative. Histoire et généalogie*, ed. Marie-Hélène Bacqué, 155–73. Paris: La Découverte, 2011.

Bacqué, Marie-Hélène, Yankel Fijalkow, Lydie Launay, and Stéphanie Vermeersch. "Social Mix Policies in Paris: Discourses, Policies and Social Effects." *International Journal of Urban and Regional Research* 35, no. 2 (2011): 256–73.

Baizán, Pau, Cris Beauchemin, and Amparo González-Ferrer. "An Origin and Destination Perspective on Family Reunification: The Case of Senegalese Couples." *European Journal of Population* 30, no. 1 (2014): 65–87.

Ballain, René, and Elisabeth Maurel. *Le logement très social: extension ou fragilisation du droit au logement?* La Tour d'Aigues: Éditions de l'Aube, 2002.

Ballard, Roger. "Migration and Kinship: The Differential Effect of Marriage Rules on the Process of Punjabi Migration to Britain." In *South Asians Overseas: Contexts and Communities*, ed. C. Clarke, C. Peach, and S. Vertovec, 219–49. Cambridge: Cambridge University Press, 1990.

Baron, Pierre, Anne Bory, Sébastien Chauvin, Nicolas Jounin, and Lucie Tourette. *"On bosse ici, on reste ici!": la grève des sans-papiers, une aventure inédite*. Paris: La Découverte, 2011.

Barou, Jacques. "Immigrés africains devant la caméra." *Journal des africanistes* 60, no. 1 (1990): 141–51.

——. "L'Islam, facteur de régulation sociale." *Esprit* 102, no. 6 (1985): 207–15.

——. *Travailleurs africains en France: rôle des cultures d'origine.* Collection Actualités-recherche. Grenoble: Presses Universitaires de Grenoble, 1978.

Barou, Jacques, Moustapha Diop, and Toma Subhi. "Des musulmans dans l'usine." In *Ouvriers spécialisés à Billancourt: les derniers témoins*, ed. Renaud Sainsaulieu and Ahsène Zehraoui, 131–61. Paris: L'Harmattan, 1995.

Barros, Françoise de. "Les acteurs municipaux et 'leurs' étrangers (1919–1984): gains et contraintes d'un détour communal pour l'analyse d'un travail de catégorisation étatique." *Genèses* 72, no. 3 (2008): 42–62.

Basch, Linda Green, Nina Glick Schiller, and Cristina Szanton Blanc. *Nations Unbound: Transnational Projects, Postcolonial Predicaments, and Deterritorialized Nation-States*. London: Gordon and Breach, 1994.

Baussant, Michèle, Marina Chauliac, Irène Dos Santos, Evelyne Ribert, and Nancy Venel. "Introduction." *Communications* 100, no. 1 (2017): 7–20.

Bava, Sophie, and Stefania Capone. "Religions transnationales et migrations: regards croisés sur un champ en mouvement." *Autrepart* 56, no. 4 (2010): 3–15.

Bear, Laura. "Ruins and Ghosts: The Domestic Uncanny and the Material-ization of Anglo-Indian Genealogies in Kharagpur." In *Ghosts of Memory: Essays on Remembrance and Relatedness*, ed. Janet Carsten, 36–57. Hoboken, NJ: Blackwell, 2008.

Beaugé, Julien, and Abdellali Hajjat. "Élites françaises et construction du 'problème musulman.' Le cas du Haut Conseil à l'intégration (1989–2012)." *Sociologie* 5, no. 1 (2014): 31–59.

Beck-Gernsheim, Elisabeth. "Transnational Lives, Transnational Marriages: A Review of the Evidence from Migrant Communities in Europe." *Global Networks* 7, no. 3 (2007): 271–88.

Becker, Howard S. *Outsiders: Studies in the Sociology of Deviance*. New York: Free Press, 1963.

Beeckmans, Luce. "Migrants, Mobile Worlding and City-Making: Explor-ing the Trans-Urban Circulation and Interconnectedness of Diasporic World-Making Practices." *African Diaspora* 11, no. 1–2 (2019): 87–100.

Béguin, Hélène. "Un dispositif spatial à la rencontre ou à l'encontre des usages? L'introduction du 'logement individuel autonome' dans les foyers de travailleurs migrants". In *Transformations des horizons urbains. Savoirs, imaginaires, usages et conflits*, eds. Frédéric Coninck and José-Frédéric Deroubaix, 129–42 Paris : L'oeil d'or, 2012.

——. "Des "Africains noirs" à la "mixité sociale". Usages paradoxaux des caté-gorisations ethniques dans les foyers de travailleurs migrants AFTAM (1962–2010)". In *Le peuplement comme politiques*, eds. Fabien Desage, Christelle Morel Journel, and Valérie Sala Pala, 15573. Rennes: Presses Universitaires de Rennes, 2014.

——. "Héberger des migrants ou gérer des logements? L'Aftam et ses 'foyers d'Africains noirs' (1962–2012)." PhD diss., University of Paris Est, 2015.

Belkacem, Lila. "Dire, penser et vivre les frontières: catégorisations et présen-tations de soi des enfants d'immigrés maliens en France." *Migrations Société* 128, no. 2 (2010): 177–92.

Bellamy, Vanessa. "236,300 mariages célébrés en France en 2015, dont 33,800 mariages mixtes." *Insee Première*, 2017.

Bernard, Tiphaine. "Habiter le foyer: approche anthropologique de la résiden-tialisation des foyers à travers l'exception' Centenaire, une résidence sociale en co-gestion à Montreuil-Sous-Bois" PhD diss., University of Paris 8, 2017.

Bernardot, Marc. "Le Grand âge dans les foyers, nouveau public, nouveaux enjeux." Paper presented at the Congrès de l'AFS, RT 7 (Vieillesse,

Vieillissement,ParcoursdeVie).Bordeaux,2006,http://www.copaf.ouvaton
.org/vieux/vieux_bernardot.pdf.

——. "Invisibiliser par le logement. De Sonacotra à Adoma." In *Les nouvelles frontières de la société française*, ed. Didider Fassin, 79–100. Paris: La
Découverte, 2012.

——. *Loger les immigrés: la Sonacotra*. Bellecombe-en-Bauges, France: Edition
du Croquant, 2008.

——. "Une tempête sous un CRA. Violences et protestations dans les centres
de rétention administrative français en 2008," *Multitudes*, 35, no. 4 (2008):
215–24.

——. "Le vieux, le fou et l'autre, qui habite encore dans les foyers?" *Revue
européenne de migrations internationales* 17, no. 1 (2001): 151–64.

Bertoncello, Brigitte, and Sylvie Bredeloup. *Colporteurs africains à Marseille:
un siècle d'aventures*. Paris: Autrement, 2004.

Biehl, Kristen Sarah. "A Dwelling Lens: Migration, Diversity and Boundary-
Making in an Istanbul Neighbourhood." *Ethnic and Racial Studies* 43, no.
12 (2020): 2236–54.

Bird, Charles S., and Martha B. Kendall. "The Mande Hero: Text and Context."
In *Explorations in African Systems of Thought*, ed. Ivan Karp and Charles S.
Bird, 13–26. Bloomington: Indiana University Press, 1980.

Blanc-Chaléard, Marie-Claude. *En finir avec les bidonvilles: immigration et
politique du logement dans la France des Trente Glorieuses*. Paris: Publications de la Sorbonne, 2016.

Blanpain, Nathalie. "L'espérance de vie s'accroît, les inégalités sociales face à
la mort demeurent." *INSEE Première* 1372 (2011).

Bledsoe, Caroline, and Papa Sow. "Family Reunification Ideals and the Practice of Transnational Reproductive Life Among Africans in Europe."
MPDIR Working Paper, February 2008.

Blum, Françoise. "Trajectoires militantes et reconversions." *Genèses* 107, no. 2
(2017): 106–30.

Bobbé, Sophie, Evelyne Ribert, and Emmanuel Terray. "Droits des travailleurs migrants: le cas des retraites." ENSANS, Environnement, santé et
société, March 2013.

Boccagni, Paolo. *Migration and the Search for Home*. New York: Palgrave Macmillan, 2017.

Boittin, Jennifer. "The Militant Black Men of Marseille and Paris, 1927–
1937." In *Black France/France Noire*, ed. Trica Danielle Keaton, T. Denean

Sharpley-Whiting, and Tyler Stovall, 221–46. Durham, NC: Duke University Press, 2012.

Borrel, Catherine, Gérard Bouvier, and Bertrand Lhommeau. *Immigrés et Descendants d'immigrés en France*. Paris: INSEE, 2012.

Bouillon, Florence. "Des migrants et des squats: précarités et résistances aux marges de la ville." *Revue européenne des migrations internationales* 19, no. 2 (2003): 23–46.

Bourdieu, Pierre. *La distinction: critique sociale du jugement*. Paris: Les Editions de minuit, 1979.

Boursin, Marie-Laure. "À l'heure de la prière: entre pratiques et expérimentations." *Ethnologie française* 168, no. 4 (2017): 623–36.

Boussad, Nadia, Nathalie Couleaud, and Mariette Sagot. "Une population immigrée aujourd'hui plus répartie sur le territoire régional." *INSEE Analyses Ile-de-France*, October 17, 2017.

Bowen, John R. *Why the French Don't Like Headscarves: Islam, the State, and Public Space*. Princeton, NJ: Princeton University Press, 2008.

Bredeloup, Sylvie. *La Diams'pora du fleuve Sénégal: sociologie des migrations africaines*. Toulouse: Presses Universitaires du Mirail, 2007.

Brettell, Caroline B. *Anthropology and Migration: Essays on Transnationalism, Ethnicity, and Identity*. Walnut Creek, CA: Altamira Press, 2003.

——. *We Have Already Cried Many Tears: Portuguese Women and Migration*. Cambridge, MA: Schenkman, 1982.

Brinbaum, Yael, Mirna Safi, and Patrick Simon. "Les discriminations en France: entre perception et expérience." Working Paper. Paris: INED, 2012.

Broqua, Christophe. "La socialisation du désir homosexuel masculin à Bamako." *Civilisations. Revue internationale d'anthropologie et de sciences humaines* 59, no. 1 (2010): 37–58.

Brun, Solène, and Patrick Simon. "L'invisibilité des minorités dans les chiffres du Coronavirus: le détour par la Seine-Saint-Denis." *De facto* [on line] 19 (2020).

Bucerius, Sandra Meike. "Becoming a 'Trusted Outsider': Gender, Ethnicity, and Inequality in Ethnographic Research." *Journal of Contemporary Ethnography* 42, no. 6 (2013): 690–721.

Byrnes, Melissa K. "French Like Us? Municipal Policies and North African Migrants in the Parisian Banlieues, 1945–1975." PhD diss., Georgetown University, Washington, D.C., 2008.

Çağlar, Ayse. "Citizenship, Anthropology Of." *International Encyclopedia of the Social & Behavioral Sciences*, 2nd ed., Vol. 3, 637–41. Amsterdam: Elsevier, 2015.

Çağlar, Ayşe, and Nina Glick Schiller. *Migrants and City-Making: Dispossession, Displacement, and Urban Regeneration.* Durham, NC: Duke University Press, 2018.

Calandre, Natacha, and Evelyne Ribert. "Les pratiques alimentaires d'hommes ouest-africains vivant en Île-de-France. Entre perpétuation de la culture alimentaire d'origine et aspiration à la modernité." *Hommes & Migrations*, no. 1286–1287 (2010): 162–73.

Carsten, Janet. "Introduction: Cultures of Relatedness." In *Cultures of Relatedness: New Approaches to the Study of Kinship*, 1–36. Cambridge: Cambridge University Press, 2000.

Castles, Stephen, and Godula Kosack. *Immigrant Workers and Class Structure in Western Europe.* London: Oxford University Press, Institute of Race Relations, 1973.

Célestine, Audrey, and Sarah Fila-Bakabadio. "Introduction to the Special Issue: 'Black Paris and the Lived Experiences of Black Subjects.'" *African and Black Diaspora: An International Journal* 10, no. 1 (2017): 1–11.

Centre d'étude des mouvements sociaux. *Sociologie des mouvements sociaux urbains: enquête sur la région parisienne.* Vol. 1. Paris: EHESS, 1974.

Centre national de la recherche scientifique, and Régie nationale des usines Renault. *Les O.S. dans l'industrie automobile: recherche documentaire et bibliographique, 02: Analyse documentaire.* Paris: CNRS, 1986.

Charsley, Katharine. "Unhappy Husbands: Masculinity and Migration in Transnational Pakistani Marriages." *Journal of the Royal Anthropological Institute* 11, no. 1 (2005): 85–105.

Charsley, Katharine, Marta Bolognani, Evelyn Ersanilli, and Sarah Spencer. "Marriage Migration and Integration: Unpacking the Arguments and Evidence." In *Marriage Migration and Integration*, 57–81. New York: Palgrave Macmillan, 2020.

Charsley, Katharine, and Helena Wray. "Introduction: The Invisible (Migrant) Man." *Men and Masculinities* 18, no. 4 (2015): 403–23.

Chaskin, Robert J., and Mark L. Joseph. *Integrating the Inner City: The Promise and Perils of Mixed-Income Public Housing Transformation.* Chicago: University of Chicago Press, 2015.

Chort, Isabelle, Flore Gubert, and Jean-Noël Senne. "Migrant Networks as a Basis for Social Control: Remittance Incentives Among Senegalese in France and Italy." *Regional Science and Urban Economics* 42, no. 5 (2012): 858–74.

CILPI. "Document cadre. Orientations pour la mise en œuvre du plan de traitement des Foyers de Travailleurs Migrants," 2018. https://www.gouvernement.fr/sites/default/files/contenu/piece-jointe/2018/12/document_cadre_cilpi.pdf.

——. "Document cadre relatif au plan de traitement des Foyers de Travailleurs Migrants, Cilpi, DGUHC, UESL et Anpeec," 2007.

Cissoko, Mahamadou. "Les relations afro-maghrébines du foyer au quartier. La fraternité islamique à l'épreuve du quotidien." PhD diss., Université Paris 8, 2019.

Clavé-Mercier, Alexandra, and Martin Olivera. "Une résistance non résistante? Ethnographie du malentendu dans les dispositifs d'"intégration' pour des migrants roms." *L'Homme, Revue française d'anthropologie*, 219–220 (November 2016): 175–207.

Clerval, Anne. *Paris sans le peuple: la gentrification de la capitale*. Paris: La Découverte, 2013.

Clerval, Anne, and Yoan Miot. "Inégalités et habitat en Île-de-France: quelles conséquences des politiques de renouvellement urbain sur le peuplement?" *Espaces et sociétés* 170, no. 3 (2017): 51–72.

Clouet, Claire. *La Diaspora de la chambre 107. Ethnographies musicales dans la diaspora soninké*. Paris: Editions MF, 2021.

Cohen, Muriel. *Des familles invisibles: Les Algériens de France entre intégrations et discriminations (1945–1985)*. Paris: Editions de la Sorbonne, 2020.

Cole, Jennifer. "The *téléphone malgache*: Transnational Gossip and Social Transformation Among Malagasy Marriage Migrants in France." *American Ethnologist* 41, no. 2 (2014): 276–89.

——. "Working Mis/Understandings: The Tangled Relationship Between Kinship, Franco-Malagasy Binational Marriages, and the French State." *Cultural Anthropology* 29, no. 3 (2014): 527–51.

Condé, Julien, and Pap Syr Diagne. *Les Migrations internationales Sud-Nord: une étude de cas*. Paris: OCDE, 1986.

Connell, R. W., and James W. Messerschmidt. "Hegemonic Masculinity: Rethinking the Concept." *Gender and Society* 19, no. 6 (2005): 829–59.

Cooper, Frederick. *Citizenship Between Empire and Nation: Remaking France and French Africa, 1945–1960*. Princeton, NJ: Princeton University Press, 2014.

Cordell, Dennis D., and Carolyn F. Sargent. "Islam, Identity and Gender in Daily Life Among Malians in Paris: The Burdens Are Easier to Bear." In *L'islam politique au sud du Sahara. Identité, discours et enjeux*, ed. Muriel Gomez-Perez, 177–206. Paris: Karthala, 2009.

——. "Samba Sylla (1948), Doulo Fofanna (b, 1947 or 1948), and Djenébou Traoré (b. 1972): The Colonies Come to France." In *The Human Tradition in Modern Africa*, ed. Dennis D. Cordell, 249–66. Lanham, MD: Rowman and Littlefield, 2012.

Cour des comptes, Rapport public annuel, vol. 1, part 2, chapter 4, section 3 "La transformation des foyers de travailleurs migrants en résidences sociales: une politique à refonder." 337–397 (Paris: 2014).

Crenn, Chantal. "Les retraités sénégalais entre Bordeaux et Dakar: 'bien vieillir' en restant cosmobiles." *Gérontologie et société* 41, no. 158 (2019): 125–38.

Cupers, Kenny. *The Social Project: Housing Postwar France*. Minneapolis: University of Minnesota Press, 2014.

Cuq, Henri. "Mission parlementaire sur la situation et le devenir des foyers de travailleurs migrants." Mission parlementaire auprès ministre chargé de l'intégration et de la lutte contre l'exclusion. Paris: 1996.

Daum, Christophe. *Les associations de Maliens en France: migrations, développement et citoyenneté*. Paris: Karthala, 1998.

David, Cédric. "Logement social des immigrants et politique municipale en banlieue ouvrière (Saint-Denis, 1944–1995). Histoire d'une improbable citoyenneté urbaine." PhD diss., University of Paris Ouest Nanterre, 2016.

Davidson, Naomi. *Only Muslim: Embodying Islam in Twentieth-Century France*. Ithaca, NY: Cornell University Press, 2012.

Dazey, Margot. "Les conditions de production locale d'un Islam respectable." *Genèses* 117, no. 4 (2019): 74–93.

De Genova, Nicholas. "Migrant 'Illegality' and Deportability in Everyday Life." *Annual Review of Anthropology* 31 (2002): 419–47.

De Rudder, Véronique. "Notes à propos de l'évolution des recherches françaises sur 'l'étranger dans la ville.'" In *Les étrangers dans la ville: le regard des sciences sociales*, ed. Simon-Barouh Ida and Simon Pierre-Jean, 60–80. Paris: L'Harmattan, 1990.

De Rudder, Véronique, François Vourc'h, and Christian Poiret. *L'inégalité raciste: l'universalité républicaine à l'épreuve*. Paris: Presses universitaires de France, 2000.

Deboulet, Agnès, and Claudette Lafaye. "La rénovation urbaine, entre délogement et relogement. Les effets sociaux de l'éviction." *L'Année sociologique* 68, no. 1 (2018): 155–84.

Dedieu, Jean-Philippe. "S'engager dans l'image. Migrants ouest-africains et journalistes français dans les années 1960." *Ethnologie française* 42, no. 4 (2012): 811–22.

——. "L'internationalisme ouvrier à l'épreuve des migrations africaines en France." *Critique internationale* 50, no. 1 (2011): 145–67.

——. *La parole immigrée: les migrants africains dans l'espace public en France (1960–1995)*. Paris: Klincksieck, 2012.

——. "The Rise of the Migration-Development Nexus in Francophone Sub-Saharan Africa, 1960–2010." *African Studies Review* 61, no. 1 (2018): 83–108.

Dedieu, Jean-Philippe, Lisa Chauvet, Flore Gubert, Sandrine Mesplé-Somps, and Étienne Smith. "Les 'batailles' de Paris et de New York." *Revue française de science politique* 63, no. 5 (2013): 865–92.

Dedieu, Jean-Philippe, and Aïssatou Mbodj-Pouye. "The Fabric of Transnational Political Activism: 'Révolution Afrique' and West African Radical Militants in France in the 1970s." *Comparative Studies in Society and History* 60, no. 4 (2018): 1172–1208.

——. "The First Collective Protest of Black African Migrants in Postcolonial France (1960–1975): A Struggle for Housing and Rights." *Ethnic and Racial Studies* 39, no. 6 (2016): 958–75.

Delon, Margot. "Faire mémoire(s) de lieux disparus. Le cas des bidonvilles et cités de transit de Nanterre." *Ethnologie française* 44, no. 2 (2014): 341–53.

Demonsant, Jean-Luc. "Family Prestige as Old-Age Security: Evidence from Rural Senegal." Department of Economics and Finance Working Papers EC200802, Universidad de Guanajuato, 2007.

Dewitte, Philippe. *Les mouvements nègres en France, 1919–1939*. Paris: L'Harmattan, 1985.

Dhume-Sonzogni, Fabrice. *Communautarisme: enquête sur une chimère du nationalisme français*. Paris: Demopolis, 2016.

Dia, Hamidou. *Trajectoires et pratiques migratoires des Haalpulaaren du Sénégal: socio-anthropologie d'un "village multi-situé."* Paris: L'Harmattan, 2015.

——. "Villages multi-situés du Fouta-Toro en France: le défi de la transition entre générations de caissiers, lettrés et citadins." *Revue Asylon(s)*, no. 3 (2008).

Diarra, Souleymane. "Les travailleurs africains noirs en France." *Bulletin de l'Institut fondamental d'Afrique noire* 30, no. 3 (July 1968): 884–1004.

Diawara, Mamadou. "Ce que travailler veut dire dans le monde mandé." In *Le Travail en Afrique*, ed. Hélène d'Almeida-Topor, Monique Lakroum, and Gerd Spittler, 67–80. Paris: Karthala, 2004.

Diémé, Yancouba. *Boy Diola*. Paris: Flammarion, 2019.

Dietrich-Ragon, Pascale, and Yankel Fijalkow. "'On les aide à partir,' Le relogement comme révélateur des contradictions du développement social dans le cadre de la rénovation urbaine." *Espaces et sociétés* 155, no. 4 (2013): 113–28.

Diop, Abdoulaye-Bara. *Société toucouleur et migration: (enquête sur l'immigration toucouleur à Dakar)*. Dakar: Institut français d'Afrique noire, 1965.

Diop, Amadou. "Tradition et adaptation dans un réseau de migration sénégalais: la communauté manjak de France." PhD diss., EHESS, Marseille, 1981.

Diop, Moustapha. "L'émigration murid en Europe." *Hommes & Migrations* 1132, no. 1 (1990): 21–24.

——. "Structuration d'un réseau: la Jamaat Tabligh (Société pour la Propagation de la Foi)." *Revue Européenne des Migrations Internationales* 10, no. 1 (1994): 145–55.

Diop, Moustapha, and Laurence Michalak. "'Refuge' and 'Prison': Islam, Ethnicity, and the Adaptation of Space in Workers' Housing in France." In *Making Muslim Space in North America and Europe*, ed. B. D. Metcalf. Berkeley: University of California Press, 1996.

Diouf, Mamadou. "The Lost Territories of the Republic. Historical Narratives and the Recomposition of French Citizenship." In *Black France/France Noire*, ed. Tyler Stovall, Trica Danielle Keaton, and T. Denean Sharpley-Whiting, 32–56. Durham, NC: Duke University Press, 2012.

Dubois, Vincent, and Marion Lieutaud. "La 'fraude sociale' en questions." *Revue française de science politique* 70, no. 3 (2020): 341–71.

Dubresson, Alain. "Les travailleurs Soninké et Toucouleur dans l'Ouest parisien." *Cahiers ORSTOM Série Sciences Humaines* 12, no. 2 (1975): 189–208.

Dufoix, Stéphane. "Nommer l'autre. L'émergence du terme communautarisme dans le débat français." *Socio. La nouvelle revue des sciences sociales*, no. 7 (2016): 163–86.

Eberhard, Mireille, Erwan Le Méner, and Emilie Segol, *Qui sont les migrants mis à l'abri ? Île-De-France (Juin 2015-Novembre 2016)*, Rapport pour la Direction régionale et interdépartementale de l'hébergement et du logement d'Île-de-France (2018).

Echenberg, Myron. *Les Tirailleurs sénégalais en Afrique occidentale française (1857–1960)*. Paris: Karthala, 2009.

Edwards, Brent Hayes. *The Practice of Diaspora*. Cambridge, MA: Harvard University Press, 2003.

Eff, Carine. "Mémoire d'un homme au foyer." *Vacarme*, no. 30 (2005): 90–93.

Englund, Harri. "Ethnography After Globalism: Migration and Emplacement in Malawi." *American Ethnologist* 29, no. 2 (2002): 261–86.

Epstein, Renaud. "La rénovation urbaine: démolition-reconstruction de l'État." Paris: Presses de Sciences po, 2013.

Escafré-Dublet, Angéline. "Aid, Activism and the State in Post-War France: AMANA, a Charity Organisation for Colonial Migrants, 1945–1962." *Journal of Modern European History* 12, no. 2 (2014): 247–61.

——. "L'Etat et la culture des immigrés, 1974–1984." *Histoire@Politique* 4, no. 1 (2008): 15.

Espéret, Gérard. *Problèmes posés par l'immigration des travailleurs africains en France*. Rapport au Conseil économique et social, 1964.

Eun, Eun-Gi. "Une gestion socialiste en matière de logement: Boulogne-Billancourt (1947–1965)." *Le Mouvement Social* 213, no. 4 (2005): 31–51.

Fainzang, Sylvie, and Odile Journet. *La femme de mon mari: étude ethnologique du mariage polygamique en Afrique et en France*. Paris: L'Harmattan, 1989.

Fall, Papa Demba. "Migration internationale et développement local dans le Nguènar sénégalais." In *Le Sénégal Des Migrations. Mobilités, Identités et Sociétés*, ed. Momar-Coumba Diop, 195–210. Paris: Karthala, 2008.

Fassin, Didier. "Compassion and Repression: The Moral Economy of Immigration Policies in France." *Cultural Anthropology* 20, no. 3 (2005): 362–87.

——. "Qu'il ne suffit pas d'être politiquement incorrect pour être scientifiquement fondé." *Revue francaise de sociologie* 52, no. 4 (2011): 777–86.

Fassin, Didier, and Estelle d'Halluin. "The Truth from the Body: Medical Certificates as Ultimate Evidence for Asylum Seekers." *American Anthropologist* 107, no. 4 (2005): 597–608.

Fassin, Didier, and Éric Fassin. *De la question sociale à la question raciale?: représenter la société française*. Paris: La Découverte, 2006.

Faty, El Hadji Adbou Aziz. "Quand les hommes haalpulaar se plaignent de la migration: La question de la précarité masculine au cœur des problématiques migratoires dans la vallée du fleuve Sénégal." In *La Migration prise aux mots*, ed. Cécile Canut and Catherine Mazauric, 209–24. Paris: Le cavalier bleu, 2014.

Faure, Alain, and Claire Lévy-Vroelant. *Une chambre en ville: hôtels meublés et garnis de Paris 1860–1990*. Grâne: Créaphis, 2007.

Feld, Steven, and Keith Hamilton Basso. eds. *Senses of Place*. Santa Fe, NM: School of American Research Press, 1996.

Feldman, Nehara. *Migrantes: du bassin du fleuve Sénégal aux rives de la Seine*. Paris: La Dispute, 2018.

Fernando, Mayanthi L. *The Republic Unsettled: Muslim French and the Contradictions of Secularism*. Durham, NC: Duke University Press, 2014.

Fesenmyer, Leslie. "'Assistance but Not Support': Pentecostalism and the Reconfiguring of Relatedness Between Kenya and the United Kingdom." In *Affective Circuits: African Migrations to Europe and the Pursuit of Social Regeneration*, ed. Jennifer Cole and Christian Groes, 125–45. Chicago: Chicago University Press, 2016.

——. "Bringing the Kingdom to the City: Mission as Placemaking Practice Amongst Kenyan Pentecostals in London." *City & Society* 31, no. 1 (2019): 34–54.

Fiévet, Michel. "Le foyer, lieu de vie économique pour les Africains." *Hommes & Migrations* 1202, no. 1 (1996): 23–27.

——. *Le livre blanc des travailleurs immigrés des foyers: du non-droit au droit*. Paris: L'Harmattan, 1999.

Fourcaut, Annie. "Bobigny, banlieue rouge." Paris: Éditions ouvrières: Presses de la Fondation nationale des sciences politiques, 1986.

Fourot, Aude-Claire. "Instruments d'action publique et régulation municipale de l'islam. Le cas de la mosquée de Créteil." *Gouvernement et action publique* 3, no. 3 (2015): 81–102.

François, Camille. "Au mépris des locataires." *Genèses* 96, no. 3 (2014): 86–109.

——. "Une discrimination au délogement." *Terrains travaux* 29, no. 2 (2016): 105–25.

——. "Disperser les ménages." *Actes de la recherche en sciences sociales* 204, no. 4 (2014): 102–17.

Frémontier, Jacques. *La forteresse ouvrière: Renault: une enquête à Boulogne-Billancourt chez les ouvriers de la Régie*. Paris: Fayard, 1971.

Gaibazzi, Paolo. "The Rank Effect: Post-Emancipation Immobility in a Soninke Village." *Journal of African History* 53, no. 2 (2012): 215–34.

——. "Visa Problem: Certification, Kinship, and the Production of 'Ineligibility' in The Gambia." *Journal of the Royal Anthropological Institute* 20, no. 1 (2014): 38–55.

Galembert, Claire de. "De l'inscription de l'islam dans l'espace urbain." *Les Annales de la recherche urbaine* 68, no. 1 (1995): 178–88.

Gallo, Ester. "Italy Is Not a Good Place for Men: Narratives of Places, Marriage and Masculinity Among Malayali Migrants." *Global Networks* 6, no. 4 (2006): 357–72.

Gallou, Rémi. "Les immigrés isolés: la spécificité des résidants en foyer." *Retraite et société* 44, no. 1 (2005): 106–47.

——. "Le vieillissement des immigrés en France." *Politix* 72, no. 4 (2005): 55–77.

Garbin, David, and Anna Strhan. *Religion and the Global City*. London: Bloomsbury, 2017.

Gary-Tounkara, Daouda. "Quand les migrants demandent la route, Modibo Keïta rétorque: 'retournez à la terre!' Les Baragnini et la désertion du 'chantier national' (1958–1968)." *Mande Studies* 5 (2003): 49–64.

Gastaut, Yvan. *L'opinion française et l'immigration sous la Vème République*. Paris: Le Seuil, 2000.

Gaullier, Pauline. "La décohabitation et le relogement des familles polygames." *Revue des politiques sociales et familiales* 94, no. 1 (2008): 59–69.

Gauz. *Black Manoo*. Paris: Le Nouvel Attila, 2020.

Gay, Vincent. "Grèves saintes ou grèves ouvrières?" *Genèses* 98, no. 1 (2015): 110–30.

Germain, Félix F. *Decolonizing the Republic: African and Caribbean Migrants in Postwar Paris, 1946–1974*. East Lansing: Michigan State University Press, 2016.

Gimat, Matthieu, and Julie Pollard. "Un tournant discret: la production de logements sociaux par les promoteurs immobiliers." *Géographie, économie, société* 18, no. 2 (2016): 257–82.

Ginésy-Galano, Mireille. *Les Immigrés hors la cité: le système d'encadrement dans les foyers 1973–1982*. Paris: L'Harmattan, 1984.

Glaes, Gillian. *African Political Activism in Postcolonial France*. London: Routledge, 2019.

Glick Schiller, Nina. "A Global Perspective on Transnational Migration: Theorising Migration Without Methodological Nationalism." In *Diaspora and Transnationalism*, ed. Rainer Bauböck and Thomas Faist, 109–30. Amsterdam: Amsterdam University Press, 2010.

Glick Schiller, Nina, Linda Basch, and Cristina Szanton Blanc. "From Immigrant to Transmigrant: Theorizing Transnational Migration." *Anthropological Quarterly* 68, no. 1 (1995): 48–63.

Goebel, Michael. *Anti-Imperial Metropolis: Interwar Paris and the Seeds of Third-World Nationalism.* Cambridge: Cambridge University Press, 2015.

Goetz, Edward Glenn. *New Deal ruins: Race, economic justice, and public housing policy.* Ithaca: Cornell University Press, 2013.

Gordon, Daniel A. *Immigrants & Intellectuals: May '68 & the Rise of Anti-Racism in France.* London: Merlin Press, 2012.

Gosselin, Anne. "Les délais pour obtenir un titre de séjour s'allongent." *De facto* [on line] 14 (December 2019). https://www.icmigrations.cnrs.fr/2019/12/09/defacto-014-04/.

Gosselin, Anne, Annabel Desgrées du Loû, Éva Lelièvre, France Lert, Rosemary Dray-Spira, and Nathalie Lydié. "Migrants subsahariens combien de temps leur faut-il pour s'installer en France?" *Population Sociétés* 533, no. 5 (2016): 1–4.

Grelet, Stany, Philippe Mangeot, Victoire Patouillard, and Isabelle Saint-Saëns. "Vingt ans après." *Vacarme* 16, no. 3 (2001): 4–14.

Groupe de sociologie urbaine de Nanterre. "Paris 1970: reconquête urbaine et rénovation-déportation." *Sociologie du travail* 12, no. 4 (1970): 488–514.

Grysole, Amélie. "De bonnes fréquentations." *Actes de la recherche en sciences sociales* 225, no. 5 (2018): 28–41.

Grysole, Amélie, and Aïssatou Mbodj-Pouye. "Bons, fax et sacs de riz. Tenir et maintenir un circuit économique transnational (France, Sénégal)." *Cahiers d'études africaines*, no. 225 (2017): 121–50.

Guérin, Laura. "L'appropriation spatiale comme résistance habitante. Ethnographie de résidences sociales issues de Foyers de Travailleurs Migrants." PhD diss., University of Paris 8, 2021.

——. "Cohabiter dans un studio de travailleurs migrants : contraintes gestionnaires et 'arts de faire.' *Espaces et sociétés*, vol. 186–187, no. 3–4 (2022): 35–50.

——. "Le portable comme 'chez-soi' dans un contexte de précarité résidentielle. Le cas des habitants de résidences sociales issues de foyers de travailleurs migrants." *Socio-anthropologie*, no. 40 (2019): 97–113.

Gueye, Abdoulaye. "The Colony Strikes Back: African Protest Movements in Postcolonial France." *Comparative Studies of South Asia, Africa and the Middle East* 26, no. 2 (2006): 225–42.

———. *Les intellectuels africains en France*. Paris: L'Harmattan, 2001.

Guillon, Michelle. "Ouvriers étrangers et français des usines Renault. Pratiques de mobilisation de la main-d'œuvre." *Espace Populations Sociétés* 6, no. 3 (1988): 455–66.

Guillouet, Jean-Jacques, and Philippe Pauget. "Les structures d'hébergement et de logements adaptés en Île-de-France en 2012." *Institut d'aménagement et d'urbanisme*, July 31, 2013.

Guyer, Jane I., and Samuel M. Eno Belinga. "Wealth in People as Wealth in Knowledge: Accumulation and Composition in Equatorial Africa." *Journal of African History* 36, no. 1 (1995): 91–120.

Hage, Ghassan. *The Diasporic Condition: Ethnographic Explorations of the Lebanese in the World*. Chicago: University of Chicago Press, 2021.

Hamel, Christelle, Bertrand Lhommeau, Ariane Pailhe, and Emmanuelle Santelli. "Rencontrer son conjoint dans un espace multiculturel et international." Working Paper. Paris: INED, 2012.

Hamès, Constant. "Islam et structures sociales chez les immigrés Soninké en France." *Social Compass* 26, no. 1 (1979): 87–98.

Harries, Patrick. "Symbols and Sexuality: Culture and Identity on the Early Witwatersrand Gold Mines." *Gender & History* 2, no. 3 (1990): 318–36.

Heil, Tilmann. "Conviviality. (Re)negotiating Minimal Consensus." In *Routledge International Handbook of Diversity Studies*, ed. Steven Vertovec, 317–24. Abingdon: Routledge, 2015.

Hendrickson, Burleigh J. *Decolonizing 1968: Transnational Student Activism in Tunis, Paris, and Dakar*. Ithaca, NY: Cornell University Press, 2022.

Hernández-Carretero, María. "Hope and Uncertainty in Senegalese Migration to Spain: Taking Chances on Emigration but Not Upon Return." In *Hope and Uncertainty in Contemporary African Migration*, ed. Nauja Kleist and Dorte Thorsen, 113–33. New York: Routledge, 2017.

Hmed, Choukri. "Loger les étrangers 'isolés' en France: socio-histoire d'une institution d'État." PhD diss., Université Panthéon-Sorbonne, Paris, 2006.

House, Jim. "Contrôle, encadrement, surveillance et répression des migrations coloniales: une décolonisation difficile (1956–1970)." *Bulletin de l'Institut d'Histoire du Temps Présent* 83 (2004): 144–56.

Hull, Matthew S. *Government of Paper: The Materiality of Bureaucracy in Urban Pakistan*. Berkeley: University of California Press, 2012.

Hunter, Alistair. *Retirement Home? Ageing Migrant Workers in France and the Question of Return*. New York: Springer, 2018.

Hutchison, Ray, and Bruce D. Haynes, eds. *The Ghetto: Contemporary Global Issues and Controversies.* New York: Routledge, 2019.

INSEE. *Atlas des populations immigrées en Ile-de-France: regards sur l'immigration.* Paris: INSEE, 2004.

Jefferson, Andrew, Simon Turner, and Steffen Jensen. "Introduction: On Stuckness and Sites of Confinement." *Ethnos* 84, no. 1 (2019): 1–13.

Jervis Read, Cressida. "A Place in the City: Narratives of 'Emplacement' in a Delhi Resettlement Neighbourhood." *Ethnography* 13, no. 1 (2012): 87–101.

Jobard, Fabien, and René Lévy. "Les contrôles au faciès à Paris." *Plein droit* 82, no. 3 (2009): 11–14.

Jolly, Cédric, Frédéric Lainé, and Yves Breem. *L'emploi et les métiers des immigrés.* Paris: Centre d'analyse stratégique, 2012.

Jónsson, Gunvor. "Migration, Identity and Immobility in a Malian Soninke Village." In *The Global Horizon. Expectations of Migration in Africa and the Middle East*, ed. Knut Graw and Samuli Schielke, 105–20. Leuven, Belgium: Leuven University Press, 2012.

Jouanneau, Solenne. "Faire émerger un 'islam français': paradoxes d'une action publique sous contrainte (1970–2010)." *Sociologie* 8, no. 3 (2017): 247–64.

Jounin, Nicolas. *Chantier interdit au public.* Paris: La Découverte, 2009.

——. "Aux origines des 'travailleurs sans papiers.' Les spécificités d'un groupe au service d'une identification généraliste." *Revue européenne des migrations internationales* 30, no 1 (2014): 131–52.

Jousselin, Brigitte, and Michèle Tallard. *Les conditions de logement des travailleurs migrants en France.* Paris: Centre de Recherches et de Documentation sur la Consommation, 1975.

Jusot, Florence, Paul Dourgnon, Jérôme Wittwer, and Jawhar Sarhiri. "Le recours à l'aide médicale de l'État des personnes en situation irrégulière en France: premiers enseignements de l'enquête Premiers pas." *Questions d'économie de la santé* 245 (2019): 8.

Kane, Abdoulaye. "Les pèlerins sénégalais au Maroc: la sociabilité autour de la Tijaniyya." In *Les nouveaux urbains dans l'espace Sahara-Sahel. Un cosmopolitisme par le bas*, ed. Elisabeth Boesen and Laurence Marfaing, 187–208. Paris: Karthala-ZMO, 2007.

——. *Tontines, caisses de solidarité et banquiers ambulants: univers des pratiques financières informelles en Afrique.* Paris: L'Harmattan, 2010.

Kane, Francine, and André Lericollais. "L'émigration en pays Soninké." *Cahiers ORSTOM. Série Sciences Humaines* 12, no. 2 (1975): 177–87.

Kane, Ousmane. *The Homeland Is the Arena: Religion, Transnationalism, and the Integration of Senegalese Immigrants in America*. Oxford: Oxford University Press, 2011.

Kanté, Nianguiry. "Contribution à la connaissance de la migration Soninké en France," PhD diss., University of Paris 8, 1986.

Karine, Geoffrion, and Viviane Cretton. "Introduction: Bureaucratic Routes to Migration: Migrants' Lived Experience of Paperwork, Clerks, and Other Immigration Intermediaries." *Anthropologica* 63, no. 1 (2021).

Khemilat, Fatima. "La construction des prières de rue comme problème public." *Confluences Méditerranée* 106, no. 3 (2018): 81–94.

Kirszbaum, Thomas, and Patrick Simon. "Les discriminations raciales et ethniques dans l'accès au logement social." Note de synthèse no. 3 du Groupe d'étude et de lutte contre les discriminations, May 2001.

Klausser, Nicolas. "La régularisation pour soins des étrangers: symptômes d'une pathologisation d'un droit de l'homme." *La Revue des droits de l'homme* 11 (2017), https://doi.org/10.4000/revdh.2890.

Kleinman, Julie. *Adventure Capital: Migration and the Making of an African Hub in Paris*. Oakland: University of California Press, 2019.

Kleist, Nauja, and Dorte Thorsen, eds. *Hope and Uuncertainty in Contemporary African Migration*. New York: Routledge, 2017.

Konaté, Moussa. "Tunga: A Study of Malian Soninke Labor Migration to France." PhD diss., University of California, Los Angeles, 1997.

Koser, Khalid, ed. *New African Diasporas*. London: Routledge, 2003.

Kuczynski, Liliane, and Élodie Razy, "Anthropologie et migrations africaines en France: une généalogie des recherches." *Revue européenne des migrations internationales* 25, no. 3 (2010): 79–100.

Lacobucci, Gareth. "Covid-19: Increased Risk Among Ethnic Minorities Is Largely Due to Poverty and Social Disparities, Review Finds." *BMJ*, October 22, 2020.

Lacroix, Thomas. "Conceptualizing Transnational Engagements: A Structure and Agency Perspective on (Hometown) Transnationalism." *International Migration Review* 48, no. 3 (2014): 643–79.

Lagrange, Hugues. *Le déni des cultures*. Paris: Le Seuil, 2010.

Lamont, Michèle. *The Dignity of Working Men: Morality and the Boundaries of Race, Class, and Immigration*. New York: Russell Sage Foundation, 2000.

Laurens, Sylvain. "De la 'promotion culturelle des immigrés' à 'l'interculturel' (1974–1980): Discours d'État sur une catégorie d'État." *Cultures & Conflits*, no. 107 (2017): 15–41.

——. *Une politisation feutrée: les hauts fonctionnaires et l'immigration en France, 1962–1981.* Paris: Belin, 2009.

Laurent, Pierre-Joseph. *Amours pragmatiques: familles, migrations et sexualité au Cap-Vert aujourd'hui.* Paris: Karthala, 2018.

Le Bris, Émile, Pierre-Philippe Rey, and Michel Samuel. *Capitalisme négrier: la marche des paysans vers le prolétariat.* Paris: Maspero, 1976.

Le Courant, Stefan. "'Être le dernier jeune.'" *Terrain. Revue d'ethnologie de l'Europe*, no. 63 (2014): 38–53.

——. *Vivre sous la menace. Les sans-papiers et l'Etat.* Paris: Le Seuil, 2022.

Le Roux, Guillaume, Christophe Imbert, Arnaud Bringé, and Catherine Bonvalet. "Transformations sociales de l'agglomération parisienne au cours du XXe siècle: une approche longitudinale et générationnelle des inégalités d'accès à la ville." *Population* 75, no. 1 (2020): 71–100.

Lebon, Hélène. "Blanc-Mesnil Noirs. Exposition Forum." *Hommes et Migrations* 1266, no. 1 (2007): 164–67.

Legrain, Jean-François. "Islam en France, Islam de France." *Esprit* 119, no. 10 (1986): 1–30.

Legru, Jacques. "Main d'œuvre noire dans la Seine." *Cahiers Nords-Africains*, no. 102 (1964): 1–57.

Lelévrier, Christine. "La rénovation urbaine, un re-peuplement des 'grands ensembles'?" In *Le Peuplement comme politiques*, ed. Fabien Desage, Christelle Morel Journel, and Valérie Sala Pala, 175–94. Rennes: Presses universitaires de Rennes, 2019.

Lems, Annika. *Being-Here: Placemaking in a World of Movement.* London: Berghahn, 2018.

Lems, Annika, and Jelena Tošić. "Preface: Stuck in Motion?" *Suomen Antropologi: Journal of the Finnish Anthropological Society* 44, no. 2 (2019): 3–19.

Lendaro, Annalisa. "Inégalités sur le marché du travail entre deux générations d'immigré-e-s." *Revue française de sociologie* 54, no. 4 (2013): 779–806.

Lendaro, Annalisa, Claire Rodier, and Youri Lou Vertongen. *La crise de l'accueil: frontières, droits, résistances.* Paris: La Découverte, 2019.

Leroux, Vincent. *Commanderie.* Paris: Temps Machine, 2011.

Leservoisier, Olivier. "L'association Pulaar Speaking à la croisée des chemins. Dynamiques migratoires et débats autour du sens à donner à l'action communautaire au sein du collectif migrant haalpulaaren (Mauritanie, Sénégal) aux États-Unis." *Revue européenne des migrations internationales* 35, no. 1 (2019): 125–47.

——. "Les héritages de l'esclavage dans la société haalpulaar de Mauritanie." *Journal des africanistes* 78, no. 1–2 (2008): 247–67.

Lévy-Vroelant, Claire. *L'incendie de l'hôtel Paris-Opéra. Enquête sur un drame social.* Grâne: Créaphis, 2018.

——. "Les sans-papiers au risque du Covid-19. Entre 'protocole compassionnel' et déni de droits," *Métropolitiques*, May 1, 2020.

Lounici, Fathia. "Les foyers de travailleurs nord-africains en banlieue parisienne: une politique de logement social d'exception (1945–1962)." *Cahiers d'histoire. Revue d'histoire critique* 98 (2006): 43–63.

Lovatt, Roland, Christine Whitehead, and Claire Lévy-Vroelant. "Foyers in the UK and France—Comparisons and Contrasts." *International Journal of Housing Policy* 6, no. 2 (2006): 151–66.

Lyons, Amelia H. "Social Welfare, French Muslims and Decolonization in France: The Case of the Fonds d'action Sociale." *Patterns of Prejudice* 43, no. 1 (2009): 65–89.

Mabanckou, Alain, and Abdourahman Waberi. *Dictionnaire enjoué des cultures africaines.* Paris Fayard, 2019.

Magri, Susanna, and Christian Topalov. "De la cité-jardin à la ville rationalisée: Un tournant du projet réformateur, 1905–1925: Etude Comparative France, Grande-Bretagne, Italie, Etats-Unis." *Revue française de sociologie* 28, no. 3 (1987): 417–51.

Mahajan, Uma V., and Margaret Larkins-Pettigrew. "Racial Demographics and COVID-19 Confirmed Cases and Deaths: A Correlational Analysis of 2886 US Counties." *Journal of Public Health* 42, no. 3 (2020): 445–47.

Mahdjoub, Dalila, and Martine Derain. *D'un seuil à l'autre: perspective sur une chambre avec ses habitants.* Marseille: Editions Transit, 2007.

Mahler, Sarah J., and Patricia R. Pessar. "Gender Matters: Ethnographers Bring Gender from the Periphery Toward the Core of Migration Studies." *International Migration Review* 40, no. 1 (2006): 27–63.

Manchuelle, François. "Background to Black African Emigration to France: The Labor Migrations of the Soninke, 1848–1987." PhD diss., University of California, Santa Barbara, 1987.

——. "The 'Patriarchal Ideal' of Soninke Labor Migrants: From Slave Owners to Employers of Free Labor." *Canadian Journal of African Studies* 23, no. 1 (1989): 106–25.

——. *Willing Migrants: Soninke Labor Diasporas, 1848–1960*. Athens: Ohio University Press, 1997.

Mann, Gregory. *From Empires to NGOs in the West African Sahel. The Road to Nongovernmentality*. Cambridge: Cambridge University Press, 2014.

——. "Immigrants and Arguments in France and West Africa." *Comparative Studies in Society and History* 45, no. 2 (2003): 362–85.

Mao-Mei, Liu. "Becoming a Man: Legal Status, Networks and Male Migration Between Senegal and Europe." MAFE Working Paper 38. Paris: INED, 2015.

Marsicano, Élise. "Mixité, inégalité, hétéroconjugalité. La formation des couples chez les migrant·e·s d'Afrique subsaharienne en France." *Nouvelles Questions Feministes* 38, no. 2 (2019): 86–106.

Masclet, Olivier. "Du 'bastion' au 'ghetto.' Le communisme municipal en butte à l'immigration." *Actes de la recherche en sciences sociales* 159, no. 4 (2005): 10–25.

——. "Une municipalité communiste face à l'immigration algérienne et marocaine." *Genèses. Sciences sociales et histoire* 45, no. 4 (2001): 150–63.

Massey, Douglas S. "Social Structure, Household Strategies, and the Cumulative Causation of Migration." *Population Index* 56, no. 1 (1990): 3–26.

Matonti, Frédérique, and Bernard Pudal. "L'UEC ou l'autonomie confisquée (1956–1968)." In *Mai-Juin 68*, ed. Bernard Pudal, Boris Gobille, Frédérique Matonti, and Dominique Damamme, 130–43. Paris: Editions de l'Atelier, 2008.

Maussen, Marcel. *Constructing Mosques: The Governance of Islam in France and the Netherlands*. Amsterdam: Amsterdam School for Social Science Research, 2009.

——. "Islamic Presence and Mosque Establishment in France: Colonialism, Arrangements for Guestworkers and Citizenship." *Journal of Ethnic & Migration Studies* 33, no. 6 (2007): 981–1002.

Mazouz, Sarah. *La République et ses autres: politiques de l'altérité dans la France des années 2000*. Lyon: ENS Éditions, 2017.

Mbodj-Pouye, Aïssatou. *Le fil de l'écrit: une anthropologie de l'alphabétisation au Mali*. Lyon: ENS éditions, 2013.

——. "Fixed Abodes: Urban Emplacement, Bureaucratic Requirements, and the Politics of Belonging Among West African Migrants in Paris." *American Ethnologist* 43, no. 2 (2016): 295–310.

——. "'On n'ignore pas la solidarité'. Transformation des foyers de travailleurs migrants et recompositions des liens de cohabitation." *Genèses* 104, no. 3 (2016): 51–72.

Mbodj-Pouye, Aïssatou, and Stefan Le Courant., "Living Away from Family Is Not Good but Living with It Is Worse: Debating Conjugality Across Generations of West African Migrants in France." *Mande Studies* 19 (2017): 109–30.

Meeus, Bruno, Karel Arnaut, and Bas van Heur, eds. *Arrival Infrastructures: Migration and Urban Social Mobilities*. London: Palgrave Macmillan, 2019.

Meillassoux, Claude. *Maidens, Meal, and Money: Capitalism and the Domestic Community*. Cambridge: Cambridge University Press, 1981.

Melly, Caroline M. "Titanic Tales of Missing Men: Reconfigurations of National Identity and Gendered Presence in Dakar, Senegal." *American Ethnologist* 38, no. 2 (2011): 361–76.

Michalon, Anissa, and Claire Soton. *Natifs de Bada. Récits d'une émigration malienne*. Cherbourg: Le Point du Jour, 2014.

Mills-Affif, Édouard. *Filmer les immigrés: les représentations audiovisuelles de l'immigration à la télévision française, 1960–1986*. Bruxelles: De Boeck, 2004.

Minces, Juliette. *Les travailleurs étrangers en France: enquête*. Paris: Le Seuil, 1973.

Monjaret, Anne. *La pin-up à l'atelier: ethnographie d'un rapport de genre*. Grâne: Créaphis éditions, 2020.

Monjaret, Anne, and Catherine Pugeault, eds. *Le sexe de l'enquête: Approches sociologiques et anthropologiques*. Lyon: ENS Éditions, 2015.

Moodie, T. Dunbar, Vivienne Ndatshe, and British Sibuyi. "Migrancy and Male Sexuality on the South African Gold Mines." *Journal of Southern African Studies* 14, no. 2 (1988): 228–56.

Moore, Henrietta L. *Feminism and Anthropology*. Cambridge, UK: Polity Press, 1988.

Morice, Alain, and Swanie Potot. *De l'ouvrier immigré au travailleur sans papiers: les étrangers dans la modernisation du salariat*. Paris: Karthala, 2010.

Morokvasic, Mirjana. "Birds of Passage Are Also Women . . ." *International Migration Review* 18, no. 4 (1984): 886–907.

Moulin, Marie-France. *Machines à dormir: les foyers neufs de la sonacotra, de l'a.d.e.f et quelques autres*. Paris: Maspero, 1976.

Narayan, Kirin. "How Native Is a 'Native' Anthropologist?" *American Anthropologist* 95, no. 3 (1993): 671–86.

Nasiali, Minayo. *Native to the Republic: Empire, Social Citizenship, and Everyday Life in Marseille Since 1945.* Ithaca, NY: Cornell University Press, 2016.

Ndiaye, Jean-Pierre, J. Bassene, and D. Germain. *Les travailleurs noirs en France: pourquoi les migrations?* Paris: Bureau d'études des réalités africaines, 1963.

Ndiaye, Pap. *La condition noire: essai sur une minorité française.* Paris: Calmann-Lévy, 2008.

N'Diaye, Sidi. "Des 'restes' résistants en milieu soninké: esclavage, sens de l'honneur et mécanismes d'émancipation." *Critique internationale* 72, no. 3 (2016): 113–25.

Neveu Kringelbach, Hélène. "Gendered Educational Trajectories and Transnational Marriage Among West African Students in France." *Identities* 22, no. 3 (2015): 288–302.

——. "'Mixed Marriage,' Citizenship and the Policing of Intimacy in Contemporary France." IMI Working Papers, no. 77 (2013): 19.

Newman, Andrew. *Landscape of Discontent: Urban Sustainability in Immigrant Paris.* Minneapolis: University of Minnesota Press, 2015.

Noiriel, Gérard. *Les ouvriers dans la société française: XIXe-XXe siècle.* Paris: Éditions du Seuil, 1986.

Noiriel, Gérard, Eric Guichard, and Marie-Hélène Lechien, eds. *Le vieillissement des immigrés en région parisienne.* Paris: Rapport au FAS, 1992.

Palomares, Élise. "Le racisme: un hors-champ de la sociologie urbaine française?" *Métropolitiques,* September 11, 2013.

Paskins, Jacob. *Paris Under Construction: Building Sites and Urban Transformation in the 1960s.* New York: Routledge, 2016.

Pasquiers, Olivier. *Merci aux travailleurs venus de loin.* Grâne: Créaphis éditions, 2012.

Patterson, Tiffany Ruby, and Robin D. G. Kelley. "Unfinished Migrations: Reflections on the African Diaspora and the Making of the Modern World." *African Studies Review* 43, no. 1 (2000): 11–45.

Pattieu, Sylvain. "The BUMIDOM in Paris and Its Suburbs: Contradictions in a State Migration Policy, 1960s–1970s." *African and Black Diaspora: An International Journal* 10, no. 1 (2017): 12–24.

——. "Souteneurs noirs à Marseille, 1918–1921: Contribution à l'histoire de la minorité noire en France." *Annales. Histoire, Sciences Sociales* 64, no. 6 (2009): 1361–86.

Pattillo, Mary E. *Black on the Block: The Politics of Race and Class in the City.* Chicago: University of Chicago Press, 2007.

Peabody, Sue. *"There Are No Slaves in France": The Political Culture of Race and Slavery in the Ancien Régime*. Oxford: Oxford University Press, 2002.

Péchu, Cécile. "Black African Immigrants in France and Claims for Housing." *Journal of Ethnic and Migration Studies* 25, no. 4 (1999): 727–44.

——. *Droit au logement, genèse et sociologie d'une mobilisation*. Paris: Dalloz, 2006.

Pelckmans, Lotte. "Moving Memories of Slavery Among West African Migrants in Urban Contexts (Bamako, Paris)." *Revue Européenne Des Migrations Internationales* 29, no. 1 (2016): 45–67.

Perron, Tangui, ed. *Histoire d'un film, mémoire d'une Lutte*. Paris: Scope & Périphéries, 2009.

Petit, Agathe. "L'ultime retour des gens du fleuve Sénégal." *Hommes & Migrations* 1236, no. 1 (2002): 44–52.

Pette, Mathilde. "Associations: les nouveaux guichets de l'immigration? Du travail militant en préfecture, Are non-profit organizations the new offices of immigration services? Activists' work in a local administration." *Sociologie* 5, no. 4 (2014): 405–21.

Petty, Sheila. "Black Mic-Mac and Colonial Discourse." *CinéAction* 18 (1989): 51–55.

Piot, Charles. *The Fixer: Visa Lottery Chronicles*. Durham, NC: Duke University Press, 2019.

Pitti, Laure. "Les 'Nord-Africains' à Renault: un cas d'école de gestion coloniale de la main-d'œuvre en métropole." *Bulletins de l'Institut d'Histoire du Temps Présent* 83, no. 1 (2004): 128–43.

——. "'Travailleurs de France, voilà notre nom.' Les mobilisations des ouvriers étrangers dans les usines et les foyers dans les années 1970." In *Histoire politique des immigrations (post)coloniales, France, 1920–2008*, ed. Abdellali Hajjat and Ahmed Boubeker, 95–111. Paris: Editions Amsterdam, 2008.

Platone, François. "'Prolétaires de tous les pays.' Le Parti communiste français et les immigrés." In *Les étrangers dans la cité: expériences européennes*, ed. Catherine Wihtol de Wenden and Olivier Le Cour Grandmaison, 64–80. Paris: La Découverte, 1993.

Poiret, Christian. *Familles africaines en France: ethnicisation, ségrégation et communalisation*. Paris: L'Harmattan, 1997.

——. "L'inclusion des familles africaines en Ile-de-France: de la catégorie 'ethnique' aux groupes 'africains.'" *Espace Populations Sociétés* 14, no. 2 (1996): 335–46.

——. "Les processus d'ethnicisation et de raci(ali)sation dans la France contemporaine: Africains, Ultramarins et 'Noirs.'" *Revue européenne des migrations internationales* 27, no. 1 (2011): 107–27.

Porquet, Jean-Luc. *Guide actuel du Paris mondial.* Paris: Le Seuil, 1992.

Préteceille, Edmond. "La ségrégation sociale a-t-elle augmenté?" *Sociétés contemporaines* 62, no. 2 (2006): 69–93.

Prost, Barbara. "Les 'saisonniers' immigrés dans le collectif de travail. Paris, fin des années 1950-début des années 1980." In *Les travailleurs des déchets*, ed. Delphine Corteel and Stéphane Lelay. Paris: ERES, 2011.

Quiminal, Catherine. *Gens d'ici, gens d'ailleurs: migrations Soninké et transformations villageoises.* Paris: C. Bourgois, 1991.

Raissiguier, Catherine. "Troubling Borders: Sans-Papiers in France." In *New Border and Citizenship Politics*, ed. Helen Schwenken and Sabine Ruß-Sattar, 156–70. London: Palgrave Macmillan, 2014.

Razy, Elodie. "Les migrants ont-ils des manières particulières d'habiter?" *Hommes & Migrations* 1264, no. 1 (2006): 77–87.

——. *Naître et devenir: anthropologie de la petite enfance en pays soninké (Mali).* Nanterre: Société d'ethnologie, 2007.

Roederer, Thomas, Bastien Mollo, Charline Vincent, Birgit Nikolay, Augusto Llosa, Robin Nesbitt, Jessica Vanhomwegen, et al. "High Seroprevalence of SARS-CoV-2 Antibodies among People Living in Precarious Situations in Ile de France." *MedRxiv*, October 9, 2020, medRxiv 2020.10.07.20207795.

Rogaly, Ben. "Disrupting Migration Stories: Reading Life Histories Through the Lens of Mobility and Fixity." *Environment and Planning D: Society and Space* 33, no. 3 (2015): 528–44.

Rosello, Mireille. "Representing Illegal Immigrants in France: From clandestins to l'affaire des sans-papiers de Saint-Bernard." *Journal of European Studies* 28, no. 109–110 (1998): 137–151.

Rosenberg, Clifford D. *Policing Paris: The Origins of Modern Immigration Control Between the Wars.* Ithaca, NY: Cornell University Press, 2006.

Rose-Redwood, Reuben, and Anton Tantner. "Introduction: Governmentality, House Numbering and the Spatial History of the Modern City." *Urban History* 39, no. 4 (2012): 607–13.

Rossi, Benedetta, ed. *Reconfiguring Slavery: West African Trajectories.* Liverpool: Liverpool University Press, 2009.

Safi, Mirna. "Le processus d'intégration des immigrés en France: inégalités et segmentation." *Revue francaise de sociologie* 47, no. 1 (2006): 3–48.

Sala Pala, Valérie. "Politique du logement social et construction des frontières ethniques: une comparaison franco-britannique." PhD diss., University of Rennes 1, 2005.

Salzbrunn, Monika. "The Place-Making of Communities in Urban Spaces: The Invention of the 'Village Saint Louis Sainte-Marthe.'" In *Between Imagined Communities and Communities of Practice. Participation, Territory and the Making of Heritage*, 185–99. Göttingen: Göttingen University Press, 2015.

Samuel, Michel, *Le prolétariat africain noir en France*. Paris: Maspero, 1978.

Santelli, Emmanuelle, and Béate Collet. "De l'endogamie à l'homogamie socio-ethnique: réinterprétations normatives et réalités conjugales des descendants d'immigrés maghrébins, turcs et africains sahéliens." *Sociologie et sociétés* 43, no. 2 (2011): 329–54.

Sargent, Carolyn F. "Reproductive Strategies and Islamic Discourse." *Medical Anthropology Quarterly* 20, no. 1 (2006): 31–49.

Sassen, Saskia. *The Global City: New York, London, Tokyo*. Princeton, NJ: Princeton University Press, 1991.

Sayad, Abdelmalek. "Le foyer des sans-famille." *Actes de la recherche en sciences sociales* 32, no. 1 (1980): 89–103.

——. *L'illusion du provisoire. L'immigration ou Les paradoxes de l'altérité 1*. Paris: Raisons d'agir, 2006.

Scafirimuto, Guglielmo. "Les films associatifs autobiographiques des migrant-e-s et l'espace de réception des foyers parisiens." In *Images et réceptions croisées entre l'Algérie et la France*. Paris: Éditions science et bien commun, 2020.

Schmitz, Jean. "Islamic Patronage and Republican Emancipation: The Slaves of the Almaami in the Senegal River Valley." In *Reconfiguring Slavery: West African Trajectories*, ed. Benedetta Rossi, 85–115. Liverpool: Liverpool University Press, 2009.

Secrétariat général à l'immigration et à l'intégration. "Atlas national des populations immigrées." March 20, 2013. https://www.immigration.interieur.gouv.fr/Archives/Les-archives-du-site/Archives-Statistiques-etudes-et-publications/Atlas-national-des-populations-immigrees.

Semin, Jeanne. "L'argent, la famille, les amies: ethnographie contemporaine des tontines africaines en contexte migratoire." *Civilisations. Revue internationale d'anthropologie et de sciences humaines* 56 (2007): 183–99.

Siméant, Johanna. *La cause des sans-papiers*. Paris: Presses de Sciences po, 1998.

Sinatti, Giulia. "Masculinities and Intersectionality in Migration: Transnational Wolof Migrants Negotiating Manhood and Gendered Family Roles." In *Migration, Gender and Social Justice: Perspectives on Human Insecurity*, ed. Thanh-Dam Truong, Des Gasper, Jeff Handmaker, and Sylvia I. Bergh, 215–26. Berlin: Springer, 2014.

Smith, Michael Peter, and Michael MacQuarrie. *Remaking Urban Citizenship: Organizations, Institutions, and the Right to the City*. New York: Routledge, 2012.

Soares, Benjamin F. "An African Muslim Saint and His Followers in France." *Journal of Ethnic and Migration Studies* 30, no. 5 (2004): 913–27.

Soton, Claire, and Anissa Michalon. "Natif de Bada. Vit à Montreuil (Foyer Rochebrune)." *Communications* 79, no. 1 (2006): 225–45.

Soukouna, Sadio. "Migrants maliens et paradiplomatie." *Monde commun* 3, no. 2 (2019): 72–85.

Spire, Alexis. *Accueillir ou reconduire: enquête sur les guichets de l'immigration*. Paris: Raisons d'agir, 2008.

——. *Étrangers à la carte: l'administration de l'immigration en France (1945–1975)*. Paris: Bernard Grasset, 2005.

Staal, Gilles de. *Mamadou m'a dit: les luttes des foyers, révolution Afrique, Africa fête*. Paris: Syllepse, 2008.

Stefanson, Blandine, and Sheila Petty. *Directory of World Cinema: Africa*. Bristol: Intellect Books, 2014.

Stoler, Ann Laura. ed. "Introduction. 'The Rot Remains': From Ruins to Ruination." In *Imperial Debris: On Ruins and Ruination*. Durham, NC: Duke University Press, 2013.

Stoller, Paul. *Money Has No Smell: The Africanization of New York City*. Chicago: University of Chicago Press, 2002.

Stovall, Tyler. *Paris Noir: African Americans in the City of Light*. Boston: Houghton Mifflin, 1996.

——. "Race and the Making of the Nation. Blacks in Modern France." In *Diasporic Africa: A Reader*, ed. Michael A. Gomez, 200–218. New York: NYU Press, 2006.

——. *The Rise of the Paris Red Belt*. Berkeley: University of California Press, 1990.

Stovall, Tyler, Trica Danielle Keaton, and T. Denean Sharpley-Whiting. *Black France/France Noire*. Durham, NC: Duke University Press, 2012.

Subhi, Toma. "Musulmans dans l'entreprise." *Esprit* 102, no. 6 (1985): 216–21.

Sy, Yaya. "L'esclavage chez les Soninkés: du village à Paris." *Journal des Africanistes* 70, no. 1 (2000): 43–69.

Tapinos, Georges. *L'Immigration étrangère en France: 1946–1973*. Paris: Presses Universitaires de France, 1975.

Tarr, Carrie. "French Cinema and Post-Colonial Minorities." In *Post-Colonial Cultures in France*, ed. Alec G. Hargreaves and Mark McKinney, 59–83. London: Routledge, 1997.

Tetreault, Chantal. "Cultural Citizenship in France and *le Bled* Among Teens of Pan-Southern Immigrant Heritage." *Language & Communication* 33, no. 4 (2013): 532–43.

Thomas, Dominic. "Afropeanism and Francophone Sub-Saharan African Writing." In *Francophone Afropean Literatures*, ed. Dominic Thomas and Nicki Hitchcott, 17–31. Liverpool: Liverpool University Press, 2014.

Tiberj, Vincent, and Patrick Simon. *La fabrique du citoyen: origines et rapport au politique en France*. INED Working Paper 175, 2016.

Ticktin, Miriam Iris. *Casualties of Care: Immigration and the Politics of Humanitarianism in France*. Berkeley: University of California Press, 2011.

Timera, Mahamet. "Hospitalité et hébergement dans un réseau migratoire d'Afrique de l'Ouest." In *Logements de passage: formes, normes, expériences*, ed. Claire Lévy-Vroelant, 51–67. Paris: L'Harmattan, 2000.

——. *Les Soninké en France: d'une histoire à l'autre*. Paris: Karthala, 1996.

——. "Trajectoires du fondamentalisme parmi les communautés soninké musulmanes immigrées en France." In *Islam et villes en Afrique au sud du Sahara: entre soufisme et fondamentalisme*, ed. Adriana Piga, 293–303. Paris: Karthala, 2003.

Tripier, Maryse. *L'immigration dans la classe ouvrière en France*. Paris: L'Harmattan, 1990.

Trouillet, Caroline. "(Dé)peindre les travailleurs migrants en photographie." *Africultures* (blog), February 17, 2013.

UGTSF. *Le livre des travailleurs africains en France*. Paris: Maspero, 1970.

UNAFO. *Le Vieillissement des résidants dans les Foyers de Travailleurs Migrants. Constats et propositions*. Paris: UNAFO, 1996.

URACA. "Annual Report 2006." http://uraca-basiliade.org/wp-content/uploads/2016/12/URACA_RapportActivites2006.pdf.

Van den Avenne, Cécile. *Changer de vie, changer de langues: paroles de migrants entre le Mali et Marseille*. Paris: L'Harmattan, 2004.

Vieillard-Baron, Hervé. "L'islam en France: dynamiques, fragmentation et perspectives." *L'Information géographique* 80, no. 1 (2016): 22–53.

Viet, Vincent. *La France immigrée: construction d'une politique, 1914–1997.* Paris: Fayard, 1998.

Vigh, Henrik, and Jesper Bjarnesen. "Introduction: The Dialectics of Displacement and Emplacement." *Conflict and Society* 2, no. 1 (2016): 9–15.

Vigna, Xavier. "Une émancipation des invisibles? Les ouvriers immigrés dans les grèves de mai-juin 68." In *Histoire politique des immigrations (post) coloniales, France, 1920–2008*, ed. Abdellali Hajjat and Ahmed Boubeker, 85–94. Paris: Editions Amsterdam, 2008.

Voldman, Danièle. *La reconstruction des villes françaises de 1940 à 1954: histoire d'une politique.* Paris: L'Harmattan, 1997.

Vulbeau, Janoé. "Les 'Nord-Africains' dans la rénovation urbaine des années 1960." *Métropolitiques*, May 31, 2018.

Wacquant, Loïc. *Urban Outcasts: A Comparative Sociology of Advanced Marginality.* London: Polity, 2008.

Wakeman, Rosemary. *The Heroic City: Paris, 1945–1958.* Chicago: University of Chicago Press, 2009.

Weil, Patrick. "Immigration and the Rise of Racism in France: The Contradictions in Mitterrand's Policies." *French Politics and Society* 9, no. 3–4 (1991): 82–100.

Weil, Patrick, and John Crowley. "Integration in Theory and Practice: A Comparison of France and Britain," *West European Politic* 17, no. 2 (1994): 110–26.

White, Luise. *Speaking with Vampires: Rumor and History in Colonial Africa.* Berkeley: California University Press, 2000.

Whitehouse, Bruce. *Migrants and Strangers in an African City: Exile, Dignity, Belonging.* Bloomington: Indiana University Press, 2012.

Wilder, Gary. *The French Imperial Nation-State: Negritude and Colonial Humanism Between the Two World Wars.* Chicago: University of Chicago Press, 2005.

Xiang, Biao, and Johan Lindquist. "Migration Infrastructure." *International Migration Review* 48, no. S1 (2014): S122–48.

Yount-André, Chelsie. "Empire's Leftovers: Eating to Integrate in Secular Paris." *Food and Foodways* 26, no. 2 (2018): 124–45.

Yuval-Davis, Nira. "Belonging and the Politics of Belonging." *Patterns of Prejudice* 40, no. 3 (2006): 197–214.

Zelizer, Viviana A. *The Purchase of Intimacy.* Princeton, NJ: Princeton University Press, 2005.

# INDEX

GPSR Authorized Representative: Easy Access System Europe, Mustamäe tee
50, 10621 Tallinn, Estonia, gpsr.requests@easproject.com

www.ingramcontent.com/pod-product-compliance
Lightning Source LLC
Chambersburg PA
CBHW022131020426
42334CB00015B/851